# Great American Anecdotes

*Also by John and Claire Whitcomb*


*Oh Say Can You See:*
*Unexpected Anecdotes About American History*

# Great American Anecdotes

John Whitcomb
★
Claire Whitcomb

William Morrow and Company, Inc.
New York

It is the policy of William Morrow and Company, Inc., and its imprints and affiliates, recognizing the importance of preserving what has been written, to print the books we publish on acid-free paper, and we exert our best efforts to that end.

Library of Congress Cataloging-in-Publication Data

Whitcomb, John.
     Great American anecdotes / John Whitcomb and Claire Whitcomb.
         p.   cm.
     Includes bibliographical references and index.
     ISBN 0-688-09473-2
     1. United States—History—1945— —Anecdotes.   I. Whitcomb,
Claire.   II. Title.
E839.4.W47   1993
973.92—dc20                                              92-37975
                                                             CIP

Printed in the United States of America

First Edition

1   2   3   4   5   6   7   8   9   10

BOOK DESIGN BY LISA STOKES

# A Coauthor's Note

How exactly did a father and a daughter living on separate sides of the Hudson (but with matching computers) come to write a book together? Families have various kinds of glue, but ours has always been a love of writing (my mother, Helen, has been writing books and articles since I can remember) and a love of history. As children my brother, Jonathan, and I spent our summer vacations in the back seat of the blue Plymouth station wagon, heading to Civil War battlefields, to log cabins with Lincoln lore.

When my father decided to retire from teaching after thirty-two years, I thought he ought to write a book. With me. The result was *Oh Say Can You See: Unexpected Anecdotes About American History*, and now *Great American Anecdotes*. Fortunately Dad and I have had plenty of unsolicited readers and supporters. Chief among them are my mother, Helen, whose fine editorial eye has been invaluable; Howard Klein, who proved our best reader; and, of course, Jonathan, Diane, and Terra, who have been our biggest cheerleaders. We also owe our heartfelt thanks to the vision of our agent, Barbara Hogenson, and the dedication of our editor, Randy Ladenheim-Gil, and everyone at William Morrow.

—CLAIRE WHITCOMB

# Contents

# Introduction

"I did some of the big things rather well," said Richard Nixon, looking back on his presidency. "I screwed up terribly on what was a little thing. . . ." He meant Watergate—a small-time, bungled break-in. In his view, he'd spent his presidency worrying about the forest and didn't notice the trees—or more precisely the tree roots—that can trip a fellow whose gaze is skyward.

This book is about the little things, the stuff that trips egos, reveals character, creates laughs. It generally doesn't make or break history, but it certainly makes history personal.

In terms of LBJ, for instance, the phrase "Great Society" is of interest for its cocktail party connotation, because it was at political parties that you'd find Johnson working the crowd, eating chicken legs from the buffet table, and stuffing the bones in his pocket. How someone eats—"I don't know how to order from those hifalutin' French menus. I like . . . turnip greens, pole beans, corn bread. . . . I'm a professional southerner," said Alabama governor George Wallace—or how someone dresses, undresses, proposes, swears, tries to get ahead, lies, or dreams is the sort of little thing that gives you a shot of character, straight up.

This book is about the stuff we all have in common. Like

mothers. "I can't understand all the fuss over Elvis. I think I have a better voice than he does," said Gladys Presley.

And fathers. "I can't believe it! I simply cannot believe Grace won," Jack Kelly said after his daughter had won an Oscar for *The Country Girl.* "Of the four children, she's the last one I expected to support me in my old age."

It's about a cross section of Americans who influenced postwar culture and events, from Patty Hearst to Patti Davis, Harry Truman to Cary Grant, Oliver North to Oliver Stone. It's of necessity quirky, eclectic, and far from comprehensive. After all, you really can't research something like "people who proposed on the first date." But if you read enough—and over the course of three and a half years we did—things start to resonate. You discover that LBJ proposed almost at first sight. You find out that Jesse Jackson said, "Hey, baby. I'm going to marry you," to a woman he hadn't even met but whom he later married. You notice the same pattern occurring in the lives of Martin Luther King, Norman Vincent Peale, Supreme Court Justice William O. Douglas, and Zsa Zsa Gabor, and you're on your way to a chapter on the art of courtship.

So that's how this book progressed: through careful listening to hundreds of lives; through a persistent curiosity about how people negotiate the very human aspects of our times. Writing it can only be called an exercise in patience.

Having written another eclectic book, *Oh Say Can You See: Unexpected Anecdotes About American History,* which covered the whole gamut of American history and drew on Dad's years of teaching, we had a pretty good idea of what our themes would be: lies and other mistruths, famous last words, what people were doing when. This book just took a lot longer and, because it covered a much narrower time period, 1945 onward, led us to discoveries we hadn't anticipated. Like the number of times we heard the word "lonely"—from those at the top, from those at the bottom, and particularly from blacks quietly trying to fight for their rights during the sixties. That led to a chapter. So did the cultural fine line between film and reality (best exemplified by Ronald Reagan). And so on.

Though clearly there's an authorial voice in this book—when little points indicated a line, we've strung quotes together into short essays—we've done our best to let those who shaped our times provide the shape of this cultural tapestry. This book is built on the fact that people really do say the darndest things. What we tried to do was listen up. We hope you will enjoy listening, too.

# Great American Anecdotes

# 1
# Growing Up in America

THROUGH THE EYES OF CHILDREN

*"Aren't you Senator Goldwater?" asked a twelve-year-old.*
*"Don't you remember me?"*
*"Well—" Goldwater hedged.*
*"I'm the kid who was riding with you on a plane going to Houston.*
*I came out of the rest room and couldn't get my zipper up.*
*You zipped up my pants!"*

Children have a decidedly different view of life. A senator is remembered not for his oratory but for his finesse with tricky bits of clothing. A first Lady's backside is seen as a terrific target for slingshot practice. Eleanor Roosevelt, leaning over a barbecue grill, inspired ten-year-old Shirley Temple to pick up a pebble, slip her slingshot out of her lace purse, and score a bull's-eye. "Mrs. Roosevelt straightened with a jerk, holding her long-handled barbecue fork upward like the Statue of Liberty," Temple wrote in her memoir. "With the other hand she reached around in back and smoothed her dress over the target area. She never even glanced over her shoulder."

Mickey Mantle encountered a child's-eye view of the world when a fan brought over his son and said, "Son, I want you to meet Mickey Mantle, one of the greatest ballplayers who ever lived." Mantle, then nearing sixty, recalled, "Well, this kid—he musta been about six or seven years old—he looks me over real careful for several seconds, then he turns to his father an' says, 'But, Daddy, this is an old man!' "

Kids, you might say, will always be kids. Which is part of their charm. When Raisa Gorbachev was scheduled to visit New York City's P.S. 6 in 1988, kindergarten teacher Joan Goldberg asked her class: "If Mrs. Gorbachev were your mother—think of her as the mom of Moscow—and you were all alone with her, what would you ask her?" Without hesitation little Molly Karp offered, "I would ask her if she loves me better than my brother."

Life beyond the immediate purview has never been a child's forte. Sometimes explaining that the USSR isn't near New Jersey is the best you can do. Try, then, tackling the moon, the place seven-year-old Ann Collins's daddy, Michael, was headed. When *Apollo 11*, the first lunar landing mission, blasted off, Ann was watching on television. The capsule's orbit wasn't even confirmed when she asked the proverbial backseat-of-the-station-wagon question—with a space age twist: "Are they on the moon yet, Mommy?" Her mother, Pat, told her, "Oh, no, honey. It takes two days to get to the moon." "Three days," corrected her six-year-old brother.

The trouble with kids is that not all the questions they ask have easy answers. Take, for instance, "Daddy, *why* do you have to go to prison?" Jeb Stuart Magruder, convicted in the Watergate scandal, was trying to explain that to his six-and-a-half-year-old son by saying that he had made a big mistake. "I make mistakes all the time, and I don't have to go to prison," the boy countered.

Or try explaining war if you're on your way overseas to Operation Desert Storm. "Mom, if you die over there, I'm coming to rescue you," was the farewell offered by Lieutenant Colonel Carolyn Roaf's six-year-old daughter.

Or prejudice if you're holding the short end of the stick. "When we become citizens, Momma, will we get blond hair and blue eyes?" asked twelve-year-old Sirhan Sirhan, who had just arrived in the United States from Palestine and grew up to be Robert Kennedy's assassin.

"Can we go to Funtown?" was the question Martin Luther King, Jr.'s daughter Yoki asked after she saw an advertisement for the Atlanta amusement park on TV. "My tongue twisted and my speech stammered," King recalled, "seeking to explain to my six-year-old daughter why the public invitation on television didn't include her, and others like her. One of the most painful experiences I have ever faced was to see her tears when I told her that Funtown was *closed* to colored children. . . ."

Of course, the hardest thing to explain—to anyone, adult or child—is death. "A bad man shot my daddy," little John Kennedy told his nanny, Maud Shaw. But the concept was as abstract as flying to the moon. When he heard a chopper arriving at the

White House, he mimicked its path with his hand. "Whoosh! Here comes my daddy, and he's landing."

Miss Shaw gently explained that John's daddy wouldn't be on the helicopter; he had gone to heaven.

"Did he take his big plane?"

"Yes, John, he probably did."

"I wonder when he's coming back?"

How many of us wished we could have given him an answer.

### THE LEGACY OF A LAST NAME

*And my son Pete [Rose] the ballplayer took a lot of static, too. I mean, he's in the minor leagues trying to make a good living. The day I got suspended he was playing in Durham. People—a whole group of people—stood up and waved five-dollar bills and that's not right.*

*Regardless of what they think about me, you can't take it out on a nineteen-year-old kid. Regardless of what his name is.*

—Pete Rose, Sr., who was banned from baseball for gambling

If you start out in life with a name like Rose or Hearst or Reagan, people treat you a little differently. They open doors— or maybe slam them. They invite you to publish books (Patti Reagan, now Davis) or refuse to carry them (Patty Hearst Shaw). When Shaw's account of her kidnapping came out, a bookstore in Berkeley declined to put it on the shelves, citing the fact that "my grandfather started the Spanish-American War," Patty said: "I don't see what the problem is; we won the war."

Ah, the blitheness of the third generation. Patty might not have found life so easy if she had been in the thick of a family-run war. Certainly the Nixon girls didn't. "It's no fun to have kids tell you your father stinks," announced Julie Nixon when she came home from school.

Richard Rusk's father, Dean, was secretary of state in the Johnson administration. He came to Cornell for a parental visit, and students demonstrated and wore death masks. Richard, whose sympathies lay with the peaceniks, found an uneasy truce at home. When he brought his antiwar friends for a visit, "Dad would say, 'Well, park your signs in the umbrella rack.'"

Even in peacetime having a prominent last name isn't a piece of cake. People assume that if you run for Congress, as Robert Kennedy's son Joe did, or if, like Bridget Fonda, you get a lead in a film, the reason has more to do with DNA than skill. "I can deal with that stuff, but I don't like it. People telling me I don't have to work hard because I have good genes," explained Bridget. "It diminishes all the effort. And they make me sound as if I were a racehorse. I mean, it's just a last name." One shared by Grandpa Henry, Aunt Jane, and Papa Peter, of course.

A name as difficult as Fonda and as complicated as Kennedy is undoubtedly Rockefeller. "When I was about eleven and at a summer camp in Maine," recalled JDR III's daughter Alida, born in 1949, "people found out who I was. One kid came up and asked if I lit my cigars with million-dollar bills. Another came up and asked for my autograph. I gave it to her."

"It's a preposterous name," said David Rockefeller's oldest daughter, Abby. "I remember as a child having it whispered that we were rich. I have vague memories of my classmates talking and then all of a sudden, of the name Rockefeller looming as something beyond. Very quickly I came to feel it wasn't my name."

A generation earlier her father also found the name unwieldy. "How would you like to go through college in the middle of the Depression," David Rockefeller asked, "and have your grandfather described by every one of your history and economics professors as 'chief of the robber barons'?" His niece Lucy said she "didn't take American history for that reason. I didn't want to hear about the Rockefellers." Her sister Marion admitted, "To be truthful, it was a great relief for me when I got married and didn't have to carry it around anymore."

Jay Rockefeller didn't mind. His father named him simply John Rockefeller, giving him the option of adding a roman numeral when he came of age. On his twenty-first birthday, the future West Virginia senator was studying in Japan. He wrote his grandfather John D. Rockefeller, Jr., requesting formal permission to use, John D. IV. "I wanted that name very much," he said years later. "I thought it represented certain levels of public service, integrity, the sense you've got to go at it, you know, that there's no such thing as leisure."

George Walker Bush didn't consider his name a cross to bear. "I'm not going to miss my forties. I'm not going to walk around worrying about being the son of a President. Oooh, how burden-some."

Patti Reagan felt differently. At fourteen she wailed, "Oh, no, how could you do this to me?" when her parents called her at school to tell her her dad had been elected governor. When she was twenty-two, she legally ditched her father's legacy, switching her name to Davis to distance herself from family politics.

As difficult as names are, it should be pointed out that not having a historic last name can be problematic, too. Angela Mc-Coy Lewis, born out of wedlock, never met her father. He was James Chaney, one of three civil rights workers murdered in Mississippi in 1964—just ten days after her birth. She found it "really strange" to sit in black history class in Meridian, Mississippi, and hear Chaney mentioned as just another chapter in the civil rights struggle. "Some parts of me wanted to stand up and yell, 'This is my father!' " but she only told her closest friends. "I didn't want to be known just as his child." Her son, however, bears a quiet legacy from his grandfather: the name of James.

### IF ONLY WE COULD PICK OUR PARENTS

*Every girl should have a daddy just like Charlie [Manson].*
—Lynette "Squeaky" Fromme, one of the murderer's followers
who tried to assassinate Gerald Ford

Though most of us may not agree with Squeaky on fatherly ideals, the impulse to trade in a parent for a new, improved version is pretty universal—unless, of course, we have the wisdom of Lee Harvey Oswald. At age thirteen he talked about his mother to a social worker, saying, "Well, I've got to live with her. I guess I love her." It may have been a good thing he never lived to learn that one of her first reactions after the Kennedy shooting was to call reporters and say, "Boys, I'll give you a story—for money."

It's hard to anticipate the moment when a parent will disappoint you, but here are a few occasions when it might have been forgivable to call a recycling service for used family members:

1. After Bess Myerson won the Miss America title in 1945, her father told the *New York Post*, "I wouldn't say Bess is bad-

looking, but maybe if I was the judge I would have chosen one of the other girls."

2. "But what do you mean you find her talented? She doesn't sing, you know. She doesn't dance," said Debbie Reynolds's mother to the Warner Bros. agent who called to ask to put the sixteen-year-old under studio contract.

3. "You would make a very competent secretary," said Harlow Davis, father of Bette, upon seeing her New York stage debut as Hedvig in Ibsen's *The Wild Duck*, which had left one Hollywood director exclaiming, "My God! She's made of lightning."

4. "To my knowledge, Mother saw only one film of mine," recalled Joan Fontaine. When the star was hospitalized for an ovarian cyst, her mother took her place at the opening of *Rebecca*. "This must be a golden moment for you, Mrs. Fontaine," columnist Louella Parsons gushed. "Mother looked coolly down her aquiline nose and replied, 'Joan has always seemed rather phony to me in real life, but she's quite believable on the screen.' "

5. "I can't believe it! I simply cannot believe Grace won," Jack Kelly told reporters after his daughter had won an Oscar for *The Country Girl*. "Of the four children, she's the last one I expected to support me in my old age."

6. "I hope not" was Ronald Reagan's response to a reporter's question on whether his daughter Maureen was running for the Senate in 1982. She did make the bid, though unsuccessfully.

7. When George Walker Bush was considering a run for the Texas governorship in 1990, his mother failed to wax enthusiastic. "I'm rather hoping he won't . . ." Barbara Bush said. "I'm hoping, having bought the Rangers, he'll get so involved he won't do it. When you make a major commitment like that, I think maybe you won't be running for governor. . . ."

Did Mom hold sway in Bush's decision not to run? "That's crud," said George W. "My mother's been telling me stuff to do for forty-four years, and I haven't done eighty percent of it."

"MY FATHER WOULD BE FOR ME IF I WAS RUNNING FOR THE
HEAD OF THE COMMUNIST PARTY"

If you're wondering whose dad would support such offbeat political calling, the answer is Joe Kennedy, Sr., a one-man cheering squad for his son John and indeed for all his energetic brood.

"If I walked out on the stage and fell flat on my face, Father would say I fell better than anyone else," said John F. Kennedy when he was running for Congress for the first time. But his father was never really put to the test.

Not so Harry Truman. His daughter, Margaret, who fancied herself a singer, embarked on a concert tour and received a poor review from *Washington Post* music critic Paul Hume. He immediately received an angry note from the President. It was written in longhand, hand-stamped, and personally carried to the mailbox so as to avoid Bess's scrutiny. Truman made it clear that if the two ever met, Hume would "need a new nose, a lot of beefsteak for black eyes, and perhaps a supporter below."

"I'm absolutely positive my father wouldn't use language like that," Margaret demurred. However the President phrased it, one thing was clear: His support was unwavering, and no muffed arpeggios would ever change that.

Richard Nixon also got a bad notice in the papers: he made the front page for accepting money from a secret slush fund. "When those headlines first came in the paper, I just wanted to hide that paper," said Nixon's mother, Hannah. "I didn't want anyone to see it. I couldn't eat. I knew that it wasn't true, but, well, what could I do?" She wasn't one to go to bat for Dick when the going got tough. And when the going was good, compliments seldom slipped through her pursed lips. To reporters who asked her if her son would make a good President, she said: "I think he would make a good President if God is on his side." When they wanted to know if she saw "a new Nixon," as was being advertised in his 1968 comeback, she replied, "No, I never knew anyone to change so little."

As parents the Carters were of the Kennedy school. "Amy's been arrested four times, three times for protesting apartheid and this last time for what she considers, and I consider, illegal activity of the CIA in Nicaragua," bragged Jimmy. When Amy, then a nineteen-year-old Brown University sophomore, participated in a protest against the CIA, she was acquitted of charges of disorderly conduct. Jimmy declared himself "a very proud father."

One of Amy's codefendants was ex-Yippie and sixties icon Abbie Hoffman, himself a father with children who trod on the wrong side of the law. His daughter Ilya once told him she got arrested, and he responded, "Great! What for?"

"I told him I'd gone camping in a graveyard," recalled Ilya. " 'Well, that's a good start,' he said. And I thought, 'Dad, you're not supposed to say that to me!' "

But it was difficult to outrebel Abbie, as his son Andrew learned. "Everything I tried—he agreed with me."

If Andrew had run for head of the Communist party, his father would *really* have been for him.

### MOTHER KNOWS BEST

1. "Sometimes when I look at my children, I say to myself, 'Lillian, you should have stayed a virgin.' "—Lillian Carter.

2. "I taught Ralph to be human . . . to think of others before he thought of himself."—Rose Nader.

3. "I can't understand all the fuss over Elvis. I think I have a better voice than he does."—Gladys Presley.

4. "If he had followed my advice years ago, he'd be a senator by now."—Regina Haig on her son, Al, who held the rank of general and was White House chief of staff at the time.

5. "I'll give him Frankie Satin with a shot to knock him cold," Dolly Sinatra told her son when his manager proposed a non-Italian stage name. "Your name is Sinatra, and it's going to stay Sinatra. So tell him to fuck off with this Frankie Satin crap."

6. "If all parents today were as strict as I was, we wouldn't have so many brats and little vandals."—Dr. Benjamin Spock's mother, Mildred.

7. "I am not a cookie-baking mother. Well, that's not true. I am a cookie-baking mother, but I'm not a traditional cookie-baking mother."—Cher.

8. "Why can't you look more like Muriel Humphrey or Pat Nixon?"—Jackie Kennedy's mother during the 1960 campaign. She was distressed that her daughter's designer fashions were intimidating the public.

9. "His father and I raised our boy as a good Christian. He was baptized and confirmed in the Episcopal Church. We taught him every Christian principle. Imagine saying he's just now become a Christian!"—the mother of Nixon protégé Charles Colson after he was publicly born again.

10. "Dear Ted: Did you ever think of eating an apple at noontime? I used to send apples to the boys at school. They are

very good in New England at this time of year and much more thinning than other types of desserts."—Rose Kennedy in a letter to her son the senator.

## YOU'RE NOT MY MOM AND OTHER DISCOVERIES THAT TEND TO BE MADE BY HAPPENSTANCE

*"I know a secret," said Michael Reagan, age four.*
*"Don't tell me. I don't want to know," said his older sister,*
*Maureen, Jane Wyman and Ronald Reagan's daughter.*
*"You're getting a blue dress for your present," said Michael.*
*Maureen burst into tears and shot back, "I know a secret, too.*
*You're adopted."*

The question of parentage tends to rank right up there with Santa Claus; telling the truth is sure to involve tears and disillusion, so no one is really eager to get the facts out on the table. That gives the Maureen Reagans of the world a lot of room in which to operate.

Poor Maureen. Not only did she spill the beans with her brother ("Your father and I chose you because you were just what we wanted," Jane Wyman explained when Michael went running to her), but she managed to reenact virtually the same scene with her half sister, Patti.

Ronnie and Nancy had just explained to their seven-year-old daughter, Patti, that Michael, who had moved in with them, was her brother, a fact she proudly announced to Maureen, then aged nineteen.

"And do you know what that makes you and me?" Maureen responded.

"No, what?" asked Patti.

"That makes you and me sisters." She thought Patti would be pleased.

The result: tears and pandemonium. Ronald Reagan's response: "Well, we just haven't gotten that far yet."

Though the management style is pure Reagan—minimal involvement, government or otherwise—it can be hard for a parent to anticipate the right time to burst a child's bubble.

"I was playing on the playground with a group of boys, and some lady called me over. She whispered to me, 'See that kid

From this Hollywood photo, it looked like baby Maureen Reagan, shown with beaming Ronald Reagan and Jane Wyman, had entered a charmed family circle. However, there were surprises to come.

over there with the curly hair, well, he's your brother.' " Seven-year-old Noah Robinson would have none of that. He went and got his father and had him take a look. The child in question: Jesse Jackson, a neighbor whom he played with. "The expression on my father's face told me that the lady was right," recalled Noah. "He held my hand all the way back to the house. He sank down in the telephone chair and explained what had happened, which I did not understand until much later."

"A tabloid called to tell me, 'We found your daughter.' I was stunned," recalled Roseanne Arnold. "They had gotten hold of the birth certificate of the baby girl I bore out of wedlock and gave up for adoption after nine days in Denver when I was eighteen. I was so pissed off." To put it mildly. Rather than have a tabloid intrude ("They had been asking questions, showing up in [her adoptive family's] garage, scaring the shit out of them"), Arnold hired a private detective to locate her daughter, Brandi Brown, with whom she had a tearful reunion in 1989. "What was really weird was that . . . everyone had known about the Browns adopting a little girl out of Denver. They were friends with a lot of my family, but nobody ever put it together."

Grade-school classmates of Jason Smith put it together, calling him Little Joe. The boy had been briefly adopted by Michael Landon, *Bonanza*'s Little Joe, but given up when Landon's marriage to his first wife, Dodie, failed. "I always wondered why Mom used to make me watch *Bonanza*," said Smith of his adoptive mother, Alma Smith, who told him the facts of his life when he was ten years old.

Gossip—many in Jason's town assumed he was Landon's love child—plagues many an "unnatural" family unit. The only way to head it off at the pass is to find a way to break the story early, which, like a good journalist, Barbara Walters did. When her adopted daughter, Jackie, was about five, the two were taking a bath. "[S]he asked about parts of my body," recalled Barbara. "I said that breasts were used by mommies to feed their babies. And she asked about her vagina. I said, 'This is where a baby comes from. There are two ways that mommies who want babies have them—through this way and through adoption.' "

Jerry Ford knew which method his mother used, and he knew Gerald R. Ford, Sr., his mother's second husband, wasn't his father. But that didn't lessen what he called the "first major shock of my life."

In the spring of 1930 he was in high school and working part-time at a restaurant. "I was behind the counter in my regular spot near the register when I noticed a man standing by the candy display case. He'd been there fifteen or twenty minutes without saying a word and he was staring at me. Finally, he came over. 'I'm Leslie King, your father,' he said. 'Can I take you out to lunch?' "

Jerry Ford, born Leslie King, Jr., "was stunned." His father, passing through town, had stopped at the high school to locate his son and been directed to the restaurant. King took Jerry to lunch, gave him twenty-five dollars, drove him back to South High, and left. That night in bed, Ford "broke down and cried."

The tears are understandable. A child can accept the facts—
the who, what, where, and when of his family tree—and still be
thrown by the whys and hows. *Why*, as in "Why did you leave
me?" *How*, as in "How come you haven't made an effort to
contact me?"

"Every birthday I thought about it. You know, my birthday's
coming and maybe she's out there and she just kind of forgot.
Those were real tough times," said David Borher, born as a result
of a brief romance between a Hollywood producer and Judith
Campbell Exner, former lover of JFK and mobster Sam Giancana.
When Borher was twenty-four and decided to contact his natural
mother, he was given an indication she was famous. But when
her name was disclosed, "Who?" was his only response. He went
to the library, read old newspapers, discovered the *People* article
recounting her affair, and borrowed her autobiography. The book
made the difference. In it she wrote that "she couldn't give me
the life that she thought I deserved"—continued FBI harassment
made Exner decide to give up her child—and she said "I wonder
about him every day . . . I constantly wanted to call the adoption
agency asking if he's all right, is there anything I can do for him."

When Borher read that, a light bulb went off. "I said, 'Yeah,
she's my mother. Yeah, this is *her*.' " She loved him. She cared
about him. That was all he really wanted to know. The rest was
gravy.

Often it's not the facts of life that are the problem; it's the
facts of love.

### VANISHED HOPES

*Suddenly, in a few seconds of radio time, it was all over. My first
son, whose birth had brought me such joy that I jumped up in the
hall outside the room where he was born and touched the ceiling—
the child, the scholar, the preacher . . . all of it gone.*
—Martin Luther King, Sr.

A few seconds of radio bulletins have changed so many families in our increasingly violent age. Robert Kennedy, who would
make radio time himself, ruminated after his brother Jack's death,
"I was just thinking out there—if my mother hadn't had more
children after her first four, she would have nothing now. . . . I

guess the only reason we've survived is that there are more of us than there is trouble."

The trouble with trouble—or at least this particular brand of trouble—is that we not only lose someone we love but lose the hopes we have pinned on our children.

"A child's death is impossible to describe," recalled Elaine Holstein. She was driving home from work when she heard on the car radio that four student demonstrators had been killed in a confrontation with national guardsmen at Kent State University in Ohio. Her son, Jeffrey Miller, was enrolled there. He had told her "he was going to a rally and might get arrested, but wouldn't get his head broken." She decided she'd better "tell him to get the hell out of there until things calmed down." Jeffrey's phone rang and rang. A stranger answered. The voice said, "He's dead."

"Sometimes I think Jeffrey's death made no difference," said Holstein. "Other times I think it may have brought the war to an end sooner. After all this time I just don't know."

What's a mother to do? Doris Tate, whose daughter, actress Sharon Tate, was killed by followers of Charles Manson, was unstrung for a long time. "It took three years to say that she had been murdered—to say she's not around. She's not in a movie in Europe. She's not working overseas or somewhere else." Then in 1988 Tate helped pioneer a program called Parents of Murdered Children, and she talked to prison inmates, trying to get them to understand crime from a victim's point of view. "I have to believe that it's all worthwhile," said Tate. "Okay, let's reverse that. If I could save Sharon, how hard would I work at it? Nothing's too monumental." Especially if it can spare other parents from vanished hopes and a few seconds of radio time.

ALL IN THE FIRST FAMILY, OR . . . THE BROTHER PROBLEM

*I got a mama who joined the Peace Corps when she was sixty-eight, I got one sister who's a Holy Roller preacher. Another wears a helmet and rides a motorcycle. And my brother thinks he's going to be President. So that makes me the only sane one in the family.*
—Billy Carter

Oh, brother! If you've got one and you're President, it's open season for trouble. "I'll make more money than Jimmy makes," said Billy Carter in 1977, "but I work harder." That year the President's brother lent his name to a brand of beer and pulled in five hundred thousand dollars in personal appearance fees and endorsements.

Jimmy's view on the subject: "I might say, first of all, I don't have any control over what my brother says or what he does. . . ."

When LBJ was a senator, he said of his brother, "Sam Houston is my chief political adviser—always has been." At the White House the President insisted his brother come to stay but kept him under a firm watch on the third floor. "It seemed, in fact, as if Sam Houston was under some sort of house arrest," commented the chief usher, J. B. West. The problem was that Sam Houston Johnson was an alcoholic. Once when Lyndon got drunk, he called his brother over and said, "I want you to take a damned good look at me, Sam Houston. Open your eyes and look at me. 'Cause I'm drunk, and I want you to see how you look to me, Sam Houston, when you come home drunk." In his will LBJ, a wealthy man, left only five thousand dollars to the family's black sheep.

Though Nixon tried to sweep his brother problems under the rug, he managed to immortalize Donald Nixon by calling him "my poor damn, dumb brother" on the Watergate tapes. In his memoirs he wrote almost nothing about the man who, when Dick was Vice President, opened a string of restaurants selling "Nixonburgers," financed with a $205,000 loan from Howard Hughes. The venture went bankrupt—and caused Richard Nixon embarrassment in his 1962 bid for California's governorship. His opponent, Pat Brown, asked whether it was "proper for a governor, morally or ethically, to permit his family to receive a secret loan from a major defense contractor in the United States."

When Dick was President, he took no chances. In September 1973 *The Washington Post* revealed Nixon had the Secret Service tap Donald's phone. In the 1974 Watergate investigation it came out that the No. 2 Nixon was also spied upon. "Look, I want a complete surveillance on Don. Keep tabs on him and all the contacts he makes. I don't want people taking advantage of him," the President told H. R. Haldeman. "I don't care how you do it— just keep him covered."

Why were there so few problems among the Kennedy brothers? For one, it may be that there were just too many of them.

One day when JFK came home from boarding school, two friends picked him up at the railroad station. Kennedy jokingly said, "I want to stop by the house for a minute and see if there's anybody new in the family." He came out and said, "By God, there is." It was Teddy.

The other reason may be that the Kennedys had a strong stage manager: their dad. As presidential adviser Clark Clifford recalled, "Joe made it clear to Jack that he wanted the President-elect to appoint Bobby attorney general. When Jack protested that 'Bobby's never practiced law a day in his life.' Joe said, 'Don't worry, he'll learn. And I'm telling you this: We all worked our tails off to make you President. Now I want Bobby to have his chance.'"

# 2
# Financial Tea Leaves: Finding Character in a Wallet

## THE VALUE OF A DOLLAR

*If you know how people feel about money, that's more revealing than*
*any other single thing I know, including sleeping with them.*
—playwright Jerry Sterner, author of the hit *Other People's Money*,
who lost five hundred thousand dollars in the 1987 stock market
crash before turning to writing full-time

Sterner has a point. Why bed down with
anyone if you're searching for character clues? Looking in a wallet
is easier. If you know Ralph Nader feels "it's always been boring
to think about money," you have Ralph's values in a nutshell.

Despite Marla Maples's statement, headlined on the front
page of the *New York Post*, BEST SEX I'VE EVER HAD, no amount of
nighttimes with Donald Trump could disclose more about his
view of women than his decision to pay then-wife Ivana "a salary
of a dollar a year and all the dresses she wants" for running the
Plaza Hotel in New York.

Money attitudes are as individual as a fingerprint. To figure
them out, all you have to do is pick up a charge-card bill.

"Lookit, Elvis," said Vernon Presley, "I know you don't like
me sayin' anythin' about your money, but I just got these from
California and I wanna check 'em with you. There must be a
mistake, because this one's from Kerr's and it says you charged
thirty-eight thousand dollars in guns there this month."

"Christmas shoppin', Daddy. That's all."

Jack Kennedy found one bill that said, "Department store—
forty thousand dollars." When he asked Jackie, "What the hell
does this mean?" she said she didn't remember.

"That Jackie is unbelievable. She thinks she can keep on
spending it forever. . . . God, she's driving me crazy, absolutely
crazy, I tell you," Kennedy said. The Kennedys' personal expenses

their first year in the White House were $145,446. "Do you realize I only make a hundred thousand as President?" he reminded her.

Not that Kennedy, the son of a millionaire, had any need to live on his salary. But a willingness to spend money is quite different from having it.

Alabama governor George Wallace refused to call out state troops to protect the "so-called demonstrators" who were marching from Selma to Montgomery in 1965. His reason: The state didn't have the four hundred thousand dollars he said would be necessary to pay the troopers.

In 1967 Martin Luther King said, "It is estimated that we spend three hundred and twenty-two thousand dollars for each enemy we kill in Vietnam while we spend in the so-called War on Poverty in America only about fifty-three dollars for each person classified as poor."

Money is just another word for values. Which is why parents endeavor early on to teach their kids the meaning of a dollar. However, the results often aren't what they'd like. For example, Huntington Hartford, heir to the A&P fortune, graduated from Harvard and was welcomed into the family firm—as a clerk. Surely it would do him good to learn things from the bottom up, the family thought. He was put in charge of monitoring sales of bread and pound cake, but anyone who monitored him quickly discovered he arrived late, left early, and liked to take naps on the floor. "There he was," said his uncle and employer, "surrounded by people who really had to work for a living, and he was receiving callers who wanted to sell him paintings." Hartford was fired when he took off yet another day to see the Harvard-Yale game. "I had an income of over a million dollars a year. Can you imagine me sitting out with a bunch of clerks?"

Clearly he'd already figured out that money entitled him to pretty much anything he wanted. But wealthy parents can instill a penny-wise message. In the case of the Rockefellers there were minor glitches—Nelson tried to illustrate one of his tax proposals by saying, "Take an average family with an income of a hundred thousand dollars"—but on the whole his family knew what was what.

John D. Rockefeller paid his son, John D., Jr., two cents for sharpening pencils. John D. III doled out allowances that began at fifteen cents when his children were five and eventually increased to five dollars a week. "There were three little jewelry boxes," recalled his daughter Alida. "I got fifteen cents to spend, fifteen cents to save, and fifteen cents to give away. Every Christmas season my father would sit down with me and we'd decide who I'd give the money in the third box to. Usually some went to Riverside Church, and always to one of the one hundred neediest cases in *The New York Times.* We read the cases together and decided which to give to. It was a real ritual, one of the times we were closest."

The Kennedys, by and large, knew the value of a dollar, even though Bobby ran into problems when he served the proverbial stint as a newsboy. He talked the chauffeur into driving him on his paper route in the family Rolls-Royce—until Rose got wind of it. "Mother thought this was all wrong, that he should walk or ride his bike. She was dead right, of course," reported Bobby's sister Eunice Shriver.

When Joseph Kennedy, Sr., set up a trust fund for each of his children, William Randolph Hearst warned him that if they were able to be independent, they would take their money and run when they came of age. Joe countered by saying, "If that's the only way to hold them, I've been a lousy father."

The value of the bequeather of dollars, like the value of a dollar, is ultimately measured in sense, not cents.

BUYMANSHIP: CHARACTER IN A WALLET

*You just remember that every man—I can buy—I, Howard Hughes, can buy any man in the world, or I can destroy him.*

Hughes may have ended up alone with his millions, but not his sentiments. "You can buy those monkeys anyway," was the view of Nixon's 1968 campaign manager, John Mitchell, on the black vote.

"I'm telling you this, and it's cold turkey," said Paul Brown, coach of the Cleveland Browns when his 1949 team lost for the first time after winning twenty-nine consecutive games. "If those of you who fell down on the job don't bounce back, I'll sell you."

George Foreman liked to say, after he was born again, "The old George Foreman is dead, and I got his money." He'd traded the boxing ring for the pulpit. It felt a little funny to have a worldly man's bank account, but who was he to complain?

Lee Iacocca didn't have even the slightest qualms about the things he did for money. "God, was I greedy! My generation wasn't looking for 'quality of life'; we were money-grubbers." If Iacocca sported his ambitions like a glittery hood ornament, Wall Streeter Ivan Boesky wore his like a monogrammed shirt. He summed up the Reagan era with "I think greed is healthy. You can be greedy and still feel good about yourself."

Fred Astaire didn't give his aspirations the soft shoe, but money clearly was the sole of his quickstep. "I am not sending messages with my feet," he said. "All I ever wanted was not to come up empty. I did it for the dough and the old applause." And Paul McCartney knew exactly what was going on when he sang for his supper. "Somebody said to me, 'But the Beatles were antimaterialistic.' That's a huge myth. John and I literally used to sit down and say, 'Now, let's write a swimming pool.' "

Sugar Ray Robinson guzzled cash like the gas for one of his signature flamingo pink Cadillacs. "I went through four million dollars, but I have no regrets." Though he died virtually broke in 1989, in his heyday he owned a Harlem nightclub called Sugar Ray's plus dry-cleaning, lingerie, and barber shops. On his boxing tours to Europe, he brought along a valet, barber/golf pro, manicurist, trainer, assorted family members, and a "fancy" or lady friend. His joyride forced him to stay in boxing long after his prime, but he said, "If I had the chance to do it over again, I'd do it the same way. I didn't gamble away my money. I used it to let people live. I took my family and my friends on trips with me. I loaned it to strangers to pay their bills, and sometimes I didn't get it back."

Understand the cash register in the brain, and you understand the man or the woman. "There was a time in my life when I spent ninety percent of my money on booze and broads. And the rest of it I just wasted," said Georgia Representative (and former *Dukes of Hazzard* actor) Ben Jones.

"I'm so naïve about finances," confessed actress Brooke Shields. "Once when my mother mentioned an amount and realized I didn't understand, she had to explain: 'That's like three Mercedes.' Then I understood."

"Shameless Exploitation in the Pursuit of the Common

Good" reads the stationery for the Newman's Own food company. Founder Paul donates all after-tax profits—an estimated eight million dollars a year—to charity. "If we stop having fun, we're closing up shop" is his theory.

"Who's a hippie? I'm Jewish," Abbie Hoffman told a guard at the New York Stock Exchange who thought he and his friends looked suspicious. The guard decided it wasn't a good idea to keep a Jew out, and Hoffman and crew signed up for a regular guided tour of the exchange. When they got to the balcony, they opened up bags of bills and showered the trading floor. They knew that quicker than you could say "cash," capitalists would be down on their knees groveling for dollars and Hoffman would be on the evening news, dancing and celebrating the end of money. Commented a tourist: "I'm from Missouri, and I've been throwing away money in New York for five days now. This is quicker and a hell of a lot more fun."

"I've always thought, and I know this sounds on the edge of arrogant," said author Robert Fulghum of *All I Really Need to Know I Learned in Kindergarten* fame, "that anyone could make money. Making a life worth living, that was the real test."

Money is a multiple-choice question. Choose an attitude; choose your friends and lovers. Choose one from column A or all the above. Just make sure you scrutinize all the clues to character a wallet offers.

EARNING THEIR KEEP: WHO GOT PAID WHAT

*25 CENTS PER QUESTION.* At the Kennedy compound in Hyannis the kids would greet tourists through the hedges and offer to answer questions like "What does Jackie eat for breakfast?" for a quarter. They also sold "Kennedy Sand," scooped up from a nearby beach, for $1 a bag.

*$1 FOR A LIFE STORY.* The original cast members of *A Chorus Line* sat around in a Manhattan loft in 1974, talking into a tape recorder and telling the tales that were developed into a musical and drew crowds for a legendary fifteen years. They signed away the rights to the stories of their lives for a dollar. The musical went on to earn $50 million on and off Broadway. "We were just stupid kids. We wanted to perform," said one cast member, Nancy Lane.

"Now we look back and say, 'Yeah, what I did for love—give me a break.' "

*$60 A WEEK.* "I took it, I was just so happy to have the job," said Bill Cosby of a six-day-a-week $60 stint at a Greenwich Village coffeehouse in 1962. "Then I started to figure out how much it would be to live [in New York]." The club owner offered lodgings in a storage room over the club. Its amenities amounted to a mattress. Cosby said, "I went out and bought DDT and sprinkled it all around. I gave the guy five dollars a month to use his bathroom, and he allowed me one shower a day."

*$1.40 AN HOUR, DOWN FROM $1,046 A MINUTE.* Even when he was sleeping, Drexel Burnham Lambert junk bond wizard Michael Milken was earning $1,046 a minute, day in and day out, in 1987. His annual salary of $550 million a year was more than the total net worth of J. P. Morgan when he died in 1913. Subsequently Milken's prison wages at Pleasonton, California, were as much as $1.40 an hour, received for chores like scrubbing toilets.

*$1,500 A PITCH.* In 1991 Roger Clemens of the Boston Red Sox was paid $28 a second or about $1,700 a minute on the mound for a total annual salary of $5.3 million. "I'll be the first one to tell you that a police officer or a teacher are the most underpaid people in the country. They should be making the dollars that we make as athletes," he said. "But there's only two hundred pitchers in the major leagues. If you . . . could throw ninety-five miles an hour from sixty feet and six inches [toward] a seventeen-inch plate at will, you'd be pushing me for my job."

*$5,000 A WEEK.* Stripper Blaze Starr, who attracted the attention of Louisiana Governor Earl Long, had a high-paying act that was so hot her red velvet couch smoked during one set; in another set, a panther, lured by strategically placed raw meat, removed her dress. Earl took one look and was a goner. "I never *used* Earl, like they said," she commented years after their affair. "I was making twice as much as he did anyway!"

*$14,000 A YEAR.* Voluptuous Elizabeth Ray, secretary to Representative Wayne Hays, Democrat of Ohio, said: "I can't

type. I can't file. I can't even answer the phone." Her salary, she claimed, was payment for sexual favors. It proved to be Hays's downfall.

*$36,000 FOR TWO SETS.* That's what rock star Jimi Hendrix earned at Woodstock. He was the highest-paid artist at the concert. The Who played for $12,500.

*$50,000 A YEAR.* Spy John Walker had retired from the Navy and active secrets gathering in favor of running his own private investigation business. "I was making fifty thousand honest dollars a year when you arrested me—you pricks."

*$110,000 A YEAR.* That was General Manuel Noriega's pay as a CIA informant.

*$350,000 A MOVIE.* John Belushi couldn't "fucking believe it. I've made it." He had already made *Animal House*, but for *1941* he received a star's salary.

*$400,000 A YEAR.* Working for Merrill Lynch sure beat being a press secretary—at least financially—until Larry Speakes published his memoir of his Reagan years. The book, *Speaking Out*, included one very expensive paragraph. After the Soviets shot down the Korean Air Lines Flight 007 passenger plane, he wrote: "Since the President had almost nothing to say [about the incident] during the national security and congressional leadership meetings, I made presidential quotes out of [Secretary of State George] Shultz's comment. . . . My decision to put Shultz's words in Reagan's mouth played well, and neither of them complained." When the book came out, the press, politicians, and much of America complained, and Speakes was out of a $400,000-a-year job.

*$1 MILLION FOR FOUR TELEVISION INTERVIEWS.* That's what earned Richard Nixon a chance to say, "Well, when the President does it, that means it is not illegal," on television with David Frost.

*$2 MILLION IN TWO WEEKS.* That was the going rate for Ronald Reagan to lecture in Japan in 1989. "I would have made a lot more money if I'd gone back to my original career making movies. I felt that would be cashing in on the presidency."

*$3 MILLION FOR A TRIP TO THE ALTAR.* After she was widowed, Jackie Kennedy realized, "I can't really marry a dentist from New Jersey." She was getting $175,000 a year from the Kennedys plus a $10,000 presidential widow's pension and protection from the Secret Service. But she would lose all that if she married. Hence financial negotiations had to take place when Aristotle Onassis proposed. Teddy Kennedy was dispatched. So were lawyers. The agreement: a cash payment of $3 million plus the annual interest on a $1 million trust for each of the children until they reached the age of twenty-one. Onassis asked his secretary, Lynn Alpha Smith, "Do you think three million dollars is too much?"

"Hell, no," she replied. "You can buy a supertanker on that, but then you have to pay fuel, maintenance, insurance, and a lot of extras." From then on Jackie was dubbed "Supertanker" around the office. Said Smith, "Onassis didn't mind. It made him laugh. 'It's Supertanker on the line,' I'd announce whenever she called."

*APPROXIMATELY $12 MILLION OVER TEN YEARS.* That's the tidy sum Time Inc. CEO Richard Munro pocketed when his company acquired Warner Communications in 1989. "That sounds like a lot of money unless you live in New York and live in the world I live in. In New York City it's like Monopoly money."

*$112 MILLION (ESTIMATED) TO END A MARRIAGE.* When TV producer Norman Lear became an ex, his divorce settlement was so hefty *Forbes* magazine had to bump him off its list of the four hundred wealthiest Americans. His wife, Frances, promptly plunked down $30 million on *Lear's*, a magazine bearing her last name. But there was plenty of change in her pocket. "For older women, like older men," she said, "money is a plus when it comes to attracting the opposite sex."

*UNKNOWN QUANTITIES.* When Mike Wallace asked H. L. Hunt, then eighty years old, to "give us a horseback guess" as to how much he was worth (estimates ranged from $400 million to $2 billion), Hunt said, "Well, you see they talk about that I have an income of a million dollars a week. . . . And that is a lot of percent erroneous."

"It is erroneous? It's bigger or smaller than that?"

"I would starve to death with an income of a million dollars a week."

*MORE THAN YOU CAN COUNT.* "The news about being the richest man in America came to me as a surprise. . . . I don't know how much money I have, I don't know how they would know," said J. Paul Getty in the late 1950s.

# 3
# Power and Politics: The Rules of the Game

## POMP AND CIRCUMSTANCES

*There is a danger that the individual comes to believe that just because his voice is amplified and reaches halfway around the world he is therefore more intelligent, more discerning than he is when his voice only reached from one end of the bar to the other.*
—Edward R. Murrow

Murrow was speaking of the vanities of television, but smoke and mirrors, ego and illusion have long surrounded the bully pulpit of the presidency. One day a man is simply a private citizen, the next the leader of the free world—with "Hail to the Chief" sounding every time he walks in the room.

"Politics is just like show business," said Ronald Reagan, who ought to know. "You have a hell of an opening, you coast for a while, you have a hell of a closing." In between he mastered the art of using the theater of office like no other president. For his press conferences he strode down a red-carpeted hallway and posed at a lectern positioned in front of open doors—the best possible camera angle. When it came to signing the historic 1981 tax cut bill, he used a different pen for each letter of his name so as to have the maximum number of souvenirs to give away. "It's times like these I wish I had a middle name," he said to press secretary Larry Speakes, who replied, "You do, Mr. President. It's Wilson."

Red carpets, a presidential plane stocked with packets of M&Ms bearing the Air Force One insignia (Reagan's innovation), a White House staffed with four florists and four calligraphers (as it was during George Bush's tenure)—it's hard to complain about the trappings of power. But most Presidents have tried to shrug off the importance of the perks.

"Now, some men, like Nixon, want power so they can strut

around to 'Hail to the Chief,' " said Lyndon Johnson while skinny-dipping in the White House pool with press secretary Bill Moyers and speech writer Richard Goodwin. "I wanted power to use it."

"[Y]ou know why I wanted it?" said Nixon. "The trappings? Hell, no. If I never had to review an honor guard, I'd have been delighted."

If anyone was truly unconcerned about the trappings, it was James Earl Carter. Sworn in as Jimmy, he walked from his inauguration to the White House and that night at the ball delighted in saying, "How many of you like my wife's old blue dress? She made it herself six years ago." He liked to wear cardigans and jeans. He sold the presidential yacht, eliminated limousines for Cabinet members, and said with utmost sincerity, "The pomp and ceremony of office does not appeal to me . . . I'm no better than anyone else, and . . . I don't think we need to put on the trappings of a monarchy in a nation like our own."

But for some pomp does have its allure. "I was eleven then. I remember reading it in *The Weekly Reader*, how Vice President Nixon planted a tree here [at the ambassador's residence in Asunción, Chile], and I always wanted to do that," said Dan Quayle, who got his wish as Vice President in 1990. "It's true. I was eleven years old. I read it."

The downside of a profession devoted to pomp: It can be hazardous to your health. John Kennedy injured his back at a tree-planting ceremony in Ottawa in 1961, and Vice President Lyndon Johnson was exuberantly shaking hands in Pakistan when an American doctor gasped, "My God! He's shaking hands with a leper!"

THE RULES OF THE GAME

*Being in politics is like being a football coach. You have to be smart enough to understand the game—and dumb enough to think it's important.*
—Eugene McCarthy

Herewith some rules of the game:
1. *Master the art of handling large, adoring crowds.* "Now here's what you do," said Dwight D. Eisenhower. "Get out there.

Don't look so serious. Smile. When the people are waving at you, wave your arms and move your lips, so you look like you're talking to them. It doesn't matter what you say; let them see you're reacting to them."

2. *Learn to wave.* Ike "greeted the crowds with both arms stretched above his head in the V for Victory sign, while Adlai only raised one hand to his ear as if he were waving a handkerchief," recalled *New York Times* reporter James Reston. When he told Stevenson that "this sissy wave would cost him a million votes," the candidate replied, "I know, but I've got bursitis and can't get my arms any higher."

3. *Get your picture taken whenever possible.* "If the cameras are at the end of the table for a picture down the line of a delegation meeting, the thing to do is lean forward. Then you cover the face[s] of the three other people between you and the President, usually more senior officials . . . and it makes you appear to be sitting right next to the President," advised Helmut "Hal" Sonnenfeldt, who served on the National Security Council in the Nixon and Ford administrations. His adroitness at getting into photographs earned him the Secret Service nickname of the Ferret; whenever he wasn't in a photo, Ford used to joke, "Where's Hal?"

4. *Mind your manners.* When young politicians came to former House Speaker Tip O'Neill for advice, he told them his Mrs. O'Brien story about his first election—a failed bid for the city council when he was a senior in college. To his surprise, the one area where he didn't get the votes he expected was his own neighborhood.

"Mrs. O'Brien met me the next day, and she said, 'My husband and I voted for you, even though you didn't ask us.' I said, 'Mrs. O'Brien, you live across the street. I shoveled your walk. I sifted your ashes. I did errands. And not only that, you taught me in high school. I didn't think I had to ask you.' She said, 'Thomas, people like to be asked, and people like to be thanked.' So when a young politician comes to me for advice, I say, 'People like to be asked, whether it's for their vote, their time, their services, their money. And when they've given you something, they like to be thanked.' "

5. *Act your age.* "One thing I remember is Ted Sorensen riding in the back seat with the senator," said White House re-

porter Marianne Means, "and the senator was chewing gum. Sorensen said, 'Presidential candidates do not chew gum in public,' and John Kennedy threw it out."

6. *Control your temper.* In 1960 Nixon was campaigning in Iowa, driving long distances to reach small towns. Furious that his planners had plotted things so inefficiently, he began to kick the back of the car seat in front of him "with both feet. And he wouldn't stop! Thump! Thump! Thump!" recalled H. R. Haldeman. "When the car stopped at a small town in the middle of nowhere, [Major Don] Hughes [a military aide seated directly in front of Nixon], white-faced, silently got out of the car and started walking straight ahead, down the road and out of the town. . . . I believe he would have walked clear across the state if I hadn't set out after him and apologized for Nixon and finally talked him into rejoining us."

7. *Don't settle for second best.* "Mr. President, I've still got a decision to make," Congressman George Bush said to Lyndon Johnson, "and I'd like your advice." Bush, who was thinking of running for Senate, explained, "My House seat is secure—no opposition last time—and I've got a position on Ways and Means. I don't mind taking risks but in a few more terms, I'll have seniority on a powerful committee. I'm not sure it's a gamble I should take, whether it's really worth it."

"Son," said the former President, pausing between pronouncements. "I've served in the House. And I've been privileged to serve in the Senate, too. And they're both good places to serve. So I wouldn't begin to advise you what to do, except to say this— that the difference between being a member of the Senate and a member of the House is the difference between chicken *salad* and chicken *shit.* Do I make my point?" Bush ended up with neither chicken dish; he lost the Senate race.

8. *Be creative in your campaign financing.* "We're going to beat them at their own game," vowed Jane Fonda in 1978. To help finance her then-husband Tom Hayden's bid for the U.S. Senate, she founded Jane Fonda's Workout Center and designated the Campaign for Economic Democracy, Hayden's political membership organization, its sole owner. The exercise salon yielded revenues of twenty thousand dollars a month, quickly filling Hayden's campaign coffers.

9. *Choose an opponent you can really whip.* "Kennedy speaks

over people's heads," said Nixon before the 1960 presidential debates. "I did pretty well with Khrushchev. I'll murder Kennedy."

10. *If you can, avoid being a woman.* "I moved into the presidential bid, and that was the worst campaign I ever went through in my life in terms of almost being destroyed by men. They never attacked me in terms of my ability and articulation. It was always an attack based on my gender. . . . I have met far more discrimination as a woman than being black in the field of politics," said Shirley Chisholm. The first black woman elected to Congress, she ran for President in 1972.

11. *Take the political pulse of the country.* "You know the first time I thought Johnson might be beaten," said Eugene McCarthy, "was when I realized that you could walk into any bar in America and insult Lyndon Johnson and no one would punch you in the nose."

12. *Rail against the deficit.* JFK: "This country has the largest peacetime deficit in history."

Richard Nixon: "Our deficit in the budget at this time would be irresponsible."

Ronald Reagan: "We call it the taxpayer's protection plan. And that's just what it is. It will reduce deficits by three hundred billion dollars over three years, bringing us within reach of a balanced budget by 1990."

George Bush: "These outrageous deficits cannot be permitted to go on and on and on and on."

13. *Don't be afraid to create your own myths.* Jesse Jackson's version of his childhood: "I used to run bootleg liquor, bought hot clothes. I had to steal to survive."

His father, Charles Jackson, a postal worker who married Jesse's mother, a beautician, and adopted him at the age of two: "We were never poor. We never wanted for anything. We've never been on welfare, because I was never without a job. We never begged anybody for a dime. And my family never went hungry a day in their lives."

14. *Never let anyone put the word "wimp" anywhere near your name.* "People want a country to be tough. If we had bombed Teheran, I think Jimmy would have been reelected, even though the hostages would have died," said Rosalynn Carter.

15. *Talk quickly—or else.* In 1968 the average television sound

bite was 42 seconds; in 1988 it was 9.8. "If you couldn't say it in less than ten seconds, it wasn't heard because it wasn't aired," complained Michael Dukakis, who never mastered the art of being short-winded.

16. *Never have pigeons at your party convention.* At 1:45 A.M. a tired, hot, and unenthusiastic Democratic party readied itself to hear Harry Truman's acceptance speech. Delegate placards read, WE'RE JUST MILD ABOUT HARRY. "Hail to the Chief" sounded, and fifty pigeons—ostensibly doves of peace—were released from a cage near a flower-covered Liberty Bell. Some of the birds, cooped up without water, fell straight to the floor, dead or dying. Others flew wildly. A few saw the bald head of House Speaker Sam Rayburn as an appealing target. He tried to shoo them away, creating a further commotion. Finally a national radio audience heard Rayburn say, "Get those goddamned pigeons out of here."

17. *Should your fortunes fade, choose a time-honored exit line.* "You won't have Dick Nixon to kick around anymore" was Nixon's famous comment to the press after losing the governor's race in California. Johnson updated the idea when he decided not to run in 1968: "You fellows won't have me to pick on anymore. You can find someone else to flog and insult."

WOULD YOU VOTE FOR THIS MAN?

1. "I've read about foreign policy and studied—I know the number of continents. . . ."—George Wallace during his 1968 presidential campaign.

2. "If you've seen one slum you've seen them all."—Spiro Agnew, campaigning for Vice President, in response to a question about the nation's urban problems.

3. "Known all over Washington as a shameless extrovert" was just one of the charges George Smathers leveled at incumbent Florida Senator Claude Pepper. He further asserted that Pepper was "reliably reported to practice nepotism with his sister-in-law and has a sister who was once a Thespian in Greenwich Village. Worst of all, it is an established fact that Mr. Pepper, before his marriage, practiced celibacy." Smathers won the 1950 race.

4. "No more bullshit" was Norman Mailer's campaign slogan

when he ran for mayor of New York in 1969. His earlier foray into New York politics, in 1960, was on the Existentialist ticket.

5. Vietnam should be bombed "back into the Stone Age. . . . We are swatting flies when we should be going after the manure pile," said Wallace's running mate, General Curtis E. LeMay. When his words provoked an outcry, he "reassured" voters that "the world won't come to an end if we use a nuclear weapon."

6. "I didn't have my hearing aid on. Tell me again."—Admiral James B. Stockdale, Ross Perot's running mate, in response to a question during the 1992 debates.

7. "Do I have any foreign policy experience? No. Did I have any experience before writing a song? No. Producing a show? No. Running for mayor? No."—Palm Springs, California, Mayor Sonny Bono, who tried to run for Senate in 1992.

8. "There is no Soviet domination in Eastern Europe, and there never will be during a Ford administration. . . ."—Gerald Ford as President during a TV debate with Democratic candidate Jimmy Carter on October 6, 1976. After the democratic changes that took place in Poland in 1989, Ford commented: "I came out pretty well as a prophet."

9. "For seven and a half years I have worked alongside him," George Bush said of Ronald Reagan while campaigning in 1988, "and I am proud to be his partner. We have had triumphs, we have made mistakes, we have had sex." (He meant to say, "We have had setbacks.")

RHETORICALLY SPEAKING

1. "Our future lies before us."—Thomas Dewey in his 1948 campaign.

2. "The question is whether we're gonna go forward to tomorrow or we're gonna go past to the back."—Dan Quayle.

3. "Don't worry, Jim. If that question comes up, I'll just confuse them."—President Eisenhower, speaking to his press secretary regarding the Taiwan crisis that was brewing. Ike was famous for his incomprehensible "Eisenhowerese," some of which may not have been innocent.

4. "I am in the mode of being deeply concerned and would like to be a part of finding a national answer."—George Bush.

5. "Oh, Hubert, you don't have to be interminable to be immortal."—Muriel Humphrey to her husband.

6. "I shall try to cut my remarks down, but after all I am a Negro Baptist preacher. You know nobody can control a Negro Baptist preacher, even God sometimes can't. But nevertheless, I shall try to make them like a woman's skirt—long enough to be respectable but short enough to be interesting."—Harlem Congressman Adam Clayton Powell, Jr.

7. "If Lincoln were alive today, he'd roll over in his grave."—Jerry Ford at a Lincoln's Birthday dinner.

8. Campaigning for President in 1980, Teddy Kennedy tried out garbled Spanish when speaking to a Mexican-American political organization. "Well, what do you expect?" commented a journalist. "It *was* the course he cheated on at Harvard after all."

9. "My position on Vietnam is very simple. I think our concepts as a nation and our actions have not kept pace with the changing conditions, and therefore, our actions are not completely relevant today to the realities of the magnitude and complexity of the problems that we face in this conflict," said Governor Nelson Rockefeller, prompting a reporter to ask him, "What does that mean?" Rockefeller replied, "Just what I said."

ON THE CAMPAIGN TRAIL

1. "You can't campaign in a drugstore anymore. People don't want you to see what they're buying."—Eugene McCarthy.

2. "I was born over a drugstore. They were short of log cabins that year."—Hubert H. Humphrey.

3. "Well, that's over," said JFK after a South Dakota speech in front of a huge but lukewarm crowd. "Fuck the farmers after November."

4. "What would you do if you *were* elected?" a reporter asked William Buckley, who was running for New York City mayor in 1965. "Demand a recount," Buckley answered.

5. "Republicans understand the importance of bondage between parent and child."—Dan Quayle.

6. "I don't want to be his mother. I want to be governor of Texas," said Democrat Ann Richards in response to Republican

candidate Clayton Williams's admission that he would feel uncomfortable running against a woman.

7. "Won't it be wonderful when we get back into the White House again?" said Jackie Kennedy when RFK declared his candidacy in 1968.

"What do you mean, *we?*" replied Ethel Kennedy.

8. In 1976 when Walter Mondale was campaigning for the vice presidency in Lewiston, Maine, a huge crowd came out to see him off. "I'm really very, very flattered," Mondale said as he was about to board his plane. "There must be about two thousand people here!"

Yes, he was told, "but to be perfectly truthful, we've never had a 747 land or take off at our airport before. Everyone turned out to see if it'll take off okay or crash."

9. "Thank God that's over," Jeb Magruder told John Mitchell after the Miami Beach City Council had finally voted four to three to host the Republican National Convention. Nixon's reelection committee had no other sites lined up. "Nothing worse than that can possibly happen to us in the rest of the campaign."

"You're wrong," Mitchell replied. "This was a tough one, but before the campaign is over, worse is sure to come along." He was right. Watergate was months away. G. Gordon Liddy was already getting his team ready for the Democratic headquarters break-in.

SO YOU THINK YOU WANT TO BE PRESIDENT WHEN YOU GROW UP

> *I mean, like, hasn't everybody thought about becoming President for years?*
> —George Bush

The truth is some have. And some haven't. When asked, "Did you ever have the standard boyhood dream of growing up to be President?", Bob Dylan replied, "No. When I was a boy, Harry Truman was President. Who'd want to be Harry Truman?"

JFK wouldn't have minded adding his own polish to Truman's shoes. Early in his career, newly defeated in his quest for national name recognition and the number two spot on Adlai Stevenson's ticket, Kennedy was lying in the sun on the French

Riveria. Why did he want to be President? he was asked. "I guess it's the only thing I can do," he said, without even opening his eyes.

"I always took it for granted I'd be President. It was always there, in the back of my mind," said Nelson Rockefeller, who, unlike Kennedy, thought he could just go to the head of the class without running on anyone else's ticket. He steadfastly maintained, "I am just not built for standby equipment." But when Gerald Ford became President, Rockefeller decided to let his ambitions idle on the vice presidential sidelines. "I go to funerals. I go to earthquakes," he lamented.

LBJ complained that the vice presidency was "filled with trips around the world, chauffeurs, men saluting, people clapping, chairmanship of councils, but in the end it is nothing." Furthermore, he noticed that "every time I came into John Kennedy's presence, I felt like a goddamn raven hovering over his shoulder."

Why would anyone accept such a grin-and-bear-it job? Dan Quayle offered an answer with the slip of a tongue: "I happen to be a Republican President—ah, the Vice President." One false slip of history and "vice" gets deleted from titles quite quickly.

LBJ knew the score. Even though he protested to Clare Boothe Luce before the 1960 convention, "Clare, honey, no way will I ever join that son of a bitch," he changed his tune within days. The reason he offered Luce for accepting the vice presidential slot: "Bird's been wanting me something fierce to slow down, and my health ain't been good lately, and, well, I thought this job might suit me for a spell."

"Come clean, Lyndon," countered Luce.

Johnson then said in a hushed voice, "Clare, I looked it up. One out of every four Presidents has died in office. I'm a gamblin' man, darlin', and this is the only chance I got."

History's invisible men—the Vice Presidents—are gamblers. Bush counted on one of the chanciest rolls of the dice. Not since 1836, when Andrew Jackson anointed Martin Van Buren his heir, had a Vice President made it to the White House on his own steam, a fact Bush recognized when he broke the 152-year curse. "I couldn't help but think that old Martin Van Buren was up there giving me the high five sign," he said. Martin Van Buren, of course, was a one-term president.

But there's more than luck and ambition to presidential success stories. One reason Jimmy Carter declared his candidacy was that "as governor of Georgia I had visits from some of the other people running for President, and they didn't seem very smart."

"I have a theory that in the United States those who seek the presidency never win it," explained Richard Nixon. "Circumstances rather than a man's ambition determine the result. If he is the right man for the right time, he will be chosen."

His theory is borne out by the fact that many who have made it to the Oval Office never expected to. "I am not available for and could not accept nomination to high political office . . . the necessary and wise subordination of the military to civil power will be best sustained . . . when lifelong professional soldiers . . . abstain from seeking high political office," said Dwight David Eisenhower, who declined to run more frequently than any other contemporary President. On another occasion he announced adamantly, "I cannot conceive of any circumstance that could drag out of me permission to consider me for any political post from dogcatcher to Grand High Supreme King of the Universe!"

"The thought of being President frightens me," said Ronald Reagan in 1973. "I do not think I want the job."

"I have no intention of seeking any public office in 1976," asserted Jerry Ford during his 1973 vice presidential confirmation hearings. "I can foresee no circumstances where I would change my mind."

The latest in the list of demurrals: "Right now I have absolutely no political ambition at all," victorious General H. Norman Schwarzkopf declared in March 1991.

"Getting all caught up in a political process that doesn't work . . . I wouldn't be temperamentally fit for it," said H. Ross Perot in February 1992.

"I'm not running for President," announced Donald Trump in 1988, "but if I did . . . I'd win."

OVAL OFFICE JOB DESCRIPTIONS

1. "It won't be long until I can sit back and study the whole picture and tell 'em what is to be done in each department," Harry Truman wrote to his wife, Bess, about his new job as President.

"When things come to that stage there'll be no more to this job than there was to running Jackson County and not any more worry."

2. "The pay is good and I can walk to work."—JFK.

3. "At last I've got a job where I can stay home nights," said President Eisenhower, "and, by golly, I'm going to stay home."

4. "Before you get to be President, you think you can do anything. You think you're the most powerful leader since God. But when you get in that tall chair, as you're gonna find out, Mr. President, you can't count on people. You'll find your hands tied and people cussin' you. The office is kinda like the little country boy found the hoochie-koochie show at the carnival, once he'd paid his dime and got inside the tent! It ain't exactly as it was advertised!"—LBJ to Nixon.

5. "I've been criticized for dealing too much in specifics and trying to learn too much about the government and how it works, how the economy functions and what the Congress does, the attitudes and organization of the Congress and the federal government agencies. But this is my nature. I think having come in to Washington for the first time to serve in the Federal government, I had an obligation to learn. I enjoy it and I obviously realize there are many things I don't completely comprehend."—Jimmy Carter.

6. "It's full-time work. It's very interesting. You meet interesting people. It's very important. It's exciting. You live in a beautiful White House. After supper, guess who we walk with? Millie! So it's not all hard work."—George Bush to a group of Chicago children.

7. "You go to bed every night knowing that there are things you are not aware of."—Ronald Reagan.

"WHAT PLEASES HIM PLEASES ME."

The comment was from Lady Bird Johnson regarding her husband. For the record (when reporters were not around, the story may have differed) most political wives have made it their policy to stand firmly behind their men. Some variations on a theme:

1. "I'm an old-fashioned wife, and I'll do anything my husband asks me to do."—Jackie Kennedy.

2. "I'll do anything Bobby wants me to do."—Ethel Kennedy.

3. "Whatever you want to do, I'll do it with you," said Joan Kennedy on one occasion. When Ted ran for President in 1980, she explained, ". . . it was the only chance I had to see him. He came home so seldom, it was like being courted again."

4. "Well, I try to be supportive of my husband. I just do whatever they tell me to do."—Nancy Reagan.

5. "But very rarely do I disagree with him. We've been married so long, and we've really grown up together. We've had the same experiences, we've met the same people; he's just better briefed than I am."—Barbara Bush.

*P.S.* A different drummer: "I made all the decisions."—Marilyn Quayle after her husband's first run for Congress in Indiana.

# 4
# Matters of Dress (and Undress)

## WHAT TO WEAR ON A DATE WITH DESTINY

*I wear a suit when I'm arrested. I think it helps to remind people*
*that this isn't a rowdy act but a carefully considered demonstration*
*that I deem worthy of great respect.*
—Dr. Benjamin Spock, an early anti–Vietnam War activist

When a historic moment arrives, most of us would like to look our best and be fresh as a lily. That's why, when Robert Kennedy was running for President, he changed his shirts as often as five times a day. And why his brother John, who relied on crutches to relieve back pain during his presidency, deftly kept them out of the public's sight. "He would hide his crutches and canes around the office," recalled presidential secretary Evelyn Lincoln. "It was hard for him to use them even in front of me. He used them mostly when he was alone. He was a very proud man. But I used to buy those athletic rubber supports for his back."

A desire to greet history with one's best foot forward explains why, on November 24, 1971, hijacker D. B. Cooper donned loafers and a business suit before boarding a Northwest Airliners 727, demanding two hundred thousand dollars and two sets of parachutes, and bailing out over a densely wooded area of Washington State. He was never heard from again—the only hijacker to escape both justice and history—but he sure looked swell while we knew him.

Looking good is more than mere vanity. The well dressed get taken seriously; the scruffy don't. That's why the students participating in the first sit-ins at a Nashville lunch counter "were dressed like they were on their way to church," as participant John Lewis, then a seminary student, recalled. ". . . We took our seats in a very orderly peaceful fashion. We stayed at the lunch counters studying, preparing our homework, because we were denied service." Even after the restaurant was closed to thwart their protest, the students sat there, the very model of propriety.

Propriety of a different sort characterizes philanthropist Brooke Astor when she sets out in her chauffeured limousine to visit those in the poor areas of New York City who might benefit from her riches. Every inch the heiress, she wears her best jewels, hats, and designer suits. "People expect to see Mrs. Astor, not some dowdy old lady," explained the woman whose husband, Vincent, left her sixty-seven million dollars in 1959, "and I don't intend to disappoint them."

Of course, not everyone has the same idea of what to wear on a historic occasion. Patti Davis's first choice would have been along the lines of jeans, but her mother, Nancy Reagan, talked her into a ruffled red Adolfo gown for the 1981 inaugural ball. Patti promptly put her foot through the dress, tearing it so that the hem had to be taped up at the last minute. "I'm not exactly grace in motion," she admitted.

When General William Westmoreland was superintendent of West Point in 1962, President Kennedy came to deliver the commencement address. Westmoreland's two daughters, "both resplendent in new dresses," showed up, but his seven-year-old son was nowhere to be seen. Westmoreland "hoped the President would fail to notice." No such luck. Kennedy promptly asked about the rest of the family, and the general was forced to 'fess up: "Mr. President, you have finally backed me into a corner. Last night I told the children I looked forward to introducing them to you but that they had to dress properly for the occasion. The girls were delighted, but my young son wanted to wear his base-ball uniform. I told him he would have to wear a coat and tie. 'Under those circumstances,' he said, 'I am not interested.' "

Equally uninterested in social niceties was Abbie Hoffman. When he was asked to testify before the House Un-American Activities Committee (HUAC) in 1968, he wore an Indian cos-tume, complete with feathers, a hunting knife, and a bullwhip. He brought along an electric yo-yo and, in his view, "dazzled the Committee with tricks like, 'Around-the Capitalist-World.' " At another committee appearance he wore a commercially made Stars and Stripes shirt and was promptly arrested for mutilating the American flag. "NBC was so worried about being indicted for showing him in a flag shirt that they didn't go below his Adam's apple with their cameras," reported William Kunstler, Abbie's lawyer in the Chicago Seven conspiracy trial. Hoffman spent a night in jail—but he made the TV news.

Douglas MacArthur was more subtle about it, but he also used dress to flout authority. When he went to Wake Island to meet Harry Truman during the Korean War, he showed up— late—"with his shirt unbuttoned, wearing a greasy ham and eggs cap that evidently had been in use for twenty years," as Truman recounted. Clearly "God's right-hand man"—Truman's term for MacArthur—didn't think this was an occasion worth getting dressed up for. The President was *not* amused.

Neither was Senator Daniel Inouye, chairman of the joint congressional committee investigating Iran-contra, when he interviewed Admiral John Poindexter. The committee's counsel, Arthur Liman, had briefed Inouye on Poindexter's character. Here was a guy who approached his job in textbook military fashion, who always consulted his superiors when making a decision. By deduction that meant that Iran-contra wasn't Poindexter's brainchild but a project approved by Ronald Reagan. Would Poindexter reveal any such chain of command? Inouye lectured him on duty, saying he didn't like to see a man in uniform dodging the truth and taking the Fifth Amendment. Poindexter's response: "I'm not going to wear my uniform."

After JFK was assassinated, Jackie Kennedy adamantly refused to change her bloodstained clothes for LBJ's swearing in on the plane back to Washington. "No," she said passionately. "Let them see what they've done." Much of America didn't, however. The White House photographer staged his picture so the stains were hidden; it was his feeling that photographing Jackie's bloody skirt would be too shocking.

There's drama to be had in defying convention, but most of us prepare to make headlines by polishing our shoes, brushing our teeth, and hoping to survive the day without a run in our stockings or a spot on our ties. Sometimes it works, and sometimes it doesn't. For example, in 1988, when Barbara Bush was on the campaign trail, a photographer asked the "woman in the red dress to get out of the picture." Mrs. Bush, not yet a household face, said "I looked down at my clothes, and realized he was talking about *me*."

Once, while Jack and Jackie Kennedy were vacationing in

the south of France, they were invited to a party on Aristotle Onassis's yacht. The guest of honor: Kennedy's hero, Winston Churchill. JFK donned his best formal wear and hovered around Churchill, hoping to make an impression. But the former prime minister was drinking and ignoring the guests, including a crestfallen young senator from Massachusetts. Afterward Jackie pointed to her husband's dinner jacket and suggested, "Maybe he thought you were a waiter, Jack."

In 1954 everyone knew Frank Costello was not a waiter, but being well dressed didn't get him anywhere either. The biggest mobster of his time, Costello was on trial for income tax evasion. His attorney warned him that his $350 suits were creating a negative impression with the jury. "Buy yourself a suit from one of those plain-pipe clothes racks," he told Costello.

"I'm sorry, but I'd rather blow the goddamn case," his client replied. He did and was sent to prison, though flashy dressing clearly wasn't his only crime.

Costello had a chance to fashion his public image, but what about those of us who are caught by the whirlwind of events without a moment to plan an appropriate outfit? "I had just gotten out of the tub, wearing nothing but a towel when I glanced at the TV set. Then I shouted, 'Ronnie!' " recalled Nancy Reagan. "He dashed from the shower, also wrapped in a towel, and together we watched in astonishment as President Carter conceded the election to him." Even though the media were declaring a Republican landslide, the timing of Carter's concession took the Reagans by surprise. The polls were still open in California, and no candidate had ever thrown in the towel when his opponent was clutching one. Reagan stood with his wife, both of them "trying to take in the amazing truth" that he would be President and she First Lady. "I don't think this is the way it's supposed to be," Nancy said quietly.

Richard Nixon didn't think this was the way it would be either. Having returned from a swim in the Pacific near his San Clemente home, he was getting dressed in his beach trailer when the phone rang. His press secretary told him that the House Judiciary Committee had voted 27 to 11 in favor of an article of impeachment charging that Nixon had engaged in a "course of conduct" designed to obstruct the investigation of the Watergate case. "That was how I learned that I was the first President in one hundred and six years to be recommended for impeachment: standing in a beach trailer, barefoot, wearing old trousers, a Ban-Lon shirt, and a blue windbreaker emblazoned with the Presidential Seal."

This is just the sort of situation your mother warned you about.

### THE NAKED AND THE NEARLY SO

*Look, I was made for the sixties. I was enormously happy when I could go to Topanga Canyon, take off all my clothes, and go out and garden. It was nothing if someone came over and you were walking around naked.*
—Patti Davis, Reagan's daughter

The necktie with polka dots or stripes? Black pumps or navy blue? The simplest answer to that nagging question of what to wear is, of course, nothing at all. God gave us birthday suits. Why argue with His design?

The cast of the 1968 musical *Hair* surely didn't, even though Diane Keaton, who made her Broadway debut in the show, was among the few who refused to bare all. "I'm not comfortable unless I have a lot of clothes on," she says of her fashion sensibility. "I don't want to reveal my body."

Neither does the puritanical majority. And as long as they persist in buttoning their collars down, the naked truth will always be that, in our society, showing a lot of skin is the fastest way to get anyone's attention. Richard Opel knew that well. In 1974, when he was a thirty-eight-year-old advertising executive, he streaked across the stage during the Academy Awards telecast, showing his natural assets to a national audience. David Niven was just about to introduce Elizabeth Taylor, who was to present the Oscar for best picture to *The Sting*, and the two stars were temporarily flustered. Niven ad-libbed, "I suppose it was bound to happen . . . the only laugh that man will ever get in life is stripping off his pants and showing [his] shortcomings." Taylor allowed, "That's a pretty hard act to follow. I'm nervous—that really upset me."

As for Opel, he said, "It just occurred to me that it might be an educative thing to do. You know, people shouldn't be ashamed of being nude in public. Besides, it's a hell of a way to launch a career."

But not everyone who flashes means to. Singer Ray Charles, who is blind, was staying at the Park-Sheraton Hotel in New York. He recalled, "I was so tired that I could barely put one foot in front of another. I got to my room, fell asleep, and drifted off to another planet. I mean, I was out." The next morning he woke up, "opened the door and stepped inside the bathroom to pee when I suddenly heard the door slam behind me. I realized I wasn't in the bathroom at all. The bathroom door didn't have no spring to it. I was in the hallway. And I was stark naked. I tried to open the door, but it was locked tight." He heard a maid and called to her. As she neared, she said, "Here I am, sir . . . sir . . . my GOD, *SIR!*"

Barbara Bush almost created a similar sensation. "I was staying at a very stylish hotel in New York City where I knew they always had a bathrobe in the closet, so I left mine at home. I had called room service for coffee, then discovered there was no robe. When the coffee came, I took a sheet off the bed and wrapped it around myself toga style to answer the door. I can imagine what the waiter thought. I can just see him going back to the kitchen and saying, 'You'll never guess what I saw in room seventeen twelve!' "

Guests at the Biltmore in New York City never could have guessed they'd see what emerged from a deluxe room: JFK in his undershorts. He'd just announced, "I'd like to find the son of a bitch who was driving," referring to the driver who, earlier in the day, had gotten his motorcade lost in the Bronx. The 1960 campaign was drawing to a close, and wasting time where crowds were thin wasn't on Kennedy's agenda. When he was told the driver was "probably outside now," he simply bolted out the hotel bedroom door, strode through the Biltmore reception room, impervious to gasps and gapes, and cornered the object of his wrath.

"Are you the driver?" Kennedy barked.

"Yes, sir."

"Well, next time get a road map," he said, and strode back as if he were as fully clad as the next fellow.

A view of politicians in their undershorts (or less) was not exactly what newly elected Congresswoman Patricia Schroeder of Colorado had in mind when she strolled out onto a members-only balcony at the House one fair spring day in 1973. "You should have seen some of those old bulls—they went crazy. They were sunning themselves with their shirts and pants off. . . . They asked me to leave."

Since underdressing in public places causes dropped jaws and gossip, conventions must be observed if you plan to hang around in the buff. If you're a dancer, for example, the Supreme Court offers this advisory: A statute insisting you wear "pasties and a G-string does not violate the First Amendment." Foreclothed is forewarned.

And if you're Marilyn Monroe, about to sing "Happy Birthday" to JFK on his forty-fifth, something a little more concealing—but no less provocative—might be in order. For her Madison Square Garden performance, Monroe asked her favorite designer, Jean-Louis, to design a gown that looked like "a second skin." Glittering with rhinestones sewn to a flesh-colored mesh, the five-thousand-dollar dress was so tight it precluded underwear. In fact, Marilyn had to be sewn into it. Afterward Adlai Stevenson wrote a friend that the outfit was "skin and beads. I didn't see the beads! My encounters, however, were only after breaking through the strong defenses established by Robert Kennedy, who was dodging around her like a moth around the flame."

As Elizabeth Taylor said at the Oscars, that's a pretty hard act to follow.

### THE POLITICS (AND POLITESSE) OF HATS

*"I can't kiss you under that hat," President Lyndon Johnson told Washington insider Alice Roosevelt Longworth, Teddy Roosevelt's daughter.*
*"That's why I wear it," she replied.*

Once upon a time everyone who was anyone wore a hat. After the 1956 Republican National Convention in San Francisco, gossip columnist and hat enthusiast Hedda Hopper reported that "some of the visiting ladies had red faces because they brought no hats; they learned the hard way that in this city a woman would sooner go without her shoes as without a hat."

Wearing a hat can have distinct advantages—especially if

you are Alice Roosevelt Longworth dealing with a touchie-feelie fellow like LBJ. But in the sixties, if you were young, Democratic, and a Kennedy, it was a stodgy accessory. When Jackie was about to enter the White House, a friend reminded her that she'd have to make concessions. "I will," she said. "I'll wear hats."

Her husband was not so accommodating, though he did go so far as to be photographed hat in hand. "I've got to carry one for a while," he told reporters. "They tell me I'm killing the industry." Indeed, industry representative Al Webb came to the White House to tempt JFK and friend Paul B. "Red" Fay, Jr., with the latest headgear. "You both look great," Webb told them as they modeled their hats. Fay and JFK took one look at each other and started laughing. "Al," asked Kennedy, "are you willing to destroy the beloved image of our country's leader just to save the hat industry?"

Senator Joe McCarthy was quite willing to ruin hat commerce to save the world from communism. After a much-publicized fistfight with Drew Pearson, McCarthy made a speech from the Senate floor, denouncing the columnist as the "sugar-coated voice of Russia." He called for Americans to boycott the Adam Hat Company, which sponsored Pearson's radio program. His tirade finished, the Senator put on his hat and walked out. In the doorway he met Pearson's assistant, Jack Anderson, who noted that McCarthy was wearing "a grey fedora which I recognized— an Adam hat, size seven and three eighths, presented to him a year before by Drew Pearson."

Over the decades hats have caused lots of controversy. Candidates have thrown them in the ring; people have cried when they dropped. "That whole year [1964] I would cry at the drop of a hat if someone mentioned Jack's name. I couldn't get over it, couldn't let it go," said former JFK lover Judith Exner.

At the FBI hats could get you fired. Once J. Edgar Hoover, whose orders were carried out on the double no matter how ambiguous they were, shook hands with a new class of agents and said under his breath, "They've got some real pinheads in that class." The following day, according to G. Gordon Liddy, "as the class was at firearms training, their lockers were opened and the snap-brim hats all were required to have were measured. The three agents with the smallest hat sizes were washed out."

But hats have caused only one known presidential dispute,

which flared up as Harry S. Truman was leaving office. Tradition prescribed top hats for the inauguration, but incoming President Dwight Eisenhower changed the dress code to homburgs. Truman was furious, but he managed to bite his tongue, vowing, "I refuse to have my last quarrel over a hat." You'd have to take your hat off to him for that.

## CLOTHES MAKE—AND UNMAKE—THE MAN

*If you and your siblings had had to go to church dressed in kilts, your friends snickering at the sight of you all in skirts . . . you could begin to understand why all of us are so close.*
—Christopher Forbes, son of the late Scottish enthusiast, Malcolm

This is the stuff that either lands people on psychiatrists' couches or in a dressing room at Bloomingdale's until, somewhere along the road to maturity, they realize that clothes make the man and that they buy the clothes.

"My white suits came about by accident," explained author Tom Wolfe. "I had a white suit made that was too hot for summer, so I wore it in December. I found that it really irritated people—I had hit upon this harmless form of aggression!"

People look at what you wear and react. If they see a flag pin on your lapel, you seem patriotic. Nixon started wearing one after aide H. R. Haldeman did. He borrowed the idea from the movie *The Candidate*.

If they look at you and don't see proper business wear, they read disrespect. "It is ridiculous to have the attorney general walking around the building in shirt sleeves," fumed J. Edgar Hoover when Robert Kennedy was his boss.

And if they see Pucci slacks, Italian hairdos, and French designer dresses—all Jackie Kennedy trademarks—they may think you're too fancy for the White House. "The American people just aren't ready for someone like you," said JFK, who initially considered her a liability. "I guess we'll just have to run you through subliminally in one of those quick flash TV spots so no one will notice." She burst into tears and fled the room.

In judging people by how they look, you can hurt people's feelings—and fail to "see beneath the boobs . . . beneath the wig" and miss the brains and the heart, as Dolly Parton points out. "I think one big part of whatever appeal I possess is the fact that I am totally another. I look artificial, but I'm not."

"*Laugh-In* came in when women were burning bras. And I came on as a wide-eyed innocent—some called it silly, stupid, vacant," said Goldie Hawn. "A lot called it the dumb blonde. Reporters always asked, 'Don't you feel what you represent is not good for women's lib?' Well, I always knew that I was smart. That I would never take money from a man—ever. I was *already liberated.*"

"I may be dressing like the traditional bimbo, whatever," admitted Madonna, "but I'm in charge. And isn't that what feminism is all about . . . ?"

Well, yes. But clothing tends to promote stereotypes, as Andrew Young, Martin Luther King's associate, knew. "Martin always wore the good preacher blue suit," recalled Young. Before the 1965 march from Selma to Montgomery, the civil rights leader received death threats. "I figured since we couldn't stop him from marching, we just had to kind of believe that it was true when white folks said we all look alike," said Young. "So everybody that was about Martin's size and had on a blue suit I put in the front of the line with him. . . . All of the preachers loved the chance to get in the front line with Martin Luther King, but I don't think to this day most of them know why they were up there."

Though many of us exercise preacher like conservativeness in our daily dress, there's one occasion when we can all be Madonnas or King Kongs or Batmen if we'd like, and that's Halloween. On October 31, 1988, George Bush celebrated on board Air Force Two. He followed his twin granddaughters Jenna and Barbara (dressed as a Juicy Fruit gum pack and a Juicy Fruit pack vampire respectively) down the aisle, wearing—surprise—a carrot-topped George Bush mask and windbreaker with his name embroidered on it. As his granddaughters extorted candy from the Secret Service agents, he delivered his famous no tax line, though no one needed to read his lips to get a laugh.

In an election year, Bush was probably smart to play himself, because when you start manipulating your fashion image, you can get caught with your pants down, metaphorically speaking. Once LBJ showed up at college with a new tie and socks. Classmate Horace Richards recalled, "I knew where he had bought them, but I asked *him* where he had bought them. He said, 'I got them over at Scarborough's in Austin. I paid a dollar for the socks and a dollar for the tie.' Scarborough's was the fanciest store in Austin, and a dollar was a whole lot of money in those days. I said, 'Lyndon, you're just lying. You were never in Scarborough's yesterday. Besides, I saw them in Woolworth's window yesterday. The socks were ten cents and the tie was twenty cents.' But Lyndon just had to lie and say he was wearing a dollar tie. It just seemed like he had to lie about everything."

Yes, you can tell a lot about a fellow from his clothes.

MUCH ADO ABOUT HAIR

*My biggest irritation was his insistence on using Brylcreem. Yeah, exactly. He would put a little dab of it in the palm of his hand and rub it into his scalp. And he had a habit, before each press conference, of slapping water onto his hair. I begged him, "Governor, some people don't use that much water when they shampoo."*
—Michael Deaver about campaigning with Ronald Reagan in 1980

Hair is the ultimate vanity. We can't lose ten pounds or ten years in time for a dinner party, but we can primp and fuss, smooth and curl—and camouflage. "I think it's just great when people get a kick out of my piece. That's why I wear it, for pete's sake," commented NBC weatherman Willard Scott on his two-thousand-dollar toupee. "I put it on and I look fantastic."

"I've come up with a system. . . . When I play Sam Malone, I wear a hairpiece," said Ted Danson of *Cheers* television fame. "When I'm an environmentalist, I don't. Somehow it sets me straight." Danson's other life includes lobbying for the American Ocean Campaign, which he founded in 1987 and over the next three years funded with an estimated seven hundred thousand dollars of his own money.

Junk bond wizard Michael Milken also developed a system about his hair-piece, though not one of his own making. When he's an investor, he sports a curly toupee. As an inmate, he goes bald—per security regulations. Had his crowning glory been natu-

Headstrong in his disregard of vanity, former
President Reagan waved to his fans after being
operated on to remove fluid from the brain.
Nancy would clearly have preferred to cap his
exuberance.

ral, prison might not have cramped his style. Singer James Brown,
who served time from 1988 to 1991 for charges including aggravated assault and possession of a deadly weapon, managed to
maintain his glamorous 'do. "During the week, when I couldn't
be there, the prison barber would put some sponge rollers on his
hair for him to sleep on," said the singer's wife, Adrienne, a
former beautician. On weekends she styled Brown's hair herself.
    Pink rollers and hair spray? Now we're getting to the good
stuff. Feminine hocus-pocus? Not really. As far as styling mousse

goes, George Bush uses it. "That way it doesn't blow if he walks across the street," said the man who tended his hair at The White House, barber Milton Pitts.

Boxing promoter Don King doesn't—or so he claims. "I don't wear my hair that way. My hair wears me," he says of his graying locks, which simulate a close encounter with an electric socket. "It's an oracle garden. My hair was just like any other black's— kinky, curly, right to the scalp. One time after a traumatic experi- ence, I come home and the bumbling in my head, my hair went up ping ping ping. And it's standing up, just the way it is now. . . . No mousse, no artificial preparation, no chemical abuse. It's *au naturel.*"

Hmm . . . There are a number of questions that only a man's hairdresser knows for sure. Is Robert Redford's color natural? One would assume so because he has said, "I have never felt my coloring. I have always felt like a dark-haired person." And what of Ronald Reagan's? He claimed it wasn't dyed, but after his 1989 surgery he appeared in public (to Nancy's horror) with half his head shaved—and the short side looking inconclusively brown. In fact, it looked gray. Reagan explained the situation on television to Barbara Walters: "When it's short, the gray is far more exposed. When it's long, the gray is kind of hidden under the brown hair." Go figure.

Reagan's cubist 'do brings us to the question of length. How long is acceptable? "I mean shit, you know, long hair is just another prop," admitted Abbie Hoffman in the sixties. "You go on TV and you can say anything you want but people are lookin' at you and they're looking at the cat next to you like David Susskind or some guy like that and they're sayin' hey man there's a choice, I can see it loud and clear."

"The thing that most people don't realize," Bob Dylan pointed out, "is that it's *warmer* to have long hair. Everyone wants to be warm. People with short hair freeze easily. Then they try to hide their coldness, and they get jealous of everybody that's warm. Then they become either barbers or congressmen. A lot of prison wardens have short hair. Have you ever noticed that Abraham Lincoln's hair was much longer than John Wilkes Booth's?"

Mirror, mirror on the wall, who can resolve questions this small? The only answer we have comes in the form of another question, this from Lily Tomlin: "If truth is beauty, how come no one has their hair done in a library?"

# 5
# Why Me? Discriminating Points of View

*"I don't even ask, 'Why me?' " said Lieutenant William Calley after being tried for the My Lai massacre. "I know as I lay in the paddies with the Vietnamese shooting at me, I didn't say, 'Oh, why was I ever born? Why me?' I lived, I got home again, and I had the Army harping on me. . . . I knew, It isn't right, but I shouldn't say 'Why me? Why me?' Why not?"*

"**W**hy me?" is the cry of the bewildered. After John Hinckley paid actress Jodie Foster the compliment of shooting Ronald Reagan in her name, the question she wrestled with was "Why me? Why not someone like Brooke Shields?"

Even Magic Johnson wondered "Why me?" when he discovered he had the AIDS virus. But after "five or ten minutes" he decided the only thing to do was to make the most of his life.

Those hit by assassins' bullets—George Wallace, Ronald Reagan—have wondered why they were singled out. And those subjected to prejudice wonder it every day. "I think it is so unfair of people to be against Jack because he is a Catholic," mused Jackie Kennedy. "He's such a poor Catholic. Now if it were Bobby, I could understand it."

"They're not like us," Richard Nixon said of Italians on the Watergate tapes. "They smell different, they look different, they act different. The trouble is you can't find one that's honest."

"Listen to what these sons of bitches are saying," said Peter Rodino, chairman of the House Judiciary Committee, as he reviewed the tapes.

Clearly Nixon had never intended his remarks to reach the ears of an Italian-American weighing his impeachment, but that's the problem with generalities. That's why prejudice surprises like a "Why me?" Or perhaps a "Why did you pull me over?" in the case of a black man driving a red Lamborghini. He happened to be basketball star Bill Russell, and he was doing twenty-five miles per hour on Los Angeles's Sunset Boulevard, so his query merited at least a semblance of an answer.

"We have a report of a car like this being stolen, and we have to check it out," the policemen told Russell. "What kind of car is it?" Russell responded, causing the cops to scramble for an answer. Since the Lamborghini's name isn't written on it, they were reduced to explaining, "You might have been one of the Brink's robbers."

But Russell knew it was "stop-the-nigger-in-the-expensive-car time," as he loudly told a gathering crowd. Ordered out of the vehicle, he unfolded himself to his full six feet plus and kept his hands up, despite the cops' pleas to keep them down. "Oh, no. I'm not going to put my hands down so you can shoot me and say I was going for a gun."

Why me? The answer: a "routine mistake." A basketball star was mistaken for a "nigger in the expensive car," a future Supreme Court justice for a loiterer. In the latter instance Thurgood Marshall, then chief counsel for the NAACP Legal Defense Fund, was standing on a train platform in Mississippi. A white man with a pistol in his pocket asked him what he was doing. Marshall replied, "I'm waiting for the next train," only to have the question repeated. "Then I remembered," Marshall recalled. "I said, 'I'm waiting for the next train, sir.'" The man responded, "You'd better be on it because the sun's not going down on a live nigger in this town."

If the man had known who Marshall was, maybe he'd have been sorry he hadn't shot him. The course of history would certainly have been very different. But for the moment Marshall was just another anonymous black in a small southern town. It's no wonder that H. Rap Brown said, "The white man don't like nothing black but a Cadillac." In those days people were better at telling Cadillacs from Lincolns than blacks from one another.

And the ignorance continues. "I've got black accountants at Trump Castle and at Trump Plaza. Black guys counting my money! I hate it. The only kind of people I want counting my money are short guys that wear yarmulkes every day," Donald Trump told his former CEO, John O'Donnell.

"What can you say about a country that tolerates homosexuals but not smokers? I never gave anyone AIDS," commented novelist Tom Clancy.

What can you say? "Until everyone knows someone who died of AIDS, this discrimination and prejudice will continue," offered C. Everett Koop, Reagan's surgeon general, after the 1990 death of young Ryan White, a hemophiliac who contracted AIDS and attracted national attention because he had been hounded out of his hometown of Kokomo, Indiana. "And I think this winsome little boy has found his way into our hearts over the past several weeks, and I think now many Americans know someone who died of AIDS and it can't help but improve the situation."

When situations get personal, the cry of "Why me?" no longer falls on deaf ears.

P.S.: A word about being vigilant against prejudice: If you aren't careful, you can go overboard with your antis. George Bush campaigned in 1988, saying "I'm anti-bigotry, anti-racist, and anti-Semitic."

LEARNING THE BLACK, WHITE, AND MINORITY BASICS

Sometimes it is the clear-eyed questions of children that point up the oddities of life. "Daddy, I go to the grocery and the grocery man's white. I go to the drugstore and the drugstore man's white. The bus driver's white. What do colored people do?" five-year-old Muhammad Ali asked his father.

How to explain the inequities of life? Civil rights leader Ralph Abernathy's parents tried by warning him never to play with white children because "every joke will be at your expense. If you wrestle or box with a white child, you will always have to let him win, otherwise he may become aggravated, and that could lead to trouble."

Other children were just left to sort their way through trouble. Actor Kirk Douglas recalls "getting beaten up going to Hebrew school after regular school, every day. Having to run the gantlet every block."

One way or another, it seems, children learn the score, as these examples illustrate:

1. *Cesar Chavez, who led the fight for American farm workers' rights.* As a child in Arizona he mentioned to his teacher that he was Mexican. She corrected him by telling him, "You are an American. All of us are Americans." The concept was unfathomable to Chavez, who thought that "an American was a white man."

When he went home from school, he said to his mother, "Mama, they tell me I'm an American!" His mother couldn't really explain why he spoke Spanish and had a whole different set of customs. "She said I was a citizen, but I didn't know what a citizen meant. It was too complicated."

2. *Richard Pryor, actor.* "One of my first big traumatic experiences was when I went to see a *Little Beaver* movie. When it was over, I tried to get behind the screen. I thought Little Beaver would be there, you know. And I wanted to talk to him. I never thought to myself, 'Little Beaver's white.' I didn't think about color—just feelings. My heroes at the movies were the same as everyone else's. I wanted to be John Wayne, too. I didn't know John Wayne hated my guts."

3. *Kareem Abdul-Jabbar, basketball player.* In the early 1950s, when he was in the third grade at a Manhattan Catholic grade school, a classmate brought in a marvel: a Polaroid camera. The sister assembled the class in front of the blackboard, clicked the shutter, and ordered everyone back to his seat. When a minute was up and the photograph ready, it was passed around the room, finally reaching Kareem. "I was shocked. I knew I was the tallest boy in the class; I had always been taller than everyone else my age." But when he spotted himself in the back row, "towering over every one as usual," he realized " 'Damn, I'm dark and everybody else is light!' I hadn't noticed and nobody had told me."

4. *Rhonda Suzanne, singer Diana Ross's daughter.* "Why is my skin brown when my girlfriend has white skin and blond hair?" This was an after-school question from an energetic five-year-old in the mid-1970s. Bending down to her daughter's level, Diana quietly explained, "That's the breaks, kid. That's the way it is. My skin is brown, too. Don't you think I'm beautiful?"

5. *Adrienne Belafonte, singer Harry's daughter.* "Mother, we've got to move! We've got to move!" Adrienne told Marguerite Belafonte. "There are Niggeroos moving into the block!"

"I stared at her wide-eyed," Mrs. Belafonte recalled. "It was apparent that she was repeating what one of her playmates had told her. And obviously, the playmate didn't understand what she was saying any more than Adrienne did." Adrienne was four in 1953, and the Belafontes were the first blacks in a white neighborhood in Elmhurst, Queens.

6. *Lee Iacocca.* "I was eleven before I learned we were Italian.

Until then, I knew we came from a real country but I didn't know what it was called—or even where it was. I remember actually looking on a map of Europe for places named Dago and Wop."

7. *Carl Stokes, elected the mayor of Cleveland in 1967—the first black mayor of any major American city.* "We were in a motorcade coming down East 55th Street and my wife, Shirley, and I were sitting on the back of the convertible. And a little black kid that was maybe eight years old, probably, came up to us as we were stopped at the traffic signal. He said, 'Are you Carl Stokes?'

"I said, 'Yes.' "

"He just gave a little leap in the air and ran down the street clapping his hands, saying, 'He's colored, he's colored!' I thought that sort of caught the sense of pride I felt as I went through the black areas of the city of Cleveland."

### SHADES OF GRAY

Q:  *How many blacks are there on your top campaign staff,*
       *Governor?*
A:  *I couldn't honestly answer you. No.*
Q:  *That speaks for itself.*
A:  *Huh?*
Q:  *That speaks for itself.*
A:  *No, because I can't tell how many people are on the staff. . . .*
Q:  *But surely you can tell black from white.*
—conversation between Mike Wallace and Ronald Reagan, 1980

Reagan did have a little trouble with things that appeared black and white to others. "How are you, Mr. Mayor? How are things in your city?" he greeted Samuel Pierce, Jr., his secretary of housing and urban development and the only black in his Cabinet. But generally Americans have been pretty good at telling black from white. In pretty colorful terms. Take Mississippi Senator James Eastland, who bemoaned the fact that "in every stage of the bus boycott we have been oppressed and degraded because of black, slimy, juicy, unbearably stinking niggers."

J. Edgar Hoover took a more cerebral view. "Everybody knows that Negroes' brains are twenty percent smaller than white people's," he said. In 1961, when Attorney General Robert Kennedy asked the FBI chief how many black agents there were,

Hoover listed five. Three were personal servants who had been appointed agents to avoid the draft; two were assigned to Miami and San Diego field offices and served as Hoover's drivers when he visited.

It's no surprise that Hoover's most enthusiastic involvement in the civil rights movement consisted of tapping the phones of Martin Luther King at hotels and motels across the country. "I want to hit him hard," King was taped saying about Hoover. "He made me hot, and I wanted to get him."

The Kennedys acquired a sterling reputation on civil rights, but as a young politician JFK didn't seem very promising. He told baseball player Jackie Robinson, "I haven't had much opportunity to learn about the Negro." Robinson's response: "He has been in Congress fourteen years, and he tried to tell me he hadn't an opportunity to learn about the Negro."

But then being too busy could be a problem. As President Eisenhower told Martin Luther King he didn't have time for civil rights. "Reverend, there are so many problems . . . Lebanon, Algeria. . . ." Which prompted this comment from King: "President Eisenhower could not be committed to anything which involved a structural change in the architecture of American society. His conservatism was fixed and rigid. . . ." After sending troops to Little Rock to integrate Central High, Eisenhower commented, "These are not bad people. All they are concerned about is to see that their sweet little girls are not required to sit in school alongside some big overgrown Negroes!"

What bothered Henry Ford II about "those goddamn coons" was their use of their cars. "They drive up and down Lake Shore Drive in front of my house. I hate them, I'm scared of them, and I think I'll move to Switzerland, where there just aren't any."

Prejudice, of course, is not a permanent issue. People can change their minds on the subject. For example, on October 20, 1965, Ronald Reagan said, "I favor the Civil Rights Act of 1964 and it must be enforced at gunpoint if necessary."

In 1968 he said, "I would have voted against the Civil Rights Act of 1964."

When Sammy Davis, Jr., told Samuel Goldwyn he was a Jew and couldn't work on the High Holy Days. "You're a *what?*" said an astonished Goldwyn. "You mean it? It's not one of your little jokes?"

"No. I'll do anything in the world for you Mr. Goldwyn, but I won't work on Yom Kippur."

"Sammy, you're a little so-and-so, but go with your yarmulke and your tallis—we'll work it out somehow." As Davis began to leave, Goldwyn could be heard saying: "Directors I can fight. Fires on the set I can fight. Writers, even actors I can fight. But a Jewish colored fellow? This I can't fight."

### TURNING A DARK CORNER

Some streets look pretty harmless, but you turn a corner and find a sign that says VOTE FOR CUOMO NOT THE HOMO, a campaign slogan that appeared in Mario Cuomo's New York mayoral campaign against Ed Koch in 1977. You know, then, that you've turned a dark corner.

Here, a sampling of locations where prejudice has been known to hide out:

1. *At the hairdresser's.* "I remember when the story about Burt having AIDS came out, my hairdresser refused to do my hair because of the story. I couldn't believe it. People and the press can be so hurtful, so vicious," said Loni Anderson, whose husband, Burt Reynolds, was falsely rumored to have AIDS.

2. *At the barbershop.* Freshly discharged from service in World War II, wearing full uniform, "the new captain's bars bright on my shoulders, four rows of ribbons on my chest, the combat infantry badge, the distinguished unit citations—and a hook where my hand was supposed to be," Daniel K. Inouye wanted to get a haircut so he could look his best before he went home. He went to a barbershop outside San Francisco but got only as far as the door. "Are you Chinese?" the future senator was asked.

"I think what you want to know is where my father was born. My father was born in Japan. I am an American," Inouye replied.

"Don't give me that American stuff," he was told. "You're a Jap, and we don't cut Jap hair."

Inouye's silent response: "To think that I had gone through a war to save his skin—and he didn't cut Jap hair."

3. *At the beach.* Singer Ray Charles "was having a ball, splashing in the ocean like a baby in a bath," at Myrtle Beach, South

Nat King Cole taught his "Sweetie," seven-year-old Natalie, piano and voice, but other lessons she learned on her own. As far as race relations went, she grew up to realize, "My dad was cool, you know. He was hip to people. People tend to think he was just a nice wimp. But he was a strong, religious man who knew what was going on."

Carolina. "I kept swimming further and further out when suddenly I heard one of the cats screaming, 'Hey, Ray, come back, man. Come back!' I thought I had simply gone out too far and the cats were worried about me drowning. But that wasn't it." The problem was, he was told, "You were about to go over to the white side, man!" Ray, who was about twenty at the time, was dumbfounded. *"White side!* Shit. Whoever heard of such a thing? I couldn't figure out how the ocean could have a white side and a black side."

4. *On an airplane*. Flying Pan Am from New York to Africa in the early 1970s, civil rights advocate Julian Bond stopped in Senegal to change planes. Until he got to Africa, "all the crew was white; the pilot was white; and almost all the people on the plane were white." But after Dakar "all the crew was black. I had never seen a black man flying a plane. I was shocked. I was surprised. The terrible thought went through my mind: *'Maybe he doesn't know how to fly!'* " Bond, who is black himself, was taken aback that you could be "twenty-five years old and still have, for a fraction of a second, the doubt in your mind that black people can fly airplanes."

5. *At a country club*. Bess Myerson, Miss America in 1945, fancied herself Scarlett O'Hara for a moment. She was on her way to a southern country club "to make a short speech and play the piano." In order to dress for the occasion, she was taken to "a gorgeous antebellum mansion" with "a winding staircase, crystal chandeliers, servants in livery." But when she zipped up her gown and swept downstairs, any dreams of being the belle of the ball were gone with the wind. At the bottom of the stairs she found her hostess "telling the members of my party that there had been a terrible mistake, the country club was restricted, and no Jewish person could possibly be welcome there." Myerson said, "I felt as though I'd walked into a stone wall." She went upstairs, changed, and took a train home.

6. *In a restaurant*. "I wanted to hang out with my buddies, but I didn't want to make things hard on them, so I stayed to myself," recalled baseball player Reggie Jackson of his time on the road in Birmingham, Alabama, in 1967. Generally he relied on room service or the hotel coffee shop for sustenance, but one night he wanted a steak. He went to a nearly empty, nearby restaurant where "the headwaiter took a long time to seat me, and as I walked through the room, I feel every eye in the place on me." What time Jackson lost waiting for a table was made up by the speed with which his waiter delivered his steak. "As he held it in front of my face, I could see that it had been barely cooked. Then the waiter just dropped the plate on the table, from a height of about three feet. Just dropped it. The steak flopped onto the tablecloth. The silverware went flying, water glass tipped over. Big racket. Loud fuckin' racket."

"Nigger," Jackson was told, "don't you *ever* come back

here." Jackson "hot-footed" it back on his hotel and ordered room service.

7. *Down the block.* In the late 1940s singer Nat King Cole moved into an exclusive white Los Angeles neighborhood. "Before I was born," recalled his daughter, Natalie, "one of the women there approached my father and told him 'Well, you know, we don't want any *undesirables* in this neighborhood.' And my father just looked at her and said, 'Well, if I see any, I'll let you know.' Another time . . . this real socialite lady . . . was having a luncheon. She invited my dad, and when he got there, they wanted him to perform. So being the gracious man that he was, he did. But he also sent her a bill for his services."

8. *At the negotiating table.* During the Arab oil embargo Henry Kissinger was sitting down with King Faisal of Saudia Arabia, listening to a torrent of anti-Zionist remarks. Kissinger spied a painting "at the far end of a long, smoke-filled hall." In an attempt to change the subject, he asked, "Is that a landscape of Saudi Arabia? I really like the desert." He was told in no uncertain terms, "That's the Holy Oasis." Later Kissinger said, "It was like going into a Catholic home and seeing the Virgin Mary on the wall and saying, 'Is that your aunt?' The remark probably caused a three-month extension in the oil embargo."

"IMAGINE MARTIN LUTHER KING HAVING A BIGOT FOR A FATHER"

It was a telephone call from the Kennedys that secured the release from jail of Martin Luther King, Jr. A very impressed Daddy King commented, "I had expected to vote against Senator Kennedy because of his religion. But now he can be my President, Catholic or whatever he is. It took courage to stand up for what he knows is right. I've got all my votes and I've got a suitcase, and I'm going to take them up there and dump them in his lap."

Later when told about Daddy King's comment, JFK mused, "That was a hell of a bigoted statement, wasn't it? Imagine Martin Luther King having a bigot for a father." And he added with a smile, "Well, we all have fathers, don't we?"

# 6
# The Art of Courtship

*He spent half of each week in Massachusetts. He'd call me from some*
*oyster bar up there, with a great clinking of coins, to ask me out to*
*the movies the following Wednesday in Washington. . . .*
*He was not the candy and flowers type, so every now and then he'd*
*give me a book.*
—Jackie Kennedy, who called her romance "a very spasmodic
courtship"

The art of courtship. Some people do it with
champagne, others with a great clinking of coins. By the time we
figure out how to do it successfully, our skills are obsolete because
by then we're at the altar. But here's a look back over the shoulder
at how to get things off the ground.

What you need for starters is a good opening line. "I was at
a party feeling very shy because there were a lot of celebrities
around," recalled Helen Hayes, no unknown herself. She was
sitting in a corner alone when "a very beautiful young man came
up to me." It was Charles MacArthur. He offered her "some salted
peanuts and he said, 'I wish they were emeralds' as he handed
me the peanuts and that was the end of my heart. I never got it
back."

Not bad for openers. But don't worry if poetry doesn't trip
off your tongue. Some very prosaic phrases have been proved to
work quite well. "I took one look at her and said, 'This is it. I'll
be back for you. Stick with me, kid, and you'll be farting through
silk'," said Robert Mitchum upon meeting his future wife,
Dorothy.

"I hate to give away secrets, but I did have a very effective
opening line," explained basketball star Wilt Chamberlain, who
claimed to have slept with some twenty thousand different
women. "It's very simple. Since I traveled the world so much,
especially throughout America, I knew my geography. I'd always
ask, 'Where are you from?' And when she would answer, I'd
pretend that I was from some small place close to it, and we

would immediately be on common ground. She might say, 'I'm from Portland, Oregon.' And I would say, 'No kidding? I was born in Lake Oswego.' She wouldn't believe me, but then I'd say, 'How could I make that up?' and she'd say, 'You're right.' That approach has worked for me all over the world."

Who needs fancy stuff when "How do you do? Why don't you shut your mouth and sit down?" can do the trick. It certainly wowed young Shirley MacLaine, a chorus girl in the theater. A friend introduced her to businessman Steve Parker at a bar near Broadway in New York in 1952. He instructed her to sit down, and "I fell in love with him immediately," she recalled. "Four hours later he asked me to marry him. Because I was a respectable lady from Virginia, I made him wait until morning for my answer."

One would have thought Lauren Bacall was born with a brash insouciance that turned men into putty. Actually it was an acquired trait. When she was eighteen and unknown, director Howard Hawks took her under his wing and invited her to a party at his house. "What's the matter?" he inquired when he noticed nobody was offering her a ride home.

"I don't get along too well with men," confessed Bacall.

"Are you nice to them?"

"I try to be."

Hawks advised her to shift into reverse. "Try insulting them and see whether maybe you do a little better."

Near the end of his next Saturday soiree Bacall announced to Hawks, "I've got a ride home."

"Good for you. What did you do?"

"I did what you told me to do. I insulted a man. I asked him where he got his tie. He said, 'Why do you want to know?' I said, 'So I can tell other people not to go there.' "

Hawks thought that was great. Who was the man she'd chosen as target practice? "Clark Gable."

Go ahead. Toss those darts and barbs. "You're rather *short*, aren't you?" Katharine Hepburn informed Spencer Tracy the first time she met him. She was five eight and liked to wear custom-made platform shoes that gave her a six-foot footing. Director Joseph Mankiewicz, who had initiated the meeting, had an inkling of just how Hepburn and Tracy would get along. "Don't worry, honey," he told her, "he'll cut you down to size."

If you can't think of anything devastating that will incite an ego-trimming duel, a perfectly fine opener is "Would you like to dance?" It isn't very original, but it enables you to hang out with that attractive whoever, to cha-cha and not worry about conversational lulls. A word of warning: If you are born with two left feet, you have to be fast on them to use your opening line and not actually have to dance.

"That's why I'm married to Barbara," explained George Bush. "I met her and they started playing a waltz. I said, 'Let's sit down, I can't do this.' It was frankness and openness that impressed her—that side of me." The two students met during Christmas break at a Greenwich, Connecticut, party. They sat out a waltz and fell in love. By the summer they were engaged. Technically it was a secret, meaning, according to George, "The German and Japanese high commands weren't aware of it."

Bush still can't dance, though apparently he's gotten one step down. "He foxtrots no matter what the tune," says Barbara.

If you're loath to polish your opening lines, it may help to get into a business like Hugh Hefner's where you can have a staff turn up research on a whole bevy of beauties. "You know, in the next ten years, I would rather meet a girl and fall in love and have her fall in love with me than make another hundred million dollars," he said in the 1970s. It was a decade later when he noticed Kimberly Conrad, *Playboy*'s Miss January 1988. "One time in the dining room," she recalled, "Hef leaned over and said, 'By the way, I looked at your data sheet. I think it's wonderful.' " What a line! They married in 1989; she was twenty-six, he sixty-three.

It should be noted that some people end up in the thick of things with absolutely no what's-your-astrological-signs, no haven't-I-seen-you-befores. For example, Ted Turner was reading the paper one day and noticed Jane Fonda was divorcing Tom Hayden. "Now there's a woman I'd like to go out with," he said. Immediately he set about finding Fonda's phone number and asked her out. She demurred initially because she "wasn't feeling peppy," but within a year she and Turner were an item.

If you're famous enough, you can pick up the phone and orchestrate your own blind date. But the time-honored way to do it is to have a friend act as an intermediary. "How would you like to meet a nice guy?" business manager David March asked

Marilyn Monroe on the telephone. "Are there any?" she replied. The guy he had in mind for her was Joe DiMaggio, who proposed on the first date and "every night thereafter until she accepted," according to Marilyn's friend Robert Slatzer. Her view on the marriage: "He can hit home runs. If that's all it takes, we'd still be married."

Luci Johnson must have looked a little like a bad version of Marilyn when she went out on a very key blind date. To give the press the slip, the First Daughter donned a blond wig and used a false name for a blind date at Marquette University in Milwaukee. The man in question: Patrick J. Nugent, her future husband.

Wigs, waltzes, long distance phone calls from oyster bars— in love anything is worth a try.

### DON'T LAUGH: LIGHTNING DOES STRIKE

*"When are you going to give me that date?" Richard Nixon was driving Pat Ryan and a girl friend home from a drama rehearsal. It was only the third time they'd met. He'd asked her out immediately. She'd demurred. Now he asked again. She giggled. "Don't laugh," he told her, pointing his finger in that Nixonian way. "Someday I'm going to marry you."*

Don't laugh. Really. Don't smirk, don't even smile to yourself. Don't think, as Pat did, he's "nuts or something." If a man looks at you and says he's going to marry you, he may well do just that.

Jesse Jackson was standing with a group of football players outside the student hall at North Carolina A&T when he yelled out, "Hey, baby. I'm going to marry you." He hadn't even met the woman. She was so startled she stepped into a mud puddle and ruined her new black suede high heels. "That put us on bad terms to start with," Jacqueline Davis recalled, "although he said he was sorry and offered to help me." When the two met later in class, "I found him to be very bright and sensitive." Jackson married her.

LBJ met Lady Bird and asked her if she'd have breakfast the next day. Why breakfast? It was a matter of being politic; Lyndon already had a date that night. Lady Bird nearly stood him up. She was late for the appointment and thought she'd just skip it. But you don't stand up Lyndon Johnson. He spotted her and "just flagged me down. So I went in." He proceeded to tell her "all sorts of things I would *never* have asked him, certainly on first acquaintance." They spent the day together, and he popped the question. "I was so surprised I couldn't believe it. I thought it was some kind of joke."

Don't laugh. Don't even let any disbelieving thoughts cross your mind. This type of man is serious. Within seven weeks Lyndon and Lady Bird were at the altar—without a wedding ring. Bird hadn't really said yes, and LBJ was so intent on hustling her to San Antonio, where a friend had set up a church service, that a few matters of protocol had slipped his mind. A ring! Luckily the Sears across the street was open late on Saturdays. LBJ's friend sprinted over to the jewelry counter. What size ring? He pointed to the cheap bands and said, "Just give me a dozen." Bird picked one that fitted and said her "I do's." As the newlyweds left, the minister couldn't help himself. "I hope that marriage lasts," he said under his breath.

Don't laugh. Don't doubt. For richer or poorer, for better or worse, when lightning strikes, some sort of fusion happens. Maybe the sheer shock of it is enough to keep people wondering for decades just what happened. For example, how would you feel if, like theologian Norman Vincent Peale, you looked up and the church doors opened suddenly, leaving a girl "framed in the golden light"? If you'd "never seen her before, did not know her name," but knew "that was the girl," you'd probably still be reeling on your fortieth anniversary. Peale fell in love with Ruth Stafford on the spot: "She was waiting for one of the girls in my committee meeting, but actually it was I who was waiting for her. And I had been waiting a long time."

A class A epiphany! Ah, you might mutter, it happens only to those who have a hot line to the other world. It probably doesn't hurt to be well connected. Muhammad Ali was in a motel when his friend Herbert brought in Sonji Roi to meet him. "I swear to God, Herbert, you know what I was doing?" Ali exclaimed, jumping up. "I was laying across the bed praying to Allah for a wife, and here she comes with the Messenger's son, so she's gotta be the one." Ali walked over to Sonji and said, "Girl, will you marry me?"

Later he asked her: "That quick? I said it that quick?"

"Just that quick," she replied.

Divine intervention, however, doesn't guarantee a marriage will last. Ali's didn't. Usually what's divine about epiphanies of the romantic sort is the way they feel. Because the transaction is essentially a plebeian affair. No matter how heavenly the results, all they involve is looking in the right direction on a day when Cupid is in the halls. That's what happened to Joe McCarthy. Jean Fraser Kerr had dropped into his office to visit a friend. The senator took one look, buzzed his secretary, and commanded, "Whoever that girl is, hire her!" Jean joined his staff a few months later and married her boss the same year.

"I loved her the first time I saw her," said Justice William O. Douglas. Love? He was sixty-six, married, and in the Three Star Restaurant in Portland, Oregon. She was twenty-two and a cocktail waitress. "A Supreme Court justice and this little girl?" gasped Douglas's friend Damon Trout with undisguised incredulity. But there's no accounting for chemistry. William O. and Cathy Heffernan met in August 1965 and were married the following year.

What's going on? Hormones? "The only reason he wanted to marry me was because he couldn't get me any other way," said Joan Kennedy of Ted. Well, particularly in the presexual revolution days, the zap and sizzle of lightning striking released enough you-know-what to fuel a rush to the altar. Sometimes even a kiss would do it. Jimmy Carter came home from a movie double date and told his mother, "She's the girl I want to marry." What he didn't tell her was, as Rosalynn recalled, that as the two rode "in the rumble seat of the car, the moon was full in the sky." Conversation flowed effortlessly, and "He kissed me! I couldn't believe it happened. I had never let any boy kiss me on my first date. My mother told me she hadn't even held hands with Daddy until they were engaged."

But a kiss, or even a full tank of razzle-dazzle, doesn't explain everything. Men—especially powerful men—seem to have a talent for seeing a woman across a school quad, across a cocktail room, across a church sanctuary, across a motel bed, and knowing she's the one. And generally they don't look back.

That doesn't mean they don't notice other women that come into their line of vision. "I'm away from home twenty-five to twenty-seven days a month," said Martin Luther King, Jr. "Fucking's a form of anxiety reduction." But when it comes to marital matters, powerful men seem to know exactly what sort of wife they need.

"Do you know what?" King told Coretta Scott the very day he met her. "You have everything I have ever wanted in a wife." King was up in Boston, where he was getting his doctorate in theology, and his social life was going nowhere fast. He complained that the women weren't of the same quality as in the South. A friend told him to call Coretta. "He had quite a line," she said later. "He was a typical man. Smoothness. Jive. Some of it I had never heard of in my life. It was what I call intellectual jive." She "kind of enjoyed it" and accepted an invitation to lunch the next day. When Martin drove her home, he dumbfounded her by saying, "The four things that I look for in a wife are character, intelligence, personality, and beauty. And you have them all. I want to see you again."

Some men, you see, think there's a rhyme and reason to what's going on. They've thought it all out, they'll tell you. Jack Kennedy explained that he'd decided at their first meeting that Jackie was the one he'd marry—when he got around to marrying. "How BIG of you" was her thought on the matter. How unromantic! How calculating! How logical!

Well, logic pshaw. Surely there must have been several other women who would have made just as suitable First Ladies. In romantic matters, rational explanations are just a thinking man's refusal to be sentimental.

Consider G. Gordon Liddy's detailed discourse on why he ended up head over heels. "When I learned Fran's job at IBM was to receive from brainstorming electronic engineers short, written descriptions of theoretically possible new kinds of computers, for which she would create a mathematical language, and that she did calculus problems for recreation the way I did crossword puzzles," he wrote later, "I knew she was the woman I wanted to bear my children. A Teuton/Celt of high intelligence, a mathematical mind, physical size, strength, and beauty, she had it all." That's longhand for saying he really liked her.

When lightning strikes, what transpires is this: A man makes a split-second decision to marry because—whether or not he can detail it—he feels he knows exactly who that woman is. Her affection for calculus is just his own version of Ali Baba's password. The fact that she might snore or hate his mother never crosses his mind. The transaction is sort of like what goes on when a guy meets a movie star. For example, Debbie Reynolds was out on a first date with her future husband, a businessman named Richard Hamlett. Over dessert—you guessed it—he popped the question. Fearing that he was "a full-blown nut," she tried to clarify the situation. "Why do you want to marry me? You don't even know me."

His reply is telling: "Yes, I do. I've known all about you all my life through the press and movies. I have loved you since *Tammy*. I just never thought I'd get a chance to meet you. But now that I have, I want to marry you."

The same thing happened to Elizabeth Taylor. "I'd seen Mike at several parties and knew him," she said of the man who was her third husband, director Mike Todd. She hadn't thought much about him until he called and insisted he meet her immediately at MGM. He marched her to a deserted office and "sort of plunked me on the couch, and . . . started in on a spiel that lasted about half an hour without a stop, saying that he loved me and that there was no question about it, we were going to be married. I thought, Oh well, he's stark, raving mad. I've got to get away from this man!"

You see, a man like this thinks he knows the score. That's why he proposes out of the blue, in the blink of an eye. But she hasn't had time to think straight. So she laughs.

But she really shouldn't. Because lightning is sex-blind. It strikes women as liberally as men. Actress Natalie Wood was only eleven when she spotted nineteen-year-old Robert Wagner in the studio commissary. "I'm going to marry that man," she announced.

"When I first met my husband," wrote comedienne Roseanne Arnold of her first spouse, Bill Pentland, "he was reading a copy of *The Sensuous Man*." She fell in love immediately. So did Lady Jane Campbell, daughter of the Duke of Argyll, upon meeting writer Norman Mailer. "The night I met him I knew I was going to marry him and have his child." She did exactly that.

"Ronnie and I went together for about a year," said Nancy Reagan, "but I think I knew from the moment I opened the door on our first date that this was the man for me."

Actress Zsa Zsa Gabor was at a party when she saw a suntanned man who looked like a diplomat. "I found myself thinking: this man I could marry. I was a little shocked: I have no idea where the thought came from. It was almost as though it had been whispered in my ear." She inquired who he was. Conrad Hilton, the hotel man, it turned out. They danced. "He took me back to the table. When I said something he liked, he slapped his knee and roared. After a moment I said, because I had to say it, 'I think I'm going to marry you.' "

Yes, he burst out laughing. " 'You sink you're going to marry me?' " he said, affecting her accent. "All right, why don't you do just that?"

Don't laugh. She did.

WOULD YOU ACCEPT ANY OF THE FOLLOWING PROPOSALS?

1. *"My huge, happy, hilarious heart is throbbing tumultuously, tremendously, triumphantly with a lingering, lasting, long-lived love for you.* As I gaze into your bewildering, beauteous, beaming eyes, I am literally lonesomely lost in a dazzling, daring, delightful dream in which your fair, felicitous, fanciful face is ever present like a colossal, comprehensive constellation. Will you be my sweet, smiling, soulful, satisfied spouse?" This was the tongue twister Oral Roberts offered Evelyn Fahnestock, who told him, "Listen, here, boy, if you're trying to propose to me, talk in the English language." He apparently did, for she married him.

2. *"It's your engagement ring, dummy."* Warren Beatty, saying he was in the mood for a snack, had induced Joan Collins to go to the refrigerator to get him some chopped liver, in which he'd stuck a gold ring encrusted with diamonds and pearls. "Does it fit?" he called to her. "Fit? Fit where, on a bagel?" she replied, confused until she brought the container out and noticed the ring. "Oh, darling, it's beautiful," she exclaimed, wiping off bits of liver. "Absolutely beautiful—what's it for?" It was for a marriage that the elusive Beatty managed to dodge.

3. *"Bill, what do you want?"* asked Patricia Taylor. William F. Buckley had called her into the library of her parents' house, interrupting the canasta game she was playing.

"Patricia, would you consider marrying me?"

"Bill, I've been asked this question many times. To others I've said no. To you I say yes. Now may I please get back and finish my hand?"

4. *"We were about to be called for a take.* Ronnie simply turned to me as if the idea were brand-new and just hit him and said, 'Jane, why don't we get married?' I couldn't think of any reason why we shouldn't," said Jane Wyman of Ronald Reagan. "I'd been wondering for a whole year—ever since I first saw him—why he hadn't asked me. I was just about to say a definite yes when we were called before the cameras. In trying to step down off my own personal cloud, I managed to muff a few lines and toss in a whispered 'Yes' after the director said 'Cut!' "

5. *"I don't think he ever did ask me, not just straight out,"* recalled Rose Kennedy. "It was less a matter of 'Will you marry me?' than of 'When we get married. . . .' " Her son John inherited his father's disinclination for scenes of passion and declarations on bended knee. JFK's close friend Lem Billings explained, "I couldn't visualize him actually saying 'I love you' to somebody and asking her to marry him. It was the sort of thing he would have liked to have happen without having to talk about it." When Jackie was sent to London to cover the coronation of Queen Elizabeth II, Jack popped the question via telegram.

6. *"The day I proposed to Alma she was lying in an upper bunk of a ship's cabin,"* said Alfred Hitchcock. "The ship was floundering in the most desperate way, and so was Alma, who was seasick. We were returning to London from Germany. Alma was my employee. I couldn't risk being flowery for fear that in her wretched state she would think I was discussing a movie script. As it was, she groaned, nodded her head, and burped. It was one of my greatest scenes—a little weak on dialogue, perhaps, but beautifully staged and not overplayed."

# 7

# The White House: Life Above the Store

*More than once during the eight years I lived there, I stood at a window looking out across the big lawn of the White House, through its black iron fence at the people strolling along Pennyslvania Avenue, and found myself envying their freedom. I'd say to myself, "You know, I can't even walk down to the drugstore and look over the magazine rack anymore. Will I ever be able to do it again?"*
—Ronald Reagan

Every day hundreds of people line up to tour the White House, and every four years grown men and women duke it out for a chance to live in the nation's only government-owned, fully staffed Georgian mansion with 132 historic rooms and a river view. Though no one, save Grover Cleveland—plagued by tourists and fearful for the safety of his baby Ruth—has taken the drastic step of living elsewhere during his term, few modern Presidents have unpacked their belongings without reservations.

The drawbacks are fairly obvious. "Honey, I'm still living above the store," Ronald Reagan said to Nancy when he heard tourists below.

"I felt like a moth banging on the windowpane," said Jackie Kennedy when she first moved in. "Sometimes I wondered, 'How are we going to live as a family in this enormous place?' . . . It's an office building."

"I hated the White House. It's like this tiny claustrophobic town. There are eyes and ears everywhere," said Patti Davis, who visited her parents four times in eight years. She brought an overnight bag with her to Reagan's second inauguration but left after the ceremony.

"It's not the kind of place you would pick to live in," said LBJ. ". . . [W]hen I'm trying to take a nap, Lady Bird is in the next room with Laurance Rockefeller and eighty ladies talking about the daffodils on Pennsylvania Avenue."

"It was the faculty leaders and professional agitators and the pampered kids on campus who were out screaming, protesting, crowding around the White House," complained Richard Nixon. "Sometimes it was so loud you couldn't even go to sleep at night."

But then, as Pat Nixon said, "Nobody could sleep with Dick. He wakes up during the night, switches on the light, speaks into his tape recorder or takes notes—it's impossible."

Her husband's habits aside, the White House was not a restful place during the Nixon tenure. "It was like living in a bunker in the White House," remembered special counsel Charles Colson. "I mean, you'd look out on the streets and you'd see thousands of people protesting. You literally were afraid for your life. There are times when I can remember saying, 'I can't believe this is the United States of America, a free country,' and here we are in the White House with barricades up and buses around the White House and tear gas going off and thousands, hundreds of thousands of protestors out on the streets and troops sitting here."

Even George Bush had problems during the Gulf War. Protesters camped across the street in Lafayette Park and beat drums around the clock. "Those damned drums are keeping me up all night," he grumbled.

Should anyone who is plagued with sleeplessness—or a dog that needs to go outside—decide to wander around at night, Harry Truman's description of the White House as "the Great White Prison" on Pennsylvania Avenue comes to mind.

Once when Jerry Ford's dog Liberty was pregnant, she licked his face in the middle of the night—her signal to go out. Ford donned his slippers and took her to the south lawn. All was well—until he tried to get back in. The elevator to the family quarters wouldn't work. Ford and Liberty, who was barely able to waddle, padded upstairs but found the second- and third-floor doors locked. As Betty Ford recounted in her memoir, "there they were, a President and his dog, wandering around in a stairwell in the wee small hours of the morning, not able to get back to bed." Finally the Secret Service agents, who normally pay attention to their closed-circuit TV monitors, noticed something was amiss and came to the duo's rescue.

Lady Bird Johnson likewise found herself stranded in her

robe and slippers. She'd left a party downstairs and changed for bed when she noticed a few lights left on, something that seldom failed to bug LBJ. In reaching for a switch in a stairway, she let go of the door to the family quarters, and it locked behind her. "I thought about all those funny ads—'I went to the Opera in my Maidenform Bra'—and I thought how awful it would be if I walked through the main entrance hall of the White House at about 1:30, in my dressing gown, and met a dozen or so of the last departing guests." To her relief she encountered "only two or three of the departing musicians and staff members. I smiled as if the whole thing were a matter of course, caught the elevator back up to my own floor, and so to bed. . . ."

When Raisa Gorbachev toured the White House, she was singularly unimpressed. "It's an official house," she told Nancy Reagan. "I would say that humanly speaking a human being would like to live in a regular home. This is a museum."

Exhibit A, she might have added, is the folks who live there. Abigail Adams realized this when she decided to hang her wash in the unfinished East Room rather than display it outside for all Washington to see. George Bush wrestled with the privacy issue when he tried to figure out where to jog.

His predecessors had managed exercise routines. When Truman was President, he rose at 5:30 A.M. and at 6:00 headed off (with the Secret Service in tow) for a brisk walk around the city (he kept a strict pace—120 steps per minute). Even privacy-conscious Jackie Kennedy, after her breakfast in bed, took an energetic walk around the White House grounds. But George Bush's predicament was a little different. Dashing around the White House at midday in his orange workout shorts would be conspicuous, to say the least. "Imagine what it would do to the traffic on Pennsylvania Avenue," said one member of the press office. He pointed out that the White House is "not a good ground for running and . . . the grounds [sixteen acres] are not as big as they look." After he first took office Bush tried driving to Fort McNair, an Army base, to jog, but his motorcade succeeded in snarling traffic. His compromise: an indoor treadmill.

Venturing out of the White House, whether in jogging shorts or a Chrysler, is seldom accomplished inconspicuously. Bess Truman tried to continue her prepresidential life, driving "my own car, the Chrysler," when she wanted to go shopping or meet with her bridge clubs. When she first asked for her car to be "brought up at two o'clock," Chief Usher J. B. West wanted to know if she'd like a driver. "Indeed no. I don't want to forget how to drive," Mrs. Truman responded. But her attempt at normality was short-lived. The Secret Service stopped her solo expeditions; she was creating too much of a stir.

Reagan found himself in a similar predicament when he went to buy Nancy a valentine. He talked the Secret Service into driving him to a nearby gift store, browsed through the racks, and bought two or three cards. It was his last shopping venture. "It caused such a commotion," Reagan said, "that I never wanted to do that to a shopkeeper again."

Eisenhower went to a store only once during his administration. In 1958, when he was vacationing at his Gettysburg farm, he stopped in at a sporting goods store to buy fishing gear for his grandson, David. When he'd picked out the rods and reels, boots and hooks that he wanted, he took his parcels and left, totally ignoring the not so small matter of payment. A reporter explained to the flattered—and flabbergasted—shop owner that the President never carried cash. If a bill were sent to the White House, it would be paid.

President George Bush went to J. C. Penney's and bought socks for himself and a sweat suit for his grandchild—and made the evening news. His wife complained, "We barely get to go to our children's homes. . . . We don't feel we can cause that kind of problem for our children," a reference to the security entourage that must travel with them. "I've never been to a grandchild's school play or an athletic event. I mean, I would go to every one that I was available for, but I just can't do that. . . . It would risk our grandchildren and I'm just not going to do that."

Jimmy Carter was determined that his daughter, Amy, would have as normal an upbringing as possible. He built her a tree house, and she skated around the big pillars in the White House entrance. When it came to school, Amy looked like the other kids, walking off to elementary school with a book bag on her back. However, a Secret Service agent followed her everywhere. Since the time of Theodore Roosevelt, no presidential children had attended public school, but to Carter that was the point. On her first day Amy entered through a mass of TV cameras, news reporters, and onlookers. Amy's grandmother, Miss Lillian, housebound when she was visiting the White House, complained, "It's so boring. . . . I just feel like I'm waiting for Amy to come home from school."

"I'm not going to tell you I didn't enjoy being President," Ronald Reagan said, looking back. "I did. But, in a way, you're a bird in a gilded cage."

"The best way to stay normal," as David Eisenhower said, "is to stay away from the White House."

### A VIEW FROM THE HELP

*"Mr. West, we have a little problem,'' Bess Truman said to White House usher J. B. West. ''. . . It's the President's bed. Do you think you can get it fixed today?'' He inquired what the matter was and was told that, ''two of the slats broke down during the night.'' Bess had just returned from summering in Missouri, and apparently Harry was very happy to see her.*

When you're on staff at the White House, you never can tell what might unfold in the course of an average working day. You might get asked about bed slats; you might hear loud barking sounds emanating from the presidential bedroom. "It surprised the shit out of me. I thought we had a fucking seal in the White House," said JFK aide Dave Powers to a startled visitor. Kennedy had been told by a doctor that if he spent a half hour barking each morning, it would deepen and strengthen his voice, and he followed doctor's orders.

"I even had to hold his undershorts for him to step into," discovered White House staffer George Thompson when he substituted for Ike's valet, Sergeant Moaney, on his day off.

As far as the latter employee went, he did have responsibilities that extended beyond the call of undershorts. When Ike took out his long irons to practice at the White House, Moaney was assigned to retrieve the presidential golf balls. "Many times while walking through the White House grounds I saw Ike hitting balls while Moaney chased them," observed staffer Traphes Bryant. When Ike hit the ball solidly, he'd say, "I got that one," ignoring the fact that a solid hit was occasionally accompanied by the sound of shattering glass from a streetlight across from the south grounds. Bryant's tasks included replacing the bulbs. Eventually, he reported, "the city got tired of replacing glass protectors and put in plastic ones."

On the rare occasions when LBJ practiced golf, he had his dogs fetch the balls. But that didn't mean he didn't expect service from his staff. As Vice President he once insisted that Secret Service Agent Jerry Kivett help him dress for a formal party. When LBJ criticized his technique, Kivett replied, "Well, sir, you have to consider that this is the first time in my life I ever dressed another full-grown man!"

Chief Usher J. B. West wasn't asked to dress a man; Jackie Kennedy had other things in mind. For a surprise party skit in honor of her social secretary, Nancy Tuckerman, she rounded up one of the nanny's uniforms and her own bouffant wig. Laughing, Jackie said, "Mr. West, you're going to wear these to the party and be Miss Ward, our housemother from Miss Porter's School. And I want you to put a sign around your neck saying, 'Miss Ward,' so people will know who you are."

West protested, "I'm not going to do it," but few could resist Mrs. Kennedy.

Besides, it's the unspoken responsibility of those who serve the presidential family to be ready for anything. Thus, when JFK stayed at his duplex penthouse in New York's Carlyle Hotel and reporters camped out in the lobby, the Secret Service helped him find another exit—through underground tunnels that led to neighboring apartment buildings. "It was kind of a weird sight," recalled JFK's friend Charles Spalding. "Jack and I and two Secret Service men walking in these huge tunnels underneath the city streets alongside those enormous pipes, each of us carrying a flashlight. One of the Secret Service men also had this underground map, and every once in a while he would say, 'We turn this way, Mr. President.' "

The Secret Service also came to the rescue when a fire broke out in the dining room of the Nixons' California house at San Clemente. Agent Dennis McCarthy, who, in his own words, was "a civil servant with absolutely no experience as a fire fighter," found himself holding a hose, "wearing one of my best suits." When the water came on, the pressure jolted him; he sprayed "just about everything in the room except the fire in the wall" and then remembered the President. "Who's got the fucking President?" he shouted.

"I'm right here," Nixon answered. "Everything is fine."

Secret Service agents may have the most adventurous jobs, but those who have the most trying jobs may well be the kitchen staff. Consider the responsibility of anticipating what a new First Family might want to eat. "For two weeks we've laid in supplies in the kitchen," mused chef Henry Haller. "I think we could open a grocery store in the pantry. We've tried to find out everything they like." It was the Nixons' first night in the White House. The President ordered steaks for the family, but Mrs. Nixon thought she'd just have a bowl of cottage cheese. There was not, recalled Haller, "a spoonful of cottage cheese in the house. And what in the world would be open this time of night—and inauguration night to boot?" A limousine was summoned, and the head butler was dispatched in search of an open deli. Cottage cheese was located—and served in due course.

The limo route was out of the question one evening when Tricia Nixon asked for a hot dog after the grocery stores had closed. Aiming to please, Chef Haller went from the second-floor kitchens to the ground-floor freezers but could find nary a wiener. Finally it occurred to him that the vending machines used by office workers in the West Wing dispatched fast food. Using change from his pocket, he bought a hot dog, brought it to the kitchen, reheated it, and presented it to Tricia, who pronounced it the best she'd ever had.

Not all chefs viewed the household's whims so agreeably. "Our food bill was astronomical," Rosalynn Carter discovered to her horror. She insisted the kitchen be stocked with the cheapest brands of food, much to the embarrassment of the staff who had to shop from her list.

Jackie Kennedy tried her own version of an economy move. "Oh, Mary," she said to her secretary Mary Gallagher, "do you know what I've just learned from Anne Lincoln? You know, all the food we buy here at the White House? Well, she told me that with the stamps the stores give us, we can trade them in for these marvelous gifts!"

Free toasters aside, the Kennedys expected life in the White House to be *haute*. Jackie induced René Verdon, formerly of the Carlyle Hotel in New York City, to take over the kitchen. Every inch the French chef, he arrived with his white hat and Italian assistant, prepared to serve trout with wine and meringue shells filled with raspberries. There was just one problem: JFK's tastes ran to fish chowder and chocolate ice cream. "He told me you had to be from New England to make fish chowder, and I believe him," said Verdon. But whatever plebeian fare the Kennedys requested was small potatoes compared with the food the Johnsons preferred.

"Chili con-crete" was Verdon's nickname for the *chili con queso* LBJ adored. "The President eats so much tapioca pudding," the chef ranted, "that Zephyr [a longtime Johnson servant] doesn't even cook it herself. She has the pot washer do it."

On another occasion Verdon cried in despair, "You don't ask a chef to serve red snapper with the skin on it, beets with cream all over them."

Not everyone considers working in the White House a dream come true. Verdon hung up his chef's hat and went back to the land of haute cuisine.

THE VAGARIES OF TASTE

*"It looks like it's been furnished by discount stores," said Jackie Kennedy after Mamie Eisenhower gave her a tour of the White House, her home-to-be. To Jackie, the downstairs was "a dentist's office bomb shelter"; the East Room curtains were "seasick green." She broke down and cried.*

Taste is in the eye of the beholder. One woman's pink—Mamie Eisenhower's, for instance—is another's Pepto-Bismol. Upon moving into a new home—whether the White House or a farmhouse—most families' first impulse is to expunge the "errors" of the previous residents.

Teddy Roosevelt undid an elaborate interior design by Chester A. Arthur protégé Louis Comfort Tiffany and even tore down a Tiffany stained glass screen. Barbara Bush turned Nancy Reagan's beauty salon into a puppy-whelping room, her gym into a guest room for visiting grandchildren. Pat Nixon substituted Monets (on loan from the Metropolitan Museum in New York) for war-painted Oto Indian chiefs.

And so it goes. Out with the old, in with the proclamations of taste, at long last. Should anyone doubt that the end results are highly subjective, consider two case studies: the strange history of the Revolutionary War wallpaper and the question of the squirrels.

First to the wallpaper, a story that begins with Jackie Kennedy. Other First Ladies have been taken aback by the condition of their new quarters. For example, Pat Nixon found faded draperies, sofas hiding shredded wallpaper, and once-white family-quarter carpeting marred by dog stains. But Jackie Kennedy found a house in which "you couldn't even open the windows in the rooms, because they hadn't been opened for years. . . . When we tried the fireplaces, they smoked because they hadn't ever been used."

When they first moved in, her husband dropped to the floor to examine the underside of a dresser, as any antiques connoisseur would. "Ken, look at this," he said to John Kenneth Galbraith, the economist. "It's not even authentic. It's not even a good reproduction."

Jackie was determined to make the White House into an American showplace, reflective of nearly two hundred years of decorative arts history. She rummaged in the basement for antiques ("I had a backache every day for three months"); she bargained with dealers. People donated important American pieces. She learned that a historic house in Maryland was being torn down and set out to rescue its wallpaper. Sheets depicting George Washington and Revolutionary War soldiers were steamed off the wall and applied to the White House dining room. In her memoir Maud Shaw, the Kennedys' nanny, wrote, "The dining room had another wonderful attribute, thanks to Mrs. Kennedy. . . . It was covered in the most fascinating wallpaper." But JFK didn't think it was so fascinating. When the newspapers reported that a reproduction paper was available in the same design, he confronted Jackie. She said the colors of the original were superior. "I don't give a damn," her husband said. "Twelve thousand, five hundred dollars is entirely too much money for wallpaper." But by then the damage was done.

Damage was exactly Betty Ford's view of the wallpaper. She had it removed from the dining room. "It was a valuable historical document, I'm sure, showing a lot of Revolutionary War scenes, but I couldn't stand to look at soldiers fainting and dying while I was eating my soup."

By the Bush administration the dreaded wallpaper was back up and considered the best of taste. However, it did pose a problem for Barbara Bush when she had Queen Elizabeth II of England over for lunch. The First Lady said she had to "mumble" when describing the wallpaper, since it depicted the vanquishing of British troops.

Eisenhower worried little about wallpaper, but vanquishing the squirrels who dug up his putting green was quite high on his agenda. Donated by the American Public Golf Association, the green was his pride and joy; he even insisted that gardeners use fishing poles to brush the dewdrops off it each morning. Thus when Eisenhower discovered bumps on the green caused by hidden nuts, he was irate. But he became apoplectic when he'd try to sink a shot and the ball would roll right up to the hole—and keep on going—because the squirrels had filled the hole with acorns. "Get those goddamn squirrels out of here," he'd bellow.

Once the White House's long-tailed rodents so annoyed him that he instructed his valet, Sergeant Moaney, "The next time you see one of those squirrels go near my putting green, take a gun and shoot it!" The Secret Service didn't think that was such a good idea. Instead, the Capital Parks Service obligingly set cages and removed the squirrels to other city parks.

Whatever lack of love the squirrels suffered as a result of Eisenhower's wrath, Ronald Reagan more than made up for. He'd bring acorns back from Camp David and toss them outside the Oval Office so he could watch the squirrels snack in the course of his day. "He used to say that by Friday the squirrels would practically nose up to the windows and give him a sad, pleading look, reminding him to bring back some more goodies after the weekend," recalled Reagan's daughter Maureen.

When Reagan told his successor of his carefully cultivated relationship with the squirrels, Bush gasped, "Oh, gosh. Millie kills squirrels." In *Millie's Book*, the First Dog reported her White House kills: one pigeon, three rats, and four squirrels.

For everything there is a season. Squirrels and wallpaper and even putting greens. The only thing, it seems, that remains constant at the White House is its exterior color.

CHIPPED BEEF, EGG NOG, AND THE BLUES: ENTERTAINING AT
THE WHITE HOUSE

*"After a few minutes, I noticed the prince was staring rather
quizzically down into his cup," observed Ronald Reagan when
Prince Charles was served tea in the Oval Office, "and I thought he
seemed a little troubled." The prince put his cup down and left it
untouched. Later he confessed, "I just didn't know what to do with
the little bag."*

In 1961 novelist William Faulkner passed up an invitation
to a White House dinner, saying it was just too far to go to eat.
He might have had a point, given some folks' experience.

Once George Bush asked Denver Broncos quarterback John
Elway over for breakfast. That night—Monday—Elway was mys-
teriously absent from the game. The reason, explained his perturbed coach, Dan Reeves, was that Bush had served the
quarterback "the worst-looking thing you can imagine: creamed
chip beef." Considering that Bush's tastes ran to pork rinds and
strip mall takeout specialties like ribs, beef jerky, and nachos, he
probably thought a Bronco like Elway was a perfect partner in
cast-iron stomach adventures.

Food wasn't the problem at the Carter White House. It was
the lack of it. One year the President spent only $1,372 of his
$50,000 entertainment allowance. And even though he had cash
to spare, he tried billing congressmen for their breakfasts. Needless
to say, that went over like burned toast. But when Carter broke
down and treated congressional leaders to breakfast in the Cabinet
Room, the grumbling didn't cease. The proffered fare—juice, coffee, and a roll—wasn't enough for 265-pound House Speaker Tip
O'Neill. "I guess you'd call it a Continental breakfast. It must be
that economy wave that's hit the White House," he complained.

The Carters' White House picnic didn't go over much better.
Gone were the embossed invitations. Senators and representatives
were sent mimeographed notices and entertained by Rosalynn's
old music teacher.

Johnson, on the other hand, did it up right when he was
trying to grease the congressional wheels and get his controversial
1964 civil rights bill passed. Finishing legislative touches were still
required on Christmas Eve, so he bellowed, "Bird"—his wife was

in another room of the White House living quarters—"let's have Congress over tonight." That meant a potential guest list of well over a thousand, counting all the representatives and their spouses. No problem. Eggnog was laced with bourbon, and a lavish party prepared. The civil rights bill passed.

Kennedy affairs were generally noted for their sophistication and wit. At a dinner for twelve Nobel Prize winners, JFK toasted his guests as "the most extraordinary collection of talent, of human knowledge, that has ever been gathered together at the White House—with the possible exception of when Thomas Jefferson dined alone." But such refinement did not always prevail. When Robert F. Kennedy was being sworn in as attorney general, the ceremony was held upstairs. Downstairs in the White House foyer a large group of guests waited to be called into the East Room. Suddenly the guest of honor dropped in—literally. RFK arrived by sliding down the curved banister of the White House's great stairway, followed by his children Kathleen and Michael, squealing with laughter.

Laughter eluded blues singer Sarah Vaughan after she performed at the White House for Lyndon Johnson and the prime minister of Japan. One of Lady Bird's aides, Bess Abell, found her sobbing in her dressing room. "Nothing is the matter," Vaughan explained. "It's just that twenty years ago when I came to Washington, I couldn't even get a hotel room, and tonight I sang for the President of the United States in the White House—and then he asked me to dance. It's more than I can stand."

# 8

# The Moral and the Immoral

*"I'm reliable. When I agree to do something, I do the best possible job. That may sound ridiculous in light of the fact that I was working for two governments at once. But the fact of the matter is . . . neither of them had a complaint. My work for the U.S. Navy was extraordinary, was exemplary. And my work for the Soviets was also exemplary."*
—spy John Walker, Jr., who, in eighteen years, made thirty successful drops of Navy intelligence for the KGB

From the time we're little, we're taught the value of work. Do a good job. Be reliable. It's a work ethic that doesn't go away—even if we venture into lines of business where churchgoers fear to tread. For example, Sydney Biddle Barrows, the Mayflower Madam who was caught running an escort service, explained, "I ran the wrong kind of business, but I did it with integrity."

Integrity in the wrong kind of business is a rationale; in the right kind, its existence is assumed, perhaps a little too blithely. After all, we live in a world where an owner of a troubled savings and loan bank, Charles Keating, can give $1.3 million to five senators and announce, "One question among the many raised in recent weeks had to do with whether my financial support influenced several political figures who took up my cause. I want to say in the most forceful way that I can, I certainly hope so."

And we live in a world where Oliver North accepts a $13,800 home security system for free but writes two letters that create the false impression he paid for them. He transgresses, but with his own brand of integrity. Rather than have people at work "see me typing a letter dated 18 May in December," he drove to a department store near his suburban Virginian house and used one of the typewriters on the display counter to write what the prosecutor at his trial called "phony letters."

"Why in a store?" North was asked.

"I didn't want the Marine Corps involved in this kind of coverup, so I went and did it in the store," he testified.

Work and ethics are on occasion a difficult pairing of words. If an employee like George Bush's chief of staff John Sununu is doing an exemplary job, what does it matter to his boss that he takes government limousines from Washington, D.C., to stamp auctions in New York City or military planes to go on ski vacations? How much do we forgive when a man's on-the-job attitude is straight-arrow Protestant ethic?

Prim and proper, Sherman Adams, a blue-blooded New Englander who served as Ike's chief of staff, crossed the line. He accepted a vicuña coat from an influence peddler and, like Sununu, was forced to resign, despite presidential protests of "I need him." Eisenhower fumed, "The trouble with these people is they don't recognize integrity." He felt a vicuña coat couldn't even begin to buy the favor of a man he trusted and valued, but the public thought otherwise.

Not that Eisenhower was without his own ethical hot potatoes. In defending Adams, he commented, "A gift is not necessarily a bribe. One is evil, the other is a tangible expression of friendship," and thus put forth a line of defense he would need. In 1957 it was disclosed that Eisenhower had accepted more than forty thousand dollars' worth of tractors, livestock, and gifts for his Gettysburg, Pennsylvania, farm. The press had a field day. Eisenhower called a news conference on July 31 and offered the peculiar explanation that "The conflict of interest laws do not apply to me." Since he announced that the farm would one day become public property, the controversy died down. Later the value of the gifts he received was revised to an estimate of three hundred thousand dollars. Six years after leaving office, he deeded the farm to the United States.

Money is the fastest way to blur any on-the-job ethical lines. Not only is there the lure of "gifts" and ill-gotten cash (despite John Walker's warning "I certainly don't recommend espionage as a second career. It's not even very profitable. It's dangerous") but for the businessmen everywhere, there's the persistent pressure of making sure a company turns a profit. How easy it would be to do the right thing—to stop dumping chemicals into rivers, to hire blacklisted actors and not fret about the TV sponsors' fury—if we didn't have to worry about the bottom line, as Henry Luce, cofounder of *Time*, knew well.

In 1960, the very week that Detroit was abuzz with rumors that a Chrysler executive was taking kickbacks, the *Time* reporter responsible for the muckraking was transferred from Detroit to the Los Angeles bureau, where he could do no more damage. "No major publication in America exists without automobile advertising," explained Luce. "Integrity is a word I left at Yale."

What's a businessman to do when he'd really like to do the right thing? Richard Rich, owner of Rich's Department Store in Atlanta, broke down in tears when he learned that the only way a sit-in at his store dining room could be resolved was if Martin Luther King and the student protesters were led out in handcuffs. Though he didn't want to see King imprisoned, he refused to drop the trespassing charges. He had his profit margin to consider: If he desegregated his store, white customers would flock to his competitors. He was just doing his job.

"Everyone's entitled to a lawyer," Edward Bennett Williams told Eunice Shriver when, in the early 1980s, she turned to him in church and asked, "How can you defend evil?" Jimmy Hoffa, Mafia don Frank Costello, Soviet spy Igor Melekh, Joe McCarthy—he'd defended them all. "In the law," he told Shriver, "there is a presumption of innocence. It is a legal concept, not a moral one. I defend my clients from legal guilt. Moral judgments I leave to the majestic vengeance of God."

"The idea was to prove that these people were Communists," said William Wheeler, a staff investigator for the House Committee on Un-American Activities. "It didn't make a hell of a lot of difference who they were, in a sense. In retrospect, I just wonder if I did what was right. . . . But you see, I was a cop. I'd been trained as a cop. And when you work for Congress you say to yourself, 'If this is what I'm assigned to do, I'm going to do it and I'm going to do a good job.' "

And therein lies one of the simplest ways to draw the moral line. If you're just doing your job, the decision isn't really up to you. It's a natural offshoot of accepting a paycheck for a certain line of work.

If you're a journalist, that means your job is to report. If you're offered a chance to cover the Gulf War from behind enemy lines, you take it, even if it means being charged with transmitting propaganda. Said CNN reporter Australian-born Peter Arnett, "I became an American a few years ago because I felt this was the one country in the world that would allow and approve what I was doing in a place like Baghdad. Freedom of speech. Understanding. Information."

When someone wrote that gossip maven Liz Smith would go to lunch with almost anyone, she thought, "Wow! Would I? Yes, of course. Hitler too. Any of them. I'm not their judge and jury."

It's her job to get the gossip, just as surely as it was Sugar Ray Robinson's to outpunch his opponents. The problem with the latter occupation was that Robinson won an eight-round knockout fight against Jimmy Doyle but lost his opponent. Doyle died from brain damage resulting from Robinson's blows. Asked at the coroner's inquest if he had intended to get Doyle "in trouble," Robinson said simply, "Mister, it's my business to get him in trouble." Said fellow boxer Sugar Ray Leonard, "We're all given some sort of skill in life. Mine just happens to be beating up on people."

When your job involves a skill like killing, the same logic applies. You're in the Army, you're in Vietnam, you're ordered to shoot. You do. But if your target is Vietnamese women and children, the moral line gets very fuzzy.

"Lieutenant Calley started pushing them off into the ravine. It was a ditch. And so we just pushed them off and just started using automatics on them—men, women, children and babies," said Private Paul Meadlo. "They was begging and saying no, no, and the mother was holding the children, but they kept right on firing. . . . Why'd I do it? Because I felt like I was ordered to do it. At the time I felt like I was doing the right thing." Though when he was shooting, he "felt good," he said "later on that day it was gettin' to me." It continued to get to him after he came home. So he brought My Lai to the attention of CBS News, turning the incident into a national scandal. "I sent them a good boy and they made him a murderer," lamented Meadlo's mother. But it was his job to murder. He and Charlie Company were just doing it a little too well.

The problem is that not everyone has the strength of character to listen to his or her conscience when history is happening. Not everyone can stand up in front of the House Un-American Activities Committee and announce as Lillian Hellman did, "I cannot and will not cut my conscience to fit this year's fashions." She could not and would not discuss her Communist friends or affiliations, no matter what the career price.

Not everyone can look the nation in the eye and forgive a President for impeachable crimes. "I don't give a damn about the criticism," said Gerald Ford when, one month after taking office, he pardoned Nixon. "I did it because it was right." He went to church to "pray for guidance and understanding," appeared on national TV, made his announcement, and went off to play golf. His favorable rating fell from 71 to 49 percent in the polls, but he slept at night.

Not everyone who thinks his boss is in error can quit his job. "President Ford was creating a double standard of justice, one for people in power, with power, and other people who then had to go to jail for various Watergate-related events," said Ford's press secretary Jerald terHorst, who resigned as soon as he heard of his boss's intentions that Sunday morning in 1974. "I had a daughter who was a schoolteacher. Try to imagine how she would explain this to her students. . . ."

We all have to find the right balance, the ethical standards we can live with, work with, love with. And oh, how good it feels when we figure out the right stance. "If it's possible to know what it means to have your soul cleansed—I felt pretty clean at that time. I probably felt better on that day than I've felt in my life," said Howell Raines, who as a student at the all-black North Carolina A&T College participated in the first civil rights sit-in, staged at the Woolworth's counter in Greensboro, North Carolina.

"Now . . . you have been with us all along, so now you go on and start back to ridin' the bus, 'cause you are too old to keep walking," Martin Luther King said to an elderly lady during the Montgomery bus boycott.

"Oh, no. Oh, no," she replied. "I'm gonna walk just as long as everybody else walks. I'm gonna walk till it's over."

"But ain't your feet tired?"

"Yes, my feets is tired but, but my soul is rested."

POWER: THE ULTIMATE APHRODISIAC

*Here, find out who owns these. They're not my size.*
—Jackie Kennedy, handing her husband a pair of panties
found in the presidential bed

Once upon a time—in 1988, to be precise—Dan Quayle was debating Democratic vice presidential candidate Lloyd Bentsen. He made the mistake of invoking a politician who likewise had sought the limelight at a tender age. Firmly he was told, "Senator, you're no Jack Kennedy," a comment that left Quayle flummoxed, unable to think of a comeback zippier than "that was really uncalled for, Senator." Subsequently, as Kennedy's sexual conquests have been chronicled and rechronicled, it may have dawned on Quayle that, at least from a moral standpoint, he was handed a compliment.

Power has a legendary corollary that Henry Kissinger turned into an aphorism. Power, of course, is the ultimate aphrodisiac. It inspires a lust for more power, and it also puts leaders in proximity with lusts of another sort.

Martin Luther King, Jr., preached that "it is through and in marriage that God gives man the opportunity to aid him in his creative activity. Therefore, sex must never be abused in the loose sense that it is so often abused in the modern world." But he, too, was seduced by the opportunities power affords.

When influential men flirt with infidelity, they play a dangerous game. J. Edgar Hoover did his best to ruin Martin Luther King, labeling him " 'tom cat' with obsessive degenerate sexual urges" and sending his wife, Coretta, a tape of suggestive noises made from King's bugged hotel rooms. Nixon tried to get Teddy Kennedy. "Catch him in the sack with one of his babes," he said, instructing Bob Haldeman to place Teddy under twenty-four-hour surveillance. Gary Hart, of course, got his. Responding to Ted Koppel's question on *Nightline* "Did you have an affair with Miss Rice?" he offered this rambling explanation: "Mr. Koppel, if the question is in the twenty-nine years of my marriage, including two public separations, have I been absolutely and totally faithful to my wife, I regret to say the answer is no . . . I've been forced to make a declaration here that I think is unprecedented in American political history, and I regret it. That question should never have been asked. . . . Never ask another political candidate that question."

But the question does get asked—except, it seems when the politician in question is able to charm more than just women, when he's able to seduce a powerful network of admirers, in both politics and the media.

"So you say to me, 'Well, what about the fact that people in bygone days were womanizers?' Hell, there wasn't anybody in Boston who didn't know that Jack Kennedy was," recalled Tip O'Neill after he had retired as Speaker of the House. "You know he brought more women into politics than any other man by having a reception and shakin' their hand twice and lookin' them in the eye. They'd say, 'You never knew what that did to us, Tip.' [Laughter] . . . It wasn't reported in those days. It wasn't *reported*."

Among those who wondered why was Pat Nixon. In 1960 she asked NBC News' John Chancellor, "What's going to happen to this country if someone with those morals gets into the White House? Why doesn't the press write about it?"

Her husband certainly had the dirt on Kennedy. Why didn't he exploit it? Years later Nixon explained, "I think we probably felt it would be counterproductive. I don't want to indicate to you that . . . we wanted to be so much above the battle and campaign only on the issues. I'm sure that he and we would have done virtually anything which might be legal in order to win." His feeling was that in 1960 "the media would have discounted it. . . . They liked him."

Kennedy managed to live a charmed life. The press turned a blind eye when women came and went during Jackie's absences at the White House. ("We were standing close to a window and I could see the Washington Monument in the distance," recalled lover Judith Exner of her first visit to the presidential home. "Then he kissed me and I forgot about monuments and parks.")

His aides were loyal. Secret Service Agent Marty Venker recalled: "When he used the pool, he always posted an agent outside the door. 'Nobody comes in,' he said. 'You understand that? Nobody.' " Aide Ken O'Donnell was convinced that "nobody" didn't include him. He "thundered" at the agent, "Are you telling me I can't see the Chief?" and followed that up with "You're nothing but a Secret Service agent, a little twerp." He charged toward the pool and "found Kennedy relaxing in the pool with two young ladies. All three were nude. Kennedy was furious."

Even Jackie, who must have had some idea of what was going on in the executive bedroom, didn't make waves. Touring the White House with a French photographer, she pointed to a staffer, saying in French, "And this is a young lady who is supposed to be sleeping with my husband." Perhaps she simply viewed the matter as very European. "I don't think there are many men who are faithful to their wives," she said on another occasion. "Men are such a combination of good and evil."

Kennedy himself was decidely blasé about the sexual perks of power, much to the frustration of J. Edgar Hoover. The FBI director thought he had a juicy scoop when he discovered that an American ambassador had departed from a woman's bedroom window in such haste that he left his trousers behind. He dispatched the news to Kennedy but heard nothing. Finally he inquired as to the President's course of action. JFK had said, according to an aide, "that from now on he's going to hire faster ambassadors."

If the President worried so little about puritanical values, it should be no surprise. He had a role model who reveled in power's candy shop: his father. Joan Fontaine described one encounter with Joe, Sr., when she was seated at JFK's left at a White House dinner. Once in Beverly Hills, ". . . Joe got up before the dessert was served and beckoned me into the living room," she recalled. He told her, "I like it. I like your guests, your children, your house. . . . Tell you what I'll do. I'll live here whenever I come to California. I'll invest your money for you . . . just as I did for Gloria Swanson."

Fontaine said: "With one eye on my guests, chatting over dessert, I listened as he continued. 'You can do what you like when I'm not here, but there's only one thing . . . I can't marry you!' I was stunned. Joe had never even held my hand. I simply laughed it off, chucked him under the chin, and returned to the table."

Kennedy's response: "Let's see . . . how old would he have been then? Sixty-five? Hope I'm the same when I'm his age!"

At forty something, he was doing pretty well himself. He had more power than his father and arguably more notches in his belt. His attitude about his affairs was, as he put it, "They can't touch me while I'm alive, and after I'm dead, who cares?"

Yes, Dan Quayle is no JFK. Once he went off on a golfing trip to Florida and an eye-catching lobbyist, Paula Parkinson, claimed he tried to put the moves on her. Marilyn quickly came to her husband's defense, saying, "Anyone who knows Dan Quayle knows that given a choice between golf and sex he'd choose golf every time."

### BARGAINING WITH THE DEVIL

*Memo from Oliver North to National Security Adviser Robert McFarlane regarding supplying the contras in Nicaragua: "There is great despair that we may fail in this effort and the resistance support account is darn near broke. Any thoughts where we can put our hands on a quick $3 million to $5 million?"*

In the halls of government the devil is no stranger. A lot of people open bank accounts with him. Interested in funding the contras, even though there's a congressional ban on such activity? No problem. The Bank of the Devil advises: Solicit funds from other countries, sell missiles to Iran at above market prices, and dispense the cash. His loan officer whispers: Don't worry about the consequences, even if the secretary of state, George Shultz, advises the President directly that "[White House chief of staff] Jim Baker said if we go out and try to get money from third countries it is an impeachable offense."

Concerned that the Watergate burglars are snapping at your heels demanding so much hush money that White House counsel John Dean terms it "blackmail"? No problem.

"How much money do you need?" Nixon asked Dean.

"I pulled out of thin air what I thought was a pretty astronomical number," Dean recalled later, "and I said, 'Well, it could cost $1 million.' And he looked at me and said, 'John, I know where we can get $1 million.' "

Generally the devil's currency is vanity—yours. He banks on the fact that you'll believe you're the one who can outsmart the system, you're the one who can thumb your nose at fate and not anger the gods.

Harlem's Adam Clayton Powell, Jr., liked to call himself "the

first bad nigger in Congress." And bad he was. His fellow congressmen eventually refused to seat him, ostensibly for tax entanglements
but arrogance played no small part. Powell played the power game
without pretense. He set off with various aides (and the first black
Miss Ohio) on an all-expenses-paid six-week junket to Europe,
ostensibly to attend a labor congress in Geneva. "Is going to night-
clubs part of committee business?" he was asked by reporters.

"I'm sure you don't go to Paris and stay the whole time in
Notre Dame. Of course, it's part of it. You're going abroad. Travel
is a very broadening form of education. And I assure you it is
practiced by every member of the House and Senate."

"Do you think having family members on the payroll is a
good thing?" he was also asked, referring to the fact that his wife
was drawing a government paycheck.

Yes, came the reply. "As long as a hundred plus members
of the House and X number of senators do it, then I'm going to
do it."

Why be a saint when the good ol' boys are riding in limousines? Everyone's doing it.

And therein lies one of the devil's best tactics: moving a sin
from the realm of the extraordinary to the commonplace, from
the realm of the criminal to the savvy.

When spy John Walker's activities were discovered by his
wife, he told her things like the information he was sending to
the KGB "is obsolete or it's shortly going to be obsolete. It's not
important. A lot of people are doing this. It's like business." Barbara Walker bought in. She didn't squeal on her husband—who
became her ex-husband—for nearly two decades. "I wanted to
believe what he was saying to me."

And why not? You'd be a fool not to.

That's what they told Charles Van Doren, son of the famous
poet, Mark Van Doren, and a lackluster academic who was re-
cruited for the lucrative *Twenty-One* quiz show to participate in a
fixed contest. According to Charles Van Doren, the producer told
him that rigging was "common practice," that the shows were
"merely entertainment"; he "also stressed the fact that by ap-
pearing on a nationally televised program I would be doing a
great service to the intellectual life, to teachers, and education in
general, by increasing public respect for the work of the mind
through my performances."

With his first TV appearance on November 28, 1956, Van Doren began winning "more money than I ever made or dreamed of making"—$129,000 in fourteen weeks plus a $50,000-a-year spot on NBC's *Today* show. His salary at Columbia University was $4,400.

*The New York Times* extolled him as "a new kind of TV idol— of all things an egghead . . . whom many a grateful parent regards as TV's own health-restoring antidote to Presley." Until the scandal broke in 1958 and Congress launched a quiz show investigation, Van Doren, rumpled in his tweeds, convinced himself he was the man *Time* put on its cover and called "The Wizard of Quiz." But such delusions are commonplace when you buy your prestige from scurrilous salesclerks.

Maybe it's the adrenaline, maybe just the intoxication of not getting caught that first or second time, but it is remarkably easy to begin to believe your own myth. "It was this incredible feeling of invulnerability, of a rush that in pushing a button—in making two phone calls, I made close to three million dollars and that's what drove it," recalled Drexel Burnham Lambert's Dennis Levine of his inside trading deals. "That was the insanity of it all. It wasn't that *hard.*"

He added, "You get bolder and bolder and bolder and it gets easier and you make more money and more money. And it feeds upon itself." Within five years he had $12.6 million stowed away in a secret bank account in the Bahamas. But in 1986 the game was up. He was arrested, tried, and treated to seventeen all-expenses-paid months at the penitentiary in Lewisburg, Pennsylvania. "And looking back—looking back I realize that I was sick, that it became an addiction. That I lived for the high of making those trades, of doing the next deal, making the bigger deal. . . . Foolishly I thought I could outsmart the system. I never thought I'd get caught."

Why didn't Van Doren just rely on being an egghead and win what he could? Why didn't Mike Milken content himself with making $5.5 million a year *on the books*? Why does someone always listen to the devil?

# 9
# Famous Last Words

*"I've got Bush by the balls," said General Manuel Noriega of Panama, indicating he had unsavory information on the man who was running for President in 1988. Two years later Bush had Noriega behind bars in Florida.*

We've all done it, succumbed to the bravado of the moment and said things in voices John Wayne would have envied. Things like "I want you to know that I have no intention whatever of ever walking away from the job that the people elected me to do." This from Richard Nixon in his State of the Union address, January 1974. In August he resigned.

Or "Fighter-bomber planes can now be put into museums"; the USSR will be "turning out long-range missiles like sausages." This from Khrushchev after *Sputnik*, the first space satellite, was launched.

Or "If anyone wants to put a tail on me, go ahead. They'd be very bored." This from Gary Hart, front-runner in the 1988 Democratic primaries, who should have known that people—reporters from *The Miami Herald*, for instance—tend to take you up, call your bluff, find blondes in your town house, and leave you with famous last words.

Politicians particularly have a talent for the foot-in-mouth syndrome. After all, they have to be schooled in bravado, in painting a compelling portrait of the future, or else we wouldn't vote for them. Hence we have George Bush playing Clint Eastwood, exhorting us to read his lips. (The applause at the Republican National Convention alone must have made it worthwhile.) And we have Lyndon Johnson promising October 21, 1964, "We are not going to send American boys nine or ten thousand miles away from home to fight." In February of the following year the Marines landed in Da Nang, Vietnam.

But famous last words aren't necessarily a by-product of hot air and chest beating. Sometimes they can be said softly and sincerely, in a voice like the one John Kennedy must have used in calming down his brother, upset that Lyndon Johnson had accepted the vice presidential slot on the ticket: "Don't worry, Bobby, nothing's going to happen to me." What makes famous last words famous is that just as you are saying them, fate is throwing you a curve ball.

A word about timing. It varies. Some words boomerang within minutes; others take a lifetime. Here is a schedule of examples.

*MINUTES.* 1. Lee Harvey Oswald, handcuffed, was being led to the fifth-floor elevator at a Dallas police station. He had undergone interrogation and was about to be transferred to a secure prison. James Leavelle, a Dallas plainclothesman, said, "If anybody shoots at you, I sure hope they are as good a shot as you are." Oswald "kind of laughed" and said, "Nobody is going to shoot me." Coming out of the elevator, he was to encounter Jack Ruby.

2. "That guy's got to stop. He'll see us," actor James Dean told his companion, a stunt man from the movie *Giant.* The two were speeding down a rural California highway in Dean's new gray Porsche. The guy didn't see them, and Dean was killed.

*HOURS.* 1. "I know the Chinese will not intervene," General Douglas MacArthur told his boss, Harry Truman, as they were conferring at Wake Island about the Korean War. "If they do, it will be one of the greatest slaughters in history. Corpses will be piled six deep." As they conferred, the Chinese were already sending troops across the Yalu River into North Korea. Corpses were piled deep, but many of them were American. The U.S. troops, taken totally by surprise, had to beat a hasty retreat south.

2."I was an utter flop," cried Richard Nixon as he threw down his cue cards after his famous 1952 Checkers speech. Charged with using an eighteen-thousand-dollar annual fund collected by California businessmen for his own personal use, Nixon went on national television—along with his wife—in an attempt to clear his name. He denied accepting any such gifts for his personal use, except for a little black-and-white cocker spaniel that his six-year-old daughter had named Checkers. "And you know, the kids love the dog, and I just want to say right now,

that regardless of what they say about it, we're gonna keep it."
In living rooms across America, people wept. But Nixon missed
the countdown signal as the program ended. "Time had run out.
I was cut off just as I intended to say where the National Commit-
tee was located and where telegrams and letters should be sent."
He was convinced he had failed, but within hours it became clear
Eisenhower had no need to dump his running mate.

*DAYS.* 1. "I'm going to live to be one hundred. Unless I'm
run down by a sugar-crazed taxi driver." So health food advocate
Jerome Rodale was quoted in *The New York Times* on June 6,
1971. The next day he died of a heart attack while discussing his
health tenets—no wheat, milk, or sugar—during a taping of *The
Dick Cavett Show.*

2."I've never been one damned bit concerned about my
safety. Nobody's going to bother me. After all, I took care of myself
all my life," said former Teamsters President Jimmy Hoffa, days
before he disappeared without a trace.

*WEEKS.* 1."Tip, I'm getting out," Congressman Jerry Ford
told the Speaker of the House as they were driving in a golf cart.
"I promised Betty I'd quit after one more term. . . . Then I can go
back to Grand Rapids. I want to practice law three days a week
and play golf the other four. I figure I can make around twenty-
five thousand in my practice, and together with the pension I'll
have a good living. Betty and I will take a vacation in the winter,
and I'll be living the life of a gentleman." Three weeks later Ford
was Vice President.

*MONTHS.* 1. In a magnanimous gesture LBJ, a candidate
angling for his party's nomination in 1960, said he would not
reject JFK as VP because "the Vice Presidency is a good place for
a young man who needs experience." Months later LBJ was
running for Vice President.

2. "I can't imagine any set of circumstances that would ever
induce me to send federal troops . . . to enforce the orders of a
federal court, because I believe the common sense of Americans
will never require it," said President Eisenhower two months
before he sent troops to ensure the integration of Central High
School in Little Rock, Arkansas.

3. "I don't answer charges; I make them." Senator Joe Mc-Carthy was used to doing just that. But within months he was answering charges and facing censure by the Senate.

4. "I believe all Americans will be helped by Mr. Reagan's changes," commented John Hinckley during the 1980 election. "He is the best President we've had this century. Let's give the man a chance." Months after his political favorite was inaugurated, Hinckley was in Washington with a .22-caliber gun loaded with Devastator bullets, aimed at the President.

5. Only a "political convulsion" could prevent Dewey from beating Truman, declared Elmo Roper of the Roper poll. He quit taking samples as early as September 9. Two months later Truman had a mandate for another term.

6. "Don't pay any attention to any of the drivel you hear about me and Jack Kennedy. It doesn't mean a thing," wrote Jackie Bouvier to her fiancé John Husted in 1952. In 1953 she was married to the subject of all that "drivel."

*AND, OF COURSE, YEARS.* 1. "I have no political ambitions for myself or my children . . ." wrote Joseph Kennedy in a 1936 book designed to get the business community behind FDR.

2. A medium "only for idiots" was Danny Thomas's view of television. When he first appeared on NBC's *All Star Revue* in the early fifties, he bombed and swore he'd never return. But in 1953 he decided to make room for *Make Room for Daddy.*

3. "I . . . recognized that my father and men like him got caught up in the web of business and constantly postponed retirement and the pleasures of leisure," said William Paley. "In order not to get caught that way myself, I made an oath to myself and a solemn vow that I would retire, no matter what, at age thirty-five." At the age of eighty-two he stepped down from CBS, the TV and radio network he had built, only to pick up the reins of power again in 1986 at age eighty-five.

4. A 1972 fitness report by spy John Walker's commanding naval officer said: "CWO-2 Walker is intensely loyal, taking great pride in himself and the naval service, fiercely supporting its principles and traditions. He possesses a fine sense of personal honor and integrity, coupled with a great sense of humor." The joke was on the Navy. From 1967 to 1985 Walker sold vital codes to the

Soviets, earning a million dollars and eventually a life sentence in prison. "K Mart security is better than anything the Navy would have," said Walker. "K Mart protects their toothpaste better than the Navy protects their top secrets."

5. "All in all, I think we've hit the jackpot," said Ronald Reagan, signing the 1982 act deregulating the nation's savings and loan institutions and ushering in an era of widespread speculation and abuse. The jackpot turned out to be billions financed by the taxpayers.

6. In January 1963, standing on the same ground where Jefferson Davis had been inaugurated, George Wallace was sworn in as Alabama governor, vowing, "From the cradle of the Confederacy, this very heart of the great Anglo-Saxon Southland, I draw the line in the dust and toss the gauntlet before the feet of tyranny. And I say, Segregation now! Segregation tomorrow! Segregation forever!"

George Wallace in 1982: "I believe that segregation is wrong. And I don't want it to come back. I see now that we couldn't live in a society like that."

ACCIDENTS HAPPEN. THEY JUST NEVER HAPPEN TO US.
THREE CASE STUDIES

1. "I really see the shuttle as a safe program," said elementary schoolteacher Christa McAuliffe, who was scheduled to be the first civilian to fly in space. Her ship was the ill-fated *Challenger*.

2. "Ah, c'mon," Mike Todd, Elizabeth Taylor's husband, said to movie producer Joseph Mankiewicz. "It's a good, safe plane. I wouldn't let it crash. I'm taking along a picture of Liz, and I wouldn't let anything happen to her. Besides, I've got three million bucks' worth of insurance. You'd be covered, too." Elizabeth Taylor got pneumonia and couldn't go, Mankiewicz begged off because he had other appointments, and Todd died when the *Lucky Liz* crashed in a storm over New Mexico in 1958.

3. "You don't understand. They don't kidnap journalists. It would be counterproductive. These people need me; I tell their story to the world. That's my job, and they know it," said journalist Terry Anderson, who worked in Lebanon, to his sister, Peggy

Say, less than a week before three men armed with automatic weapons kidnapped him as he returned from a 1985 tennis game. He was held hostage for more than seven years.

### AND THEN THERE ARE THOSE WHO WERE RIGHT

Sometimes you sound like a petulant kid if you say something like "To hell with your daddy. I wouldn't marry you or anyone in your whole goddamned family. . . . And you can tell your daddy that someday I'll be President of this country." But if you're Lyndon Johnson, that kind of statement may be something to take into account. Carol Davis, LBJ's first love, took the young Texan's bravado seriously and was considering defying her father, who had forbidden her to marry into "that no-account Johnson family . . . one generation after another of shiftless dirt farmers and grubby politicians." But LBJ talked her out of it—with a ringdinger that ended up being true.

Others have stumbled on the truth of the matter in uncanny ways. When Mary Jo Kopechne, who had been a campaign worker for Robert Kennedy, was going up to Martha's Vineyard for a reunion and regatta weekend, her mother told her, "Honey, be careful of the water." Mary Jo replied, "Mother, you know me. I only like to sunbathe." Three days later, on July 18, 1969, her daughter drowned—when Senator Ted Kennedy's rented Valiant dived off a bridge at Chappaquiddick.

"I am going to die in a car crash," novelist Margaret Mitchell wrote to a friend. "I feel very certain of this." She was right. In 1949 she hurried across Peachtree, a busy Atlanta street, to see the movie *Canterbury Tales,* and was hit by an off-duty cabdriver who had twenty-three prior traffic violations.

Others have been alarmingly precise about knowing when they were going to be gone with the wind. "This is going to happen to me, also," Martin Luther King told his wife, Coretta, after JFK's death. "You know, I don't think I will live to reach forty because this country is too sick to allow me to live." He died at thirty-nine.

"Of course, somebody's gonna get George sooner or later. I've accepted that," said George Wallace in the 1960s. "My only consolation is, when it happens, he'll be doing the only thing he's ever cared about doing anyway."

Bobby Kennedy was equally superstitious about the advent of an assassin in his life, but a lot wiser about what his motivation might be. "I am pretty sure there'll be an attempt on my life sooner or later. Not so much for political reasons," he said. "Plain nuttiness, that's all."

Nuts tend to rule the day as far as killings go. But every now and then someone knows for sure he's played a hand in his fate. Malcolm X broke with the Black Muslims because their leader, Elijah Muhammad, was not "the man he is cracked up to be. His morals aren't what he would have you believe. He has weaknesses of the flesh that disillusioned me." He explained all this to Mike Wallace on television along with the following comment: "They're out to get me, Mike. They're going to try to kill me. . . . I know too much about Elijah." His conversation with Wallace took place in fall 1964. In February 1965 three Black Muslims turned his premonition that "I probably am a dead man already" into a reality.

The moral of the story: sometimes it may be better to bluster and be wrong than to be so amazingly dead right.

### REALLY REALLY LAST WORDS

What do you say for an exit line? If you're Medgar Evers, a civil rights worker who has just been felled by an assassin's bullet, "Turn me loose" is about as fitting—and as eloquent—as they come.

"Goddamn the whole friggin' world and everyone in it but you, Carlotta"—said by W. C. Fields on Christmas Day 1946 to his mistress Carlotta Monti—isn't really very pleasant, but it's hard to script a parting shot, unless of course, you're planning a suicide.

"Paul said there is a man born out of this season," Reverend Jim Jones said on November 18, 1978. "I've been born out of this season just like all of you are, and the best testimony we can make is to leave this goddamn world." With such oratory he persuaded his flock of followers to sample cyanide- and tranquilizer-laced strawberry Kool-Aid.

Here's how others, without benefit of cue cards, have handled their final acts:

1. "Where the hell is Giacalone? I'm waiting for him," Jimmy

Hoffa barked to his wife on July 30, 1975. He called to complain that he had been waiting for a half hour in the parking lot of the Machus Red Fox Restaurant where he was supposed to have a peace-making powwow with Anthony Giacalone of the Detroit Mafia and teamster Anthony Provenzano. But "Where the hell is Jimmy?" turned out the more appropriate question. Hoffa left home wearing dark blue pants and a casual blue shirt and was never seen again.

2. "Hey!" Roger Chaffee shouted. He, Gus Grissom, and Ed White were aboard *Apollo I* in 1967. "We've got a fire in the cockpit." On the TV monitor, flames and smoke were visible. Ed White, in his silver spacesuit, could be seen trying to open the hatch. "Blow the hatch!" pleaded an observer. "Why don't they blow the hatch?" But the hatch was too awkward to maneuver. The crew was trapped. The flames spread. Chaffee yelled, "We're burning up. . . ." A cry of pain was the last ground control heard from them.

3. At the 1948 premiere of *The Babe Ruth Story*, the man who inspired the movie was too weak to sit through the film. He was dying of cancer. On August 16 he knew the end was near. "Don't come back tomorrow, I won't be here," he told a visitor at the hospital. That evening the doctor found him crossing the room. "Where are you going, Babe?"

"I'm going over the valley," he replied. Within two hours he was dead.

4. After a civil rights march from Selma to Montgomery, Alabama, in 1965, Viola Gregg Liuzzo, a white volunteer from Detroit, was driving home demonstrator Leroy Moton, a young black. In the dark of night a car with four Klansmen drew up beside Liuzzo's car. Moton remembered that he "reached over for the radio and that's when I felt this glass and everything hit me in the face, and the car goin' off the road. Mrs. Liuzzo, last thing she said was, 'I was just thinkin' of this song, "Before I'll be a slave, I'll be buried in my grave." ' By the time she got 'grave' out, that's when she was shot. That's when the glass started hittin' me in the face."

# 10
# How to Succeed, With or Without Trying

*We had no idea what was going on financially. We actually closed*
*one day to pay our bills. We put up a sign that said,* WE'RE CLOSED
BECAUSE WE'RE TRYING TO FIGURE OUT WHAT'S GOING ON.
—Jerry Greenfield, one half of Ben & Jerry's, on their first ice-
cream shop in Vermont

In America unlikely things happen to un-
likely people all the time. A five-dollar investment in an ice-cream
correspondence course, purchased by two childhood friends ("the
two slowest, chubbiest guys in the seventh grade," said Jerry),
leads to a fifty-eight-million-plus enterprise. A school paper describing an overnight delivery company earns a C in a Yale economics course—and becomes the germ of Federal Express. "The
professor didn't understand how the goddamn world worked . . .
that America was spreading out technologically . . . that the effi-
ciency of our society is to be smarter, not work harder," said
FedEx founder Fred Smith.

Getting ahead the Horatio Alger way, the nose to the grind-
stone route, certainly works. But if you can swing it, being lucky
is a far better idea. Take Fred Smith. He was lucky enough to
have four million dollars of his own to invest in what Yale thought
was a marginal idea, but two years later, in 1973, Smith's professor was looking prescient. Federal Express had 150 employees—
and trouble meeting its payroll. Workers were asked not to cash
their checks while Smith went to Chicago in a vain attempt to
raise capital. Depressed about coming home empty-handed, he
looked up at the departures board at the Chicago airport and
spotted a flight leaving for Las Vegas. That night he won twenty-
seven thousand dollars at the blackjack table. Federal Express met
its payroll.

Luck some would say. Guts. Even foolhardiness. But it sure beats inching your way up the corporate ladder and worrying about wearing the right ties.

Here are some ways to create opportunities of your own and a reminder that as Dan Quayle has said, "If we don't succeed, we run the risk of failure."

1. *Don't be afraid to take your apron off and sing. You never can tell who might be listening.* "This very thin guy with swept-back greasy hair had been waiting on tables. Suddenly he took off his apron and climbed onto the stage. He'd sung only eight bars when I felt the hairs on the back of my neck rising. I knew he was destined to be a great vocalist." Harry James was listening to Frank Sinatra, whom he later hired for seventy-five dollars a week as the featured male vocalist in his band.

2. *If you can, inflate your ego at an early age.* Lines like "I always knew I was born for greatness" (Oprah Winfrey), "I'm one of the world's great humans" (Muhammad Ali), or "I'm going to heaven" (Johnny Cash) all seem to work pretty well.

3. *Look for a role model.* "Everyone wants to be Cary Grant. Even I want to be Cary Grant," said the one man who was.

4. *Feel free to ignore perfectly good advice.* When a young Barbara Walters told CBS's Don Hewitt, "I want to be a broadcaster," he replied, "Barbara, we're good friends, so I'll give it to you straight. With your voice, no one is going to let you broadcast."

5. *Contradict yourself if it's convenient.* "If I ever went to work for the EEOC or did anything directly connected with blacks, my career would be irreparably ruined," said lawyer Clarence Thomas. Two years later Ronald Reagan appointed him head of the Equal Employment Opportunity Commission, responsible for enforcing Federal laws against discrimination—and sexual harassment. A decade later, at the age of forty-three, he was appointed to the Supreme Court.

6. *If negotiations get tough, sleep on it.* "Paley and his programming people were . . . tossing around some very big figures," recalled Jackie Gleason, describing a lunch meeting with the CBS chairman to renegotiate his eleven-million-dollar contract. Nursing a "terrible hangover," Gleason had "a couple of Bloody Marys" and dozed off. "Paley looked over at me fast asleep in the midst of these heavy negotiations, turned to his programming

people, and said, 'If that's the way he feels, you better give him the money.' "

7. *If you're launching a new enterprise, hedge your bets.* Hugh Hefner decided to leave the date off the first issue of *Playboy*. "I was so uncertain about the magazine's chances, I figured, well, if it doesn't sell out in the first month, we'll leave it on the stands a second month."

8. *Know the laws of supply and demand; anticipate the market.* "If you ever hear of anybody that ever has a Woodstock or festival like that, remember one thing you want to buy: peanut butter and jelly," advised Arthur Vassmer, a local shopkeeper who lived through the 1969 happening. "That's the first thing I run out of. I should have put fifty cases of peanut butter and fifty cases of jelly. I found out later that peanut butter is very good for you."

9. *Worry not about your skills.* "I made over a million dollars this year, but I'm no musician at all. I can't play the guitar, and I never wrote a song in my life. Yet I get my name on songs, and I collect a third interest of *all* the songs I sing. There doesn't seem any point in my studying music," said Elvis Presley.

10. *Answer those magazine contests.* In 1953 Helen Gurley Brown was a thirty-one-year-old advertising secretary and, in her opinion, not a very good one. She entered a *Glamour* magazine contest called "Ten Girls with Taste." "I had about as much taste as a giraffe. I could write pretty well. And I was one of their ten winners. On the questionnaire it said, 'What are your goals?' All I wanted was to continue to be Mr. Belding's secretary and not get fired. But it didn't sound like it would be a good idea to say that. So I said I wanted to be a copywriter." She got the chance, was stolen by another advertising agency, and with newfound confidence in her literary skills penned *Sex and the Single Girl*. That, in turn, led to the editorship of *Cosmopolitan* magazine. What happened to the other nine girls with taste is unknown.

11. *Try talent shows.* When fifteen-year-old Ella Fitzgerald stood up at Harlem's Apollo Theater on its famous amateur night, she intended to dance. She had, in her view, "the skinniest legs you've ever seen," and they froze. The audience began to snicker, and Ella, who knew she had to do *something*, began to sing two of the only three songs she knew, memorized from her mother's recordings of Connee Boswell. She won the twenty-five-dollar first prize, and her singing career was launched. "I wanted to be

a doctor when I was eleven," she said later, "and I kept right on wanting to be a doctor until I won that amateur show at the Apollo."

12. *If you're up for a prize, know your judges.* "The Pulitzer is judged by people who are undergoing two extremely stressful things at the same time. One, they're in New York City; and two, they're reading Pulitzer Prize entries . . . hundreds of heavy, huge entries . . ." explained *Miami Herald* columnist Dave Barry. "And that makes them really hostile towards journalism in general. Then they have to go out into the streets of New York and get into the subway at rush hour. . . ." His 1989 entries comprised "a vicious and unfair attack on New York City" in addition to "a vicious and unfair attack on the Pulitzer Prizes." He won the brass ring, a prize for distinguished commentary. "Let's be honest," he maintained afterward. "Nothing I've ever written fits the definition 'distinguished commentary.'" But distinction, like beauty, is in the eye of the beholder.

13. *Never rule out divine intervention.* Conductor Arthur Rodzinski told young Leonard Bernstein, "You may know that I am about to take over the New York Philharmonic. I begin in October or late September. It is a month away, and I am going to need an assistant conductor. I have gone through all the conductors I know in my mind, and I finally asked God whom I should take and God said, 'Take Bernstein.'"

Bernstein: "I had recommendations from Aaron Copland, Roy Harris, and—but, I mean God! I don't know how Rodzinski had managed to find access to this extraordinary recommender, but I didn't ask. I just said, 'Yes, of course!'"

KEEP YOUR EYES OPEN. YOU CAN NEVER TELL WHERE
INSPIRATION WILL STRIKE

1. *At dinner.* The check came, and Frank McNamara, a credit specialist who was wining and dining clients in Manhattan, reached into his pocket. His wallet was empty, his wife was in the suburbs, and he had to wait while she drove in with money. McNamara got to thinking about credit, and soon he and his lawyers talked two dozen restaurants into accepting a card in lieu of cash. It was called Diners Club.

2. *At the scene of the crime.* When Ralph Nader saw "a little girl almost decapitated in an accident when the glove compartment door flew open and became a guillotine for the child as she was thrown forward in a fifteen-mile-an-hour collision," the idea for *Unsafe at Any Speed* was born.

3. *In the shower.* Inspiration usually strikes fashion designer Donna Karan "in the shower . . . I don't know why. I have these wonderful glass doors that fog up and I draw on the doors in the morning. It's my time to think."

4. *On vacation.* "I recall a sunny day in Santa Fe when my little [three-year-old] daughter asked why she could not see at once the picture I had just taken of her. As I walked around the charming town, I undertook the task of solving the puzzle she had set me. Within an hour, the camera, the film, and the physical chemistry became so clear to me," recounted Dr. Edwin H. Land, inventor of the Polaroid camera.

5. *In the margins of your college notebooks.* Theodor Seuss Geisel was studying at Oxford and planning to be a teacher when he met a certain Helen Marion Palmer, a fellow student fascinated by his doodles. "Ted's notebooks were always filled with these fabulous animals," recalled the woman who became his wife. "So I set to work diverting him; here was a man who could draw such pictures; he should be earning a living doing that." Using his middle name, Dr. Seuss set out to entertain America's children. He intended to publish novels and serious works with his surname, but his first attempt, his 1939 *The Seven Lady Godivas,* met with little success. "I'd rather write for kids," he explained later. "They're more appreciative; adults are obsolete children, and the hell with them."

MANAGEMENT STYLE, OR WOULD YOU HAVE THIS MAN
OR WOMAN FOR A BOSS?

Sometimes you can spend as much time managing your boss as doing your job. Here, a short course in the varieties of personalities workers can face:

*TYPE NO. 1. OBSESSED WITH THE BEST.* "He'll ask for a paper, and after he gets it he'll call the writer in and say, 'Is this

the best you can do on this?' The guy says, 'Well, I'll try again.'
A couple of days later, the writer returns with another draft. The
same ritual is repeated. After about five or six times, the writer,
weary and frustrated, takes in another draft, and Kissinger asks
again, 'Is this the best you can do?' The writer finally replies,
'Yes, dammit.' 'Good,' says Kissinger, 'now I'll read it.' "—Henry
Kissinger's aide Winston Lord.

*TYPE NO. 2. NEEDS TO BE PUT ON A PEDESTAL.* In meeting
J. Edgar Hoover for the first time, new FBI agents were coached
on the director's quirks. Not only did he resent people stepping
on his shadow, but he liked that shadow to be as long as possible.
Five feet nine and sensitive about his height, he devised a method
to increase his stature: He stood on a box when receiving visitors
in his office. As one new agent was told, "Of course, it's just a
small one, only six inches high. Pretend you never even notice it!
Not long ago we had a new agent who for some reason just
couldn't keep his eyes off it. He was fired." Other taboos: letting
your voice quiver or standing with your hands in your pockets.
"Deviates do that," agents were advised.

*TYPE NO. 3. REQUIRES UNDIVIDED ATTENTION.* "Listen,
I called your (expletive deleted) house five times yesterday; now
if your wife thinks you are (expletive deleted) dunsky or if she's
a (expletive deleted) dunsky and you're gonna disregard my (expletive deleted) phone calls, I'll blow you and that (expletive
deleted) house up." Forget about your personal life. With a boss
like reputed Mafia crime boss John Gotti, who was taped telling
the above to underling Anthony Moscatiello, you'd be well advised to be at his beck and call, night and day, day and night.

*TYPE NO. 4. CONCERNED WITH APPEARANCES.* "You
would be amazed what people think they need to wear to get a
job like this. They think, cut down to here and up to here,"
exclaimed Mayflower Madam Sydney Biddle Barrows. "They've
got it all wrong. Half those girls wouldn't have gotten to [the
restaurant] 21 on a slow day. I told them if you don't look like
you are either the wife or the daughter of the richest man at
the Pierre [Hotel], you don't belong working for me." Barrows
instituted a training program, "Everything you always wanted to
know about being a call girl," and insisted her girls watch *60*

*Minutes* and read *Time* or *Newsweek.* "What you have to remember is the longer the young lady stayed with the client, the more money she made. . . . So it's in her best interest to have a lot to say."

TYPE NO. 5. DELUSIONS OF GRANDEUR. "What did you say? I run this White House and don't you ever forget it. Don't ever let that happen again," said Nixon's chief of staff Alexander Haig, berating his staff for not informing him of a call from Democratic Senate Majority Leader Mike Mansfield to Nixon.

TYPE NO. 6. RUNS A FAN CLUB. "We were handed a box of popcorn, and that was it. Then we were forced to sit and watch home movies of his trips to Morocco and Spain. We had to stay for two hours, and people who didn't want to go to the party were made to feel awful," said a *Forbes* magazine staffer about the late Malcolm Forbes's annual staff Christmas party.

TYPE NO. 7. OUT FOR BLOOD. "I'd make them prove what they had in their veins, blood or spit, one way or the other," said Paul "Bear" Bryant, Alabama's football coach, explaining how he disciplined players. When Jim Baker was Ronald Reagan's secretary of the treasury, he took the same approach. Budget Director David Stockman was on the verge of being fired when he publicized his doubts about Reagonomics. Baker saved his job but made it clear "the menu is humble pie and you're going to eat every last motherfucking spoonful of it." Yum.

SEX AND SUCCESS

*I'm a woman like everyone else. Ask me how the match went*
*instead.*
—tennis player Renee Richards, formerly Dr. Richard Raskin,
who underwent a sex change and took up professional tennis.
In 1977 she entered the U.S. Open after the New York State
Supreme Court ruled she was a woman.

Whatever sex we are—or choose to be—can't help having an impact on the course we chart in life. If you're a woman, certain things stand out. "Big breasts, big ass, big deal," complained Marilyn Monroe. "Can't I be anything else?" If you're a man, life may not be all that much different. When John F. Kennedy, Jr., fresh out of New York University Law School, was hired at Brooklyn Family Court, the supervising judge feared that "Every woman will leave her desk to see him." He lectured his staff, "Don't make it any worse for him. Try not to drool till he's gone. I want to give the young man a chance to grow up in his profession. He has a right to that."

It isn't a piece of cake being thought of as cheesecake, though on occasion it can speed your way up the ladder of success—or at least give you a good spin around the wheel of fortune. Vanna White, resident glamour girl of the game show of that name, admitted, "It's not the most intellectual job in the world, but I do have to know the letters."

"When I started modeling, it was like part of the job. All the girls did it," explained Marilyn Monroe of a pre-AIDS sideline. ". . . It wasn't any big dramatic tragedy. Nobody ever got cancer from sex."

"Hollywood's wonderful," enthused Jane Fonda in her younger days. "They pay you for making love."

For those of us who aren't in the sex object league, sex still can influence success. "No question. If I was a man, I would have been press secretary to LBJ," commented Texan Liz Carpenter, a journalist who said she took care of "dogs, daughters, and delphiniums" as press secretary to Lady Bird.

What would life be like if we'd been allotted different dosages of X and Y chromosomes? It's interesting to speculate. "Show me a woman who doesn't feel guilty and I'll show you a man," said writer Erica Jong. "It's a good thing that I was born a woman, or I'd have been a drag queen," commented Dolly Parton. But most of us, unlike Renee Richards, choose to accept the genes we are given and make the best of it.

For much of our journey through life, it doesn't make much difference. "Once, power was considered a masculine attribute," said *Washington Post* owner Katharine Graham. "In fact, power has no sex." As comedienne Roseanne Arnold put it, "The thing women have got to learn is nobody gives you power. You just take it."

Well, yes, but you can't always just put your hand in the cookie jar. Access to power has certain prerequisites. For example, if you want to be a lawyer, there's that thorny issue of passing the bar, something John F. Kennedy, Jr., failed to do repeatedly—leading to newsstands full of THE HUNK FLUNKS headlines. But Kennedy's biggest worry was penciling in the right answers on the test. Marilyn Quayle had an additional problem. The due date for the birth of her first child neatly coincided with the date of the bar exam. Her solution: She induced labor and aced the test.

"If you give us women a chance, we can perform," said future Texas Governor Ann Richards at the 1988 Democratic National Convention. "After all, Ginger Rogers did everything Fred Astaire did. She just did it backward and in high heels."

Though some women never need to dance backward, if they do, it's often at the point in the road where a sign advises, TURN THIS WAY IF YOU WANT CHILDREN.

Sometimes they reach that fork quite by accident and, lacking either the emotional resolve or the family support of a Marilyn Quayle, decide having a child would involve too much fast footwork. For example, actress Polly Bergen was seventeen and "living in Los Angeles, trying to make it in show business, singing with bands. The man I'd been seeing disappeared when he heard that I was pregnant. . . . I really didn't know what to do." Terrified and alone, she opted for an illegal abortion. So did journalist Linda Ellerbee when she was twenty: "The man came to my apartment at midnight wearing a black raincoat. He had alcohol on his breath. I didn't die. I was one of the lucky ones." Joan Collins, engaged to Warren Beatty in 1961, said she had an abortion because Beatty felt parenthood would "wreck both our careers." Bette Davis's first husband, bandleader Harmon Oscar Nelson, Jr., insisted she have two abortions to keep her career from being derailed. Said Davis: "That's what he wanted. Being the dutiful wife that's what I did."

"It is only work that truly satisfies," Davis felt. She was twice divorced, once widowed, and harshly portrayed by her daughter, B. D. Hyman, in *My Mother's Keeper*. "I think I've known this all my life. No one could ever share my drive or vision. No one has ever understood the sweetness of my joy at the end of a good day's work. I guess I threw everything else down the drain."

"Work is something you can count on, a trusted lifelong friend who never deserts you," commented Margaret Bourke-White, a star photographer for *Life* magazine. Even Blondie, Dagwood's faithful helpmate, went out and got a job in 1991.

Explained Dean Young, writer for the comic strip and son of its originator, Chic Young: "We have a recession going on. Money's tight, and you know, Dagwood, he's been going in there trying to get that raise from Mr. Dithers for sixty-one years and I'm not so sure he's ever going to get that raise."

Blondie was lucky enough to find work as a caterer close to home. When a job involves following a star that leads you away from home and children, life can be star-crossed. Sergeant Cheryl Steward of the 202d Military Intelligence Battalion, who was deployed in the Gulf War, said she and her husband, a former Army infantryman, "were as close to divorce as we've ever been." He was not pleased at being left at home with the couple's two daughters, aged two and a half and ten months. "He had a problem with his male ego," Steward said. "He felt he should have been here [in the gulf] and I should have been at home. He had a big case of the guilts."

So did actress Whoopi Goldberg, who became a mother when she was a teenager living in the projects. "This was my lifelong dream. I wanted to be in movies and do the things I've gotten to do. And it came to me on a silver platter. Handed to me. I wish I could say I would have done it differently. But damn it, I wouldn't have. This was my shot. I got a shot and I took it. A lot of people paid the price for it. But nobody more than my kid."

Other women have made other choices. "When we were married, my husband wanted me to stay home and have babies," said Roseanne Arnold of her first husband, Bill Pentland, whom she divorced after her television show took off. "And I tried to do that for him. He was happy back in Denver when I was just really housebound—but it was a horrible time in my life. Still, I loved him and wanted to make him happy. I was like every other wife. And I loved my kids. Bill supported my career because he didn't think it was ever really going to happen."

Some never felt Arnold's angst at being a housewife. "It's obvious that I'm fully liberated. That's what drives them up the wall," said Phyllis Schlafly of the feminists she battled in the ERA wars. ". . . I've got a lovely husband, six children—I breast-fed them all—and I do what I want to do."

Mused Mamie Eisenhower: "I never knew what a woman would want to be liberated from."

Princess Grace had firm views on the matter. "Women's natural role is to be a pillar of the family. It's their physiological job," she felt. "They should make themselves interesting for their families. Women only work to get off the hook and avoid responsibilities. Emancipation of women has made them lose their mystery."

Barbara Bush, who at one point said, "It seems to me I spent my life in car pools, but you know that's how I kept track of what was going on," was forced to formulate her views on the questions of career and family when she spoke at Wellesley's 1990 commencement. One hundred and fifty seniors signed a petition protesting her appearance because her public eminence was due to the man she dropped out of Smith to marry. Bush told the graduates, "As important as your obligation as a doctor, a lawyer or a business leader may be, your human connections with spouses, with children, with friends, are the most important investment you will ever make. At the end of your life, you will never regret not having passed one more test, not winning one more verdict or not closing one more deal. You will regret time not spent with a husband, a child, a friend or a parent." She continued, "Who knows? Somewhere out in this audience may even be someone who will one day follow in my footsteps and preside over the White House as the President's spouse. And I wish him well."

FOUR STUDIES IN LOYALTY

Lyndon Johnson may have upstaged Webster in defining "loyalty." Newswriter Jack Gwyn made the mistake of describing it as "If you hire a man eight hours a day, he owes you eight hours a day." Johnson quickly set him straight. "I don't mean just that kind of loyalty, I mean *real* loyalty. Look at John Connally. I can call John Connally at midnight, and if I told him to come over and shine my shoes, he'd come running. *That's* loyalty."

With LBJ in mind, we present four true loyalists.

1. *The case of the literalist.* "Boy, it'd be nice if we could get rid of that guy," Jeb Stuart Magruder commented about columnist Jack Anderson, who had written yet another piece slanted against the Nixon administration.

G. Gordon Liddy, who had been in his office, left, and Magruder's administrative assistant Bob Reisner rushed in. "Did you tell Liddy to kill Jack Anderson?" he asked Magruder.

"What?"

"Liddy just rushed past my desk and said you'd told him to rub out Jack Anderson."

Reisner ran after Liddy and located him before he left the building, fortunately. "Gordon," Magruder told him, "I was just using a figure of speech, about getting rid of Anderson."

"Well, you'd better watch that," Liddy said. "When you give an order like that, I carry it out."

2. *The overly eager beaver.* "You just give me the word and I'll turn that f------- island into a parking lot." Secretary of State Alexander Haig was referring to Cuba at a National Security meeting with Ronald Reagan. Commented Nancy Reagan: "Ronnie just didn't care for him, and we were relieved when Haig finally left."

3. *She would dress in anything for success.* "I started pulling documents out of my boots and my back. They started chuckling. They couldn't believe I'd gone to the extremes of putting documents in my boots and back," said secretary Fawn Hall after smuggling papers pertaining to Iran-contra out of the White House on November 25, 1986, with Oliver North and a lawyer. "Sometimes you have to rise above a written law" was Hall's interpretation of her job description.

4. *No shred of evidence.* The woman who manned the FBI director's files labeled "Official and Confidential" and "Personal and Confidential"—the files one bureau official described as "full of political cancer"—was Helen Gandy. As Hoover's administrative assistant she promised her boss that when he died, she would destroy the worst evidence of his hard-core snooping. After Hoover's death in 1972 Acting Director L. Patrick Gray 3d announced that "there are no dossiers or secret files. There are general files, and I took steps to keep their integrity." Meanwhile, Helen Gandy had moved dozens of file drawers that she claimed contained Hoover's personal correspondence to his house. In his basement she shredded loyally.

YOU KNOW YOU'VE MADE IT WHEN . . .

1. *You have mess privileges at the White House.* When Christopher Buckley started working as a speech writer for Vice President George Bush, he thought his peers would "want to know if I'd

read Samuel Eliot Morison's three-volume history of the American people or how long I'd been interested in arms control." Instead the first question he was asked was "Did you get mess privileges?" He didn't.

2. *Your hometown puts up a sign.* Those entering Weatherford, Texas, are advised that this is the "home of watermelons and Mary Martin." Said the actress of the honor bestowed upon her by the town where she used to sing at firemen's balls, churches, and clubs: "I never got top billing in my hometown."

3. *You get cover billing.* "Do you know what this means?" Air Force jet pilot Captain Edward Dwight, Jr., asked when he received a letter from President John Kennedy in 1961 requesting that he enroll as the first black in the astronaut program. "If I do this I have a chance to go on the cover of *Ebony* magazine."

"What's *Ebony* magazine?" asked his commanding officer.

Dwight did get on the cover of *Ebony,* but after Kennedy's death was abruptly transferred out of the astronaut program. Space flights were not integrated until 1983.

THOUGHTS ON SUCCESS

1 "Everything I have, I owe to spaghetti."—Sophia Loren.

2. "I learned in New York that there is no deodorant like success."—Elizabeth Taylor.

3. "Success for me is having ten honeydew melons and eating only the top half of each one."—Barbra Streisand.

4. "Show me success without ego."—Ivana Trump.

5. "I believe very strongly in the philosophy of staying hungry. If you have a dream and it becomes a reality, don't stay satisfied with it too long. Make up a new dream and hunt after that one and turn it into reality. When you have that dream achieved, make up a new dream."—Arnold Schwarzenegger.

6. "But for [affirmative action laws], God only knows where I would be today. These laws and their proper application are all that stand between the first seventeen years of my life and the second seventeen years."—Supreme Court Justice Clarence Thomas in a 1983 speech.

7. "My mother drew a distinction between achievement and success. She said that achievement is the knowledge that you have studied and worked hard and done the best that is in you.

Success is being praised by others, and that's nice, too, but not as important or satisfying. Always aim for achievement and forget about success."—Helen Hayes.

8. "For the Kennedys it's either the shit-house or the White House—no in between."—Joseph Kennedy, Sr., just before the 1960 Democratic National Convention.

9. "It's not a question of money. After you reach a certain point, money becomes unimportant. What matters is success. The sensible thing would be for me to stop now. But I can't. I have to keep aiming higher and higher—just for the thrill."—Aristotle Onassis.

10. "Well, I think it's kind of an empty bag, to tell you the truth. . . . But you have to really get there to really know that. . . . I've always said I was more an adventurer than I was a businessman. I mainly did CNN just to see if it would work. And the same with the superstation. . . . Just out of personal curiosity to see if it could be done."—Ted Turner.

11. "Most people in my position say, 'Listen, you don't have to do any of that. Just kick back, man. Just enjoy your riches. Go get a house in Tahiti. Why do you keep getting yourself into trouble?' It's not my nature to just kick back. I am not going to be anybody's patsy. I am not going to be anybody's good girl. I will always be this way."—Madonna.

12. "Of course, if I had known Michael was going to be so successful, I would have been much nicer to him when he was young. Be nice to your kids. You never know how they're going to grow up."—Kirk Douglas.

### THE ROAD NOT TAKEN

1. "If it hadn't been for my interest in music, I'd probably have ended in a life of crime."—Frank Sinatra.

2. "Whoever heard of Casablanca? And anyway, I don't want to star opposite an unknown Swedish broad."—George Raft, who refused Bogart's role opposite Ingrid Bergman. Later he said, "It was the biggest mistake of my life."

3. "If I had gotten that Montgomery Ward job, probably I'd still be working in a store in Dixon, Illinois."—Ronald Reagan, who lost out on a job in managing the sports department.

4. "My daddy had seen a lot of people who played guitars

and stuff and didn't work, so he said, 'You should make up your mind—either about being an electrician or playing a guitar. I never saw a guitar player that was worth a damn.' "—Elvis Presley.

5. "Personally, if I hadn't been published in *The New Yorker*, I would have been condemned to a life of announcing Mozart symphonies. I would never have gotten to do dumb comedy on public radio. There's a real museum aspect to public broadcasting because we have to raise money from rich people. Rich people don't donate money to enable somebody to tell fart jokes, but they'll give a lot of money to hear Mozart's piano concertos played over and over. It's a terrible life to announce Mozart."—Garrison Keillor, radio raconteur and writer of tales from Lake Wobegon.

6. "I would have made a good pope."—Richard Nixon.

7. "If I hadn't become President, I sure would have made a helluva good piano player in a whorehouse."—Harry S. Truman.

# 11
# Only in America

*So this is America. They all seem out of their minds.*
—Ringo Starr at Kennedy International Airport, arriving in
1964 for the Beatles' first tour

Welcome to America, the land of opportunity, ingenuity, and all those other laudatory words that end up spelling "unique." We're a nation where the Alamo has served a stint as a dry goods store and 80 percent of the bulk of Plymouth Rock has been chiseled away by souvenir hunters. We're a nation that has lost the remains of patriot Thomas Paine (last traced to the estate of an English furniture dealer, who acquired Paine's coffin in 1844) and a nation that nearly had an advertisement for Castoria laxative decorate the Statue of Liberty (when funds to build the base were scarce in the 1880s, Castoria offered to come to the rescue with its own version of a billboard). In America anything is possible.

Lest anyone need more evidence to support that premise than Ringo Starr found at Kennedy Airport, it should be pointed out that only in America can you "pull out a Barbie from any year over the last thirty and see how the country has changed," as Don Clarke, a Mattel executive, explained. The year 1959 brought Barbie the model; 1963 saw Barbie the career girl; 1973, Barbie the surgeon, and 1984, Barbie the aerobics instructor. Barbie's other roles included an astronaut and a disco queen.

Only in America can the president's dog earn more than the president. In 1991 First Pet Millie raked in $889,176 in royalties on her book (they were donated to charity after taxes), while First Pet Owner George Bush garnered $2,718 in royalties on his book *Looking Forward*. When Jane Wyman, Ronald Reagan's ex-wife, went back to work at age sixty-seven on the TV show *Falcon Crest*, she earned a reported $770,000 annually. The presidential paycheck: $200,000.

Only in America can a visiting dignitary be denied a visit to Disneyland for security reasons. "Why am I not allowed to go?

Do you have rocket-launching pads there?" Nikita Khrushchev exploded on a 1959 visit to California. ". . . Is there an epidemic of cholera there or something? Or have gangsters taken hold of the place that can destroy me?" Disneyland was then only four years old, and Mrs. Khrushchev, too, was disgruntled at being barred from the Magic Kingdom, a fact she made obvious at a party attended by four hundred Hollywood stars. Frank Sinatra's solution: He turned to David Niven and said, "Tell the old broad you and I will take 'em down there this afternoon."

Why was Disneyland so dangerous? Don't second-guess officialdom. It has a logic of its own. Take Grenada, a skirmish that was over in three days. The Army alone—never mind the Navy or the Air Force—issued 8,612 decorations when there were never more than 7,000 troops on the island. Two thirds of the American casualties were either accidental or the result of friendly fire. No matter. The Pentagon awarded 152 Purple Hearts, even though only 115 were reported wounded.

Jackie Kennedy ran into trouble with the military mind as her husband's funeral neared. She wanted an eternal flame on his grave.

The first obstacle: figuring out if there already was a flame at the Tomb of the Unknown Soldier. ("I don't *care* if one is there. We're going to have it anyway," Jackie insisted.) There wasn't. That left obstacle number two: an Arlington cemetery official who told Kennedy aide Richard Goodwin, "We can't do it. . . . We'd have to fly to Europe. That's the only place they know about them."

Goodwin didn't blink. The official backed down and called in an Army engineer, obstacle number three.

"What's eternal?" he wanted to know.

"Eternal means forever," Goodwin barked.

"She can't light it," said the engineer.

"*Why not?*"

"There's too much danger. It might go out."

"Listen," said Goodwin, "if you guys can design an atomic bomb, you can put a little flame on the side of that hill, and you can make it so she *can* light it." But the military establishment couldn't figure out how to do that. Finally the engineer turned to the yellow pages. He found his answer under "Gas Companies."

In the 1950s the CIA was looking for a perfect mind control

drug, hoping to drop it into an enemy water supply in order to disable towns, and in so doing, it "funded and supported and encouraged hundreds of young psychiatrists to experiment with this drug," recalled one of the most eager researchers, Dr. Timothy Leary. "The fallout from that was the young psychologists began taking it themselves, discovering it was an intelligence enhancing, consciousness-raising experience." His firm belief: "I give the CIA total credit for sponsoring and initiating the entire consciousness movement counterculture events of the 1960s."

Only in America. Strange but true.

### THE RICH ARE DIFFERENT FROM YOU AND ME

*"I walked into Carl's apartment, and there he was with this enormous pile of cash buying Boardwalk for five hundred dollars." As a friend discovered, corporate raider Carl Ichan liked to play Monopoly with cash.*

Of course, the rich are different from you and me. They can afford to be. Who else can play Monopoly with cash? Who else tosses cats out the window with abandon? "We had a twelve-thousand-dollar alarm system at the house," said millionaire Seward Mellon's wife, Karen, "and I would occasionally open the bedroom window on the second floor and toss the cat out so that I could watch the arrival of the security company and the police department."

Who else can build a museum to house his two-hundred-million-dollar art collection and not visit it? "It cost me almost seventeen million dollars to have the new J. Paul Getty Museum built," reflected the man whose name was over the door. "Since its opening, the museum has cost me over a million dollars a year for operating expenses alone," the oil magnate wrote in 1976. "Although I have never personally seen the new museum, I feel the money was—and is being—well spent. . . ."

Who else can install a refrigerator in the bathroom to chill perfumes? Or take a limo to aerobics classes? Those are but two of the vanities of Susan Gutfreund, wife of John Gutfreund, who was chairman of Solomon Brothers before scandal sent him packing.

And who else could get away with gardening by photograph?

When Doris Duke, dubbed the richest woman in America, was in Hawaii or California, she'd have her head gardener at her New Jersey estate take hundreds of photographs and send them off by air express. "Tony, what is all that purple in the French garden?" she'd telephone to ask.

"Miss Duke, those are violets you wanted put in yesterday."

"Oh, no, no, no, no! Tony, what is wrong with you? This is not what I wanted at all." The staff would then dash about, digging and transplanting so Tony Gesell could take new photos and then send them off again. Then came the call. She preferred yesterday's arrangement. In a frenzy everything would have to be undone and redug.

Anybody who's transplanted violets five days in a row or been in charge of stocking the perfume fridge—in short, anyone who's been in the employ of someone with bucks—knows the rich are no average citizens. But some of them surprise more than others. Mell Stewart was an ordinary barber brought in to cut Howard Hughes's hair. "You can make signs, but you are not to say a word to him," he was instructed. He also had to scrub himself and wear rubber surgical gloves. Well, okay, that's a little weird. Stewart knew the situation wasn't going to be run-of-the-mill, but he was flat out astonished when he "found a skinny, bare-assed naked man sitting on an unmade three-quarter bed. His hair hung about a foot down his back. His beard was straggly and down to his chest. I tried not to act surprised, as if I was used to meeting naked billionaires sitting on unmade beds." He proceeded to follow instructions and don the surgical gloves. Suddenly Hughes barked, "What the hell are you going to do with those gloves on?"

"I began to feel like Alice in Wonderland," Stewart recalled. ". . . Hughes asked me a question, and I didn't know how to make signs that would explain why I was putting on the rubber gloves." He decided he had to talk, no matter what the repercussions. He offered an explanation and proceeded with the haircut. The sky didn't fall in. He pocketed a thousand dollars for his work.

As long as we're paid well, who cares how eccentric the rich are? Probably no one, but even so, it should be some comfort to underlings everywhere that those who travel in well-heeled circles are sometimes surprised by their friends. For example, CBS Chairman William S. Paley was watching television with his aristocratic brother-in-law Jock Whitney, chairman of the *International Herald Tribune.* "Where's your clicker?" Paley asked. Whitney didn't bat an eye. He buzzed for his butler, who promptly changed the TV channel.

Spiro Agnew also had his moment of astonishment. "Frank thinks you should pay," said Mickey Rudin, Sinatra's lawyer. Agnew, forced to resign the vice presidency in 1973, owed the IRS $150,000 in back taxes, interest, and penalties.

"Well, damn it, Mickey, I don't have the money. I can't pay."

"What is your bank and account number? Frank has directed me to put two hundred thousand dollars in your account."

"That's wonderful. But where is the promissory note?"

The question was met with a dismissive laugh. "Don't insult the man. I wouldn't even dare ask him about that. He knows you will pay him back when you can. That's all he needs." Agnew paid back Sinatra's trust—and the money.

If you are thinking you can avoid the surprises resulting from hobnobbing with the rich by taking lessons from shows like *Dynasty*, think again. "Rich people don't carry their money in wallets or Gucci this-es or Valentino thats," Andy Warhol discovered. "They carry their money in a business envelope. In a long, business envelope. And the tens have a paper clip on them, so do the fives and the twenties. And the money is usually new. It's sent over by special messenger from the bank offices. . . ."

In fact what can be most astonishing about mingling with the moneyed is that sometimes they don't carry cash at all. "I want them to know I'm a generous candidate. Slip me a ten," said JFK, who was running for the House, to a friend who was sitting with him in church. "I remember another strange thing. Jack never had any money," said one old girlfriend, Angela Greene. "When we went to St. Patrick's, I think I put the money in the collection box. Money meant absolutely nothing to him."

"We met at 21 for dinner," recalled Elizabeth Drake, whom Kennedy dated in New York. "We went from there to the theater to see *Brigadoon*. We took a cab. I had to pay for it because he didn't have any money—no cash. He was okay at places like 21 where he could sign the check, but he never had any cash. He wasn't chintzy at all, he just didn't think about money."

The pattern persisted even into his presidency. "Oh, Dad, I don't have a cent of money." JFK was at the family home in

Hyannis and on his way to Vienna to meet with Khrushchev. Joe
Kennedy sent his secretary upstairs for a packet of bills. "I'll get
this back to you, Dad," the President said cheerily as he left for
the helicopter. "That'll be the day," his father grumbled.

As far as actually spending money goes, there seem to be two
patterns. The rich are both cheaper and more generous than you
and I. Regarding the former trait, J. Paul Getty installed a phone
with a coin box in Sutton Place, his English country estate, and
marked it "Public Telephone." And he had all house phones
equipped with special locking devices because he felt "people
attending parties . . . were casually picking up the telephones they
found scattered around the house and placing calls here, there
and everywhere."

And Rose Kennedy didn't think twice about cross-examining
her chauffeur, Frank Sanders. "Is that my coffee . . . that you're
drinking? Is it Kennedy coffee?" When he indicated it was, she
continued, "Coffee is very expensive now, you know. In the
future, Frank, you are to bring either your own coffee in a thermos
. . . or you can pay for the coffee you drink in my house. Is that
understood, Frank?" This from a woman who once had the family
house in Palm Beach painted in the front only in order to save
money.

"I love quality, but I don't believe in paying top price for
quality," said Donald Trump, referring to his two-million-dollar
ten-seat French Puma helicopter, which he claimed was worth
ten million. He then noted one exception: "My pilots are all the
best, and I pay whatever it takes. When it comes to pilots, doctors,
accountants, I don't chisel."

For the rich, saving a dollar here or there can be a sign of the
power of their position—especially when the dollar is designated
for Uncle Sam. Of course, we know that hotel queen Leona
Helmsley said, according to her housekeeper, "Only the little
people pay taxes." Industrialists certainly don't like to. "You've
got to be a fool to pay income taxes," declared Henry Ford II in
1979. The real statement ought to be: You'd be a fool not to have
great tax shelters and great lawyers. And you'd be a fool not to
use force of personality whenever you can.

When shopping at Saks Fifth Avenue with her secretary in
the early seventies, Barbra Streisand stopped to buy some Louis

Vuitton luggage. "I don't pay sales tax," she told the saleswoman.

"No problem, ma'am. We will ship the merchandise to you in California."

Well, that wasn't the right answer. "No! I want to take the pieces with me and I am *not* paying the tax. I'm Barbra Streisand; I usually get what I want."

Generally, however, the rich get what they want by paying for it—handsomely. What's different is they want things ordinary folks can't begin to think about. Things like curing cancer. Armand Hammer was sitting at home watching Walter Cronkite's *21st Century*. Jonas Salk was being interviewed about his new Salk Institute. Hammer immediately made an appointment to meet him. "Can you possibly tackle cancer the same way you beat polio?" he asked.

"Theoretically," Salk replied. "It ought to be possible to develop a vaccine. But it would cost a tremendous amount of money."

"How much?"

"Five million dollars, for a start."

"All right. I'll give you five million dollars. Go to work."

The rich can dream of things like being governor even when they've had very little experience. Jay Rockefeller, who received a call from "Uncle Nelson offering me Bobby Kennedy's seat" in New York State after RFK was assassinated in 1968, was determined to make it on his own in West Virginia. He ran for governor in 1972 and lost. He came back to win in 1976. In 1980 he secured a second term, spending nearly twelve million dollars, enough to buy a six-dollar dinner for every man, woman, and child in the state. When he ran for the Senate in 1984, he outspent his opponent, a political novice, twelve to one. JFK, who had similarly deep family pockets tried to make light of his resources. When he ran for the Senate in 1958, he joked that his father wired him: "Don't buy a single vote more than is necessary—I'll be damned if I'm going to pay for a landslide."

And the rich are able to dream of great museums for art. Walter Thayer, a fund raiser who was being courted to head a drive to raise thirty million dollars for New York's Museum of Modern Art, knew how to make those dreams a reality. He called

William S. Paley and said, "Bill, I've thought about this, and I'll do it on one condition. I'll direct this fund-raising drive if you and David [Rockefeller] each donate five million to start the ball rolling." Paley gasped—and agreed.

And the rich can make history happen. In 1946 the newly conceived United Nations was homeless. Nelson Rockefeller was head of a committee appointed by Mayor William O'Dwyer to get the UN to locate in New York. The problem was, no one could come up with a site. The deadline of December 11 neared. Nelson offered the family's New York Pocantico estate and even cleared it with his brothers and father, though they were understandably loath to have their country homes compromised. But the UN wanted an urban site. Someone mentioned property that real estate magnate William Zeckendorf was developing on the East River. Nelson called his father. It was just before dinner. "Well, I think that's all right," John D., Jr., said finally. "If you can get it at that price, Nelson, I'll give it to the United Nations." The price in question: $8.5 million.

"Why, Pa!" Nelson exclaimed.

Zeckendorf and his partner, Harry Sears, were located at the Monte Carlo nightclub late that night. Over the beat of the dance band, the two and Rockefeller aide Wallace Harrison negotiated. They unrolled the blueprints. Harrison outlined the potential site with a red pencil. Zeckendorf picked the pencil up and wrote: "8.5 million—United Nations only, December 10 for 30 days." That was his formal option. The United Nations was coming to New York.

Of course, the rich are different from you and me.

THE VIETNAM SYNDROME

*Of course he [Johnson] would have been wiser not to escalate the war. But throughout history, even the most intelligent leaders have not always been masters of their fate.*
—North Vietnamese General Vo Nguyen Giap

When Ronald Reagan was President, he said, "For too long, we have lived with the 'Vietnam syndrome.' . . . It is time we recognized that ours was, in truth, a noble cause."

On March 1, 1991, when Saddam Hussein's forces crumbled,

George Bush announced, "It's a proud day for America and by God we've kicked the Vietnam syndrome once and for all."

This was different from kicking a little ass in a campaign; this was punting the word "wimp" out of the Oval Office. After all, Bush had blustered just before the first warplanes took off, "If we get into an armed situation, [Saddam] is going to get his ass kicked." And he did.

But what made Saddam Hussein so different from Ho Chi Minh? Sounding remarkably like Bush, LBJ once said, "Everything I knew about history told me that if I got out of Vietnam and let Ho Chi Minh run through the streets of Saigon, then I'd be doing exactly what they did in World War II. I'd be giving a big fat reward to aggression."

Just cause wasn't the problem in Vietnam for much of the war. On April 7, 1954, Ike explained, "You have a row of dominoes set up, you knock over the first one, and what will happen to the last one is the certainty that it will go over very quickly." Most of America believed that the Communist bogeyman, the very fellow who lurked in many a domestic closet, could set those dominoes tumbling quite easily.

"Whatever happens in Vietnam," Eisenhower declared, "I can conceive of nothing except military victory."

Neither could President Kennedy. After the Bay of Pigs fiasco, he met with Nikita Khrushchev in Vienna and told *The New York Times'* James Reston: "I think he thought that anyone who was so young and inexperienced as to get into that mess could be taken, and anyone who got into it, and didn't see it through, had no guts. So he just beat the hell out of me. I've got a terrible problem. We have a problem in making our power credible, and Vietnam is the place."

"I call it the Madman Theory, Bob," President Nixon told Haldeman. "I want the North Vietnamese to believe I've reached the point where I might do *anything* to stop the war. We'll just slip the word to them that 'for God's sake, you know Nixon is obsessed about Communism. We can't restrain him when he's angry—and he has his hand on the nuclear button'—and Ho Chi Minh himself will be in Paris in two days begging for peace!"

What was different about Ho and Saddam was that the North Vietnamese leader wasn't interested in compromise.

"We were not strong enough to drive out a half-million

American troops, but that wasn't our aim. Our intention was to break the will of the American government to continue the war," said General Giap long after the war. "Westmoreland was wrong to expect that his superior firepower would grind us down. . . . In war there are the two factors—human beings and weapons. Ultimately, though, human beings are the decisive factor. Human beings! Human beings!"

Commented General William C. Westmoreland: "Any American commander who took the same vast losses as Giap would have been sacked overnight."

"I'm not going to go down in history as the first American President who lost a war," vowed Lyndon Johnson. Nixon echoed his thought almost word for word. Even Kennedy had said, "We cannot accept a visible humiliation."

So what's the Vietnam syndrome? Not following the advice of Barry Goldwater? If he were President, he said, "First I'd drop leaflets on North Vietnam, then drop five-hundred-pound bombs. Make a swamp out of North Vietnam. The war would have been over in two or three weeks."

Was the problem the length of the war or the fact that we never got to the point where we could toss ticker tape out of skyscrapers and say we won?

We did win, at least according to General Westmoreland. He asserted in 1991, "We won the war in effect. One of our great strategic aims was to stop the Communist advance in Southeast Asia, and when you look at Southeast Asia today, the Communists have made no gains. . . . Today, Vietnam is a basket case run by a bunch of old men and is a threat to no one but itself."

# 12
# Life-Styles

## DRIVING STYLES

*He had this terribly disconcerting habit while he was driving along at seventy miles per hour of peering around to address everyone on the bus without looking at the highway. Everybody was constantly on the edge of their seats. Also, he'd lean out the window at every opportunity and wave to people and announce, "I'm Muhammad Ali. I'm the greatest."*
—Edwin Pope of *The Miami Herald*, touring with other sportswriters on Ali's bus to promote a 1964 fight

There's a reason why they coined all those phrases like "driven to distraction." A man and his car can do it pretty easily.

Soviet leader Leonid Brezhnev did it to Richard Nixon when the President presented him with a dark blue Lincoln Continental—donated by the manufacturer—during an American visit. "Brezhnev, a collector of luxury cars . . . got behind the wheel and enthusiastically motioned me into the passenger's seat," Nixon recalled. "The head of the Secret Service detail went pale. . . ."

Speeding over "the narrow roads that run around the perimeter of Camp David," they came to "a very steep slope with a sign at the top reading, 'Slow, dangerous curve.' Even driving a golf cart down it, I had to use the brakes in order to avoid going off the road at the sharp turn at the bottom. Brezhnev was driving more than fifty miles an hour. . . ." Despite Nixon's pleading, he didn't slow down. Afterward he pronounced, "This is a very fine automobile. It holds the road very well." Lucky for both of them it did.

"He got into the driver's seat and I sat next to him," recalled Desi Arnaz of a visit with former President Harry Truman in Independence, Missouri. "Just the two of us, not even a Secret Service man." As you might expect, Truman gave other drivers hell. "He drove pretty flamboyantly and talked very colorfully.

Though modern presidents tend to be a chauffeured breed, Harry Truman showed his driving style in 1945 when Henry Ford II presented him with this new Ford Tudor.

Such as, 'Get out of the way, you sonofabitch [sticking his head out the window]. What are you doing with that truck?' The truck driver recognized him, laughed like hell and shouted, 'Okay, Harry.' "

Johnson, a paper cup of Pearl beer in hand, liked to show reporters and visitors the LBJ ranch in Texas by careening along dusty roads in his cream-colored Lincoln Continental, which was equipped with a cow horn to summon cattle. If anyone admitted terror at his ninety-mile-an-hour speeds, he'd take off his five-gallon hat and use it to hide the speedometer. Once when he forced an oncoming car off the road, a passenger muttered, "That's the closest John McCormack has come to the White House yet." McCormack, Speaker of the House, was next in line since LBJ didn't have a Vice President in his first term.

When George Bush had to have his picture taken in a car fueled by ethanol, Barbara Bush expressed trepidation at driving with him. For most of his official career, Bush had been chauffeured in government cars. His driving experience was by and large behind the wheels of golf carts.

Indeed, it's a rare President who drives at all. Normally, as Ronald Reagan noted, "you're always somewhat apart. You spend a lot of time going by too fast in a car someone else is driving, and seeing the people through tinted glass. . . ." The problem with that is, as he told a reporter, "you forget where things are. When I used to be able to drive my own car I'd have some sense of where things are geographically located . . . where the hotels and monuments and such are. But now, being driven everywhere in the back of the car and not navigating—it's the oddest thing, but you lose track of where things are."

When Kissinger was in government, he even lost track of his house. A reporter asked what street he lived on in Georgetown, and Kissinger didn't know. His wife, Nancy, had found the house. He simply got into a limousine in the morning and at night got out where it let him off. Such things as street addresses were left to the Secret Service.

Betty Friedan left those details to the taxi service. As a young mother in the New York suburbs, tired of ferrying her children everywhere, she used to send a taxi to pick them up at school.

But cars with paid drivers behind the wheel are a rarity for most of us. The average American tends to have an intimate relationship with both geography and his or her car.

Jack Ruby, for instance, practically lived in his 1960 Oldsmobile. After he shot Lee Harvey Oswald, police found it parked—and locked—in downtown Dallas. Its contents included: his dachshund, Sheba; two sets of lightweight metal knuckles, one set worn from, one would assume, hitting people; a pistol holster; unpaid parking tickets; $837.50 in a paper bag; an empty wallet; a bathing cap; a left golf shoe with a dollar bill in it; hundreds of pictures of a stripper named Jada; a roll of toilet paper; a can of paint; a gray suit; and a November 20 newspaper showing Kennedy's motorcade route.

Though Medgar Evers didn't live in his car, he knew his life depended on it. The first thing he did when he was promoted to NAACP field secretary in 1954 was buy a car with a V-8 engine so he could outrun Klansmen searching for "race agitators" at night.

In Montgomery, Alabama, during the bus boycott, just being

black and having a car was cause for harassment. "Everybody had been told, 'Drive carefully, don't speed. Stop,' " recalled Jo Ann Robinson, president of the Women's Political Council. "One time I stopped at a corner right above the college where I lived, and a policeman drove up and said, 'Well, you stayed there too long that time.' And the next day or two I'd come up, 'Well, you didn't stay quite long enough this time.' There was no need of arguing, we just took them. We just paid them. I got thirty tickets, and there were people who got I don't know how many."

Nobody, but nobody, was going to mess with Sugar Ray Robinson in his famous flamingo pink Cadillac, a flight of fancy inspired by the birds he saw at a Florida racetrack. The color was so remarkable he couldn't get it out of his mind. Back in New York, he attended a boxing banquet and discovered Willie Pep's manager, Lou Viscusi, was wearing a flamingo pink tie. Robinson promptly commandeered it ("My wife made me wear it," Viscusi admitted) and the next day showed it to a Cadillac salesman in the Bronx. "Are you crazy?" he was told.

"Man, I ain't crazy," Robinson shot back. "I just want my new car painted this color. It's my car, ain't it?"

Well, it was. "When my car arrived, it was not only exclusive, it was a symbol. When people think they recognize a celebrity, they hesitate a moment. But when they saw me in that car, they didn't have to hesitate. They knew. There was only one like it— Sugar Ray's pink Cadillac. Most people called it pink, but to me it was always more than pink, it was flamingo pink."

"Nothing stops him from doing what he wants to do," Ray Charles, Jr., said of his father, the singer, who once owned a '63 Corvette. "Gorgeous car. I loved that car." Once when Charles, Sr., was coming home, he told his valet he wanted to drive, an unusual request since Charles is blind. "Mr. Charles, you know this is an intersection," said the valet.

"Who bought the car?" countered Charles.

"So my father gets in the driver's seat," recalled Ray, Jr., "and we're all in the house right, and we hear this BAM! Come out, the Corvette's tore up. It's gone. The car is almost totaled out, right. Father jumps the clutch and pulls out in the intersection and just totals out the Corvette. So the police come, right, and they're talking to the valet. They're about to arrest him." The valet kept insisting he wasn't driving. "They're saying, 'Now look, we're going to arrest you if you don't stop lying to this poor blind man' . . . and my father finally told them, 'I was driving the car.' He was never scared of anything.''

BATHROOM ADVENTURES

*When you go to the lavatory on an airplane, [a Secret Service] agent is standing right by the door. I remember once a plane was about to land, and it was getting very rough as we went down. Frank Domenico, one of my agents, was yelling through the door, ''Sit down, Mrs. Ford, please sit down,'' and I had to yell back, ''I am sitting down.''*
—Betty Ford

It's a fact of life. History—domestic and otherwise—happens behind certain closed doors. "He was in the tub. I went in with my calendar and sat on the john seat. That's the only time he ever talks to me," complained Joan Kennedy about her then-husband, Teddy, during the 1980 presidential primary.

"We'd better talk alone in the bathroom," Kennedy told his right-hand man Kenny O'Donnell, who was outraged that JFK had offered the vice presidency to LBJ. Away from the crowds in the hotel suite, Kennedy explained, "I'm forty-three years old, and the healthiest candidate. . . . So the vice-presidency doesn't mean anything."

"Mr. Ghorbanifar took me into the bathroom," recalled Oliver North when he was negotiating the sale of arms to Iran at a 1986 meeting in London. "And Mr. Ghorbanifar suggested several incentives to make the deal work. Ghorbanifar offered me a million dollars." North refused but thought it was a "neat idea" when the Iranian middleman suggested giving the money to the Nicaraguan rebels.

In political circles, bathrooms often mean business—and they don't necessarily mean refinement. Once LBJ summoned McGeorge Bundy, "one of the delicate Kennedyites," into the bathroom and discovered Bundy "found it utterly impossible to look at me while I sat on the toilet. You'd think he'd never seen those parts of the body before. For there he was, standing as far away from me as he possibly could, keeping his back toward me the whole time, trying to carry on a conversation. . . . It certainly made me wonder how that man had made it so far in the world."

Michael Forrestal thought he was about to get pretty far in the world when JFK, newly elected as president, asked to talk privately with him. Forrestal, a protégé of Averell Harriman, who had just lost the New York governorship, suggested the bathroom. Certain that he was up for a major appointment, he was all ears awaiting JFK's question, which turned out to be: "Do you think you can get Averell to wear a hearing aid?" Harriman had a notorious hearing problem. When he first met with JFK, he'd been asked a complicated question and responded with "Yes."

Peggy Say, sister of AP journalist and former hostage Terry Anderson, wasn't doing any better than Harriman at figuring out who was on first when she went to meet with Yasir Arafat in Tunisia in 1990 to try to secure the release of her brother. She found herself seated at a long dinner table with used cutlery and unappetizing fare ("Arafat leaned over and with his hands plopped a huge hunk of lamb onto my plate"). She realized this "was obviously not the time for a discussion. In fact, Arafat was not addressing me at all. Suddenly he gave a grunt, leapt out of his chair, and started striding across the living room next to where we were eating. I thought, 'Now we're going to have our meeting.' " She raced after him, reporters dashing in her wake, but "at the end of the hall I lost him. . . . Behind us a woman was screaming, 'What are you doing? The chairman is going to the bathroom!' The PLO boys with their automatic weapons were just about rolling on the floor with laughter."

Laughter—polite, raucous, or just plain old embarrassed—is often the outcome when two cultures clash over bathroom linguistics and logistics. "Would you like to wash your hands?" President Reagan asked Soviet Ambassador Andrei Gromyko, showing him the private bathroom off the Oval Office. They were pausing for a lunch break.

"No," Gromyko replied.

"Would you like to use the facilities?" Reagan ventured, and still received a negative reply.

"What I mean is, would you like to go to the toilet?"

"Oh, *da*, all right," the ambassador finally allowed.

"Chuck, c'mere a minute, look at this thing," Billy Graham called to fellow preacher Chuck Templeton when they were young and staying at the ritzy Dorchester Hotel in London. "What in the world is that for?" Templeton studied the object and concluded, "Man, it's the place where you wash your feet."

"I tell you this place has *everything!*" said Graham in wonder. The two were admiring a bidet.

Other people's toilets, no matter what their shape, can cause a lot of trouble. "I went to a high school to talk about the subject 'Life in the Governor's Mansion.' I was met at the front door and presented with a large corsage," recalled Rosalynn Carter. Before her speech she made a stop in the ladies' room, where she found herself trapped. The stall lock had jammed. "I thought about screaming, but I was too embarrassed. There was no room at the bottom of the door. . . . The only exit was over the top—corsage and all—scared to death that someone would come in and find me suspended five feet off the floor. No one did, and I walked calmly out to deliver the speech as though nothing had happened."

"I looked from the second story glassed-in window to a yard of concrete below. No outhouse. Where did one go?" mused Eartha Kitt, who moved from the rural South to New York at the age of seven. "I knew it had to be on the first floor outside the building someplace, but how would I find it?" Unable to locate any such outbuilding, she finally consulted her aunt, who brought her into a tiny room with "weird looking bowl-like things made out of what looked like white stone . . . if there was a place to go to the bathroom there, I couldn't find it." When the mysteries of modern plumbing were explained, she thought: " . . . It seemed to me awfully unsanitary to go to the bathroom right inside your house. . . ."

Young Shirley Temple knew what to do in the bathroom, but she couldn't always do it on cue. Her Lloyd's of London twenty-five-thousand-dollar accident insurance policy required regular submissions of urine samples. Generally that meant that "each Friday a drab little man would bustle into the cottage, usually mopping his head with a handkerchief, and wait for me to accommodate." Once he showed up unannounced, and Shirley kept him waiting and waiting until she spotted "a tall urn-shaped bottle of Shalimar toilet water, light yellow-colored." The perfect solution: "substitution." Naturally she was found out by both Lloyd's of London and her mother, who reminded her sharply,

"Those samples are needed by the four hundred and eighty-eight prominent people who signed your insurance policy, including seventeen lords and earls."

Earls weren't Shelley Winters's problem; it was a prince. While filming in London, she "dashed into what I thought was the unisex English restroom (they had those there at that time)," changed, and "was standing in my hat, half-slip, and bra, putting on my false eyelashes, when I noticed in the mirror two distinguished gentlemen in morning suits. I grabbed my lime-green chiffon dress to cover myself, and as I turned, stunned and paralyzed, I realized one of the gentlemen was Prince Philip." Winters mumbled, "Your Majesty," curtsied, and stood stunned as the prince made small talk. Finally his companion offered, "Shall I zip you up, Miss Winters?" He did—and she "barely whispered, 'Thank you,' and dashed out. . . ."

Though meeting royalty is a rarity, celebrities are accustomed to bathroom adventures. After all, public facilities are the great equalizer. Everyone needs them, famous or otherwise.

"Do you want door number one, door number two, or door number three?" is the question former *Let's Make a Deal* host Monty Hall finds himself invariably asked.

"I was at Kennedy Airport very early in the morning, sleepy. I was about to go home to California from New York. A well-dressed man said, 'Excuse me, aren't you Pearl?' " recalled Pearl Bailey, who replied, "Yes, but I've got to wee-wee." The man, she reasoned, "had followed me, without knowing, I'm sure, into the ladies' room. He smiled, shook my hand, and left."

"Being a hero in France had its surprises," said Sugar Ray Robinson. "At a nightclub once, I was in the men's room, standing at a urinal, when I noticed a middle-aged woman stroll through the door. 'Your autograph, monsieur,' she said. I was in no position to sign her menu. 'At your convenience,' she suggested."

Convenience is another issue of import. Everyone's individual needs aren't always timed with, say, meetings. After one long session presided over by Jimmy Carter, Vice President Walter Mondale complained that his boss had "a bladder the size of a football."

Presidents, of course, call the shots when it comes to bathroom matters. Driving around the LBJ Ranch, Johnson liked to make pit stops. Dutifully, a Secret Service agent would stand at the Lincoln Continental door to camouflage the roadside happening. One time, however, an agent named Henderson felt something warm on his pants. "Mr. President," he said incredulously, "you're pissing on my leg."

"I *know* I am" came the reply. "That's my prerogative."

Lauren Bacall decided to exercise her prerogative at the worst moment possible. She was about to get married to Humphrey Bogart. Bogie's friend George Hawkins knocked on her door and said, "Are you ready, Baby? . . . Hope's at the piano, ready to start. Bogie's very itchy standing with Louis, who is also very itchy. . . . Shall I give the signal?" She gave her assent and then "made my last dash for the john." The wedding march started. Bogie asked where she was. "George's romantic reply: 'Hold it—she's in the can.' "

## THE AMERICAN DIET: FROM POLE BEANS TO EXPLODING TURKEYS

*I don't know how to order from those hifalutin French menus. I like simple southern cooking—turnip greens, pole beans, corn bread, iced tea, everything southern. I'm a professional southerner.*
—George Wallace

It was health food pioneer Adelle Davis who helped popularize the phrase "You are what you eat" ("A woman who wants to murder her husband can do it thoroughly in the kitchen. There won't even be an inquest," she said). But a quick look at the dinner plates of many an American reveals truths she didn't anticipate.

For example, after countless state dinners, Ronald Reagan still considered macaroni and cheese his favorite White House dish.

"I eat cottage cheese until it runs out my ears . . . I put catsup on it . . . catsup disguises almost anything," said Richard Nixon.

J. Edgar Hoover lunched day in and day out at the same table at Harvey's restaurant on Connecticut Avenue. His meal of choice: cottage cheese, grapefruit, and black coffee.

Jackie Kennedy generally breakfasted in bed on orange juice, toast and honey, coffee and skim milk.

At parties Lyndon Johnson would work the crowd, eating

chicken legs from the buffet table and stuffing the bones in his pocket.

In Vietnam star AP reporter Peter Arnett and his photographer, Horst Faas, didn't eat American. Whenever they could, they'd chow down with the South Vietnamese troops. "They had incredibly good food," recalled Faas. "They would find a chicken or something and make a feast out of nothing. Peter and I would go out on those patrols with cans of Beaujolais on our hips. It was a good life."

As an Italian-American Lee Iacocca grew up eating pizza. But in 1933 in Pennsylvania Dutch country his fellow third graders laughed when he tried to explain his family food. "What kind of dumb dago word is that?" they jeered. In his autobiography Iacocca had the last laugh: "Those guys grew up on shoofly pie, but I never once laughed at them for eating molasses pie for breakfast. Hell, you don't see shoofly pie huts all over America today."

If you're American, regardless of your patrimony, it's pretty hard to avoid the national bird, the turkey. But "a white lady who came to our door once around Thanksgiving time" made the mistake of trying to deliver one to Dick Gregory's family.

"Is it cooked?" Dick asked.

"No, it's not. . . ."

"We ain't got nothing in the house to cook with, lady," said the boy, slamming the door.

The employees of the U.S. Embassy in Kuwait fully expected to cook their turkeys. But after the Iraqis invaded and left the embassy stranded without electricity on August 24, 1990, food that was fresh rotted and the frozen turkeys exploded. "They sounded like 105-mm shells going off," said Barbara Bodine, deputy chief of the mission. "We worried the Iraqis would think we were firing, so we had to bury them or burn them in an outdoor pit."

*A special aside to cooks*: Should anyone be tempted to toss dinner into an outdoor pit, he or she should take heart. Jackie Kennedy felt just that way as a newlywed. "Jack's secretary called and said he was leaving the office so I started everything," recalled Jackie Kennedy of the first dinner she cooked after her marriage. ". . . I don't know what went wrong, you couldn't see the place for smoke. And when I tried to pull the chops out of the oven, the door seemed to collapse. The pan slid out and the fat spattered. One of the chops fell on the floor but I put it on the plate anyway. The chocolate sauce was burning and exploding. What a smell!! I couldn't get the spoon out of the chocolate. It was like a rock. And the coffee had all boiled away."

The scene was straight out of Lucille Ball. Jackie even burned her arm. She confessed that she was "always so grateful when we happen to have an invitation to dinner on the cook's night out."

THE HIGH LIFE

*I wonder if demons don't exist so that angels might appear, to sort of joust with them, to do battle you might say, thereby inspiring us with their wonder and beauty.*
—playwright Tennessee Williams

Those who cavort with demons, who gather them around to foster creativity or lure the angels, know that dark characters require special care and feeding. The diet traditionally prescribed by writers, poets, and even politicians: alcohol and drugs.

"I used alcohol as the magical conduit to fantasy and euphoria, to the enhancement of the imagination," wrote novelist William Styron.

"Well, with one martini ah feel bigger, wiser, taller, and with two it goes to the superlative, and ah feel biggest, wisest, tallest, and with three there ain't no holding me," southerner William Faulkner explained to Lauren Bacall.

"For me marijuana has been an intellectual stimulant . . . a useful tool in breaking down . . . conceptual boundaries," said William Novak, Nancy Reagan's comemoirist.

"It was astounding. I lay back, listening to music and went into a sort of trance state . . . and in a fantasy much like Coleridge's world of Kubla Khan, saw a vision. . . . Rather beautiful images also of Hindu-type Gods dancing on themselves. This drug seems to automatically produce a mystical experience. Science is getting very hip," poet Allen Ginsberg wrote to his father in 1959 after taking LSD in a research experiment at the Mental Research Institute at Palo Alto. ". . . You would enjoy it and it's not exhausting. Good as a trip abroad."

"An insulator against the pain of racism" was what Louis Armstrong called pot. He was busted for possession of it in Hollywood early in his career but smoked it all his life.

"Drugs have been very creative and very destructive. They certainly freed my mind up very much in the sixties. It would be wrong from a 1990s perspective to say drugs were horrible. They weren't. They taught us a lot," said filmmaker Oliver Stone.

"Marijuana is like sex. If I don't do it every day, I get a headache," explained singer Willie Nelson.

"I don't care if it's horse piss. It works," said President Kennedy when the drugs prescribed by show business's Dr. Feelgood, Max Jacobson, turned out to contain amphetamines and steroids, according to analyses by both the FDA and the FBI.

As the above litany attests, the high life has its fans. But like champagne that has sat too long in a glass, it is a life that can lose its sparkle over time. For example, Styron came to realize that alcohol, the "invaluable senior partner of my intellect," was "a means to calm the anxiety and incipient dread that I had hidden away for so long somewhere in the dungeons of my spirit."

"I probably encouraged my husband to drink. He was such a reserved man it was difficult for him even to tell me he loved me—he had proposed by saying, 'I'd like to marry you.' I wanted him to loosen up, so when he got in from work, I'd encouraged him to have a beer or a martini to relax him," recalled Betty Ford. But she was the one who became dependent on the evening's elixir.

"The combination of the drama over the death of John Kennedy and the drama of working for another president would drive me every night . . . to drink a bottle of whiskey and get totally drunk to survive that day and then make it back to the White House the next day," recalled Pierre Salinger, JFK's press secretary. He tried to quit his job after the assassination, but LBJ would have none of it. "Every day while I was working there, I was thinking of what I could do in a nice way, not an insulting way—how I could leave the White House. And to be honest with you, that's why I decided to run for the United States Senate in California."

"I used to drink. Mad Dog, 20/20, Bacardi one fifty-one, Don

'Q.,' Brass Monkey, heavy stuff, *cheap* heavy stuff, gasoline. I'm talking about *straight*, fucking *straight*," said boxer Mike Tyson. "I didn't get drunk, really, but I was out of my fucking mind." He was also ten years old in Bedford-Stuvyesant, Brooklyn, New York.

"I drank nail polish remover and hair spray and anything that had alcohol in it to give me relief. I just wanted to sleep and didn't want to face another empty difficult day," recalled Kitty Dukakis about Christmas 1989, when she was on leave from a rehab center.

"I felt hypocritical. Here I was living in Topanga Canyon, a vegetarian learning about herbs, hiking in the hills, tending my vegetable garden, chopping wood because my house was heated with wood stoves . . . and yet I liked cocaine," said Patti Davis, Reagan's daughter. "What's wrong with this picture?"

"Only thing wrong with coke is that they'll bust you for it. That's it. . . . The anxiety in snortin' cocaine—it'll finally dawn on you that you're doin' something illegal, and it'll fuck with you," said jazz legend Miles Davis. "You can't enjoy it. And you'll hide it to keep from being busted. . . . You get paranoid. So you take it *all*. You get fucked up. Plus, you can't make love with it."

"See that? It's a hole, completely through to the other side," said Ike Turner of his nose. The singer was imprisoned in 1989 on drug charges. ". . . I was on a fifteen-year party. This hole in my nose was so bad that when I would go to sleep it would be hurtin' so much that I would be tryin' to get my hand up behind my eyeballs. . . . *Pain*. The first thing I'd want to do when I got up was get cocaine and put it in my nose. That would deaden the pain."

"Never once, until I got out of prison, did I ever record, perform, or do anything any way except stoned. I did it all stoned," said singer David Crosby, who was convicted of drug possession in Texas in 1983. "The only thing that saved my life was being physically, forcibly separated from my stash."

"When I was very young, I had to work so late and so hard. After I'd work, I'd be wide awake and I couldn't go to sleep, and I had to get up in four hours and start all over again. So I was given . . ." Actress Judy Garland faltered, explaining her drug addiction to her daughter Liza Minnelli. She continued, "I was given . . . a pill to help me go to sleep and help me get up. And after years of doing this, my system functions well on these. I find they make me feel better. So I kind of need them—like vitamins."

She died from too many "vitamins." So did singer Janis Joplin, whose feeling was "Yeah, life's groovy. Sometimes it ain't groovy enough." Robert McFarlane, Reagan's national security aide and Oliver North's boss, tried to follow suit. On February 9, 1987, he attempted suicide by swallowing Valium pills. Two years later he was sentenced to two years' probation and fined twenty thousand dollars for withholding information to Congress about the Iran-contra affair.

After country music star Hank Williams died in 1953, Elvis mused, "Can you imagine that? He OD'ed on drugs. Drugs! Can you imagine that? What a tragedy, and now his little son has to live with it." Elvis, of course, came to a similar fate.

*   *   *

*A VOICE OR TWO OF SOBRIETY.* "I was walking down Fifth Avenue and all of a sudden I see all these faces I knew from Studio 54 coming out of a church. Lots of them. Same people. I knew them," said Steve Rubell, cofounder of the Manhattan disco Studio 54, in the late eighties, ten years after his club's heyday. "Then I looked at the bulletin board of the church, and they were coming out of an AA meeting."

"The hardest thing is waking up in the morning and realizing that's as good as you're going to feel all day," said Sammy Davis, Jr., of sobriety.

Drugs were "the reason ninety percent of the women in prison with me were there," said Patty Hearst Shaw. "Now, when I see a friend who wants to smoke a joint, I say, 'Don't you know that by doing that you are enslaving a black person in Harlem?' "

George Bush told schoolchildren that as leader of the country he didn't have much trouble avoiding drugs. "Some drug guy," he explained, wouldn't even try to get him high because "Now, like I'm President." He would have been on grammatically safer ground if he'd chosen just to say no.

TIMES FOR TEARS

*You know, a man ain't worth a damn if he can't cry at the right time.*
—Lyndon B. Johnson

People cry over lots of things. LBJ used to cry when he told stories. The TV show *Little House on the Prairie* moved Ronald and Nancy Reagan to tears.

"Sometimes I feel so sorry for myself I could cry," Ike announced when, three weeks into his presidency, the February skies precluded golf.

Marilyn Monroe recalled how her first real love, musician Freddy Karger, would say, "You cry too easily. That's because your mind isn't developed. Compared to your breasts, it's embryonic." She added, "I couldn't contradict him because I had to look up that word in a dictionary."

When life overwhelms us, sometimes crying is the only thing to do. At least it was for Norma McCovey when she read the newspaper one day in 1973. "Don't tell me you knew Lyndon Johnson," said a friend who was surprised at her tears. LBJ's death was on page one along with the Supreme Court decision in *Roe* v. *Wade*.

"No. I'm Roe," said McCovey. It was the first time she had told anyone that she was the woman in the famous abortion case. She officially revealed her identity in a 1980 interview with a Dallas television reporter ("another woman, another Virgo, I decided to do it"), crying all the way through. Nine years later, standing on a speakers' platform at an abortion rights march on Washington, "I looked out at all those people, men and women and so many people brought their children and they were all there because of me and I started to cry. I thought I was going to lose my lunch."

"One night they said I was going home and dressed me in nice clothes," recalled Father Lawrence Jenco, who was held captive in Lebanon for 564 days. "When I dressed, they said, 'Just kidding,' and laughed. I started to cry."

"Grant after Shiloh went back and cried. Sherman went back and cried," said General Norman Schwarzkopf after the Gulf War. "I mean—and these are the tough old guys. Lee cried at the loss of human life, at the pressures that were brought to bear. Lincoln cried. And frankly, any man that doesn't cry scares me a little bit."

Politicians are generally loath to agree, aware that when Maine Senator Edmund Muskie cried in the 1972 New Hampshire primary, his political career was over. But no amount of manly resolve can ensure that a public figure will make it into the history books without reaching for a Kleenex.

As Nixon's career was plummeting, he gave a television address on April 17, 1973, then "walked only a few feet—just far enough to be out of sight of the office—when he abruptly stopped, leaned against one of the columns, and began to cry. I felt completely helpless," recalled Secret Service Agent Dennis McCarthy.

"I never cry except in public," Nixon told David Frost four years later in a television interview.

If George Bush cries, it's likely to be on a Sunday. "I do that in church," he explained while trying to cover up for a very public bout of weekday tears. He was giving a speech about the start of the Gulf War, and his script called for him to say, "And like a lot of people, I have worried a little bit about shedding tears in public, or the emotion of it. But as Barbara and I prayed at Camp David before the air war began, we were thinking about those young men and women overseas. And the tears started down the cheeks, and our minister smiled back, and I no longer worried how it looked to others." At that point in the speech he started to cry and, flashing the cameras an embarrassed grin, said, "Here we go."

Whether Mario Cuomo was a crying kind of guy was something a radio reporter wanted to ascertain after Cuomo's son, Andrew, married Kerry Kennedy. "What does cry mean?" asked the New York governor.

Interviewer: "You know, wet around the . . . You know where you're . . ."

Cuomo: "Do you mean tears? Do you have to have tears to cry? Can you cry internally? Are you asking me, is there just a little bit of regret when people are married, or is it all joy on the part of the parents? 'This is wonderful. He won't be around as much as he used to be. He won't be there when I call all the time at six-thirty in the morning. I won't see him on the weekend all the time to play basketball. But this is great because now they go on to a new full life.' Is that what you're asking me?"

Interviewer: "No."

Cuomo: "Okay."

Interviewer: "Did you cry, I ask you now, for all of New York wants to know."

Cuomo: ". . . None of your business. Do I look like a guy who would cry?"

Interviewer: "Yes."

Cuomo: "Great big nose, great big hands."

Interviewer: "Yeah."

Cuomo: "Bags under his eyes. Forget about it. I'm not the crying type."

# 13
# Life in the Public Eye

## IMAGEMONGERING

*Now I have to admit that I one time tried to change the image of
John Kennedy. I was getting all kinds of letters from women who
were complaining that John Kennedy was walking and that Jackie
was behind him, not beside him. So I went to the President one day
and I said, "I'm getting all these letters and we've got to deal with
this problem because the people are seeing this badly." He said,
"Tell Jackie to walk faster."*
—JFK's former press secretary Pierre Salinger

Imagemongering is an age-old art. Those
who make their living at it—press secretaries and publicity men—
sometimes luck out with a boss who's naturally charismatic and
only occasionally contrary—a Kennedy, in short. But usually they
earn their keep. Once a national magazine reported that FBI Director Hoover was short, fat, and effeminate. Quickly Hoover's
in-house publicity man, Louis B. Nichols, came to the rescue. He
made sure a rival magazine carried an article telling Americans
that Hoover's "compact body . . . carries no ounce of extra
weight—just 170 pounds of live, virile masculinity."

When Jerry Ford made television appearances, his personal
TV director, Robert Mead, a former CBS producer, picked out the
President's shirts and ties, held up signs that said "Stand up" or
"Sit down," and forbade Ford to eat for two hours before TV
appearances to avoid televised belches.

The PR man's motto: Leave nothing to chance. But no matter
how many precautions are taken—Ronald Reagan used to spend
two days rehearsing for his press conferences in the White House
movie theater—serving the President is often a white knuckler.

"We'd always be in the East Room sitting on the edge of
our chairs," said Patrick J. Buchanan, Reagan's communications
director. "At his first press conference, he just came crashing
through and began talking about how 'the Soviets reserved to

themselves the right to lie, cheat and steal.' Even after two days of rehearsals, you were never sure exactly what would come out. It was exciting."

"I remember one time in San Clemente, the White House press corps said, 'We've got to get a picture of President Nixon walking on the beach.' So I arranged for all of the press photographers to get up on the bluff a long distance away from the President," recalled press secretary Ron Ziegler, who was eager to reverse Nixon's image as remote and formal. "At the proper time, he came walking down the beach with his loving dog King Timahoe."

"Good Christ," said a photographer. "He's wearing *shoes*." Bostonian blacks, to be precise. Said Ziegler: "That was our last attempt to deal with that situation."

Nixon had his own ideas about shaping his public image. Once he wrote H. R. Haldeman a memo suggesting that a public relations campaign be launched emphasizing "the courage of the President . . . the character of the lonely man in the White House." He added, "The missing link now is the profile in courage idea"—i.e., the Kennedy aura—"and it's not coming through." Before he headed off to China in 1971, he memoed Henry Kissinger, saying, "One effective line you could take in your talks with the press is how RN is uniquely prepared for this meeting. . . . A man who takes the long view, never being concerned about tomorrow's headlines but about how the policy will look years from now." Just being helpful, you might say.

But then we can all use a little help. Once when George Bush was asked a tough question at a press conference, he turned to his cue card and read, "I just have to be vague about the answer, but I certainly empathize with the problem." At a conference of Christian educators in 1991, questions came to him in a different order from that which his script called for, and he complained, "Something's going awry here. I mean, if I just listen to the question, I can answer whatever it is. But if I think it's going to be on here [meaning cue cards], I don't listen to the question." But that wasn't his only problem: His mike was still open, and the press heard his entire complaint. "These things are scripted," admitted his press secretary, Marlin Fitzwater. "It was never intended to be spontaneous. It's not like the press, where they get points for stumping the boss."

But getting friendly reporters to ask planted questions is a time-honored presidential practice. Jimmy Carter held "issues briefings" before his press conferences, and Ike's press secretary, Jim Hagerty, regularly hosted powwows with selected journalists to plan what the president would be asked. JFK handled the press with such ease ("Gentlemen, I am ready for the questions to my answers," he liked to say, repeating a line from Charles de Gaulle) that LBJ was convinced his conferences were orchestrated and, according to George Reedy, LBJ's press secretary, asked for scripts of his own when he first got into office.

Dan Quayle, perhaps the most overscripted public official in recent time, offered this advice on how to handle the press: "You smile discreetly. Look like you're enjoying yourself, like you're getting ready to get down to serious business. You've got to be careful what you say."

But as Quayle's staff knew, there are some things that script-writers can't buy: a natural acting talent. If you think we're about to bring up Ronald Reagan, you're wrong. We're thinking of the man who said, "Sincerity is the quality that comes through on television"—Richard Nixon. After he gave his Checkers speech, a wet Kleenex classic, and Ike decided to keep him on the vice presidential ticket, Nixon wept openly. Watching him on TV, Albert Upton, Nixon's drama coach at Whittier College, cheered, "That's my boy! That's my actor!"

SCOOPED, OR LIFE IN AN ELECTRONIC AGE

*That bite of sandwich popped right out of my mouth.*
—Pat Nixon, who was sitting in a restaurant when a television
broadcast came on announcing that her husband had accepted
the vice presidential nomination in 1952

Years ago the town wag was all you had to worry about. If you were famous, there may have been a yellow journalist to watch out for. But however the news traveled—over the back fence or newsstand to newsstand—its pace was reassuringly slow.

Not so in the electronic age. Pat Nixon, mother of two young daughters, thought she'd talked Dick out of dabbling in national politics, but found out otherwise—on television.

During the 1976 Republican National Convention, CBS's

Mike Wallace asked Nancy Reagan if she had expected to be a candidate's wife. "No, I didn't," she replied. "I heard it over television."

"He came back and said, 'I have to go. I can't tell you where.'" It was a Sunday in October 1983, and Brenda Schwarzkopf's husband, Norman, then a major general, was called off on assignment. She'd learned not to ask too many questions. Two days later she turned on the television and discovered that the United States had invaded Grenada.

"I just saw your father on television," a Princeton coed announced to sophomore Wendell Colson, son of Watergater Charles Colson. "He is one of us; he has accepted Jesus Christ as his personal savior."

"Oh, no! Dad's a Jesus freak," said Wendell, letting out a sigh of disbelief.

Tom Brokaw gave Laura Walker, daughter of retired naval officer John Walker, Jr., the surprise of her life. Laura was making tacos: "With my mind fixed on slicing onions, I paid no attention to the droning voice of the newscaster. Suddenly my senses were alerted by the urgent tone of the announcer. . . . I reacted in time to catch the end of his statement: '. . . Walker, Jr., a former naval warrant officer, was arrested for espionage.' I had no awareness of my rushing into the family room; I seemed completely detached from my surroundings. Surely I had not heard correctly." But it was true. Though she'd had some inkling of what her father was up to—and she'd been aware the FBI was asking questions—it was Tom Brokaw who let her know her father's jig was up.

Walter Cronkite was the one who shook up Melba Pattillo Beals's world. It was late August 1957, and Beals was visiting relatives in Ohio. She planned to go home and get ready for school at Little Rock's Central High. She didn't think the fact that she was black and the school all white would be much of a problem. But as she was sitting with her mother on a couch, "Walter Cronkite came on television and said that Central High School was going to be integrated . . . that they were already beginning to have difficulty with the white Citizens' Council and the Ku Klux Klan, and that these were the children who were going, and he mispronounced my name. My mother said, 'What did he say?' And that was it, my mother started making phone calls back home." Beals was headline material.

So was Dr. Benjamin Spock. "As I got into the Lexington Avenue subway the man standing next to me was reading a *New York Post* with a headline in four-inch letters, SPOCK INDICTED. I tried to peek over his shoulder to see what it said but I couldn't read the rest. I wanted to tell him, 'That's me, buddy. Do you mind if I see what it says?' But I didn't think he'd believe me." Spock, who opposed the Vietnam War draft, had been arrested for "interruption of the induction process."

"A headline caught my eye on the front page of the *Los Angeles Times*, stacked neatly on the steps outside the restaurant," recalled Joan Collins. It read: ACTOR SUES ACTRESS FOR $1,250 SUP-PORT PER MONTH.

"Oh, darling, buy a paper. I wonder who it is?" she said to her companion as they went into Chasen's. Then from their booth came a cry of "Oh, my God!" just as the headwaiter asked for their drink orders. It was followed by Collins's exclamation "Christ, that rotten bastard"—her ex, Maxwell Reed, to be ex-act—"has gone and sued me. What am I going to *do*?"

Scooped again. It happens to the best of us. J. Edgar Hoover phoned Desi Arnaz to tell him that he was a father; the FBI director knew Lucille Ball had missed a few periods. General Douglas MacArthur heard that Truman had fired him when he and his wife, Jean, were at an embassy luncheon in Tokyo. He said he learned "of the action through a press dispatch over the public radio." Truman sent the general's relief order via the Army, but Tokyo radio outpaced military channels. "Jeannie," MacAr-thur said to his wife with characteristic calm, "we're going home at last."

"Hey, I didn't know your mother killed herself," said a class-mate reading a movie magazine to thirteen-year-old Jane Fonda.

"She didn't. She had a heart attack."

"So why does it say she committed suicide?" asked the stu-dent.

Jane's mother, who had been depressed and in and out of sanatoriums, had slashed her wrists the previous year. "It seemed easier on the kids not to tell the whole truth," said Henry Fonda. "But the bottom line of it is: I wasn't telling the truth."

Gossip columnist Louella Parsons had the honor of letting the world know that Jane Wyman was divorcing Ronald Reagan—before her ex-to-be got the formal ax. "I arrived home from the

Washington [HUAC] hearing to be told that I was leaving," Reagan explained it.

Nobody hated being scooped more than LBJ; he was even known to cancel the appointments of government officials if the word had gotten out that they'd been selected. Thus he was understandably peeved when he read the news ticker and found out that his daughter Luci was engaged to marry Patrick Nugent. Luci and her fiancé had flown home to tell LBJ their news but decided against it because Johnson was recovering from a gallbladder operation. Three weeks passed, and finally the President came to Luci and said, "What's all this I read in the papers?" As she tells it, "That was when we sat down and reasoned together." Whenever Luci "reasoned" with her father, she was almost sure to get what she wanted.

On March 31, 1968, LBJ was determined to be scoop-proof. He was scheduled to give a major speech but wanted to add his own ending, which he wrote by hand and kept tucked in his pocket. "When he got to what I knew was the end, I got up and said, 'Well, let's turn it off [the TV] and talk about it,' " said aide McGeorge Bundy. "And I moved toward the set and then came the sayonara." Johnson announced: "I shall not seek, and I will not accept, the nomination of my party for another term as your President."

"I—I couldn't believe it. It was like a—it was like a percussion grenade going off in that room and I was stunned," recalled another aide, Roger Wilkins.

LBJ had delivered the surprise of the decade.

CELEBRITY AT GUNPOINT: A KILLER'S INSTINCT

*In America, heroes are meant to be killed. Idols are meant to be shot in the back. Guns are neat little things, aren't they? They can kill extraordinary people with very little effort. But don't say a word about this to the NRA.*
—John Hinckley

If you want to make it into the history books, the simplest way may be to pick up a gun and aim it at someone famous. As these quotes indicate, an assassin's true target may be the six o'clock news.

1. "Now, everyone will know me."—Lee Harvey Oswald at the Dallas police station.

2. "From everything I know . . . and the events that transpired, I can conclude that he wanted in any way, whether good or bad, to do something that would make him outstanding, that he would be known in history."—Lee Harvey Oswald's wife, Marina, to the Warren Commission investigating John Kennedy's murder.

3. "But, hell, I gained something. They can gas me. But I am famous. I achieved in a day what it took Kennedy all his life to do."—Sirhan Sirhan.

4. "I've decided Wallace will have the honor of—what would you call it? . . . SHIT! I won't even rate a T.V. enteroption [*sic*] in Russia or Europe when the news breaks—they never heard of Wallace."—Arthur Bremer in his diary, before shooting the Alabama governor. After his arrest, he told a cop: "Just stay with me, and you'll be a star, just like I am."

5. "I did not want to kill somebody, but there comes a point when the only way you can make a statement is to pick up a gun."—Lynette "Squeaky" Fromme, a follower of Charles Manson who tried to kill President Ford.

6. When Hinckley was arrested, he asked the FBI if the shooting had made TV. He was told yes. His next question: Would it preempt the Academy Awards that evening?

PRESIDENTS MEET THE PRESS

1. "I know every one of those men. Not one of them has enough sense to pound sand in a rathole."—President Truman on hearing that a newsmagazine polled fifty political writers who all picked Dewey as winner of the 1948 election.

2. "I would get hell," protested Eisenhower's press secretary, Jim Hagerty, if he followed orders and made the statement about the Taiwan crisis that his boss wanted him to make. Ike gave him a friendly pat on the back: "My boy, better you than me."

3. "You know, when I get downstairs . . . those reporters are going to lean over my stretcher. There's going to be about ninety-five faces leaning over me, and every one of those guys will say, 'Now, Senator, what about McCarthy?' " John Kennedy, ill with back problems, was leaving the hospital and heading for Palm

UPI/BETTMANN

"Thirty years ago," Herbert Hoover told Dwight Eisenhower on a 1954 fishing trip, "we used to believe there were only two occasions on which the American people would protect the privacy of the President—that was prayer and fishing. I now detect that you have lost that last one." As evidence of changed times, Ike heads off to fish with his seven-year-old grandson—and a press pool.

Springs. He was the only Democratic senator who had failed to vote for the censure of Joe McCarthy. To avoid dealing with the press, he said, "Do you know what I am going to do? I'm going to reach for my back and I'm going to yell ooow, and then I'm going to pull the sheet over my head and hope we can get out of there."

4. "If you'll cover me every day," said LBJ to a reporter when he was Vice President, "I'll leak to you like a dog on a hydrant." He did, but according to *New York Times* reporter James Reston, LBJ "regarded the press as a conveyor belt that should carry, without question, any baggage he wanted to dump on it." When things were going well, he said, "I trust the press. I trust you as much as I trust my wife." When things were looking grim, Dan Rather would get a call at CBS News. "Rather, are you trying to fuck me?"

5. "The press aren't slobs as some people think. They are not inaccurate as many people think . . . the press generally is biased. Many of them try very hard to keep the bias out of the reporting, but when it is a liberal bias, it's extremely difficult. . . . In the period of the Vietnam War, my press conferences were really shootouts."—Richard Nixon.

6. "The story had gotten out that the President made his own breakfast, didn't require a Navy steward to fix his muffins for him," recalled Ford press secretary Jerald terHorst. "And so I said, 'Well, we'll send a [press] pool up there.' And it certainly seemed to have worked." The nation reveled in the fact that Ford knew the ins and outs of the White House toaster.

7. "There is in the press, as there is in politics, some irresponsibility, and some absence of integrity, some deliberate distortion. . . . But I would say in general the press has treated my administration fairly. They and I are trying our best, but we all make mistakes, not because of evil intent, but because we're human."—Jimmy Carter in 1977.

8. "There's some good in everyone."—Ronald Reagan when the Sandinistas fired on a press helicopter near the border.

9. "You may have read that the pups are sleeping on *The Washington Post* and *The New York Times*. The first time in history that those papers have been used to prevent leaks."—George Bush after First Dog Millie had puppies.

# 14
# What's It All About?: Life and Death, Etc.

*I have a simple philosophy. Fill what's empty. Empty what's full.*
*And scratch where it itches.*
—Alice Roosevelt Longworth, daughter of Teddy Roosevelt and
Washington social doyenne

Wat's it all about? If anybody knows, he or she's not telling. In lieu of a definitive answer, it may help to find some words to live by. These, for example:

1. "I like thinking big. If you're going to be thinking any way, you might as well think big."—Donald Trump.

2. "Life is to be lived. If you have to support yourself, you had bloody well better find some way that is going to be interesting. And you don't do that by sitting around wondering about yourself."—Katharine Hepburn.

3. "I believe that every woman over fifty should stay in bed until noon."—Mamie Eisenhower, who practiced what she preached.

4. "Christ says, 'Don't consider yourself better than someone else because one guy screws a whole bunch of women while the other guy is loyal to his wife.' "—Jimmy Carter in *Playboy*.

5. "Never doubt that a small group of thoughtful committed citizens can change the world. Indeed, it's the only thing that ever has."—anthropologist Margaret Mead.

6. "Service is the rent that you pay for room on this earth."—Shirley Chisholm, the first black woman elected to Congress, who ran for President in 1972.

7. "If there is one thing worse than having an artistic temperament, it is thinking you have one."—Henry Miller, author of *Tropic of Cancer*.

8. "Retire? No one in the Bible ever retires. Why should I?"—evangelist Billy Graham.

9. "The meek shall inherit the earth, but not the mineral rights."—oil billionaire J. Paul Getty.

10. "You gotta take the sour with the bitter."—movie mogul Samuel Goldwyn to Billy Wilder after one of their films flopped.

11. "You've got to have something to eat and a little love in your life before you can hold still for any damn body's sermon on how to behave."—blues singer Billie Holiday.

12. "You can never enslave somebody who knows who he is."—Alex Haley, author of *Roots*.

13. "I enjoy shopping. It's kind of a hobby to help my nerves. It's better than a psychiatrist."—Tammy Faye Bakker, ex-wife of the TV evangelist.

### MONEY CAN'T BUY YOU LOVE

*If you can give it away, why can't you sell it? This is a capitalist country.*

—Sydney Biddle Barrows, the so-called Mayflower Madam

Everyone knows money can't buy you love. It can't even buy you a substitute—legally. Oh, sure, Massachusetts Congressman Barney Frank paid prostitute Stephen L. Gobie eighty dollars for a one-night stand in 1985, and Lieutenant William Calley signed up for a back rub and more for fifteen dollars in Vietnam. Despite the market for amorous services, everyone knows there are some transactions between human beings that can't be bought and sold.

For example, "If they said to me . . . for ten dollars you can have your brother, I wouldn't pay a dime. We have paid . . . years in pain and suffering," said Peggy Say, sister of journalist Terry Anderson, who was taken hostage in Beirut on March 26, 1985. The years of his life from age thirty-seven on "are years Terry Anderson will never get back. I have seen his daughter born and ready to start school, and he has not. And his eldest mature into a teenager. Who can give that back to Terry?"

On Thursday, "the day before the Negro payday . . . [t]he teacher was asking each student how much his father would give to the Community Chest," recalled comedian and civil rights activist Dick Gregory. ". . . I decided I was going to buy me a Daddy right then. I had money in my pocket from shining shoes and selling papers, and whatever Helene Tucker pledged for her Daddy I was going to top it." Helene said her daddy would give $2.50, which was easy for Dick to best. The problem was the teacher never called his name. He raised his hand. "You forgot me."

"I don't have time to be playing with you, Richard." She turned to the blackboard.

"My daddy said he'd give . . . fifteen dollars."

"We are collecting this money for you and your kind, Richard Gregory. If your Daddy can give fifteen dollars you have no business being on relief. . . . And furthermore," she said, "we know you don't have a Daddy."

By then Helene Tucker was crying, and so was Dick Gregory.

Even if you're seven years old, it's a shock to realize that no matter how much shoeshine money you have, it's never enough.

"The United States government was well aware of what they were sending us into—we were used as radioactive guinea pigs," said Bill Griffin, a marine who served in Nagasaki after the atom bomb had been dropped. "I don't know what the thunder I was supposed to be guardin'! It was several square miles of nothin' but rubble about that high. There wasn't no people, they was all in the countryside or dead." Griffin came home to Illinois in 1946 and began to notice gum bleeds, hair loss, tooth loss—textbook reactions to radiation. But what wasn't expected was the leukemia that killed his son Patrick at the age of eight. "I feel they should repay me in some way," he said. "But what do you charge for a little boy?"

What do you charge for a husband? For a lover? In December 1969 the FBI raided the Black Panthers in Chicago and sprayed their apartment with bullets while everyone slept. Deborah Johnson, eight months pregnant, shook her lover, Fred Hampton, and said, "Chairman, Chairman, wake up! The pigs are vamping. The pigs are vamping." Hampton and fellow party leader Mark Clark were killed. The police billed it as a shoot-out until evidence showed that *all* the bullet holes were going in one direction— toward the rooms where the Panthers slept. The families of Hampton and Clark and the survivors of the raid sued. In 1982 they received a $1.85 million settlement out of court.

Money can't buy you life. But still it is the currency with which we pay our respects. After Policeman J. D. Tippet was shot by Lee Harvey Oswald, Tippet's widow, Marie, received $643,863 in the mail—contributions sent by sympathetic Americans. Jackie Kennedy sent a photograph of the Kennedy family with this inscription: "There is another bond we share. We must remind our children all the time what brave men their fathers were."

Oswald's widow got $70,000 in donations and did her best to cash in on her fifteen minutes of fame. She hawked Oswald's Russian diary for $20,000, peddled a picture of him holding *the* gun for $5,000, and even tried to obtain the actual gun so she could market it as a souvenir. Oswald's mother, Marguerite, who had been rather indifferent about her son while he was alive, also eagerly milked the limelight. Though she complained, "Moneywise I got took," when the Warren Commission failed to pay her for her testimony, she sold his letters to *Esquire* and bought a new two-toned Buick and an enormous reproduction of Whistler's "Mother" framed in brass. And she treated herself to a gold statuette of the Virgin Mary, which she wore around her neck.

Money can veil anybody in images of motherhood and saintliness, it can make sure a Christmas tree is piled with presents, but if love isn't in the package, everyone knows instantly. "Our parents gave us tons of presents, but never any that were for *me*," said Laura Rockefeller, daughter of Laurance. At Christmas only the servants gave the children thoughtful personal gifts—things they knew were chosen with love.

Likewise, Charlotte Ford, daughter of Henry II, complained, "We didn't see much of my father. He was always away or coming in from work after we had gone to bed. We had a Christmas tree and presents and all that. But looking back on it, I think I'd have been happy to have fewer presents and more parents."

Money can't make up for so much that goes wrong between human beings, but still we try. In 1957, when radio star and humorist John Henry Faulk was blacklisted, he sought recompense in the courts. He sued Aware, Inc., a media watchdog group that had deemed him pro-Communist. Aware got its power by insisting on screening all actors' names (or else sponsors' products would be boycotted) and charging a pretty penny for its service.

Faulk was determined to expose its racket—at enormous personal cost. After five years of unemployment his case came to trial. Faulk watched the jury file out to deliberate and went to dinner with his lawyer, Louis Nizer. "Lou, you poured it on. Hell, you had me," Faulk told him. ". . . but two million dollars? Lou . . . they're liable to think . . . I'm doing it for the money." No sooner had he expressed that opinion than a runner summoned them back to the courtroom. The jury filed in, and the judge asked whether they'd reached a verdict. "No," came the response. "We have a question we want to ask. Can we give more than two million?"

Recalled Faulk: "[O]l' sweet Louis Nizer, he sat there like somebody'd caught him between the eyes with a ball peen hammer. He'd made a lot of mistakes in his legal career, but asking for too little never had been one of them. And they went out and thirty minutes later came back with a three and a half million dollar judgment."

Upon appeal, the verdict was cut down to $500,000, and Faulk saw only $175,000 of that because, among other reasons, the primary defendant died the night the jury began to deliberate. But Faulk was able to pay back lawyers and friends. Few had expected compensation. When Edward R. Murrow chipped in for Faulk's legal fees, his comment was "I'm investing this in America, not you."

When John F. Kennedy was inaugurated, he vowed, "We shall pay any price, bear any burden, meet any hardship . . . to assure the survival and the success of liberty." Without money, cases wouldn't come to trial, many acts of bravery would never succeed. But despite the dollars a government spends, the price of freedom is generally paid by people like Faulk in years of unemployment. Or by Martin Luther King in harassment and petty arrests. Even when King could avoid jail by, for example, paying a $10 fine and $4 court fee in Montgomery in 1957, he refused, knowing that a cash payment would preserve the status quo. Police Commissioner Clyde Sellers knew this, too. He anted up $14 ostensibly to "save the taxpayers the expense of feeding King for fourteen days."

"I am a graduate of the University of Mississippi," wrote James Meredith, who had been enrolled with the help of the National Guard, to Robert Kennedy in September 1963. "For this I am proud of my Country—the United States of America. . . . I believe that I echo the feeling of most Americans when I say that 'no price is too high to pay for freedom of person, equality of opportunity, and human dignity.' "

Ultimately things like love or freedom or opportunity can't be purchased without a very human price being paid. Money simply isn't enough.

### A MOMENT OF SELF-REFLECTION

1. "I have been called indispensable and a miracle worker. I know, because I remember every word I say."—Henry Kissinger

2. "Deep down, I'm pretty superficial."—Ava Gardner.

3. "I've never had a really unhappy day in my life."—JFK.

4. "You know, nobody will believe it, but I'm really an egghead."—Richard Nixon.

5. "My mouth as overshadowed my ability."—Muhammad Ali, noted for one-liners like "I'm so fast I cut off the light switch and was in bed before the room got dark."

6. When Yogi Berra was taking on the job of manager for the Yankees in 1963, he was asked, "What will be your biggest problem next season, Yogi?"

"If I can manage."

"How have you prepared yourself for this job?"

"You can observe a lot by watching."

7. "There are two sorts of women, the female and the broad. The female marries for security. The broad is more forthright. I'm a broad."—Bette Davis.

8. "Being the author of *Gone With the Wind* is a full-time job."—Margaret Mitchell.

9. "What's wrong with being a boring kind of guy? . . . I think to kind of suddenly try to get my hair colored, dance up and down in a miniskirt or do something to show I've got a lot of jazz out there and drop a bunch of one-liners . . . we're talking about running for the President of the United States. This is serious business. . . . I kind of think I'm a scintillating kind of fellow."—George Bush in the 1988 campaign.

10. "I'm a classic late bloomer. Some develop a sense of seriousness earlier in life than others. I was clearly late in that category."—Dan Quayle.

11. Joe Kennedy: "Caroline is very bright, smarter than you were at that age."

John F. Kennedy: "Yes, but look at who *she* has for a father."

12. Asked in court to name the world's best architect, Frank

Lloyd Wright cited himself. "I was under oath, wasn't I?" he said later.

*Looking back on my life, I would have liked it if society had
protected me from myself.*
—Arthur Bremer, George Wallace's would-be assassin upon
his sentencing in court

At certain times in our lives, we pause to look back over our shoulders at roads taken—and not taken. Here we stand in the shoes of some of those who shaped our times.

1. Asked what the greatest lesson of Watergate was, Richard Nixon said, "Just destroy the tapes."

2. "The great tragedy of my life was that I survived the last battle."—General George Patton.

3. "If I could have planned his weekend schedule, I think I would have scheduled it differently."—Lee Hart, after her husband, Gary, was discovered entertaining Donna Rice.

4. "I took my own journey in my own times on my own terms. My whole life has been a reaction to the hurtful parts of my Puritan heritage; it has been an attempt to put sex back into the Puritan ethic. It is, after all, the one part left out!"—*Playboy* founder Hugh Hefner.

5. "I didn't belong as a kid, and that always bothered me. If only I'd known that one day my differentness would be an asset, then my early life would have been much easier."—actress Bette Midler.

6. "If I'd known I was going to marry you, I would have asked my mother to let me stay up to see your show."—Lorna Adams, fashion designer, who at fifty-one married eighty-three-year-old comedian Milton Berle.

7. "Fuck the law! If every man had the right to work, equality and justice, none of this would have happened."—Sirhan Sirhan, RFK's assassin.

8. "I worry sometimes now. I lie awake, and I think of My Lai and say, *My god. Whatever inspired me to do it?* But truthfully: there was no other way. America's motto there was 'Win in Vietnam,' and in My Lai there was no other way to do it. No

wonder an Army officer is so aggravated today. He has trained hard to forget, *To kill a man's wrong.* He psychs himself up, . . . he has that mission and he accomplishes it. . . . You shouldn't teach us killing then."—Lieutenant William Calley, convicted of murder in the My Lai massacre in Vietnam.

9. "There's nothing like a week in Chicago to clear the mind of adolescent machismo fantasies."—Todd Gitlin, ex-president of the SDS (Students for a Democratic Society) after its encounters with the police at the 1968 Democratic National Convention.

10. "I was just loony. There is no rational, sensible explanation for it. You either have to believe that I wanted to do all of this, and it was secretly my life's ambition and I was so happy I was kidnapped so I could finally get together with some nice people who had the same ideas I had. Or that I lost control of my ability to make decisions for myself or say anything about anything."—Patty Hearst Shaw looking back on her kidnapping by members of the Symbionese Liberation Army.

11. "It was inconceivable to me that he could be unhappy," said Jack Hinckley, father of Reagan's would-be assassin, John. "Why, our kids had everything—a yard to play in, a TV set in the living room, water skiing on weekends with our outboard motorboat. We were the family whose American dream had come true."

12. It "made me realize that probably I'm a lot deeper person than I thought I was."—Oliver North's secretary Fawn Hall, on the Iran-contra affair, in which she dutifully shredded documents for her boss.

13. "There's no doubt about it. I have never had any question about that at all. Had the hostages been released before November the fourth, I would've been reelected without any problems. In fact, even a week before the elections, Reagan and I were neck-and-neck."—Jimmy Carter.

14. "I didn't have the balls to vote against my father, but I couldn't vote for him either. . . . Still, I was horrified my father got re-elected. From the homeless to the environmental neglect to the rise in racism—if you have an elitist atmosphere, you have a racist atmosphere—I couldn't believe what was going on." —Reagan's daughter Patti Davis.

15. "Was there anything that the Secret Service or that Clint Hill could have done to keep that from happening?" Mike Wallace

asked the Secret Service agent who had helped guard John Kennedy the day of his assassination.

Hill: "Clint Hill, yes."

Wallace: "Clint Hill, yes? What do you mean?"

Hill: "If he had reacted about five-tenths of a second faster or maybe a second faster, I wouldn't be here today."

Wallace: "You mean you would have gotten there and you would have taken the shot."

Hill: "The third shot, yes, sir."

Wallace: "And that would have been all right with you."

Hill: "That would have been fine with me."

Wallace: "But you couldn't. You got there in less than two seconds, Clint. You surely don't have any sense of guilt about that?"

Hill: "Yes, I certainly do. It was my fault. . . . If I had reacted just a little bit quicker . . . I could have, I guess I'll have to live with that to my grave."

### DARK SHADOWS

Sometimes it's death that casts the shadow that illuminates what we care about. Among those who have looked the inevitable in the eye are the following:

1. "Like anybody, I would like to live a long life, longevity has its place. But I am not concerned about that now. I just want to do God's will. And He's allowed me to go to the mountain. And I've looked over. And I've seen the promised land. I may not get there with you. But I want you to know tonight that we as a people will get to the promised land. And I'm happy tonight. I'm not worried about anything. I'm not fearing any man. Mine eyes have seen the glory of the coming of the Lord."—Martin Luther King, Jr., the night before he was shot.

2. "A long life deprives man of his optimism. [Better] to die in all the happy period of unillusioned youth, to go out in a blaze of light, than to have your body worn out and old and illusions shattered."—Ernest Hemingway the year he died.

3. "He drank himself to death. Which is only another way of living, of handling the pain and foolishness that it's all a dream, a great baffling silly emptiness, after all."—Allen Ginsberg on Jack Kerouac's death in 1969 at the age of forty-seven.

4. "It wasn't suicide. It wasn't sleeping pills, it wasn't cirrhosis. I think she was just tired, like a flower that blooms and gives joy and beauty to the world and then wilts away."—Liza Minnelli in a statement after Judy Garland's death in 1969.

5. "Before takeoff they asked me if I wanted to take this little silver dollar with me. It wasn't an ordinary silver dollar; I knew it had some poison concealed in it. . . . I'd been told that if I went down, maybe they'd think it was a good-luck charm and let me keep it. I looked at the silver dollar, and I said, 'Now that's the most idiotic thing I've ever heard.' "—Francis Gary Powers, pilot of the U-2 spy plane shot down over the USSR in 1960. He didn't avail himself of the "dollar."

6. "I wouldn't mind dying in a plane crash. It would be a good way to go. I don't want to die of old age or OD or drift off in my sleep. I want to feel what it's like. I want to taste it, hear it smell it. Death is only going to happen once, right. I don't want to miss it."—Jim Morrison, lead singer of the Doors, in 1969. He was found dead in a bathtub full of water in Paris in 1971. No one knows exactly how he died.

7. "It's not that I'm afraid to die. I just don't want to be there when it happens."—Woody Allen.

8. "I think about death a lot, maybe because I don't know about life after death. So I strive as hard as I can to suck every drop out of life. The great thing about being an artist is that artists are immortal by the fact that they leave their work behind them. There is something comforting knowing that my life was not just a waste."—Madonna.

9. "But, a friend told me, 'Don't be upset, you'll be Scotty long after you die.' "—James Doohan, who played Scotty on *Star Trek* and felt producers couldn't see him in another role.

10. "I had a vision. In a split second my life was gone. Far away as I could see, Nothing, nothing, nothing! And this horrible smell, like a dumpyard of sorrow was there. And I said, I don't care if this is death, I still believe there's a God. And when I said that, I was alive in that dressing room. I started screaming that Jesus Christ was coming alive in me. That's when it all started. It shamed me. It embarrassed me. And yet it happened. I had no mind for religion at all."—Boxer George Foreman, who was born again after losing a comeback fight against Jimmy Young.

11. "You know, when I drop dead, people are gonna interpret

the shit outta my songs. They're gonna interpret every fuckin' comma. They don't know what the songs mean. Shit, *I* don't know what they mean."—Bob Dylan.

12. "Hey, life is life. We're here for a short time. When we're gone, most people don't care, and in some cases they're quite happy about it."—Donald Trump.

# 15
# Who's Not Who: Mixups, Identity Crises, and Bloopers

*George Bush: "Yes, things went wrong and I've admitted it and,*
*Dan, I'll take all the credit."*
*Ted Koppel: "Dan's the other fellow."*
—Exchange on *Nightline*, 1988

It must be tough remembering all those names. You can understand it if a coup has just turned things around in what used to be the USSR and there's a whole new cast of characters who all sound alike. "I talked to Jim Baker who had talked to . . . who was it Jimmy had talked to, Yanayev?" George Bush wondered aloud. "No, not Yanayev. Yakovlev is who we had talked to."

But even in ordinary times it's tough to be President and keep everyone straight. "Prime Minister Lee, I want you to meet Beverly Sills," said Jerry Ford. "She's our most famous professional." To which Betty Ford whispered, *"Opera star!* Dammit, Jerry, she's an *opera* star!"

Eisenhower created a Cabinet post—the HEW—for Oveta Culp Hobby but kept calling the department "Health, Welfare, and Whatnot," leaving "Education" out of the equation.

"Could you explain to the members of the jury who General Vessey was?" Ronald Reagan was asked during the Iran-contra trial of Admiral John Poindexter, former national security adviser.

"Oh dear, I could ask for help here. The name is very familiar. I am wondering if . . ."

"This is in connection with a trip by the Joint Chiefs of Staff," offered Poindexter's lawyer.

"Well, that—I don't—I don't think this was my military aide. . . ." The right answer: John W. Vessey, Jr., was Reagan's chairman of the Joint Chiefs of Staff from 1982 to 1985.

Sometimes it's all you can do to remember who you are. For example, after President Kennedy died, acting press secretary Malcolm Kilduff needed to make an announcement to the press. But first he had to get LBJ's okay. He coughed and tried to get Johnson's attention. "Mr. President . . ." LBJ turned around and "looked at me like I was Donald Duck." It was the first time anyone had so addressed the former VP.

Jimmy Carter knew who was on first. The problem was the White House operator. "Jimmy who?" was the response Rosalynn got when she first asked to be connected to "Jimmy."

Identity crises plagued JFK throughout his congressional career. His first week in the House, a longtime congressman looked at him and ordered him to get him a copy of a bill. "Where do I get it?" Kennedy replied with a grin.

"How long have you been a page?" the congressman barked. Kennedy, who was a mere twenty-nine years old and wearing a dark suit typical of those worn by pages, replied, "Hell, I'm a congressman."

But confusions persisted. In 1948, when he went to a Truman rally, the Secret Service refused to admit him until it could find someone who would vouch for the fact that he really was a congressman. Even as a senator, he tried to use a phone and was stopped by a guard. "Sorry, son. These are reserved for senators."

Tip O'Neill, one of the most powerful men in Congress, also had trouble getting respect. One day he went to address a meeting of the National Organization for Women. He pulled into a parking space marked "Reserved for the Speaker." The guard knocked on the window and ordered, "Get that car out of here. This space is reserved for the Speaker."

"I *am* the Speaker," explained O'Neill.

"Mr. Rayburn. I didn't recognize you." Rayburn had been dead for some twenty years.

How is anyone, from an operator to a Senate guard to a President, supposed to keep it all straight? These pointers might prove helpful.

1. *Take note of appearances.* "Mr. Speaker, I am very honored that you recognize me," said Daniel Inouye of Hawaii to Sam Rayburn.

"Come on, how many one-armed Japs do we have around

here?'' came the reply. The congressman and future senator had lost his arm in World War II.

2. *If you stumble, correct yourself immediately.* "To . . . the great people of the government of Israel—Egypt, excuse me." That was the toast President Ford offered Egyptian President Anwar el-Sadat.

3. *Study who's on your staff.* Jim Brady, who later was Reagan's press secretary, learned his skills as a field rep for Senator Everett Dirksen. Brady brought one press conference to a close by saying, "The Senator has time for just one more question." It was duly answered and then, as he recalled, "Dirksen in his slow, majestic voice said, 'My pilot says I have to be going now.' "

Dirksen rarely recognized any but his closest staff members. "If I'm your pilot, Senator," Brady told him, "you're in trouble."

4. *Finally, if you're really stuck, get help.* "*You*, I've been looking for *you*," Vice President Lyndon Johnson said to *New York Times* reporter Russell Baker, who knew LBJ well. Johnson dragged him into his office and launched into an hour and a half tirade about everything from Washington to his busy schedule. Midway through, LBJ scribbled something on a paper and buzzed his secretary. She returned with another bit of paper. LBJ glanced at it and kept right on talking. On his way out Baker asked a staffer if he knew what Johnson had written. "Who is this guy I'm talking to?" it said.

### IDENTITY CRISES, OR YOU THOUGHT ELVIS HAD PROBLEMS

When Governor Earl Long had a raging argument with his wife over, among other things, his affair with stripper Blaze Starr, she arranged to have him committed. He was furious. After all, he was "the governor of the great state of Louisiana," as he announced to another patient in the mental hospital. The patient nodded sympathetically. "Yeah, I used to think I was President Eisenhower."

What a mixed-up place the world can be! Unless you keep your guard up, it's pretty easy to feel like Earl Long, stuck where no one is who you—or they—think he or she is.

Bennett Cerf, founder of Random House publishers, thought he was on home turf when he was taking a woman on a tour of the office. He stopped in to see his son, Chris, a fledgling editor. Instead he found Chris's author Abbie Hoffman in the process of writing *Woodstock Nation* on the office floor—"stripped to the waist, smoking a joint," as Chris recalled. Cerf, Sr., looked in with his guest and started to stammer, "That's not my . . ." just as Abbie grinned and said, "Hi, Pop!"

Movie producer David Selznick asked CBS Chairman William Paley, "Do you mind if we bring Truman along?" as a houseguest. Paley was flattered—until everyone boarded his private plane. Trotting down the aisle was a small man with a scarf dangling off one shoulder. Paley turned to Selznick. "You know, when you said Truman, I assumed you meant Harry Truman," he said. "Who is this?" It was Truman Capote, who became one of the Paleys' closest friends.

Ray Charles also had a confusing plane ride. He was flying from New York to Los Angeles when a woman sat next to him and started "telling me she knows my music, which songs she likes, and how long she's been digging me. She rattles on. About an hour and a half into the flight, I interrupt her. 'Look, you've been talkin' so much about me. What about you? I don't even know your name.' "

"Well, I'm Judy Garland."

"Come on, Mamma. Tell the truth and shame the devil."

"It's true, Ray. I'm Judy Garland."

Ray had an excuse: He was blind. But shame the devil, a lot of others have been totally blindsided by life. Famous people are particularly vulnerable. They expect to be recognized. It's a surprise when they aren't. That's why Tip O'Neill, then Speaker of the House, didn't think twice when a man came up and said hello at Denver's Stapleton Airport. "Isn't this a beautiful city?" Tip volunteered. "Those mountains are twenty miles away, but you can almost reach out and touch them."

"You don't know me, do you?"

"Listen. You recognize me because I'm on television every day and I'm in politics. I have white hair, a big, bulbous nose, and cabbage ears. Everybody knows this face. So what's your name anyway?"

"Robert Redford."

Tell the truth and shame the devil! It isn't easy being famous. People you've never met are always waving, saying howdy, calling you by name. You start to expect that everyone who greets you is a stranger. Doris Day didn't even bat an eye when a man stopped her as she was walking down Beverly Drive. She gave him a cursory hello.

"Don't you remember me?" he asked.

"No, should I?"

"Well, you didn't have that many husbands."

"George? My God, you're George!" And so it was, George Weidler, her second husband.

She wasn't alone in her predicament. Shelley Winters was helping out at the Actors Studio just after Lee Strasberg's death in 1982, checking off students' names. She noticed "a tall, sort of familiar, middle-aged, handsome man. . . . I asked him if he was an observer or a member of the Actors Studio."

"Yes, I'm a member," he said. They chatted. She noticed he was "getting very red and staring at me."

"Shelley," he said, "don't you remember me—Tony, your friend, your ex-husband?"

"When I block, I block," wrote Winters later. ". . . I truly did not remember him. I wasn't pulling a number or anything like that. I'm sure I got as red as he did, so I said, 'Please, Mr. Franciosa, take a seat. I'm a little confused.' "

A lot of the rest of us have turned totally red over the mixups of life. E. Frederic Morrow, an aide to President Eisenhower, was at a governor's reception in Topeka. "Later in the evening," he recalled, "I was standing around, balancing a teacup, when one of the female guests came running up to me and said: 'Boy, I am ready to go now; go outside and get me a taxi.' " Another official dashed over and explained to her that Morrow, who was black, was an Eisenhower assistant. "She was overcome with remorse and embarrassment," noted Morrow.

Jackie Robinson didn't have a chance to notice any reddening of the cheeks. He was a lieutenant and morale officer at Fort Riley, Kansas. The Post Exchange where GIs went for snacks had only a few seats for blacks. Robinson phoned Major Hafner, provost marshal, to inquire about the situation. The major, unable to see who he was talking to, said, "Lieutenant, let me put it to you this way. How would you like to have your wife sitting next to a nigger?"

The best of us, however, have gotten our wires totally crossed.

Larry Hagman was the hottest thing on *Dallas* when he stopped at a New York restaurant, Nadine's, and started chatting with the bartender. "Everyone sitting at the bar was staring at Larry and putting out their cigarettes because they know he hates smoke," recalled a waiter. "But the bartender herself had *no* idea who he was. At one point Larry asked her, 'Where are you from?' and she replied, truthfully, 'Dallas. Have you ever been there?' Later that night Larry took a photograph of her. He probably shows it around as a picture of the only person in the world who doesn't know who he is."

Shirley Temple faced a photo opportunity of a very different sort. It was summer, the ragweed was in full flower, and her husband was letting off sneeze after sneeze. "Obediently I borrowed a tractor fitted with a sickle mowing bar, donned work clothes, and bound my hair tightly under a red bandana," wrote Shirley. "Clattering off in a cloud of diesel fumes, I began to chop our front pasture." She worked away until suddenly she noticed a family "who had parked their car at the roadside and were now all arranged by size along our board fence." The man waved at her and shouted, "Get out of the way. . . . Move away, you're lousing up my picture."

"What picture?" I called.

"A picture of her house. That's where Shirley Temple lives."

"Oh, her," Shirley replied, and backed her tractor up.

Humphrey Bogart backed up just as smartly when he realized he missed an opportunity to meet a screen idol. He was out boating and a crewman got injured. They stopped for help. "You know, Mr. Bogart, that man in the house was Roy Rogers," he was told.

"Roy who?" asked Bogart.

"The cowboy actor. Roy Rogers."

"You're kidding."

"No, I'm not. He had a gun belt on and boots and a hat. That was Roy Rogers."

"You're right. Let's go back to the house."

They did. Bogart apologized for not recognizing Rogers and suggested they have a drink.

"Sure," said Rogers, "but please don't say anything in the papers about all this."

"What papers?" asked Bogart.

"Well, ain't you a newspaperman?"

If you take a good look at the way the world works, is it any surprise that people keep spotting Elvis everywhere? As one tourist at Graceland said, "Of course, that's silly. Everyone knows Elvis is in Hawaii."

### A SHORT LIST OF BLOOPERS

*I am looking forward to talking with you balls to balls.*
—Soviet Foreign Minister Andrei Gromyko, referring to
Secretary of State Dean Rusk's comment, "We're eyeball to
eyeball and I think the other fellow just blinked," made during
the Cuban missile crisis.

Ooops! Some things just don't translate without a round of titters. At a White House dinner for François Mitterrand, Ronald Reagan was having a few troubles with the language barrier. He was on his way from the East Room into the state dining room. All the guests were standing. Nancy had led the French president to his table. Reagan was escorting Mme. Mitterrand. But she wouldn't budge. The butler waved her on. "We're supposed to go over there to the other side," Reagan said softly. She whispered something in French. He didn't get what she said. She repeated it. No luck. The translator dashed over. "She's telling you that you're standing on her gown."

"To err is human," said Mae West, "but it feels divine." The following gallery of errors isn't quite what she had in mind.

1. *Out on a limb.* One week before the 1948 election *Life* published a picture of Thomas E. Dewey with the caption "The Next President Travels by Ferry Boat over the Broad Waters of San Francisco Bay." When Dewey lost to Truman, a reader inquired, "How does it feel out on that limb?" The answer from the editor: "Crowded."

2. *Irony abounds.* "The funnyest [*sic*] thing happened to me when I arrived in N.Y. just after I got off the plane. I forgot my guns!" wrote Arthur Bremer in his diary on April 4, 1972. "I was in a washroom when I heard my name over the loudspeaker. WOW! The captain of the plane smiled & nodded as he gave me them. . . . Irony abounds."

3. *A giant step back for grammar.* "I had a hand in the first sign

As far as missteps go, President Ford was in a category of his own. As this 1975 photo illustrates, he often bumped, stumbled, and tripped his way into the news. Once an elevator door attacked him in Sacramento; on the golf course, his wayward shots sent caddies running for cover.

and it contains a glaring grammatical error.'' In 1969 William Safire, a Nixon speech writer, helped compose the following message: "Here men from the planet Earth/ first set foot on the moon/ July 1969 A.D. We came in peace for all mankind." As he was "sternly informed" afterward, A.D. must precede—not follow— the date. "My guilt is on the grand scale," admitted the man who now makes his living as a "word maven."

4. *What happened while Ike slept.* "You see, my nose was all stopped up and I had a jar of Vicks on my bedside table," explained Mamie Eisenhower. "So during the night when I woke up, I reached over to put some in my nostrils. Well, it seemed to just get drier, instead of moister, so I kept applying more and more. I didn't want to wake up Ike, so I didn't turn on the light. Then this morning I discovered that I was using *ink* to cure my cold." She also discovered that there were black splotches all over her, Ike, the sheets, headboard, and pink dust ruffle.

5. *Timing is everything.* President Gerald Ford's guest of honor at a White House party was Elizabeth II of England. Just as Ford took the queen out for a spin on the dance floor, the orchestra struck up "The Lady Is a Tramp."

# 16
# Living the Lonely Life

*The question a reporter posed to James Meredith, the first black admitted to the University of Mississippi, was "How is school and are you lonely?" The answer: "I've been living a lonely life a long time."*

It had taken two years, a Supreme Court ruling, a speech by President Kennedy, nearly twenty-five thousand troops, and a night of gunfire to register James Meredith at Ole Miss. At 8:00 A.M. on October 1, 1962, when he quietly filled out all the admissions forms—including one for late registration—he'd more than demonstrated he had the essential prerequisite for studying at an integrated Ole Miss: a talent for living the lonely life. It's a talent—and a mixed blessing—shared by those who decide to lead, to break the mold, to try to make the world a better place for those who follow them.

"When I traveled, during those early days," recalled Jackie Robinson, the first black in major-league baseball, "unless Wendell Smith or some other black sportswriter happened to be going along, I sat by myself while the other guys chatted and laughed and played cards."

"I was completely isolated," said Lena Horne of her experience in Hollywood. "Me and the shoeshine boy were the only two black people out there at the studio most every day."

Benjamin O. Davis, Jr., who as a three-star general served as the highest-ranking black in the Air Force until he retired in 1971, went through total isolation at West Point. When he was appointed to the school in 1932, the cadets held a meeting on the subject of "What to do about the nigger." The upshot: Davis was to be exiled socially. No one would live with him, eat with him, ride with him, or speak to him outside the classroom. He couldn't even get his Red Cross lifesaving badge because no one would be his buddy. "The only effect that that had on me," said Davis, "was to make me more and more determined to stay there for four years and to be graduated and go into the army."

In the White House, Nixon liked to bowl game after solitary game, sometimes in the wee hours of the morning. At Camp David, where military personnel had to be posted behind the automatic pin setters in case something went wrong, a twenty-four-hour guard turned out to be necessary. "The essence of this man is loneliness," said Henry Kissinger. That can have its benefits: No one notices if your foot is over the line.

In recent years the lonely life has been perhaps most dramatically—and most patiently—lived by blacks quietly seeking their rights, but it is a life that's open to anyone willing to take the high road even if it involves a singular journey.

"It was almost like getting up every morning and going to war," recalled Tracy Amalfitano, a parent who didn't join the whites' boycott of South Boston and Roxbury schools after a judge had mandated busing in 1974. In the first two years of desegregation, almost a third of the white students left the system. "Many days," said Amalfitano, "I would come home and I would think about all the liberals that got on the buses and went south for sit-ins and boycotts, and I really would come home and wonder, Where were they now?"

"It's a very strange kind of feeling to be blacklisted," recalled radio personality John Henry Faulk, who refused to play Senator Joseph McCarthy's game and find Communist flaws in his friends. "I'd go down to Colby's, which was the eating place at CBS . . . or . . . Toots Shor's . . . my headquarters over there on Fifty-first Street. . . . I knew everybody who came in. Toots had a table for me and all." The problem was that people would start leaving—"getting up and having to rush out"—when he showed up. "I finally quit doing it, because it got embarrassing to see them get up and move away from the bar when I'd sit down. . . ."

Restaurants also fell silent in the small town of Willard, Utah, when Roger Boisjoly and his wife, Roberta, walked in. Boisjoly was a whistle-blowing engineer at Morton Thiokol, the firm that manufactured the rocket boosters that doomed the space shuttle *Challenger.* He and a few colleagues had argued passionately that the O rings were not designed to function in cold weather, but the company's management—and NASA—were intent on an on-time liftoff. When Boisjoly's worst fears came true, NASA termed the event an "accident."

"I can't characterize it as an accident at all," Boisjoly said later. "It's a disaster, a horrible, terrible disaster, but not an accident. Because we could have stopped it, we had initially stopped it, and then that decision was made to go forward anyway." Congress investigated the matter, and against the advice of Morton Thiokol lawyers, Boisjoly told all he knew. His honesty won him no friends in Willard, where he had once been mayor. A dead rabbit was left in his mailbox; twice a car forced him off the road on his daily walks. "I had times when I would go to town. People would see me coming and they'd turn their backs," said his wife. In January 1987 Boisjoly took disability leave, and while he was on leave, his employment was terminated.

The world can be a very lonely place if you don't play the game. But the truth is, it can be just as desolate if you do. "A major public figure is a lonely man. . . . [Y]ou can't enjoy *the luxury* of the intimate personal friendships," said Richard Nixon. "You can't confide absolutely in anyone. You can't talk too much about your plans, your personal feelings."

There's an odd similarity between those who buck the system and those who ride it to the top. Both often have a talent for being a kingdom of one. Just as it takes formidable inner resources to go it alone and integrate a school, so it takes incredible stamina to be famous, to campaign for President and see your wife once a week, to leave your family and do a film on location.

"Her strength? Jane has a fantastic capacity for surviving. She learned long ago how to be lonely," said Jane Fonda's former husband French film director Roger Vadim. "She can be very—in French we say *solide*."

"You know, I always thought if I got good reviews I'd be happy," Rita Hayworth said in the early 1950s. "It's so empty. It's never what I wanted, ever. All I wanted was just what everybody else wants, you know—to be loved."

"I am lonely sometimes . . . sometimes I think I haven't got any friends left at all," Bette Midler once said. "I traded in big friendships for the love of a great, huge number of people. But you can't take ten thousand people home to bed with you."

Lyndon Johnson tried, more or less. When he invited journalists over for lunch in the family quarters of the White House, he'd talk right through to his last bite of diet tapioca pudding. Then he'd signal reporters to follow him up to his bedroom, where he'd change for his daily nap, chatting all the while. Only when he decided to shut his eyes did the interviews draw to a close.

"I think he just became lonely and wanted to talk," recalled press secretary George Reedy of another of LBJ's ploys for company—his Saturday morning interview sessions. "Bureau chiefs were pleading with me to get him to stop," said Reedy. Few papers published on Sunday; it was too late for the newsmagazines; other papers complained about the overtime costs. "I finally asked Johnson to stop." And finally he did.

"I was always very lonely," LBJ said near his death. But it wasn't for lack of people in his life. The problem came with his job description. As Nixon said, "The decisions that are important are the decisions that must be made alone."

Sometime after the Bay of Pigs fiasco, a distraught JFK walked his friend Charlie Spalding to the White House gate, "to that big fence on Pennsylvania where I was getting a cab," Spalding recalled. "He actually came out on the street with me, with Secret Service men scrambling all over the place, and he said to me, 'Charlie, what's out there? What's out there?' and I said, 'There's people out there. People and places to go.' And he said, 'Tell me, am I missing something? What am I missing?' "

Yes, of course, it's lonely at the top. Once Nelson Rockefeller remarked to an aide who had a lame leg because of polio, "Carl, if you think that's a handicap, you ought to try living with my name. At least you know who your friends are."

After Reagan's inauguration, Nancy called an old friend, Colleen Moore, and confided, "Colleen, I'm so scared, so scared and lonely."

"Oh, Nancy, you aren't a movie star now, not the biggest movie star," Moore said. "You're the star of the whole world. The biggest star of all."

"Yes, I know, and it scares me to death," Nancy replied.

When Jackie Kennedy told a friend she was going to marry Aristotle Onassis, she gasped, "Jackie, you're going to fall off your pedestal."

"That's better than freezing there," said the former First Lady.

And some people do freeze—at least emotionally. Once Howard Hughes invited Shelley Winters back to his house late one night. "My houseboy is still awake," he said, proposing they have a turkey sandwich. "And I have a pool in my living room if you'd like to take a dip."

"You have a *what*? Aren't you afraid one of your family or friends might get drunk and fall in and drown?" Shelley asked.

"I don't have any family or friends," he replied.

". . . [D]on't be silly. Everybody's got friends."

"I suppose so." He thought about it for a minute and said, "I have TWA."

"I never said, 'I want to be alone,' " claimed Greta Garbo, this century's most famous *femme solitaire*. "I only said, 'I want to be left alone.' "

But as she knew, solitude is not always a bad thing. What determines the quality of a life as much as friends, as much as family, as much as a career is a feeling that it's all worthwhile.

"You know, sometimes I envy the bastard," said Robert Kennedy about Cuban revolutionary Che Guevara. "At least he was able to go out and fight for what he believed. All I ever do is go to chicken dinners."

"Oh, boy! Listen to that!" said Senator Lyndon Johnson,

leaving the stage after a speech, his face radiant, amid thundering applause. "It even beats screwing."

"I miss what we had during that time," said Medgar Evers's widow, Myrlie, of the civil rights movement. "A sense of purpose, people coming together, meeting the challenges head-on, a kind of solidarity you don't find anymore."

"I don't miss the anarchy," said former Black Panther Eldridge Cleaver about the sixties. "But I do miss the innocence and the honesty."

"You know, Bob, there's something I've never told anybody before, not even you," Nixon whispered to H. R. Haldeman as Watergate was unraveling his administration. "Every night since I've been President, every single night before I've gone to bed, I've knelt down on my knees beside my bed and prayed to God for guidance and help in this job. Last night before I went to bed, I knelt down and this time I prayed that I wouldn't wake up in the morning. I just couldn't face going on."

The lonelist turn life can take is when you lose your dreams.

THE POLICEMAN'S LAMENT: NOBODY LOVES ME

*Be kind to cops; they're not cops, they're people in disguise who've been deceived by their own disguise.*
—poet Allen Ginsberg at his first Vietnam protest in 1963

Though children are brought up to believe that the policeman is their friend, few of those under thirty clung to that belief in the 1960s. Cops, or "the pigs," depending on your point of view, were the ones called upon to quell demonstrations, enforce drug laws, and deal with the clashes that resulted from the disparate ideals of those with hair long and short. As a result, officers of the law were left feeling very sorry for themselves.

After the Watts riots in Los Angeles in 1965, Police Chief William H. Parker called his staff "the most downtrodden, oppressed, dislocated minority in America."

"The better we do our job of enforcing the law the more we are attacked. . . . Subtly, too many so-called objective news writers attempt to excuse the actions of minorities [and cause] the police to be singled out by virtually all factions as the symbol of all of society's failures," lamented Quentin Tamm, executive director of the International Association of Chiefs of Police.

"Arresting them doesn't seem to help because they don't care. . . . It's been my experience that they beat me out of the court back onto the street. I believe that one good crack on the head does more good. If you give them a headache, they go home and usually stay there," said a policeman after the first riot at the Chicago Democratic National Convention, 1968.

Chicago Mayor Richard Daley's thoughts: "What would you do if someone was throwing human excrement in your face, would you be the calm, collected people you think you are? What would you do if someone was biting you? . . . What do you think they [the police] were supposed to do?"

J. Edgar Hoover's: "The police are human. They are supposed to be both lawyers and sociologists, as I said, but they are still human. I don't think any of us . . . would be restrained if we had been hit with some of the things they had been hit with."

THE THINGS THEY DID FOR LOVE

*He was never mine, totally. He belonged to his people, the struggle, and his country. In a way Medgar constantly prepared me not only to survive but to be able to live and achieve without him.*
—Myrlie Evers, widow of the civil rights activist and the first black woman to be appointed commissioner of board of public works in Los Angeles, 1987; field secretary for the NAACP, 1954–63

Some men are available for women to have and to hold; others belong to the world. It's just the way things are.

Once JFK and Jackie were on a plane. "Where will we be buried when we die, Jack?" she asked.

"Hyannis, I guess. We'll all be there," he answered.

"Well, I don't think you should be buried in Hyannis. I think you should be buried in Arlington. You just belong to all the country."

Yes, but that's hard to remember if you're left behind and the sink is piled with dishes. "George was off on a trip doing all these exciting things," Barbara Bush said of her husband, a Texas oilman turned congressman, "and I'm sitting home with these

absolutely brilliant children who say one thing a week of interest."
She was so mired in diapers and dishes that her confidence vanished; she once cried at the prospect of having to address the Houston Garden Club.

"I spent my time bailing him out of jail. I'm not saying this was the greatest thrill," said Abbie Hoffman's second wife, Anita Kushner. "But I saw my role as a real helpmate, so he was free to do his own thing. I didn't feel I knew who I was."

"It was not the right time of life for us," said Jackie when her husband was serving in the Senate and laying the groundwork for the presidency. "We should be enjoying traveling, having fun. . . . I was alone almost every weekend. It was all wrong."

"I hardly ever see him at night anymore since he took up sex," complained Clara Kinsey, the wife of Alfred Kinsey, the workaholic author of *Sexual Behavior in the Human Male.*

"I saw him just once that year," Brenda Schwarzkopf recalled regarding her husband, Norman, who had volunteered for a second tour of duty in Vietnam. She flew to Hong Kong to meet him. Six months later he was wounded. "We had only one or two phone calls that entire year. It was one of those, 'Hi, how are you? Over.' And I would say, 'Fine, how are you? Over.' You know the operator can listen in, so it's a very strained conversation. Instead we sent tapes back and forth. . . ."

"The loneliness, the being left to yourself at night, is what makes marriages crack, makes liquor more attractive . . ." wrote Betty Ford of her life as a congressional wife in the 1960s. "During the time when Jerry was gone so much I developed a problem, and I quit drinking for a couple of years." She later developed quite a severe problem.

"I remember the loneliness of the first year I was married to Elvis," recalled Priscilla Presley. "After our wedding, on May 1, 1967, we had a two-month honeymoon in Palm Springs, which was wonderful. But as soon as we went back to his house, Elvis had to leave to make a movie on location. We'd already learned I was pregnant, so it didn't seem wise for me to accompany him. . . . The hit-and-run, hello–good-bye existence that was to become our life started then. I tried to believe it was a temporary thing, that I wasn't always going to be alone. I kept thinking it would work itself out—not really. Not ever. Now I realize that Elvis didn't belong to me, he belonged to the world."

If life in the limelight surprises a woman who marries the heartthrob of America, imagine the feelings of women who were thrust there unexpectedly. When Bess Wallace, a small-town girl, agreed to marry an aspiring haberdasher with a head full of dreams, her future husband asked her, "How does it feel being engaged to a clodhopper who has ambitions to be governor of Montana and chief executive of the U.S.?" Harry Truman went on to answer his own question, saying, "He'll do well if he gets to be a retired farmer." No reasonable person Bess knew—including Harry—gave any serious thought to the prospect of life in the White House, a place he loved but she hated.

But there are those who are able to marry a public man and still carve out a universe that belongs to lovers alone. "Knowing her, being married to her," Ronald Reagan said, "is kind of like coming into a warm, firelit room when you've been out in the cold. . . ."

"Some people think I overdo it, but I love to look at Ronnie," wrote Nancy in her autobiography. "Ever since he first ran for office, people have mocked the way I focus on him while he's giving a speech, and for years now the press has referred to it as 'the gaze.' A friend of mine once said, 'Nancy, people just don't believe it when you look at him that way. It's as if you're saying, 'He's my hero.' 'But he *is* my hero,' I replied. And so he is."

Sometimes the hundred other people in the room are of little consequence.

# 17
# Lies and Other Mistruths

*If you can't lie, you'll never go anywhere.*
—Richard Nixon

Well, to tell the truth, Nixon's probably right. Where would Santa Claus, the tooth fairy, or Ronald Reagan be if all of us didn't appreciate a bit of clever mythmaking?

"Now you hear a lot of jokes about Silent Cal Coolidge," Reagan said when he was President, "but I think that the joke is on people that make jokes, because if you look at his record, he cut the taxes four times. We had probably the greatest growth and prosperity that we've ever known."

Coolidge's legacy, of course, was the Great Depression, but who needs to remember that when the good times are rolling? Why listen to a doomsayer like Walter Mondale, who in 1984 told the Democratic National Convention: "Taxes will go up. Let's tell the truth. It must be done. It must be done. Mr. Reagan will raise taxes, and so will I. He won't tell you. I just did." Mondale lost in forty-nine states. Reagan ran the nation on credit.

George Bush rode into the White House on Reagan's coattails, urging us to read his lips, which eventually moved to call for revenue enhancements. When the T-word became a reality in 1990, Michael Dukakis, who had favored a tax increase, said, "I told the truth, and I paid the price."

The lesson of history is that honesty is not always the best policy. In 1952 Adlai Stevenson reminded the nation that "Sacrifice, patience, understanding, and implacable purpose may be our lot for years to come. Let's face it—let's talk sense to the American people. Let's tell them the truth, that there are no gains without pains." He lost miserably.

In 1976 Jimmy Carter won. He promised a nation reeling from the deceptions of Watergate, "I'll never lie to you." The problem was, he meant it. Before taking office, he asked his staff to make a list of all his campaign promises so that he could be sure he never went back on them. The document was 112 pages long. To Carter's chagrin, the press got hold of it and for the next four years kept track of all that the President wasn't able to do. As his term ended in 1981, two journalists wrote, "Today much of the President's official list of promises reads like a page out of an H. G. Wells science-fiction novel."

Well, if being a stickler for the truth is no way to succeed, does that mean lying is your only option? Certainly not. There is a whole spectrum of shades of gray with which a politician—or just an ordinary citizen—can cloud any issue. Jimmy Carter's mother demonstrated that when a reporter asked her, "Miss Lillian, is it true that your son never told a lie?"

"Well, now, what do you mean by a lie?" she countered.

"Well, didn't he ever tell a lie?"

"Well, sometimes a white lie."

"What do you mean by a white lie?"

"Do you remember when you came in and I said how glad I was to see you?"

White lies make the world go around. Once Truman was steaming mad because he felt that Soviet Ambassador Nikolai Novikov had insulted Mrs. Truman by declining a social invitation at the last moment. As he ranted that the ambassador should be thrown out of the country, Undersecretary of State Dean Acheson tried to do damage control by calling Bess. According to Margaret Truman's biography of her mother, Acheson "did something very clever. He put words in Bess's mouth. He repeated aloud things she was not saying. 'Above himself—yes. Too big for his britches—I agree with you. Delusions of grandeur.' Dad snatched the phone away from him. 'All right, all right,' he said to Bess. 'When you gang up on me I know I'm licked. Let's forget about it.' "

In political circles, putting words in someone's mouth is generally a very up-and-up practice. Speech writers do it all the time, and people like Bush, who are prone to saying things like "I see this glass not half empty but half full and more," are eternally grateful. (Bush's famous "read my lips" line came from star writer Peggy Noonan, who had to fight to keep Bush's handlers from cutting the reference.) But things can get sticky. When a President's staff gets used to the fact that he rarely utters an original phrase, serving as ad hoc scripters becomes very seductive. For example, after Reagan's first meeting with Mikhail Gorbachev, press secretary Larry Speakes told a thousand journalists that Reagan had said, ''The world rests easier because we're meeting here today.'' In fact, the President, trained not to ramble off the cuff, had said almost nothing when he and Gorbachev emerged from their meeting. Feeling that the Soviet president had used the occasion to knock one-liners ''out of the ballpark at 450 feet,'' Speakes decided to come to Reagan's rescue. And no one complained until Speakes related the incident in his memoir.

Where would the world be without lies that are white—or even distinctly gray? Ron Nessen, who worked for Gerald Ford as press secretary, recalled that ''one time, President Ford wanted to play golf in Florida and we had to dream up some community meeting for him to attend and address. And, of course, everybody knew he was going to go down to play with Tip O'Neill and some others in some pro-am tournament down in Florida, and I just couldn't bring myself to look the press corps in the eye and say, 'He wants to play golf and he's going to Florida to play golf.' ''

On the whole, the truth, rather than being stranger than fiction, is just more boring. When a successful conductor like Leonard Bernstein says, ''My childhood was one of complete poverty,'' his past has some zing to it—even though he grew up with maids and chauffeurs and went to prestigious Boston Latin School and Harvard.

''The idea that the key to Nixon was his early poverty is ridiculous,'' said his cousin, writer Jessamyn West. ''The Nixons had a grocery store, two cars, and sent their son to college. By some they were considered rich.''

Once LBJ took a group of reporters on a tour of his ranch, and when he came to a forlorn shack, his voice cracking, he cited it as his boyhood home. Finally his mother, who was on the tour, chimed in, ''Now, Lyndon, you know we had a nice house over on the other side of the farm.''

When he was President, LBJ told servicemen in Korea, ''My great-great-grandfather died at the Alamo.'' Biographer Doris Kearns questioned him on that fact, and he launched into a tirade. ''God damn it, why must all those journalists be such sticklers for detail? Why, they'd hold you to an accurate description of the first time you ever made love, expecting you to remember the color of the room and the shape of the windows. That's exactly what happened here. The fact is my great-great-grandfather died at the Battle of San Jacinto, not at the Alamo. When I said Alamo, it was just a slip of the tongue. Anyway, the point is that the Battle of San Jacinto was far more important to Texas history than the Alamo."

In fact, his great-great-grandfather died at home in bed. But the truth is such a lackluster bedfellow.

### TRUTH OR CONSEQUENCES

*All right now, Doc, let's come to grips with something. I've got the toughest decision to make that ever hung over my head. I'm in the Marine Corps Reserves. Since the war in Korea started, I've felt this thing closing down around me. Suppose they call me up and we come to the loyalty part: "Are you now or have you ever been a member of the Communist Party?" What do I tell them? If I say no, I perjure myself. If I say yes, and the word gets around, then I'm dead.*
—actor Sterling Hayden to his psychiatrist during the heyday of McCarthyism

When truth has its consequences, silence is a man's best friend. If no one asks a thorny question, there's no need to lie. For instance, when Adam Clayton Powell, Jr., son of a Harlem Baptist minister, went off to Colgate, everyone assumed that the tall hazel-eyed freshman was white. And Powell did little to dispel such assumptions until a routine background check revealed that he was black.

Silence also suited Phil Masi of the Boston Braves. In the first game of the 1948 World Series, a Cleveland Indians pitcher attempted to pick Masi off at second base. But in a cloud of dust— and controversy—Masi was ruled safe. He went on to score the game's only run. As for the questionable play, he would say only that he thought it was close. But before his death, in March 1990, he autographed a child's baseball and wrote, "I was out."

Ronald Reagan didn't need to worry about dodging questions of consequence. He honestly couldn't remember what happened anyway. At the Iran-contra trial of his national security adviser, John Poindexter, Reagan said, "I don't recall," or a similar phrase 150 times in his testimony. At one point he said, "May I simply point out that I had no knowledge then or now that there had been a diversion." In fact, the diversion—the transfer of funds from Iranian arm sales to the contras in Nicaragua—had been documented in detail by the President's own Tower Commission.

Since most of us don't have Reagan's conveniently faulty memory, telling the truth presents a few stickier wickets. Yet there is still one last way around them. As Yogi Berra said, "When you come to a fork in the road, take it."

Poindexter took such a path in 1983, when press secretary Larry Speakes asked him if the United States was about to invade Grenada, a question that had been put to Speakes by a CBS reporter who knew British newspapers were reporting an imminent invasion. Poindexter's comment: "Preposterous."

"I related that exact word to the reporter, 'Preposterous,' " recalled Speakes. "And the next morning, U.S. troops went ashore in Grenada. So I learned. . . . If you ask, 'Are we going to invade Grenada today?' and they say, 'No,' remember, 'What about tomorrow morning?' "

When Alexander Butterfield, an aide to H. R. Haldeman who had installed Nixon's taping system, was called to testify before the Senate committee investigating Watergate, he recognized the fork in the road. "I had made up my mind that as remote as the possibility was that anyone would ask about the tapes, I would be vague if the question were vague. I would be precise if the question were direct and precise," he told Sam Donaldson on *Prime Time Live*.

Butterfield's 1973 appearance was "just one of those pro forma interviews," recalled Republican counsel Fred Thompson. "I'd never heard of Butterfield. No one on the minority staff had ever heard of Butterfield. Someone on the majority staff scheduled him."

The likelihood of anyone's asking Butterfield if Nixon had a taping system was remote. But out of the blue, according to Thompson, "One of our guys . . . on the minority staff said, 'By the way [John] Dean had said something about the President walking to the corner of the office or something and saying something in an almost inaudible tone. Is there any reason to believe there is an electronic eavesdropping device in the Oval Office?' "

Butterfield mulled it over. "Well, that was not a vague question, and I remember distinctly thinking that's fairly direct, that's fairly precise, so I said—I think my first words were 'I'm sorry you asked that question. Yes, there was.' "

Butterfield knew full well that his testimony had the potential to topple a presidency—until Congress learned of the taping system, Watergate was a case of John Dean's word against the President's—but he believed that telling the truth and taking the consequences were his only choice.

Not so Oliver North. He deliberately misled Congress about his dealings on Iran-contra and, when called to explain his perjury in 1986, wrapped himself in the flag. "I want you to know that lying does not come easy to me," he testified. "I want you to know that it doesn't come easy to anybody, but I think we all had to weigh in the balance the difference between lives and lies.

"I had to do that on a number of occasions in both these operations. And it is not an easy thing to do." He was so convinced of the justness of his mission that he said: "I knew it wasn't right not to tell the truth about those things. But I didn't think it was unlawful."

"I lied. And worse that that, I don't have any regrets about it," said Carter's press secretary, Jody Powell, referring to an incident a week before the administration had scheduled a hostage rescue attempt in Lebanon. A reporter had gotten wind of the situation, and Powell not only publicly denied the administration's plans but "went to great lengths to explain why we wouldn't be doing something like that." He acknowledged that he could have told the truth and asked the reporter to hold the story but "frankly didn't think I had the right, if you will, in a moral sense to play with the lives of people on that operation and to add that extra element of risk to their undertaking."

Truth or consequences. It's never an easy decision, and each man or woman has to come to it on the basis of his or her conscience.

Actor Sterling Hayden opted for the truth; he named Communists' names to HUAC and regretted it all his life. Nancy Reagan opted for cover-up. When astrologer Joan Quigley asked the First Lady, "But what will I do if someone asks about sensitive matters?" Nancy didn't miss a beat. "Lie if you have to. If you have to, lie."

Wrote Quigley in her memoir: "Nancy never called again.

After seven years of being constantly in touch, the last word Nancy ever said to me was, 'Lie!' ''

## LIAR'S POKER: JFK AND ADDISON'S DISEASE

1. "A couple of weeks later I got back from the south of France. I saw Dr. Davis and he said to me, 'that young American friend of yours, he hasn't got a year to live.' It was the first time they discovered that Jack had Addison's disease."—Pamela Churchill, a Kennedy family friend in London in 1947. Addison's disease, a failure of the adrenal gland, had commonly been considered fatal.

2. "No one who has the real Addison's disease should run for the presidency, but I do not have it."—JFK to Arthur Schlesinger, July 1959.

3. "The Senator does not now nor has he ever had an ailment described classically as Addison's disease."—RFK, referring to his brother, July 4, 1960.

4. "Your friends on the *New York Post* are going to print the story tomorrow that I have an incurable disease, and this will hurt me badly in the campaign. I think you ought to tell them that it isn't fair, and that I am not using any suppressant drugs, and that I really am wholly healthy and able to take this job." —JFK to prominent liberal Joseph Rauh, 1960.

5. "I have never had Addison's disease."—JFK to *The New York Times*, November 10, 1960.

6. "The clinical diagnosis of Addison's disease" was Dr. John Nichols's verdict on JFK, published in the *Journal of the American Medical Association* on July 10, 1967. Dr. Nichols described the ailment as "formerly fatal" and "an honorable disease and not a disease to be concealed."

7. "What happened was that Addison's disease used to be fatal," explained Sargent Shriver more than a decade after Kennedy's death. "But in the period 1950 to 1960 treatment developed for the disease. If you had put out [a statement] that Jack Kennedy had Addison's disease, everybody would have said, 'He's going to die.' Therefore, you had to explain what the situation was in such a way that was not dishonest but would not arouse a reaction that was dishonest in view of medical advances. So they said yes, he had a disability, but it was treatable. Eunice has

Addison's disease. She and Jack were physiologically alike. So I've lived with it for ten years. Seeing how it's treated and what its effects are. It's like being a diabetic. As long as you have your treatment you are in no more danger than a diabetic is."

CAUGHT WITH THEIR PANTS DOWN: GREAT MOMENTS IN LYING

1. *Gary Powers and the U-2 spy plane.* "The gentleman informed us that he was having difficulty with his oxygen equipment. Now our assumption is that the man blacked out. This is absolutely no—N-O—no deliberate attempt to violate Soviet airspace. There never has been," announced spokesman Lincoln White at the State Department's noon briefing in May 1960.

In fact, the United States had been flying spy missions routinely over the Soviet Union, each one approved by President Eisenhower. So why did the State Department lie when Nikita Khrushchev accused the United States of spying? First of all, the Soviet Union was in the habit of trumping up charges and the United States didn't think there was much to this one. As far as it knew, the Soviets didn't have a rocket capable of downing the U-2 spy plane. Furthermore, the U-2s were equipped with self-destruct buttons, and the pilots were each given poison. The problem was that in order for the system to work, a pilot had to hit the button and take the poison. Instead Gary Powers bailed out over Russia. The United States never dreamed Khrushchev had him—and all the plane's spy equipment—in hand.

"I was awakened early in the morning, May 1," Khrushchev later told American businessman Armand Hammer. ". . . I personally gave the orders to shoot it down. This was done with our rockets. I also laid a trap by withholding the announcement to see what the U.S. authorities would say. When they lied, I exposed them. We caught them as you would a thief with a hand in your pocket."

2. *The trapping of Alger Hiss.* For those hot on the trail of Communist infiltrators, Alger Hiss was a prize. A debonair Harvard Law School graduate, a protégé of Justice Oliver Wendell Holmes, and a former State Department official, Hiss was the epitome of the eastern establishment elite—until a confessed spy named Whittaker Chambers claimed Hiss had been involved with him in a Communist spy ring in the 1930s. Hiss vehemently

denied he had turned over classified papers in 1938, and he denied having seen Chambers after 1937, but the House Committee on Un-American Activities, led by an unknown congressman from California, Richard Nixon, pursued Hiss relentlessly.

Much of what Chambers testified to regarding Hiss could have been gathered from reading newspapers or magazines. The committee was wary until Chambers was asked if Hiss had any hobbies. "Yes, he did," Chambers said. "They [Alger and Priscilla Hiss] both had the same hobby—amateur ornithologists, bird observers. They used to get up early in the morning and go to Glen Echo, out on the canal, to observe birds. I recall once they saw, to their great excitement, a prothonotary warbler." That was all the committee needed.

MR. NIXON:   What hobby, if any, do you have, Mr. Hiss?
MR. HISS:   Tennis and amateur ornithology.
MR. NIXON:   Is your wife interested in ornithology?
MR. HISS:   I also like to swim and also like to sail. My wife is interested in ornithology, as I am, through my interest. Maybe I am using too big a word to say ornithologist because I am pretty amateur, but I have been interested in it since I was in Boston. I think anybody who knows me would know that.
MR. MCDOWELL:   Did you ever see a prothonotary warbler?
MR. HISS:   I have right here on the Potomac. Do you know that place? . . . They come back and nest in those swamps. Beautiful yellow head, a gorgeous bird.

A hush fell over the committee chamber. The committee was now convinced that Hiss was lying, that he knew Chambers far better than he was letting on. Eventually a jury agreed, and Hiss served forty-four months in jail for perjury. Had the statute of limitations on spying not run out, he would have been sentenced for that, too.

3. *The arrogance of Richard Nixon.* "Tell the truth. That is the thing I have told everybody around here—tell the truth! . . . That Hiss would be free today if he hadn't lied. If he had said, 'Yes I knew Chambers and as a young man I was involved with some Communist activities but I broke it off a number of years ago.'

And Chambers would have dropped it. If you are going to lie, you go to jail for the lie rather than the crime. So believe me, don't ever lie." So Richard Nixon advised the White House counsel, John Dean, on April 16, 1973. Unfortunately for Nixon, Dean took his advice.

Dean was assigned to head an in-house investigation of Watergate, but when he balked at participating in a cover-up, he was fired. Convinced there was "a cancer on the Presidency," he decided to tell all when testifying before congress.

"I believe the biggest mistake that Richard Nixon ever made was firing John Dean," said Sam Dash, chief counsel of the Senate Watergate Committee. "John Dean was a loyalist. If he had not fired John Dean and he had kept him on—and I'm using the words of the White House—on the reservation—that was the term, you were either on the reservation or you were off the reservation—if he had kept him on the reservation and stroked him—which is another term they used—John Dean would have never broken. He would have stayed behind Nixon all the way. . . ."

4. *The lies of Vietnam.* "Lyndon Johnson really did not tell very many, if any, lies [about] Vietnam," said LBJ's press secretary, George Reedy long after the war. "What he did was to accept the very optimistic assumptions, and after a while the whole federal government stopped sending him the pessimistic assumptions."

Jane Fonda had tried to publicize that situation. She went to Hanoi in 1972 and read Communists propaganda scripts designed to reach U.S. servicemen via Radio Hanoi: "This is Jane Fonda in Hanoi. . . . All of you in your heart of hearts know the lies. You know the cheating on the body counts, the falsified battle reports, the number of planes that are shot down and what your targets really are."

In 1981 Mike Wallace brought up the subject with General William Westmoreland when he interviewed him for a *CBS Reports* documentary.

WALLACE:   Isn't it a possibility that the real reason for suddenly deciding in the summer of 1967 to remove an entire category of the enemy from the order of battle—

a category that had been in the order of battle since 1961—was based on political considerations?

WESTMORELAND:   No, decidedly not. That—

WALLACE:   Didn't you make this clear in your August twentieth cable?

WESTMORELAND:   No, no. Yeah. No.

WALLACE:   I have a copy of the August twentieth cable—

WESTMORELAND:   Well, sure. Okay, okay. All right, all right.

The cable said: WE HAVE BEEN PROJECTING AN IMAGE OF SUCCESS OVER THE RECENT MONTHS. THE SELF-DEFENSE MILITIA MUST BE REMOVED OR THE NEWSMEN WILL IMMEDIATELY SEIZE ON THAT POINT THAT THE ENEMY FORCE HAS INCREASED. Westmoreland sued CBS for libel and lost.

## SMOKE AND MIRRORS

*You can fool all the people all the time if the advertising is right and the budget is big enough.*
—movie producer Joseph E. Levine

If you don't have access to a big budget, smoke and mirrors will do quite nicely. Magicians use them. So do politicians. It's easy. All you do is stir up a lot of hot air and confusion, make people look in the wrong direction, and presto, they never notice facts of the matter. For example, in 1968 before the Democratic National Convention in Chicago, the Yippies vowed to get the city high by dumping LSD in the water supply. The threat was pure theater, and even the city knew it because Commissioner Jardine had calculated that five tons of LSD or nine billion tabs would be necessary to contaminate the water. But the possibility struck such a chord that policemen were sent to guard Chicago pumping and filtration stations just the same.

Senator Joe McCarthy got his start pulling one of history's most notorious rabbits out of a hat. In Wheeling, West Virginia, on February 9, 1950, he blustered that "While I cannot take the time to name all of the men in the State Department who have been named as members of the Communist party and members of a spy ring, I have here in my hand a list of two hundred five that were known to the Secretary of State as being members of the Communist party and who nevertheless are still working and shaping the policy of the State Department." He didn't, in fact, have any such thing in his hand, but that didn't matter much. He gave voice to America's deepest fears; his accusations *felt* true.

So did Phyllis Schlafly's when she protested the Equal Rights Amendment by insisting it would "authorize homosexual marriages. In regard to the co-ed restrooms, there's no way you can tell me it won't cause that."

As Richard Nixon once told an aide, "People react to fear, not to love. They don't teach that in Sunday school, but it's true." Fear fueled his first campaign for Congress. It was 1946, and he was running against a well-liked liberal, Jerry Voorhis. "Just before the election," Voorhis recalled in 1977, "a good many people came and told me, do you know about the telephone calls that are being made and I said I didn't. Well, they said, I was called on the phone by an unidentified person who simply said that, 'Do you know that Jerry Voorhis is a communist and you should vote for Mr. Nixon because of that fact.' "

"Of course I knew Jerry Voorhis wasn't a communist," Nixon later told a Voorhis aide. "But I had to win. That's the thing you don't understand. That's the important thing."

He applied the same tactics in running for the Senate in 1950 against an actress turned politician, Helen Gahagan Douglas. She called him Tricky Dick. He called her "pink right down to her underwear" and printed anti-Douglas literature on pink sheets. In 1979, looking back on her defeat, she commented, "The essence of that kind of campaign is this. To avoid the issues you work up bogus issues trying to play on the fears of the people. Because if you talk about the real issues, you may lose votes. It's as simple as that."

Smoke and mirrors. The shortcut to success.

# 18
# The Heck with It: Oaths of Office and Other Locations

*Goddamnit! I don't curse. I just use some words as adjectives.*
—Dwight D. Eisenhower

The heck with trying to be a Puritan. How lackluster life would be if the men and women who raise their hands and solemnly swear on Bibles limited their oaths to the ones that they must say to take office. Swearing—while seldom advised by those who practice it—is undeniably colorful. If you're out campaigning and you say, "By darn, we're going to win it"— as Reagan did when stumping for Bush in 1988—the white-haired ladies may love you, but your sentiment lacks a certain *je ne sais quoi.*

On the other hand, if you find out that North Korea has invaded South Korea, and you declare as President Truman did, "We've got to stop the sons-of-bitches no matter what," your words have a decidedly macho resolve. Which is not to doubt Reagan's Rambo quotient. When he got wind of death threats emanating from Libya's Muammar al-Quaddafi, he told his Vice President: "Hey, by the way, George! I don't know how you feel about it. But I'm ready to call Quaddafi and tell him I'll meet him over on the Mall and we'll settle this thing." What we're talking about here isn't intent. It's phrasing. For example, if you're LBJ and are trying to convince the governor of Alabama, George Wallace, that he has the power to stop the civil rights protests in Selma, you might begin with "You know, George, you can turn those off in a minute. You go out there in front of those television cameras right now, and you announce you've decided to desegregate every school in Alabama." And if he demurs by saying, "Oh, Mr. President, I can't do that, you know. The schools have got school boards, they're locally run. I haven't got the political power to do that." Then *"Don't you shit me, George Wallace"*—the re-

Some people don't resort to four-letter words to get certain feelings across. Vice President Nelson Rockefeller, heckled at the Binghamton, New York, airport in 1976, managed to express his view of the demonstrators without uttering a single syllable.

sponse LBJ chose—leaves no room for argument. Indeed, Wallace said afterward, "If I hadn't left when I did, he'd had me coming out for civil rights."

On occasion an undeleted expletive has a power no Sunday school-approved words can rival. Abbie Hoffman was arrested at the 1968 Democratic Convention in Chicago for writing "FUCK" on his forehead. And he knew that he was being incendiary when he got out his writing implement. After all, the Yippie (Youth International Party) call to Chicago prescribed dancing in the streets, love in the parks, "singing, laughing, printing newspapers, groping and making a mock convention and celebrating the birth of FREE AMERICA in our own time." This was not a time for tried and true images like wearing your heart on your sleeve. As Hoffman's fellow Yippie Jerry Rubin said, "I support everything which puts people in motion, which creates disruption and controversy, which creates chaos and rebirth . . . people who burn draft cards . . . burn dollar bills . . . say FUCK on television. . . ." An "egads" clearly wouldn't do the trick.

Partly because of the accursed power of forbidden words, politicians generally chastise those who don't edit their language. For example, Harry Truman gave 'em hell—not to mention damn and SOB—so liberally that Nixon campaigned in 1952 vowing to clean up the executive vocabulary. (Of course, Harry's feeling was "I never gave them hell. I tell the truth and they think it's hell.") But when Nixon was able to partake of the privacy of the Oval Office himself, he worried little about blasphemy. Deleted expletives peppered the Watergate tapes, making this earlier Nixon statement look like a speech writer's fiction: "I see mothers holding their babies up . . ." Nixon said as Vice President, "and it makes you realize that whoever is President is going to be a man that all the children of America look up to or look down to and I can only say that I'm proud that President Eisenhower restored dignity and decency and, frankly, *good language* to the conduct of the Presidency of the United States."

Mothers holding up their babies tends to remind people that they don't want little children growing up and saying things like this from three-year-old Caroline Kennedy: "What did that goddamn lady do to make Daddy so mad?" Her father, the President-elect, had just yelled, "Shut this goddamned woman up before she opens her mouth again."

Over the years women have been around enough cussing and hollering to do a pretty good job themselves. When a man accused Congresswoman Bella Abzug of calling him a four-letter word, she replied, "Now isn't that ridiculous? A-S-S is only three letters." And Rose Mary Woods, Nixon's secretary, didn't mince words in telling Alexander Butterfield what she thought of him. "You dirty bastard," she said after Butterfield had revealed the existence of a White House taping system to the Senate Watergate Committee. "You have contributed to the downfall of the greatest President this country ever had."

When Patty Hearst and her SLA kidnappers were robbing the

Hibernia Bank in San Francisco, a fatigue-clad Hearst aimed her machine gun at the bank customers and told them to "get down or I'll blow your motherfucking heads off." That's the kind of statement that convinces innocent bystanders this is not the moment to ask for Patty's autograph.

But generally "Who does that dame think she is?"—Nancy Reagan's comment on Raisa Gorbachev—is about as strong as women's language gets—at least on the record. Men can call each other SOBs right and left, but if a woman even waltzes near the B word, she ends up with a huge stir on her hands. After George Bush's debate in 1984 with Geraldine Ferraro, Barbara Bush called his vice presidential opponent a "four-million-dollar—I can't say it, but it rhymes with rich." She got so much press that she apologized and announced "the poet laureate has retired."

A word about being a bitch: One sure route to being one is to divorce your husband. Jackie Kennedy's father, Jack Bouvier, said of his former wife, "My whole life has been ruined by that bitch," a statement that ignored his alcohol problem (he was too drunk to give Jackie away at her wedding) and his penchant for womanizing. No matter how badly men behave, many a woman ends up in the bitch category faster than she can blink a mascara-coated eyelash. Marlo Thomas has said, "A man has to be Joe McCarthy to be called ruthless. All a woman has to do is put you on hold." Madonna explained it this way: "I'm tough, ambitious, and know exactly what I want. If that makes me a bitch, okay." Leona Helmsley, jailed queen of the Helmsley hotel outfit, rationalized: "I'm a woman in business and I'm an executive. If I were a man, they would say you're a fantastic executive. But I'm a woman, so they label me a bitch."

If "they" who are doing the labeling are of the male sex, women should take heart. Men swear at each other with such regularity that nearly everyone acquires a less than favorable adjective if he hangs around long enough. In politics alone the chain of obscenities is more complicated than DNA.

Consider this short circuit of SOB name-calling: When General Douglas MacArthur made an unauthorized offer to end the Korean conflict, Harry Truman vowed, "I'll show that son of a bitch who's boss. Who does he think he is—God?" He fired MacArthur "because he wouldn't respect the authority of the President. That's the answer to that. I didn't fire him because he was a dumb son-of-a-bitch, although he was, but that's not against the law for generals. If it was, half to three-quarters of them would be in jail."

Truman's action caused Senator Joe McCarthy to declare, "The son-of-a-bitch should be impeached." McCarthy himself would be called "a real son-of-a-bitch" by Senator John Bricker, who added that "sometimes it's useful to have sons-of-bitches around to do the dirty work." And so it goes, on and on, a ring of compliments of an uncertain nature until finally someone like JFK, after winning the presidency, is forced to make peace with someone like Truman, who opposed his candidacy. "I guess he will apologize for calling me an SOB," said JFK, "and I will apologize for being one."

To take this chain just one step further, Truman sympathized with the fact that in his view, everybody thought JFK's brother Robert was a son-of-a-bitch, saying, "I understand that because everybody thinks I'm a son-of-a-bitch."

The rule of thumb, it seems, is that it takes one to know one. Unless, of course, you're General George Patton, who averred: "My private opinion is that practically everybody but myself is a pusillanimous son-of-a-bitch."

A few fine points on SOB etiquette. There are certain people who don't qualify for the term, as Harry Truman knew. He said he "would never call Nixon a son-of-a-bitch because he claims to be a self-made man." And there are ways of getting your feelings across—and being perfectly proper at the same time. When Robert Kennedy was a senator, he commented, "President Johnson and I are very courteous and correct in our correspondence these days. I address my letters to him at the White House and he writes to me at the Senate Office Building. Sometimes he only uses the initials."

And finally, you may be able to rank your place in history by your SOB usage. Consider this exchange between JFK and a friend and neighbor on Cape Cod. "How do you think I handle the press?" Kennedy asked.

"Gee, I think you handle it like no other President, probably since FDR."

"Do you think I do better than FDR?"

"Yes, you haven't called anybody a son-of-a-bitch in *public* yet."

Well, the heck with it. Propriety may count for something after all.

Sometimes nothing sums up the situation like a certain four-letter word, as evidenced by the following situations:

*CASE NO. 1. MARITAL PROBLEMS.* "Guess what's happened?" asked Steve Smith, husband of Jean Kennedy Smith. He had summoned JFK's former press secretary, Pierre Salinger, for an urgent meeting. The problem, Smith explained, was marital: "Jackie's going to marry Onassis." Jean was paving the way for Jackie to call Rose Kennedy that evening, and Steve was trying to "figure out some kind of a statement for the family to put out." He asked Salinger, "Have you got any idea of what you want to say?"

Salinger was silent. He lit a cigar. Smith answered his own question. "How about," he suggested, " 'Oh shit!' "

*CASE NO. 2. A SPY RING UNRAVELS.* When John Walker's spy ring, which included his son, his brother, and his best friend, Jerry Whitworth, unraveled, the FBI held a prosecution meeting. Afterward young Navy Lieutenant James Alsup came up to John L. Martin, chief of the Internal Security Section, and said, "Sir, I think something bad is happening. I think in Washington they're covering up or not facing the facts. I'm not an expert. But I know something about crypto and communications. I'll tell you, if we knew one tenth as much about Soviet crypto and communications as Whitworth could have told them about ours, then the Soviets wouldn't have any secrets from us. I think there's been a catastrophe, and we're not doing nearly enough about it."

"I'm not sure I understand. Could you explain?" responded Martin.

"Do you have an hour?"

"I have all night if necessary."

Alsup went over Whitworth's postings and described the type of information he had access to and the types of secrets he might have stolen. When he finished, Martin said, "You mean the Soviets may have built duplicates of our machines and with the keys [codes] read all the traffic, that they might have learned enough to read the traffic without keys?"

"Yes, sir."

"Then they could still be reading it?"

"That's possible, sir."

"Holy shit!"

*CASE NO. 3. THE BUNGLED BREAK-IN.* "There's flashlights on the eighth floor." It was 2:00 A.M. at Washington's Watergate Hotel, and G. Gordon Liddy was on the walkie-talkie. One group of his men was about to place a bug in the Democratic national headquarters; another group was stationed at an observation post. "Now they're on the seventh floor," the men at the observation post radioed Liddy. The flashlights, everyone assumed, signaled a guard check that should not prove to be any difficulty. Liddy's men would not be spotted from a hall patrol.

"Hey, any of our guys wearin' hippie clothes?"

"One to three. Negative. All our people are in business suits. Why?" Liddy responded.

"They're on the sixth floor now. Four or five guys. One's got a cowboy hat. One's got on a sweat shirt. It looks like . . . *guns*! They've got guns. It's trouble!"

"Shit!" said Liddy. The events that would bring down the Nixon presidency had been set in motion.

*CASE NO. 4. FINDING OLLIE'S ACHILLES' HEEL.* Oliver North had shredded whatever he could in anticipation of just such a moment. William Reynolds and John Richardson were sent by Attorney General Edwin Meese III to look through North's files involving arms sales to Iran in return for the release of hostages. Neither suspected a contra link.

Reynolds said: "I was rather bored. I thought it was the third draft of a document I had seen before. I started turning the pages, and they looked the same. I damn near didn't bother to turn to the next page." When he did, he let out a "Holy Jesus." He had found the Iran-contra connection, as he explained over lunch with Attorney General Meese. "We found a lot of documents," said Reynolds. "And this one you won't believe. There's a document that says they would take twelve million dollars from the arms sales to Iran and give the money to the contras."

Meese: "Oh, shit."

*CASE NO. 5. TROUBLE IN LIZ TAYLOR'S SUITE.* "Good evening, the Plaza Hotel," the operator answered. Debbie Reynolds explained who she was and asked for Elizabeth Taylor's suite, where she suspected her husband, Eddie Fisher, was snuggling up. After a long wait the operator informed her that there was no answer in Miss Taylor's suite.

Reynolds called back, putting on her best secretarial voice.

"Long distance calling for Mr. Eddie Fisher."

"Who shall I say is calling?" the operator asked.

"Mr. Dean Martin calling from Beverly Hills."

"One moment, please."

Indeed, a moment later Fisher picked up the phone. "Well, hiya, Dean, whatcha doin' calling me at this time of night?"

"It's not Dean, Eddie, it's Debbie."

"Oh, shit. . . ."

That was the end of a marriage.

# 19
# Your Tax Dollars at Work

<small>GREAT MOMENTS IN AMERICAN JUSTICE</small>

*It was not my class of people. There was not a producer, a press*
*agent, a director, an actor.*
—Zsa Zsa Gabor on the jury that convicted her of slapping a
Los Angeles cop who had pulled over her Rolls-Royce
Corniche because it had expired tags

There's a reason those marble statues—the
nymphlike figures who hold the scales of justice in courthouses—
wear blindfolds. Who would really want to watch the American
justice system in full swing day in and day out?

Imagine having to witness the 1989 trial of an aged starlet
who, despite her willingness to do battle with the courts ("I have
enough clothes [even] if this lasts a year"), was convicted and
sentenced to more than 120 hours of community service at a
shelter for homeless women. "Russia can't be worse than this,"
Zsa Zsa announced after hearing the verdict. Among those who
might have given that statement minor credence was Theresa
Carter, a mother of six whom Gabor counseled.

"I wanted someone to say, 'Come on, I'm going to sponsor
you and your kids and you go to work or to school,' or something
like that," said Carter. "She was telling me about I had to get my
hair done because I wear it kind of strange sometime. And was
telling me about my tooth and in order for me to get a job I had
to really correct that. And she said a little makeup won't hurt."

In 1962 singer Ray Charles had commissioned a West Coast
headquarters for his band. Even though he was blind and the
building was unfinished, he insisted on checking its progress. The
police weren't too pleased to discover two black men nosing
around a construction site. Charles "told 'em it was my building,"
but that didn't put the matter to rest. "They wanted to know how
a cat like me had enough bread to own a building" and were far
from satisfied with what they thought was "a wise-ass" answer:

When Yippie Jerry Rubin, imprisoned during the Chicago Seven trial, had to have his long locks shorn, Abbie Hoffman (*right*) organized a hair-raising campaign. Here he and friends take a publicity short cut.

"I work for a living, every day of the week." So Charles proceeded straight to headquarters. "When I walked in the station, all the police who were milling around screamed out. 'Hey, that's Ray! Ray Charles! That's Ray Charles!' But it took the little desk sergeant an hour or so to be convinced. In fact he even asked me for my driver's license. Feature that."

Or feature this. In 1965 the Reverend Ralph Abernathy, Martin Luther King, Jr.'s right-hand man, was leading a voter registration drive. All the rest of his group had failed to pass the four-page literacy test. Abernathy theorized it was because they'd failed to fill in all the blanks—even when the question was irrelevant. So he wrote wherever he could, "This does not apply to me."

Then he went up to the voting inspector. "She took my

examination and thumbed through it, expecting to be able to say, 'You didn't fill in all the blanks,' but as she flipped from page to page she found all the questions answered. Her eyes glazed over. And it was in that moment that I understood what was going on. She didn't know the answers to the questions herself!"

The inspector begrudgingly admitted he'd passed the test but then added a new obstacle—an oral question. "Recite the Thirteenth Amendment," she ordered. Abernathy didn't know it word for word but didn't think she did either. He proceeded to recite the Pledge of Allegiance. He got to vote.

Abbie Hoffman got to smoke. He "was responsible for me making the first marijuana motion I have made in any court," recalled Chicago Seven lawyer William Kunstler. It all began very innocently when Hoffman and Kunstler opened a package of hair. (Codefendant Jerry Rubin had had all his hair shaved off in jail, and the Yippies had sent out a circular requesting hair for Jerry and for the judge, who was bald. Packages of hair—from all parts of the body—flooded the courtroom.) One particular package held marijuana. Abbie said, "Move the judge to get this grass." And Kunstler did. The judge told him, "You're a very enterprising attorney, I'm sure you can dispose of it."

"Your Honor," Kunstler replied, "I can give you my solemn assurance it will be burnt tonight."

Many a colorful character has been in a courtroom. But the award for turning the legal system into theater surely has to go to Abbie Hoffman, as this excerpt of his Chicago Seven trial illustrates:

MR. WEINGLASS: Will you please identify yourself for the record?

THE WITNESS: My name is Abbie. I am an orphan of America.

MR. SCHULTZ: Your honor, may the record show it is the defendant, Hoffman. . . .

MR. WEINGLASS: Where do you reside?

THE WITNESS: I live in the Woodstock Nation.

MR. WEINGLASS: Will you tell the court and jury where it is.

THE WITNESS: Yes, it is a nation of alienated young people. We carry it around with us as a state of mind in the same way as the Sioux Indians carried the Sioux Nation around with them. It is a nation dedicated to cooperation versus competition, to the idea that people should have better means of exchange than property or money, there should be some other basis for human interaction. . . .

THE COURT:   No, we want the place of residence, if he has one, place of doing business, if you have a business. Nothing about philosophy or Indians, sir. Just where you live, if you have a place to live. Now you said Woodstock. In what state is Woodstock?

THE WITNESS:   It is in a state of mind, in the mind of myself and my brothers and sisters. It is a conspiracy. Presently the nation is held captive in the penitentiaries of the institutions of a decaying system.

MR. WEINGLASS:   Can you tell the Court and jury your present age?

THE WITNESS:   My age is 33, I am a child of the sixties.

MR. WEINGLASS:   When were you born?

THE WITNESS:   Psychologically, 1960.

MR. SCHULTZ:   Objection, if the court please, I move to strike the answer.

MR. WEINGLASS:   What is the actual date of your birth?

THE WITNESS:   November 30, 1936.

MR. WEINGLASS:   Between the date of your birth November 30, 1936, and May 1, 1960, what if anything occurred in your life?

THE WITNESS:   Nothing. I believe it is called an American education.

FILLING OUT THE PRISON FORMS

If there's a place where bureaucratic conformity and individuality collide, it's prison. Among the inmates whose stories didn't fit neatly on any dotted line are these five:

1. *"You Watergate?"* "Whatcha name?" asked the man filling out the form for incoming prisoners of G. Gordon Liddy. His succeeding questions included: "Where ya live onna street?" (address); "Whatcha do onna street?" (occupation); "Whatcha make onna street?" (income). Recalled Liddy: ". . . the form didn't provide for anything but an hourly wage. So I gave him what I

charged when I last practiced law—a hundred dollars an hour—and he didn't believe me. . . . When I told him I had a doctorate in law he couldn't handle that either. The form was designed to record only years of schooling, so I added it up for him and answered 'twenty.' . . . Finally he . . . screwed up his features and asked: 'You Watergate?' "

2. *A rebel with a cause.* "Occupation?" the woman at San Mateo Prison asked Patty Hearst, who couldn't think of an appropriate response. Before her kidnapping by the Symbionese Liberation Army, she'd been a college student in Berkeley, California.

"Occupation?" the attendant repeated. "You *have* to give an occupation."

"Urban guerrilla," Hearst answered.

3. *By God.* In 1971, when Charles Manson was booked at Terminal Island Prison for the Sharon Tate murders, he was no stranger to prison. He'd been in and out of prisons and reformatories his whole life. Previously he'd been released from Terminal Island and pleaded with the officer, "You know what, man, I don't want to leave! I don't have a home out there! Why don't you take me back inside?" After the Tate murders, he signed in as "Manson, Charles M., a.k.a. Jesus Christ, God."

4. *Not crazy about prison.* "So they put me in this same nut factory again and I can't get out for thirty days," said New York Mafia boss Joey Gallo, who was imprisoned on assault and coercion charges in the 1950s. "I get shown something with a lot of marks. 'What's it look like?' they say. 'It looks like somebody threw ink on it,' I tell them. '*What?* It looks like something?' So they say, 'Draw a house.' 'Draw a tree.' So I do what they tell me. Then they say, 'Would you like to live in a house like this?' 'Is this tree alive?' 'How old is it?' Jesus. If I could answer questions like that, I *would* be crazy."

5. *Psyched out.* When drug aficionado Dr. Timothy Leary was sentenced to ten years in prison on drug possession charges—he'd been caught with a small amount of marijuana—he was given a battery of psychological tests. "It seems we have a little problem here, Doc. The classification program here is partly based on psychological tests that you developed," the official in charge told him.

"That will teach me to mind my own business," Leary replied. He filled out the forms so as to "appear normal, non-impulsive, docile, conforming. My vocational tests revealed aptitudes in forestry and farming together with hopeless incompetence in clerical tasks. I was angling for a transfer to a minimum-security prison where escape would be possible." He got the transfer—and did escape.

GOVERNMENT IN ACTION

*That's fine, Don.*
—Ronald Reagan to Treasury Secretary Donald Regan after casually flipping through a proposed budget as thick as a Los Angeles telephone book

If budgets are the next best thing to Sominex, you can understand why Reagan, who already had a reputation for dozing off at meetings, wouldn't be eager to sit down and read several hundred pages or so. Government, up close, can be a bit of a yawn. At one meeting during his presidency George Bush resorted to passing a note saying, "Throw a spitball at the general and wake him up." Most people are interested in the power and the perks, not in all that nitty-gritty stuff—stuff like, say, the fine points of the Constitution.

"To be very frank with you, that day when I mentioned the Twenty-fifth Amendment I could see eyes glazing over in some parts of the Cabinet," recalled White House counsel Fred Fielding after Ronald Reagan had been shot. "They didn't even know about the Twenty-fifth Amendment." For those who are in the same boat, it authorizes an emergency transfer of power if a President is temporarily disabled. Undergoing surgery for a gunshot wound was clearly in that category. "The Twenty-fifth Amendment," said Reagan's physician, Dr. Daniel Ruge, "should have been invoked, no doubt about it. . . . This was not a cold or diarrhea."

Secretary of State Alexander Haig knew that: "Constitutionally, gentlemen, you have the President, the Vice President, and the secretary of state in that order. . . . As of now, I am in control here, in the White House, pending return of the Vice President, and in close touch with him. If something came up, I would check with him, of course."

After giving this statement to reporters, Haig returned to the

Situation Room, where Secretary of Defense Caspar Weinberger kidded him about the statement. "You'd better read your Constitution, buddy," Haig barked back and, turning to Fred Fielding, said, "Isn't that right, Fred?"

"No, Al, it isn't."

The Constitution mentions only the President and the Vice President. In terms of succession, the Speaker of the House comes next by law.

Reading the Constitution? Who would want to spend time doing that when there are so many more interesting things to do? Ronald Reagan admitted to watching *The Sound of Music* on television rather than reading his briefing books for the economic summit at Williamsburg in 1983.

When Dan Quayle was a senator, his New York colleague Daniel Patrick Moynihan had to compete with a golf game on TV when he stopped by on a Saturday to give Quayle a briefing.

"Have a brew," offered Quayle, and then, as they talked, punctuated his comments with "Oh, look at that." Moynihan recalled, "At one point, he said, 'Why don't we just wait for a station break?'"

There are no station breaks during a Senate filibuster, but Hubert Humphrey and seventeen fellow senators decided to take one anyway. While the southern Democrats speechified on April 17, 1964, hoping to prevent a vote on LBJ's Civil Rights Act, Humphrey's crowd went out to the ball park. The Washington Senators—the team, not the elected officials—were playing the California Angels. Lyndon Johnson threw out the first ball, and all was well until the end of the third inning when a call came over the loudspeaker: "Attention, please! All senators must report back to the Senate for a quorum." Aware that the ranks had thinned, the conservatives were calling for a quorum, hoping to find too few senators to do business. However, Humphrey and his pro-civil rights colleagues jumped into waiting limousines and made the one-mile trek back to the Senate in time.

The filibuster in question—the longest in Senate history—ran 534 hours, 1 minute, and 51 seconds. Getting key senators to agree to end it took all the political savvy that was in town. "I would get Everett Dirksen's agreement in the evening over bourbon," recalled recalled Deputy Attorney General Nicholas Katzenbach, "but by the next morning he had forgotten it. I almost ruined my liver in the process." Senator Hubert Humphrey said, "I courted Dirksen almost as persistently as I did Muriel."

Voting to end the filibuster required a two-thirds majority—and every senator, able-bodied or otherwise. Moments before the vote, Clair Engle of California, weak with terminal cancer, was wheeled into the Senate chamber. When his name was called, he didn't have the strength to say a word but raised his hand and feebly pointed to his eye—three times. At last the Senate clerk realized he was voting "aye." The filibuster was curtailed—with four votes to spare.

The House of Representatives has no provision for filibustering, so members of that governing body have had to take other creative routes to get attention. As a congresswoman, Barbara Boxer of California, tired of the same old song and dance she was getting when she proposed allowing women equal time in the men's gym, resorted to a song. She stood up at a House leadership meeting and, to the tune of "Has Anybody Seen My Gal?," sang: "We're not slim, we're not trim/Can't you make it her or him/ Can't everybody use your gym?" It worked, but she added, "The women's lockers are still two floors below, and we have to go through a garage to get to them. Essentially, I can't work out if the House is in session, because it would take me at least twenty minutes to get back to the lockers and get dressed. . . ."

The gym is not entirely a symbolic issue. The House has, according to Congresswoman Pat Schroeder, a "locker-room male ethos." She added, "It's a very physical place, and your male friends show their approval by punching you in the arm. Many nights I go home black and blue."

Were she invited to a pickup game of basketball, she'd find less of a difference between the locker-room ethos of the playing arena and the legislative one. As far as basketball goes, "No politician feels he can't score from any given point on the court once he has his hands on the ball. There is virtually no passing," according to North Dakota Representative Byron Dorgan. "If there was an election for most valuable player, everyone would get one vote," said Congressman Michael Oxley of Ohio.

The games members of congress play on the legislative floor generally have been codified into decades of tradition. However, every now and then someone invents a new sport. For example,

Harlem's Adam Clayton Powell, Jr., excelled at what might best be called legislative chess. The mere presence of the second black congressman seated since Reconstruction provoked the ire of John Rankin of Mississippi, who termed Powell's election a disgrace and vowed he'd never sit near him. This only raised Powell's bad boy instincts. Whenever the southerner entered the chamber, Powell would sidle right up, surprising Rankin like a knight emerging from behind two pawns. The press reported that Powell forced Rankin to change seats five times in one day.

Powell also mastered the art of delivering checkmates. He slapped an amendment onto any bill he could that denied federal funds to segregated facilities, thus causing the downfall of many bills to fund education or housing. "Whenever a person keeps prodding, whenever a person keeps them squirming, whenever a person is an irritant, it serves a purpose," said Powell. "It may not in the contemporary history look so good, but as times roll on, future historians will say he served a purpose."

Though LBJ might have agreed with Powell's goals, he believed in a totally different approach to the field of play: He intended to define it by sheer force of personality. "The telephone," said aide Jack Valenti, "was his Excalibur." Once he called a senator at five in the morning and said, "Hi, what are you doing?" The reply: "Oh, nothing, Mr. President, just lying here, hoping you'd call." If the person he wanted wasn't in, "he'd talk to the wife and if the wife wasn't home, he'd talk to the children and tell them to tell their daddy to support the President," said speech writer Richard Goodwin.

Johnson was a master at the art of negotiation. Jack Valenti, who was assigned "to handle" Republican leader Everett Dirksen, recalled how Dirksen would make an appointment to have a drink with the President. Then he'd "rise in the Senate at about three o'clock in the afternoon and accuse Johnson of every crime that the most depraved mind could be capable of committing and then at six o'clock, he'd show up and . . . the President would say, 'Everett, I wouldn't talk about a cur dog the way you did me in the Senate.' . . . And they would laugh and then they would recount some old, long-fought battles. And then finally the President would say, 'Now Everett, I've got to have three Republican votes and you know who they are.' . . . And Dirksen would say,

'Well, Mr. President, I happen to have here some names of likely nominees to the Federal Power Commission and the Federal Communications Commission and a few other commissions.' "

Government in action. It's not what they teach you in Political Science 101, and it's probably just as well. "When we got into office, the thing that surprised us most," said JFK, "was that things were as bad as we'd been saying they were." Why lose sleep over a system that's tottered on for more than two hundred years? That's the job of those we elect.

# 20
# School Days: Learning the ABCs of Life

*Filming* The Conspirator *was a peculiar experience. In between playing passionate love scenes with a man old enough to be my father, I had to fit in three hours of lessons before three in the afternoon, otherwise production would be closed down for the day. The entire film was wired to my ABCs. I nearly went crazy. Some afternoons my teacher would walk out on the set, grab me out of Robert Taylor's arms, and say, "Sorry, Elizabeth hasn't finished her schoolwork." And then she'd lug me off to the little schoolroom created especially for me and we'd start on social studies or geometry. Talk about humiliating.*
—Elizabeth Taylor

From the time we are old enough to carry a lunch box off to the school bus we are enrolled in the process of learning both our three Rs and the ABCs of life. Sometimes the twain never meet inside a classroom, and people like Elizabeth Taylor are stuck reading geometry books, and wondering what this has to do with plotting the course of their lives. As singer Billy Joel said, declining to attend summer school after twelfth grade—even though it meant not getting his diploma—"I'm not going to Columbia University. I'm going to Columbia Records." What's school got to do with it? Sometimes very little. "I was never really *in* school," said Cher. "I was always thinking about when I was grown up and famous and where I'd want to live or where I'd want to go, or what dresses I'd wear when I got there."

To judge by her wardrobe today, her time was pretty well spent. Elizabeth Taylor's was, too. The playing of passionate love scenes, for example, proved so compelling Liz went on to earn a veritable graduate degree in romance, garnering the title of Mrs. eight times. "Lemme tell ya," husband number three, Mike Todd, said. "Any minute this little dame spends out of bed is wasted,

Eleven-year-old Elizabeth Taylor, schooled in Hollywood, wasn't worried about starring in the classroom.

totally wasted." Clearly Liz was a woman not meant for social studies in the usual sense of the word.

Not that romantic research can't take place in the classroom. "She sat behind me in the sixth, seventh, and high school grades, and I thought she was the most beautiful and sweetest person on earth," said Harry Truman of Bess.

"Mrs. Livingston thought I was wonderful. She encouraged me and kept me after school . . ." said Kirk Douglas of his "tall, patrician" English teacher. "We sat at her desk next to the window, looking out over the beautiful autumn landscape, in the light that precedes dusk. . . . Her hand reached under the desk and clutched my hand close to her thigh. . . . [O]ur relationship endured through high school, college, New York, and Hollywood, even though we saw each other less and less and the letters became fewer as we grew older and I traveled to different countries making movies. I helped take care of her until she died."

As far as Douglas was concerned, Mrs. Livingston "changed my life. She introduced me to the world of poetry—Byron, Keats, Shelley. She became my confessor and listened to the dreams I didn't dare tell anyone else."

Ida Anderson, Edward R. Murrow's speech teacher, listened, too. "She taught me to love good books, good music, gave me the only sense of values I have . . . ," he said. "She knows me better than any person in the world. The part of me that is decent, that wants to do something, is the part she created. I owe the ability to live to her. . . ." Of Murrow, Anderson commented: "You are my masterpiece."

In teachers we can find mentors; in rooms lined with blackboards and presided over by pointers and flags we can find magic to last a lifetime. For example, decades and decades after fourth grade, writer Eudora Welty still remembered Mrs. McWillie's reading sessions on winter rainy days. Since it was too dark to see the blackboard, the teacher "would let her children close their books, and she would move, broad in widow's weeds like darkness itself, to the window and by what light there was she would stand and read aloud 'The King of the Golden River.' " Eudora didn't realize till much later that "the treat" of those story hours was actually a necessity; the school lacked funding for electric lighting, and the teacher had no alternative. But the magic never went away. "When in time I found the story in a book and read it to myself, it didn't seem to live up to my longing for a story with that name; as indeed, how could it?"

HOW TEACHERS SCORE ON THE CRYSTAL BALL POP QUIZ

When you're a teacher, there's plenty of room for error, and not everyone who stands at a blackboard would get an A for foresight when it comes to spotting talent in their classrooms. For example, Billy Graham's fifth-grade teacher said, "I just couldn't get him to say a word in class. I remember once, he just sat there looking at me after I asked a question, and I finally burst out in exasperation, 'Billy Frank, don't just sit there—say *something*. Please, just say *something*.' Not a sound.

"And to tell you the truth," she continued, "I just forgot about him after he passed on out of school. Then, I don't know how many years later it was, I saw him for the first time on one of his television crusades. I simply couldn't believe it."

Graham's view of education: "I could see no point in going to school at all." In high school he flunked French and struggled with literature, but as his principal noted, "There was never actually any question of his graduating. . . . [H]is daddy happened to be chairman of the school board." (To Graham's credit, as a grown-up he prided himself on learning new words like "eschatological"—and using them. But it was a dangerous practice. One night he stood up and said, "Yes, ladies and gentlemen, it was just one eschar—eschat—aw, shucks, folks I've never been able to get that word right.")

Shucks, folks. Teachers haven't been able to get a lot of things right either. Gene Hackman studied acting at the Pasadena Playhouse (one of his classmates was Robert Duvall), but said he was given "absolutely no encouragement at all. They used to grade us. You would have an average on make-up and movement and characterization and all that. . . . Out of 4 or 5 points I would get maybe a 1.1 or something like that. . . . I said, 'Well, they obviously don't know anything. I'll go off to New York.' I think it was eight years before I had my first job."

Jackson Pollock's art teacher, the well-known Thomas Hart Benton, thought that his seventeen-year-old student "was incapable of drawing logical sequences. He couldn't be taught anything."

Diana Ross's teacher at Cass Technical School was probably supremely surprised when the dreamy-eyed student she caught mooning over a newspaper made it big. What was Diana reading in study hall? Mary Constance demanded. Diana handed her an article from the *Detroit News* on the Primes. "You *know* I'm going to be a singer, *don't you*?" Diana told her. "I know these guys. And *I* sing on weekends myself."

"I looked at her," Constance recalled, "and said to myself, 'Oh, you poor child. You'll never make it.' "

Fortunately she kept her comments to herself. Others haven't been so judicious. When Malcolm Little (who later took the last name X) told an eighth-grade teacher he wanted to be a lawyer, he was advised, "You've got to be realistic about being a nigger." Malcolm's response was to drop out of school, even though he had been in the top of his class and elected class president by his white peers.

But sometimes teachers can be prescient. In prep school George Bush recieved a 67 (60 was flunking) in English composition. His teacher, Hart Leavitt, felt Bush "showed no imagination or originality."

Joe McCarthy's law professor said that the future senator "knew very little when he got here and very little when he left, but got through on his memory." McCarthy's lowest grade was in a course in legal ethics. Hmm . . .

LIKE A SPITBALL BETWEEN THE EYES

*Son, I watched ya out thar the whole time t'day. And I wanna tell*
*ya sumptun' I hope'll stay with ya the whole rest of your life.*
*'Cause if it does, it'll be of no small value to you. You're little.*
*And you're yellow!*
—football coach at Houston State Teachers College to Dan
Rather, who had his heart set on a sports scholarship that he
clearly didn't get

You may be fifty years old, but the heebie-jeebies are as tangible as acne: the snickering of the girls, the tedium of the clock inching from 2:58 to 2:59 to the release of 3:00, the time you were called a sissy or a mama's boy (Rather, who was often bedridden with rheumatic fever, earned both nicknames from a junior high school gym coach), the slings and arrows of school days. Perhaps because we are small when we begin to learn our three Rs, school persists in looming larger in memory than in life. We may remember the good things, surely, but the occasions when we are ridiculed manage to sting like a spitball between the eyes—even in adulthood.

For example, George McGovern chose this to include in his autobiography: "I had been postponing a visit to the rest room rather than raise my hand and ask to be excused." Young George was shy, you see, and we all know what happens when we let shyness get the better of us. "After a painful hour of repressing the forces of nature, a trickle appeared on the floor below my desk. This brought an excited shriek from Dorothy Nash, a girl with a high-pitched voice who sat next to me: 'Oh, look what he's doing!' " Wrote McGovern: "I have never been closer to total heart failure."

And it didn't just happen to George. Eve Arden remembered being six, "neatly dressed in white middy-blouse, navy pleated skirt and bloomers to match, over long white stockings (my mother dreaded colds)," and trying "in vain to catch the teacher's eye." Her outstretched arm and waving hand went unacknowledged, and the inevitable happened. "The giggle around me rose to a crescendo and stiffened my backbone," Arden explained in her autobiography. "I pierced the teacher with a daggered look and strode from the room."

Dealing with passes for the bathroom is only Chapter 1 in the annals of school day affrights. For example, there's long division. "This was just too much for my brain. I broke down and cried each day," recalled Dr. Benjamin Spock.

And there's disciplinary action. "In the third grade, a nun stuffed me in a garbage can under her desk," said Bruce Springsteen, "because, she said, that's where I belonged."

And then there's just plain old boredom. "You'd leave your house on a cold, wet winter morning . . . leave the comforts of your little bed and your radio and the things that were so wonderful," recalled Woody Allen. ". . . The guys would be standing in line—there would be the fat kid that you hated in front of you, and the one with his nose running behind you, and these wretched little girls in the other line. And everybody would be standing there dreading that in a few minutes you'd march up to your class and go through hours of boredom and intimidation."

It's the lot of children to follow the rules, to stand in line, to be continually tested, and—in short—to fit in until they are big enough to call the shots. In the meantime, those who are a little on the shy side, a little on the smart side, a little rebellious, or simply different often have a bumpy time of it.

"The closer we got to school," Marion Rockefeller, Laurance's daughter, remembers, "the lower we sank into the back seat of the car. By the time we were almost there, we were begging the chauffeur to please drive a few blocks further and let us out so we could arrive at school on foot, anonymously."

"All the other kids in my class was like little babies, but they could talk English and I didn't know what the fuck they was sayin'," explained Mafia *capo* Lucky Luciano. "Maybe that's why I fought so hard to get outa school, out into the streets where alotta people spoke Sicilian-Italian."

But even someone who seems cut out for school, a shy little bookworm named Truman Capote, for instance, can end up in the school of hard knocks. He recalled a first-grade teacher "who had a thing against me because I could read so well." Capote, who could read at the age of four, made the mistake of chiming in expertly when it came to reciting the alphabet. "And the teacher would say, 'Hold out your palms.' And she'd *whack* me across my palms with this ruler and I got a psychosis about it." From that time on he was unable to recite the alphabet.

In arithmetic class in junior high school food writer Craig Claiborne didn't fill out a line in a form stating what sport he was interested in. His teacher, who happened to be the school's athletic coach, responded by announcing, "We've got a sissy in the class." Wrote Claiborne in his autobiography: "To this day, in all my life, I have rarely known a more stunning and vivid pain. I have never known a moment more devastating or emasculating . . . and to this day I cannot add, multiply, divide, or subtract with anything remotely resembling facility."

Sometimes, however, a teacher is sure he's delivering an ego blow—and he isn't. Of JFK's time at Choate, headmaster St. John said, "Well, we reduced Jack's conceit, if it was conceit, and childishness, to considerable sorrow. And we said just what we thought, held nothing back, and Mr. Kennedy was supporting the school completely. I've always been very grateful to him." The problem was that Jack formed a club he named Muckers, borrowing the headmaster's term for goof-offs, and created a school discipline problem. The student body was called to the chapel for a lecture on the evils of the club, but the Muckers persisted. St. John called Joe Kennedy down for a conference, and Joe backed him up—at least in public. But as soon as St. John was out of earshot, Joe leaned over and whispered, "My God, my son, you sure didn't inherit your father's directness or his reputation for using bad language. If that crazy Muckers Club had been mine, you can be sure it wouldn't have started with an M." Prep school antics weren't going to be cause for suspension—not so far as the bond between father and son went.

WHO'S THAT IN THE THIRD ROW?

*When I was a Brownie, I ate all of the cookies. From the start
I was a very bad girl. I already knew that people were never going
to think of me as a nice girl when I was in the fifth grade. I tried
to wear go-go boots with my parochial school uniform. I wanted to
do everything everybody told me I couldn't do.*
—Madonna. In high school, she made the cheerleading squad,
but refused to shave her armpits.

Donald Trump's music teacher is probably having the time of his life at cocktail parties telling stories about a hotheaded second grader. And what are the nuns saying about Cher? Nothing compared with what she's saying about them, but certainly they've got to confess they saw it coming. And probably you would have, too, if you'd been sitting by the window observing that kid in the third row. Here we take you back to that vantage point, seat you in a desk with appropriately carved initials, and pose a purely academic question: Do we need to spend all those years maturing or should we simply fast forward from second grade to adulthood?

*MYSTERY KID NO. 1.* "Even in elementary school, I was a very assertive, aggressive kid. In the second grade I actually gave a teacher a black eye—I punched my music teacher because I didn't think he knew anything about music, and I almost got expelled." Adult identity: Donald Trump.

*MYSTERY KID NO. 2.* His mother wrote his themes for him right through college. He got a D in argumentation, though to his credit he did make the debating team. The yearbook ran a picture of a jackass with his name under it and the caption "As he looks to us on the campus every day." Adult identity: Lyndon Johnson.

*MYSTERY KID NO. 3.* A classmate told her mother she was "the very worst behaved girl in school" and that she had to go see Miss Ethel Stringfellow, the headmistress, "almost every day."

UPI/BETTMANN

If school were as interesting as horses, young Jackie Kennedy Onassis, shown here at age five, wouldn't have had problems with Miss Stringfellow.

This led a curious mother to inquire, "What happens when you're sent to Miss Stringfellow?"

"Well I go to the office, and Miss Stringfellow says, 'Jacqueline, sit down. I've heard bad reports about you.' I sit down. Then Miss Stringfellow says a lot of things—but I don't listen." Adult identity: Jackie Kennedy Onassis.

*MYSTERY KID NO. 4.* "I went to school where you couldn't wear patent leather shoes because there was some old lady who had some neurosis about it." A teacher there "was afraid your underpants would be reflected off the patent leather shoes and someone would peek. They were really sick. Once a nun beat me to a pulp. It wasn't nice what I said about her, but it was the truth." Adult identity: Cher.

*MYSTERY KID NO. 5.* "I quit school in the sixth grade because of pneumonia. Not because I had it, but because I couldn't spell it. We stole everything that began with an *a*—a piece of fruit, a bicycle, a watch, anything that was not nailed down.

"It took me nine years to get through the fourth grade. When I got into television commercials, I had to take a crash course in reading. I was thirty-two years old, and I couldn't read the cue cards." Adult identity: Rocky Graziano, boxer.

*MYSTERY KID NO. 6.* The May Queen and the editor of the school paper, she was nicknamed the class sarc for "firing off one-liners." She said, "I also did voices, so I'd call as my mother and excuse myself from school for a doctor's appointment." Her father was a famed ventriloquist. Adult identity: Candice Bergen.

*MYSTERY KID NO. 7.* His major was economics; his grades were strictly Cs. "Most of my high school and college career, a C-average was eligibility for sports and I figured that that was the standard to shoot at to remain eligible," he reasoned. Adult identity: Ronald Reagan.

*MYSTERY KID NO. 8.* "I entered Harvard in 1950 at the age of eighteen. During the second semester of my freshman year I made a mistake. I was having difficulty in one course, a foreign language. I became so apprehensive about it that I arranged for a fellow freshman of mine to take the examination for me in that course." Adult identity: Ted Kennedy, who was asked to "withdraw" from Harvard in 1951. He returned in 1953.

*MYSTERY KID NO. 9.* "I am so wicked. We had this young priest in catechism—you had to pass catechism. He had just been ordained, and who knows what problems he was going through? We used to write the answers to the catechism on our legs, up real high. We would slide up our dresses, and he would turn his face away, and we would copy down the answers." Adult identity: Linda Ronstadt, who went to parochial school through the eighth grade.

*MYSTERY KID NO. 10.* A computer whiz, he programmed the class schedule at his private high school in Seattle. "There was a shortage of girls," he recalled, so he rigged his history class so "there were myself and two other guys and then thirteen girls, which statistically would never happen. Other than that we were very normal." Adult identity: Bill Gates, cofounder of Microsoft Corporation.

*MYSTERY KID NO. 11.* "I got straight As in U.S. history and never learned there had been a depression, race revolts, Indian massacres, people like Sacco and Vanzetti or the Rosenbergs, or that blacks were getting lynched in America." He was the first male cheerleader at Brandeis, where he accused the university of having an "edifice complex." Adult identity: Abbie Hoffman.

# 21
# Believe It or Not at the White House

*I do not like broccoli and I haven't liked it since I was a little kid and my mother made me eat it. And I'm President of the United States, and I'm not going to eat any more broccoli!*
—George Bush

At first glance broccoli may seem like a small matter to attract the attention of a grown man, especially one who has been elected to the highest office in the land. But as many a President has found out, compared with broccoli, Congress and budgets are a piece of cake.

Truman's Waterloo was brussels sprouts. When he began his term, the housekeeper, Henrietta Nesbitt, who had been brought to the White House by Eleanor Roosevelt, simply ignored the fact that FDR was no longer in office. She served up brussels sprouts as usual, but Truman pushed them away. His daughter, Margaret, told Mrs. Nesbitt "that my father did not like brussels sprouts. The next night we got them again. Somewhat tensely, I informed Mrs. Nesbitt, again, that the President did not like the vegetable. The next night we got them again." But there was no correcting Mrs. Nesbitt's notions of what should be on a menu. Exasperated, Margaret called her mother, who was out of town, and "exploded" with "If you don't come back here and do something about that woman, I'm going to throw a bowl of brussels sprouts in her face!"

After his first formal state dinner Nixon analyzed everything, soup to nuts, "as if it had been a major military battle," observed his aide H. R. Haldeman. But the soup was clearly the thorny issue. "We've got to speed up these dinners," Nixon announced. "They take forever. So why don't we just leave out the soup course? . . . Men don't really like soup."

Sensing there was more to the story, Haldeman asked Nixon's valet, Manolo Sanchez, "Was there anything wrong with the President's suit after that dinner last night?"

"Yes," he said. "He spilled the soup down his vest." Never again was soup served at a Nixon state banquet.

John Kennedy negotiated soup; classical concerts were his weak point. He never was sure when to clap, so he and Jackie's social secretary, Letitia Baldrige, devised a system. As a finale neared, she'd open the door of the East Room an inch or two. Then Kennedy would applaud presidentially and, with Jackie on his arm, head to the stage to congratulate the performers.

A President may be in the limelight at a concert, but at least he's sitting down. At state galas, after the band tunes up, he's expected to dance. Jerry Ford was adept at a two-step that he used no matter what the song, but he preferred dancing to "In the Mood" and Glenn Miller arrangements. At a gala for the foreign minister of Ireland, the first number of the evening was, as Betty Ford phrased it, "some far out jazz thing." Next came a jig. The President was visibly perturbed. He summoned aide Bob Barrett and announced, "If they won't play some music I can dance to, I'm just not gonna come to these things anymore." Barrett hurried off and instructed the bandleader, "You've got to play 'Star Dust' or 'Bad Boy Leroy Brown.' "

The bandleader rose to his full height and said, "I've been playing in the White House for twelve years, and I just don't understand."

He complied, but Ford was far from mollified. After the guests left, he said, "Now listen, Barrett. I'm the President of the United States, and I should be able to have some music I can dance to."

But sometimes even being President doesn't mean you'll get your way. When LBJ was campaigning in 1964, he liked to dance with every woman in the room so that she could tell her friends, "I danced with the President." But at one White House party, when his inclination to twirl pretty woman after pretty woman showed no signs of diminishing at 3:00 A.M., Lady Bird Johnson asked the band to play "Goodnight, Sweetheart," as a signal for the guests to leave. LBJ responded by stopping in the middle of the dance floor, glaring at the pianist, and sticking out his tongue. The pianist stuck to his good-bye tune, and the party broke up.

THE WHITE HOUSE CALLING

*"Pierre, I have a problem you can help me with. Could you step into my office for a minute?" said White House Special Counsel Theodore Sorensen over the phone to JFK press secretary Pierre Salinger.*
*"Do you have any idea where I am, Ted?" Salinger answered.*
*"No. I just told my secretary to get you on the line."*
*"Well, she got me all right. I'm in Air Force One, looking down on Paris."*

White House operators are legendary. They are reputed to be able to get anyone anywhere. Kennedy boasted of their ability one night when Ben Bradlee of *The Washington Post* and his wife Toni were over. He dared them "to come up with a name of someone the operators couldn't find," Bradlee recalled. "Jackie suggested Truman Capote, because he had an unlisted telephone number. Kennedy picked up the telephone and said only, 'Yes, this is the President. Would you get me Truman Capote?'—no other identification. Thirty minutes later, Capote was on the line. . . not from his own unlisted number in Brooklyn Heights, but at the home of a friend in Palm Springs, California, who also had an unlisted number."

When Reagan was President, he discovered the crackerjack phone system extended beyond the White House. Once he helicoptered over for lunch at the home of newspaper columnist James Kilpatrick, who informed him, "Your fellows have been here all week installing your phones." That was news to the President, but he decided to check the system out. When he learned that his hosts' son was stationed on a destroyer in the Mediterranean, he put through a call. Quartermaster Kilpatrick later wrote the President telling him that amid the profusion of radio signals during maneuvers he and his shipmates heard a voice saying, "White House calling."

"What code is that?" said another voice on the radio.

"Maybe that's no code, maybe it's the White House calling," yet another voice suggested.

"Not even Hollywood could have silenced the airwaves as quickly as they were silenced," Kilpatrick wrote. The White House had found "a lowly quartermaster on a tin can"—Navy slang for a destroyer.

You can understand that with the proficiency of the White House operators, a President wouldn't worry much about phone matters. Thus, when Eisenhower left office on January 20, 1961, and settled on his Gettysburg farm, he didn't think twice about picking up the phone to call his son. He expected an operator to answer; that's the way things worked the last time he'd placed a call himself, in 1941. But this time he heard only a buzzing. Annoyed, he shouted for an operator, slammed the receiver, and fooled with the dial but nothing worked. Finally he called Secret Service Agent Flohr: "Come show me how you work this god-damned thing."

Flohr explained that you didn't use the dial as if it were a combination lock, moving it back and forth to the correct numbers, but you put your finger in the holes and let the dial spring back. "Oh! So that's how you do it!" Ike said happily. He'd negotiated his first transition to civilian life.

SIX ABSOLUTELY TRUE WHITE HOUSE TALES

1. *What was under the rug*? David Eisenhower, who at age five asked his grandmother Mamie, "Why did you build yourself such a big house?" was not entirely content that his family had to leave the White House. But he grew up, married Julie Nixon, and on inaugural night 1969 found himself showing the President and Mrs. Nixon a hidden door in the family quarters. It opened onto a passageway to the third floor. He led the family upstairs and lifted up a rug. Underneath was a note saying, "I will return," which David had written eight years earlier.

2. *A match for any tourist*. Maureen Reagan was thrilled by the matchbooks at the White House, which read "The President's House" in deference to its original name. Shamelessly she "rounded up as many matchbooks as I could reasonably get my hands on. . . . I needed about twenty of them to send home. . . . Finally I looked around the West Hall, where we were staying, and the tables really looked bare. . . . and so I said to Dennis [her husband], 'Well, maybe if I just take them all, they'll think they didn't put any out.' " She pulled off her match trick.

3. *Rats!?* That should have been what Barbara Bush cried

Willie Nelson never told his long-time fan Jimmy Carter what transpired on the White House roof.

when she was swimming in the White House pool and saw "a tremendous rat" paddling in front of her. Instead she screamed and called her husband, who "got the rat in the net and did him in." Of the acknowledged White House rodent problem, Bush said later, "We're relying heavily on Millie to cut that down."

4. *A safe place to smoke dope.* Lady Bird Johnson sunbathed there. Eisenhower barbecued. But the White House roof found its most unusual use when singer Willie Nelson came to visit the Carters. There he went "late at night with a beer in one hand and a fat Austin Torpedo in the other. . . . My companion on the roof—it couldn't do him any good to use his name, except I should say President Carter knew nothing about this and would not have condoned it—was pointing out to me the sights and the layout of how the streets run in Washington. . . . I guess the roof of the White House is the safest place I can think of to smoke dope."

5. *An even safer place.* What's better than the White House roof? The President's bedroom—if he's sharing the dope with you. In July 1962 Jackie Kennedy's friend—and JFK's lover—

Mary Meyer brought along "a small box with six joints," according to James Angleton, director of covert operations for CIA and a confidant of Mary's. "They shared one and Kennedy laughingly told her they were having a White House conference on narcotics in a couple of weeks. They smoked two more joints and Kennedy drew his head back and closed his eyes. He refused a fourth joint. 'Suppose the Russians drop a bomb,' he said."

6. *The presidential finger.* Late one night when Vietnam protesters were holding a vigil at the Lincoln Memorial, a restless Richard Nixon decided to go reason with them. He summoned his Secret Service agents, who drove him to the memorial, and under the starlit night stood and talked. When he decided to leave, a bearded protester came up to the limo and gave the President the finger. Nixon, eye to eye with the dissident, responded in kind. "The SOB," he said to Manolo Sanchez, his valet, "will go through the rest of his life telling everybody that the President of the United States gave him the finger. And nobody will believe him!"

# 22
# The American Love Story: Themes and Variations

*I married the first man I ever kissed. When I tell this to my children,*
*they just about throw up.*
—Barbara Bush

Traditionally there is only one love story. Boy sees girl (or vice versa), wants girl (or vice versa), gets girl (or vice versa). It begins with a kiss and ends with wedding bells. "He stopped dead in his tracks and said like a general giving an order, 'Tammy, kiss me!' He said it with such force that I never questioned if I should or shouldn't," recalled Tammy Faye of evangelist Jim Bakker. "I had never given a boy a kiss on the first date, but that wasn't going to stop me now." Bakker asked her to go to church on the first date, to go steady on the second, and to get married on the third.

That's romance in a nutshell. The beginnings of the story may vary—"I leaned over the asparagus and asked her for a date," said Jack Kennedy; "There was no asparagus," corrected Jackie—but the end of the first chapter is usually the same: white dresses and rice.

"We got to talking about civil rights, the South and so on," recalled Abbie Hoffman of a girl named Anita who walked into Liberty House, where he was working in 1967, and offered to volunteer. "She asked me about drugs. I asked if she had ever taken LSD. When she responded that she hadn't, I threw her a white capsule. She juggled it the way you would a lighted firecracker." In that sixties way, one thing led to another—first to drugs, then to bed, and, three months later, to Central Park and a wedding with everyone "dressed all in white with daisies in our hair."

But if that were all there were to the love story—two people sit in the first row of tax class at law school, as did Marilyn and Dan Quayle, and get married ten weeks later—generations of

If any photo illustrates the tangled web of love, it is this one. The woman whose hand Jack Bouvier holds is not that of his wife, Jackie Onassis's mother, Janet (*above right*); it belongs to Miss Virginia Kernochan with whom Jack had disappeared for the better part of the afternoon. After this photograph appeared in the New York *Daily News,* Janet was no longer willing to turn a blind eye to her husband's philandering, and the marriage disintegrated. Her daughter, as we all know, married a man cut from Jack Bouvier's cloth.

gossip columnists would be out of a job. It would be nice if we could stick to the main plot—and a lot of us try—but fate tends to hand out lives full of variations on the theme.

A girl's daddy tells you you're no good, as happened to Lyndon Johnson with his first love, Carol Davis. Or you're the governor of Louisiana and you fall in love with a stripper. Or you finally get Mr. Right to pop the question (after systematically making a list of the most eligible bachelors in town and putting his name at the top) and your first baby is born seven months later. You name her Patti Reagan and tell her she was premature.

"An eight-pound preemie?" questioned Patti. ". . . [W]hen I found out what a baby's normal birth weight is I said, 'Excuse me?' I didn't ask my parents about it because they'd made such a point of saying I was premature. . . . Growing up in the sixties, I actually thought it was kind of cool."

"Love is a many-splendored thing," the song reminds us. More accurately, it's many-tangled. There's no telling who might win your heart—or become a target for your passion—even after you've reached the altar and the curtain has supposedly dropped on the drama that is your love life. "I have committed adultery in my heart many times," announced Jimmy Carter while campaigning for President in 1976. A lot of people haven't let it go at that.

"The big trouble was . . . I kept calling her Kay. That tore it," explained General Dwight D. Eisenhower to Kay Summersby, his staff driver, after spending a week or so at home with Mamie following the North African campaign in World War II.

"What?" responded Kay.

"I kept calling her Kay. Every time I opened my mouth to say something to Mamie, I'd call her Kay. She was furious."

So was General George Marshall, who, according to Harry Truman, threatened to run Ike "out of the Army" and prevent him from "ever drawing a peaceful breath" if he came back to the United States and divorced Mamie, as he had discussed in a letter. Like a good soldier, Eisenhower followed orders, left Kay in Europe, came home, and went about his life. She gave him her diary, as he requested. When he was elected President, she sent him a note. When she remarried, he sent "happy tidings."

The other woman is never an easy role to play, even if for a jubilant moment he can't get his wife's name straight.

"I wanted to love and be loved on a daily basis, but I was closing the door to that possibility," mused Judith Exner, an ex-Sinatra lover, on her affair with Jack Kennedy. "You can't find it by going with a married President, not in a million years." Yet how does a woman like Exner get herself into such a predicament? "I was just living my life. It seemed so *normal* to me."

Just living your life begets some unlikely situations. One day the mail arrives with the requisite assortment of bills and a letter that begins "Hi." It continues, "This note shall remain anonymous for obvious reasons. Since we have had intimate sexual contact. . . , I feel it only fair to tell you that I have just found out I have AIDS. I am most sorry to tell you this. I suggest you have tests made to make sure you're OK. Most sincerely." The name that was left off was Rock Hudson's. He sent out three identical letters—but not one to his live-in companion, Marc Christian, who successfully sued Hudson's estate for millions because he was not apprised of his lover's condition.

The mail could also bring a letter like this: "Jodie, I would abandon this idea of getting Reagan in a second if I could only win your heart and live out the rest of my life with you. . . . By sacrificing my freedom and possibly my life I hope to change your mind about me. This letter is being written an hour before I leave for the Hilton Hotel." John Hinckley penned but never mailed one last effort to woo actress Jodie Foster before shooting Ronald Reagan. Later in his hotel room, investigators found a postcard with a picture of the Reagans and the following note to Jodie: "Don't they make a darling couple? Nancy is downright sexy. One day you and I will occupy the White House and the peasants will drool with envy. Until then, please do your best to remain a virgin. You are a virgin, aren't you?"

Ah, yes, virginity, the central theme of Act I in any person's romantic life. Madonna's father used to tell her, "If there were more virgins, the world would be a better place."

"Remember—never give anything away. No man really wants that. Every man wants his wife to be a virgin when he marries her" was the "nice Jewish girl upbringing" Lauren Bacall's mother "pounded into my head constantly."

But the lure of passing from innocence to experience is such that the burning question often ends up being not whether to deviate from the prescribed plot but *when*.

"I was fourteen and she was forty-two," recalled Burt Reynolds. "She was a very wealthy lady, in Palm Beach where I grew up. I used to go to her store and look around. She was always very nice to me. Then one day it just happened. . . . She taught me a lot that year, one I remember with great fondness."

"This guy in the neighborhood, Sandy, kept trying to have sex with me," said Roseanne Arnold. "He said, 'Let's smoke some pot and do what comes naturally.' I had smoked maybe two times in high school, and nothing happened, so I thought I was highly evolved and wouldn't feel anything this time either." They went to the bedroom. ". . . I still didn't know what you were supposed to do. I thought of something like an article from *Seventeen*. 'Why, what you do, Roseanne, is you lay there poised and smile.' "

"Naturally I lost my virginity in the back seat of a car. This was the fifties, right?" said singer Tina Turner of a high school beau. "I think he planned it, the little devil—told me there was nothing playing at the movies that night. I guess I knew by then he could get into my pants. . . ."

When opportunity knocks, however, not everyone responds. Elvis refused to consummate his relationship with Priscilla until their wedding night. Bette Davis, asked by Dick Cavett on television when she stopped being a virgin, counted to ten and decided to answer him. "I said, 'When I married my first husband.' Then, after a long silence, I said, 'And it was *hell* waiting.' "

Among those who should have had more of her resolve is Roman Polanski. "It is very easy to say it now. One should have thought about it before, but when you find yourself with a girl in certain situations, you don't exactly think about it," he said of an afternoon frolic with a thirteen-year-old girl that led to his arrest. "I was about to make a series of photographs of young girls of that age for a French magazine called *Vogue Homme*, and I find it quite an interesting enterprise because I like girls of that age and they like me. And it just went too far. . . . The next day I was stopped in the lobby of the hotel by a man who identified himself as a Los Angeles policeman, and I was booked. . . ." Rather than serve out a prison term, Polanski skipped the country.

The romantic plot always thickens when sex is in the air. But not all variations on the theme end up in tragedy. It all depends on your point of view—and sense of humor. When Reagan's son Ron was seventeen, he was caught with the wife of singer Ricky Nelson—in his parents' bed. "The good news," Michael Reagan told his father, is that ". . . you found out he isn't gay."

Despite our times and its temptations, there are those who never let go of the old-fashioned love story. Chief among the faithful: Elizabeth Taylor. Eight months after she said, "In today's society you don't need to be married. You don't need to tidy up. Not at my age anyway," she was engaged to be married for the eighth time. The lucky guy: Larry Fortensky, a thirty-nine-year-old former construction worker whom she met at the Betty Ford Center in 1988.

Just to recap, after she wed first husband Conrad "Nicky" Hilton in 1950, she said, "I love him better every day."

"I just want to be with him, to be his wife," she commented before her 1952 marriage to Michael Wilding.

"Thirty or forty years" was how long she thought her honeymoon with fourth husband, Eddie Fisher, would last. She married him one year after the 1958 death of hubby number three, Michael Todd, the man she took to the altar in 1957.

"This marriage will last forever," she said when she tied the knot with Richard Burton in 1964. "We are stuck together like chicken feathers to tar," she said when they remarried in 1975.

In 1976, wed to John Warner, she felt "I have never been so happy."

In 1991, announcing the Fortensky nuptials, she said, "With God's blessings, this is it, forever."

## COMING HOME TO MAMA AND PAPA

*I certainly told that Father Tucker. I told him off. I said, I didn't want any broken-down Prince who was head of a country over there that nobody ever knew anything about to marry my daughter.*
*I didn't want it and I didn't intend to get involved.*
—Grace Kelly's father's thoughts on being an in-law to a prince, expressed to Father Tucker, Rainier's personal chaplain

How much simpler life would be if we never had to get the parental stamp of approval on a newly minted romance. While many parents come around once all the I do's are said, that first promenade through the family portal can be a white knuckler. "The Prince comes up to Grace's titties," observed Jack Kelly, a self-made Philadelphia millionaire who had his own problems with social standing. A former bricklayer, he was forever excluded from the *Social Register*—something that would never plague a princess, even if she reigned over a "country over there that nobody ever knew anything about."

In America the closest thing we have to princesses—besides Hollywood stars—is presidential daughters. The Nixon girls had a terrible time getting the presidential seal on their romances. Tricia Nixon kept her engagement to Edward Cox a secret for two years before deciding to broach the marriage question with her father in 1971. "Eddie was white as a sheet when he went in to see the President," she said. "We had been watching *The Greatest Show on Earth* and we got so nervous that we had to go out and take a walk around the grounds. Then he talked to my father." Nixon "was speechless for a moment, but you know how fathers are."

Speechlessness was exactly the situation Julie Nixon encountered when she ventured into her father's office to announce her engagement to David Eisenhower. Nixon had responded to the news with nothing more than a nod. She fled in tears. However, that night on her pillow she found a note of congratulations from the future President.

Tears—and later congratulations—seem to be a persistent pattern when marriage is in the air. "I think I've met a man I could marry," opera singer Beverly Sills announced to her mother. Beverly had talked the night away with Peter Greenough and was ecstatic. So was her mother, initially. "Then I told her that Peter was still married, had three children, was twelve years older than I, and wasn't Jewish."

"Why does everything have to happen to my baby?" her mother sobbed. Beverly "had figured she wouldn't be overjoyed" but married Peter anyway.

"My family warned me about men, but they never said a word about women," commented Tallulah Bankhead, a line Martina Navratilova could well have borrowed when her father confronted her by saying, "I think you and [novelist] Rita Mae [Brown] are living as man and wife." As far as he was concerned, he'd rather she "slept with a different man every night than sleep with a woman."

A woman was what was bothering Allen Ginsberg's father, Louis. Maretta came for a visit equipped with meditation paraphernalia, including finger cymbals, crystals, a metal dorje, incense, and a dog-eared paperback, *The Tibetan Book of the Dead.* "What's with this Maretta?" Mr. Ginsberg asked. "Why can't you bring home a nice Jewish girl?"

"For the love of God, Louis," Allen countered, laughing, "here for years you've been saying, 'Please just bring home a *girl* for a change,' and now that I do, you want a *Jewish* one?"

ON THE SUBJECT OF MARRIAGE

"Marrying a man is like buying something you've been admiring for a long time in a shop window. You may love it when you get it home, but it doesn't always go with everything else."—playwright Jean Kerr.

"Communication, separate bedrooms, and separate baths. I think that gives you a chance."—Bette Davis.

"The problems were never in the bedroom. We were always great in bed. The trouble usually started on the way to the bidet."—Ava Gardner on Frank Sinatra.

"My wives married me. I didn't marry them."—oil billionaire J. Paul Getty.

"I think paperwork in marriage means more to women than it does to men."—Willie Nelson, who married wife Connie without divorcing wife Shirley.

"The person you want with you in Intensive Care."—Kirk Douglas's view of the ideal wife, after he had to go into surgery for implanting of a pacemaker.

"After all, I have a wonderful family and a pretty good wife."—Richard Nixon.

"Husbands are like fires. They go out when unattended."—Zsa Zsa Gabor.

"Some of us are becoming the men we wanted to marry."—Gloria Steinem.

"A man's home may seem to be his castle on the outside; inside it is more often his nursery."—playwright, congresswoman, and ambassador Clare Boothe Luce.

"Living with Marlon is like an afternoon at the races—short periods of orgiastic activity followed by long periods of boredom and anticipation."—Marlon Brando's first wife, Anna Kashfi, who met him before the filming of *The Teahouse of the August Moon* and left him after a year of matrimony.

"I went through a period when I felt like a total failure—as any good Catholic girl would. But I'm over it now. I don't feel like a failure anymore. I just feel sad. Every once in a while at night I'll wake up and go, 'My God! I was married once. I was married and he was the love of my life.' It is like a death to deal with. It's very, very difficult."—Madonna on her divorce from actor Sean Penn.

LOVE NOTES

"If love is the answer, could you please rephrase the question?"—Lily Tomlin.

"I was telling a white girlfriend of mine once that when she's in love, she hears violins and stuff like that. But me, when I'm in love, I hear James Brown, you know? 'Get on up,' that's what I hear. Some Prince, and it goes bom da boom da boom boom. Drums. But on the white side it's this da de da de da da and 'I love you so much, and I'm crying and shit.' Black people don't do that. We go to the Castle Ballroom, get some barbecue, that kind of stuff."—jazz trumpeter Miles Davis.

"The love of the old and the middle-aged is a theme that is recurring more and more in my works of fiction. Literature has neglected the old and their emotions. The novelists never told us that in love, as in other matters, the young are just beginners and that the art of loving matures with age and experience."—Isaac Bashevis Singer, in his author's note to *Old Love*.

"Love does not exist without reciprocation, hugging that person and feeling the meeting of two minds, two hearts, two souls, two bodies. Obsession is pain and a longing for something that does not exist. John Hinckley's greatest crime was the confusion of love and obsession. The trivialization of love is something I will never forgive him."—Jodie Foster in 1982.

"Love is the invention of a few high cultures . . . it is cultural artifact. To make love the requirement of a lifelong marriage is exceedingly difficult, and only a few people can achieve it. I don't believe in setting universal standards that a large proportion of people can't reach."—Margaret Mead.

"Few people know what they mean when they say 'I love you.' . . . Well, what does the word love mean? It means total interest. I think the reason very few people really fall in love with anyone is they're not willing to pay the price. The price is you have to adjust yourself to them."—Katharine Hepburn.

SEXUAL TENSIONS

"In my sex fantasy, nobody ever loves me for my mind."
—writer Nora Ephron.

"When a woman walks across a room, she speaks with a

universal body language that most men intuitively understand. Men hardly ever ask sexual favors of a woman from whom the certain answer is no."—anti-ERA activist Phyllis Schlafly.

"I thought of sex as a duty, not a pleasure. You know, there should be a school to teach sex. It's so important, and yet we have no teachers, no classes."—Debbie Reynolds.

"These are sexy pictures of real women. Why do people think they are empty-headed? I grew up in a world where if you were pretty, you could not be smart, and if you were smart, you could not be pretty. That's just a dumb way to look at the world." —Christie Hefner, daughter of Hugh and the CEO of Playboy Enterprises.

"Porn killed stripping. And now with those tape rentals, well, nudity seems like nothing at all. But in my day, nudity was so rare—so special."—stripper Blaze Starr, who had an affair with Louisiana Governor Earl Long in 1959 and believed that "if there is such a thing as getting nude with class, then I did it."

"A lot of girls think that wow, here's an opportunity . . . to meet these wealthy fabulous terrific guys. In fact it was just the opposite. The men used to fall in love with the women on a regular basis. Here was Miss Perfect. She was always there for him. She never had an opinion—practically—on her own. She was sexually willing to do just about anything. He thought she was perfect, not realizing she was there doing a job. I had many girls come back to me and say I just can't see Mark anymore. He really wants a girlfriend. I'm not willing to do that."—Mayflower Madam Sydney Biddle Barrows.

"I wasn't blown over or anything. . . . I've been with priests and others in public office. . . . It was just kinda strange."—prostitute Stephen L. Gobie on paid sex with Congressman Barney Frank of Massachusetts in 1985.

"I visited him twice at the White House, the first time for only fifteen minutes in a small room off the Oval Office. His secretaries didn't so much as blink when they saw me. They showed me in and out as naturally as they would the Secretary of State. On my second visit, I met him upstairs in the living quarters. A Secret Service agent ushered me into a dark and somber room filled with heavy wood furniture, and said, 'Make yourself comfortable, he'll be with you shortly.' He motioned to an enormous, intricately carved rosewood bed. 'That's Abraham

Lincoln's bed,' he said. 'You mean,' I said, 'I'm to lie down on *that*, on Abraham Lincoln's bed?' 'Lady,' he said, 'it's the best we've got.' "—Leslie Devereux, a New York call girl set up for JFK by Peter Lawford.

"If someone is stroking your little breasts, you get a sexy, physical feeling. It can be a good feeling, and so it's confusing, because you then blame yourself for feeling good, not knowing that you had nothing to do with that kind of arousal. A child is never to blame."—Oprah Winfrey, who was sexually abused as a child by a male teenage cousin and other male relatives and friends. "It was not a horrible thing in my life. There was a lesson in it. It teaches you not to let people abuse you."

"I view it as a nightmare that the sodomites are so brazen. . . . These obnoxious, repulsive people are anything but 'gay.' " —Senator Jesse Helms, 1988.

In 1959 John Griffin dyed his skin black and roamed the South, gathering material for what would become the best seller *Black like Me*. Hitchhiking from Mobile to Montgomery, he found that the drivers, with the exception of two, all "picked me up the way they would pick up a pornographic photograph or book. . . . Some were shamelessly open, some shamelessly subtle. All showed morbid curiosity about the sexual life of a Negro, and all had, at base, the same stereotyped image of the Negro as an inexhaustible sex-machine with oversized genitals and a vast store of experiences, immensely varied."

"I think I am a sexual threat, and I think, if anything, there is a prejudice against that. I think that it is easier for people to embrace people who don't frighten them and poke at their insides and make them think about their own sexuality."—Madonna.

"I never particularly wanted to make simply sex movies. If I had wanted to make a real sex movie I would have filmed a flower giving birth to another flower. And the best love story is just two lovebirds in a cage."—Andy Warhol.

# 23
# Matters of Semantics

## A LOGIC OF THEIR OWN

1. "Nobody goes there anymore, it's too crowded."—Yogi Berra.

2. "We had to destroy that town in order to save it."—U.S. military officer to AP reporter Peter Arnett during the Vietnam War.

3. "We're going to have the best educated American people in the world."—Dan Quayle.

4. "I knew that flying over the Soviet Union without permission was spying," said U-2 reconnaissance pilot Francis Gary Powers after he was returned to the United States. "I *knew* that it was. But I really didn't think that in a true sense of the word spy I ever considered myself a spy. I was a pilot flying an airplane and it just so happened that *where* I was flying made what I was doing spying."

5. "I am very patriotic. I've only committed one crime in my life."—Soviet spy John Walker to the FBI.

6. "If we didn't have bonuses, we wouldn't have had anybody working for us."—a Drexel Burnham Lambert spokesman explaining why the firm paid out multimillion-dollar bonuses days before filing for bankruptcy in 1990.

7. "Mayor Daley, do you know a federal judge by the name of Judge Lynch?" lawyer William Kunstler asked Richard Daley during the Chicago Seven trial.

Daley:   "Do I know him?"
Kunstler:  "Yes."
Daley:   ". . . We have been boyhood friends all our
lives."
8. "I didn't have cancer. I had something inside of me that
had cancer in it, and it was removed."—Ronald Reagan.
9. "We are dealing in facts, not realities!"—movie mogul
Samuel Goldwyn to Walter Winchell.


QUESTIONS OF ADDRESS


*"Ah, here is my blind date. I am going to call you Alice," said Joe
McCarthy, putting his arm around Washington insider Alice
Roosevelt Longworth.*
*"No, Senator McCarthy. You are not going to call me Alice. The
truckman, the trashman, and the policeman on my block may call
me Alice, but you may not."*


Even those of us who regularly mind our ma'ams and our
sirs, our pleases and thank-yous can find the world of social
niceties tough sledding. As these examples illustrate, conversational forays must be launched with care.
1. "I wish she wouldn't call people 'kiddo.' She called me
'kiddo' just the other day, and frankly I can't stand it."—Alice
Roosevelt Longworth about Pat Nixon.
2. "Sweetheart, listen, Lady Bird and I want to see you over
here at our next White House dinner party. Jack was a great man,
but you've got to start living again," Lyndon Johnson told Jackie
Kennedy over the telephone. Her response: "How dare that over-
size, cowpunching oaf call me sweetheart. Who the hell does he
think he is?"
3. "What's shakin', Chiefie baby?" Supreme Court Justice
Thurgood Marshall once joked to Chief Justice Warren Burger.
4. "Boy, show me your license," a policeman said to Martin
Luther King, Sr. "Do you see this child here?" said Daddy King,
his voice resonant as only a preacher's can be. He pointed to
his young son, Martin, and said, "He's a boy. I'm a man." The
policeman, though surprised, gave him the ticket anyway.
5. "We're not royal highnesses. I don't want to be king. . . .

All day long they call me Mr. President. I wish they'd just call me Lyndon sometimes . . .," lamented LBJ.

6. "I am King . . . and the King can do no wrong!" Henry Ford II liked to say to himself every morning as he eyed himself in the mirror.

7. "Would you like to remind me too?" Supreme Court Justice Sandra Day O'Connor asked an attorney who said, "I would like to remind you gentlemen," of a legal point. When O'Connor joined the court, she eliminated the use of "Mr. Justice," which meant redoing the brass plaques on each of the nine justices' chambers. "Now we're all known as Justice so-and-so," she explained.

8. "The one thing I do not want to be called is First Lady. It sounds like a saddle horse," Jackie Kennedy told her secretary. "Would you notify the telephone operators and everyone else that I'm to be known as Mrs. Kennedy and not as First Lady?"

WHAT TO SAY WHEN YOU'RE ABOUT TO MAKE HISTORY

*You can't imagine how glad I am to see you. I've thought about this moment for a long time, and now it's here, and I'm scared to death. I don't know what to say.*
—journalist Terry Anderson greeting a roomful of former colleagues after being released from seven years of captivity in Lebanon

The spotlight is on you, the flashbulbs poised, the journalists' pencils sharpened. What do you say? "What can you say about a day when you have seen four beautiful sunsets?" said John Glenn after he became the first American astronaut to orbit the earth.

What can you say when you lose an election by landslide margins? Adlai Stevenson could only compare himself with the little boy who stubbed his toe in the dark: "He was too old to cry, but it hurt too much to laugh."

What can you say when you've won the Nobel Prize for literature? Isaac Bashevis Singer learned the news when he came back from breakfast and "saw people were standing with cameras around my place." The reporters "all asked me the same question, were you surprised? Were you happy? So since I did not want to have a discussion with them about what happiness is, I said yes. Yes, I was surprised and I was happy and this went on for about ten or fifteen minutes." When another reporter repeated the question, "I said how long can a man be surprised and how long can a man be happy? I've already been surprised. I've already been happy. And I'm the same schlemiel as I was before."

Dan Quayle found himself in a happy and surprising predicament when George Bush called to tell him he was on the vice presidential ticket. Thrilled, Quayle jumped in the shower, changed, and wondered, "Well, now what am I going to say?" He headed over to the convention and gave his answer. After being introduced amid massive fanfare, he grabbed Bush's shoulders, fraternity-style, and shouted, "Let's go get 'em. All right? You got it."

That should have been the nation's first clue to Quayle's real-guy approach to statesmanship, which was further evidenced when he toured Alaska's oil-soaked coasts after the spill from the Exxon *Valdez*. He told emergency workers to "have a great day. . . ."

"You all look like happy campers to me," he greeted a delegation in Pago Pago when he visited American Samoa in 1989. "Happy campers you are, happy campers you have been, and, as far as I am concerned, happy campers you will always be."

Quayle wasn't a fellow prone to rail about the "nattering nabobs of negativism" or "pusillanimous pussyfooting," as did vice presidential predecessor Spiro Agnew. But with a boss like George Bush, who prided himself on his "red meat" vocabulary, it probably wasn't smart to try to sound like the "egghead academicians," "smart-aleck columnists," or "mournful pundits" that Bush used to go "ballistic" about. As Quayle himself pointed out, "Verbosity leads to unclear, inarticulate things."

How then to make it safely into the history books? A sense of humor helps. "Why don't you roll me under the table and I'll sleep it off while you finish the dinner," Bush mumbled after he threw up on the prime minister of Japan in 1992.

"Honey, I forgot to duck," Ronald Reagan deadpanned from his hospital bed, surrounded by blood, discarded bandages, and the remains of a new pin-striped suit. His wife, Nancy, had just arrived after the 1981 assassination attempt.

"I am leaving *The Tonight Show*. There must be a better way of making a living than this," Jack Paar, fighting off tears, announced on camera in 1960 after he was prevented from using a joke that mentioned a water closet. Three weeks later he was back on the air: "As I was saying before I was interrupted . . ."

Sometimes, like Paar returning to NBC, we know we're going to be in the glare of publicity and have a chance to think of an appropriate line. Take "I am not a crook," which is what Richard Nixon told the nation as the credibility of his administration crumbled. Or "You killed the President, you rat!," Jack Ruby's parting shot as he pointed his .38 into the stomach of Lee Harvey Oswald.

"Here I am saying it can happen to anybody, even me, Magic Johnson," the basketball player said in announcing he was infected with the HIV virus.

"I feel like a pawn in a chess game being played by giants," Oliver North told Congress during the Iran-contra hearings.

"We would call G. Gordon Liddy into executive session," recalled Sam Dash, chief counsel of the Senate Watergate Committee. ". . . He doesn't sit, he stands. He salutes us and says, 'I have only to give you my name, rank and serial number. I consider myself captured by the enemy.' "

Wowing the world isn't something you can always do on cue. Nixon knew that and tried to make sure his family wouldn't lack for charisma. "It occurs to me that from time to time you may be asked for anecdotes . . ." he memoed Tricia and Julie on July 24, 1972. "On a personal side, you might mention some of our Christmas parties where I played the piano for group singing, etc., always by ear. . . . Another personal note that could be made is that when I come in to dinner at the White House—before dinner I will often make phone calls [to] people who may be sick, who have hard luck like losing an election or not getting a promotion. . . . These calls never, of course, are publicized because they are personal in nature." He signed the memo "the President."

JFK was prepared to meet history when he went to West Berlin. "Today in the world of freedom, the proudest boast is '*Ich bin ein Berliner*,' " he told the wildly cheering crowd that greeted him in a city that stood as a lone outpost of democracy in Communist Germany. "*Ich bin ein Berliner* was not my idea; it was his," adviser McGeorge Bundy recalled. "I just told him how to say it in German. He had no feeling for the German language. He had no feeling for any foreign language. That's because he had no sense of music, no *ear*. So there we were in the goddamn airplane, coming down on Berlin, while he repeated the phrase over and over again—I don't know how many times. But they knew what he said, and it worked. God, how it worked!"

What works often is a sense of history—and poetry. "Don't shoot. We are your children," Abbie Hoffman cried outside the Democratic National Convention in Chicago in August 1968 as protesters faced police.

"I have a dream," Martin Luther King, Jr., improvised before a hundred thousand civil rights marchers in Washington, D.C., on August 28, 1963. "I have a dream today that my four little children will one day live in a nation where they will not be judged by the color of their skin but by the content of their character. I have a dream today. . . ."

Later he said, "I started out reading the speech just all of a sudden—the audience was wonderful that day—and all of a sudden this thing came to me that I have used—I'd used it many times before, that thing about 'I have a dream'—and I just felt that I wanted to use it here. I don't know why, I hadn't thought about it before the speech."

General Douglas MacArthur had thought about it before when he addressed a joint session of Congress in 1951. He'd just been fired by Truman, and he closed his speech with "The world has turned over many times since I took the oath on the Plain at West Point and the hopes and dreams have long since vanished. But I still remember the refrain of one of the most popular barrack ballads of that day, which proclaimed, most proudly, that 'Old soldiers never die. They just fade away.' And like the soldier of the ballad, I now close my military career and just fade away— an old soldier who tried to do his duty as God gave him the light to see that duty." Then came a hushed "Good-bye." There was pandemonium and sobbing in the House chamber.

Watching on television, President Truman, who was never inclined to poetry, commented, "One hundred percent bullshit." The Truman tactic—refusing to mince words—is another tried and true way to greet history. It works. But you're far less likely to end up in *Bartlett's*.

FESSING UP IS HARD TO DO

If anything will tie a man's tongue, it's admitting lapses in moral judgment. Here, a stammerer's gallery of confessions:

1. "Now I find it as I have stated that I have that the conduct that—that evening in in this as a result of the impact of the accident of the—and the sense of loss, the sense of hope and the sense of tragedy and the whole set of—circumstances, that the er-ah-behavior was inexplicable. . . ."—Teddy Kennedy talking about Chappaquiddick to Roger Mudd on TV.

2. "I'm not proud of this period. Ah . . . I didn't handle it well. I messed it up."—Richard Nixon explaining Watergate to David Frost on TV.

3. "I sorrowfully acknowledge that seven years ago, in an isolated incident, I was wickedly manipulated by treacherous former friends and then colleagues who victimized me with the aid of a female confederate."—PTL minister Jim Bakker's resignation statement.

4. "It was suggested I have this picture taken with Miss Rice. This attractive lady whom I had only recently been introduced to dropped into my lap. I was embarrassed. I chose not to dump her off and the picture was taken. I should not have been in that situation. . . . It was a very serious mistake."—Senator Gary Hart explaining on *Nightline* 1987 how he ended up being photographed with Donna Rice aboard the boat *Monkey Business*.

5. During the 1992 campaign, Governor Bill Clinton explained on *60 Minuees* that he had "acknowledged wrongdoing. I have acknowledged causing pain in my marriage." Refusing to elaborate, he said, "Anybody who's listening gets the drift of it, and let's get on and get back to the real problems of this country." His wife Hillary's view: "If that's not enough for people, then heck, don't vote for him."

GEORGE BUSH AND THE LANGUAGE THING

*Poor George is hopelessly inarticulate. He never finishes a sentence or puts in a verb.*
—Nancy Ellis, the former President's sister

Like most sisters, George's has a point. Reporters, let alone grammarians, had trouble deciphering the presidential intent when Bush did things like announce he had "New Hampshire values"—a 1992 campaign ploy in New England—and then explain them by saying, "Remember Lincoln, going to his knees in times of trial and the Civil War and all that stuff."

Once asked what a summit with Gorbachev would mean for the world, Bush answered, "Grandkids. All of that. Very important."

At an Alaskan stopover on the way to Tokyo he was asked if he would present "new initiatives" in Japan. His reply: "We're ready to roll, yeah."

Pleased when he defended his China policy at a press conference, he said, "So, I'm glad you asked it because then I vented a spleen here."

Bush got himself into various forms of linguistic "deep-do-do" effortlessly, but if anything gave him the "big mo," it was the word thing. Quite simply he had a thing for it, a fondness he made obvious whether referring to "the stomach thing" (his diplomatic upset in Japan) or "the vision thing" (his cross to bear in the 1988 election). Herewith a few of his favorite things:

1. "But let me tell you, this gender thing is history. You're looking at a guy who sat down with Margaret Thatcher across the table and talked about serious issues."

2. "Dear Ollie," Vice President Bush wrote Oliver North in November 1985, "As I head off to Maine for Thanksgiving, I just want to wish you a happy one, with the hope you get some well-deserved rest. Your dedication and tireless work with the hostage thing and with Central America really gives me cause for great pride in you and thanks. George Bush."

3. "Did you come here and say, 'The heck with it, I don't need this darn thing?' Did you go through a withdrawal thing?"—at a Newark, New Jersey, drug clinic in 1988 to a recovering addict.

4. "How was the actual deployment thing?"—chatting by phone with astronauts on the space shuttle *Atlantis*.

5. "Cancel the word 'thing.' "—a correction added after he referred to a New York shelter for homeless youths as "the Covenant House thing."

THEY

*If they want to get me, they'll get me. They got Jack.*
—Robert F. Kennedy

"They" can be just a loose way of talking. As in "Boy, they were big on crematoriums, weren't they?"—George Bush's comment after visiting Auschwitz in 1980. Or "I shall stop flying in first class when they invent something better," as Jimmy Carter's special envoy for trade, Robert Strauss, explained to the "little twerp" at the White House who tried to book a coach ticket. Or "I hate it when they call me ugly, when they say I'm homely. I'm the one who's in the *body*. I'm the one who has the *face*. I can't have plastic surgery on my *heart*," said Bette Midler.

Sometimes "they" is invoked to personify authority. As in "They fill your head with all sorts of details, technicalities and statistics as if you were getting ready for an exam . . ." This was Ronald Reagan's explanation of why he fumbled through his 1984 debate with Walter Mondale.

But often "they" is an ominous word, conspiratorial because of lack of antecedents. "They even told us we could take our clothes home, with all that stuff on it, so my wife could wash them with the family clothes," said Keith L. Prescott, who worked for eight years at the Nevada desert site where the government tested nuclear weapons. He came down with multiple myeloma in 1969.

"We went swimming in the water—a lot of dead fish around, but we went swimming in the water," said Navy crewman John Smitherman, stationed at the Bikini atoll during the first underwater atomic bomb tests. "This water was also used for pulling through water from the bay or lagoon there into the condensers of the ship to make our own drinking water. We used the water to wash our clothes with. We wasn't warned about it because they continued to tell us not to worry about any of this." He later lost limbs as the result of radiation.

"They seem to forget that before I was a civil rights leader, I answered a call," said Martin Luther King, Jr., after he followed his conscience and came out against the Vietnam War. "A good man never has enough enemies," he believed, and "they" is often the sum of them.

"I gave them a sword. And they stuck it in. And they twisted it with relish. And I guess, if I'd been in their position, I'd have done the same thing," said Richard Nixon after his resignation.

"I feel like a hound bitch in heat in the country," LBJ once complained. "If you run, they chew your tail off. If you stand still, they slip it to you."

But as those enemies become abstract, larger than life, "they" is a word that gives voice to fear. "They are drugging you" is what black youths are told by Nation of Islam Minister Louis Farrakhan, who believes "there is a purposeful destruction of the black community."

"They're going to shoot my ass off the way they shot Bobby," Teddy Kennedy felt.

"He's dead, they've killed him—oh, Jack, oh, Jack, I love you," cried Jackie Kennedy en route to the hospital in Dallas.

"What if when they called a war, no one went?" asked Abbie Hoffman. What if we lived in a world where we didn't have to use the word "they"?

WHAT'S IN A NAME?

*How could anyone defeat a man called Ike with a name like Adlai?*
—Adlai Stevenson

What do you name your pride and joy, the baby who is to carry on your family heritage? "I think Egbert is not happy with his name," Edward R. Murrow's mother realized when her son was in college. "If I had known how it looked when written out, I wouldn't have given it to him. It didn't look pretty." She called him Sonny; he opted for Edward.

Parents approach the task of naming names in various ways. Jane Fonda and Tom Hayden stressed symbolism. They called their baby Troy in memory of the Vietcong martyr Nguyen Van Troi, who had tried to kill Secretary of Defense Robert McNamara when he visited South Vietnam in 1966.

Charles Manson's mother ignored the whole matter. "On November 12, 1934, while living in Cincinnati, Ohio, unwed and only sixteen, my mother gave birth to a bastard son. Hospital records list the child as 'no name Maddox.' The child—me,

Charles Milles Manson—was an outlaw from birth," wrote Manson.

Boxer George Foreman simplified the decision-making process. He named all five of his sons "George" and distinguished them by roman numerals. "I couldn't name just one after me," he said. "It wouldn't have been fair." Even Foreman's daughters are Georgetta, Freeda George, and Judy George.

General H. Norman Schwarzkopf was named after his father, who was also a general. The general part was okay with Norm, but bearing his father's first name—Herbert—was too much. The younger Schwarzkopf had his name legally changed, keeping only the initial H. Which brings up an important point. You can name them anything—something innocuous like Karen Johnson, for instance—but there's no guaranteeing it will stick. Karen Johnson is "like a Tupperware lady . . . but Whoopi Goldberg is a persona," says the woman who goes by the latter moniker.

Walker Smith, Jr., borrowed an ID card from a retired boxer and fought an amateur match using the other fellow's name, Ray Robinson. "That's a sweet fighter you've got there," a newsman told Smith's manager after another bout. A lady fan added her own compliment: Smith was "as sweet as sugar." The compliment stuck, and he became Sugar Ray Robinson.

Louis Armstrong ended up as Satchmo by mistake. When he went to England, an editor misheard his nickname, Satchel Mouth, and the rest is history.

Charles Manson acquired a new middle name on purpose. He changed "Milles" to "Willes" so that, if each syllable of his name is pronounced distinctly, it becomes "Charles' will is man's son."

"I got a call in the middle of the night. I was told, 'The clothes are wonderful, the pictures are wonderful, and you have a new name,' " recalled fashion designer Arnold Isaacs. It was 1955, and he had gotten his first break—an assignment to design gowns for car ad models. The stylist had christened him Scaasi—Isaacs spelled backward. He liked it, and with Scaasi as his legal name, his career flourished and his assignments included designing for First Ladies from Mamie Eisenhower to Barbara Bush.

"The academy has fought stoically to claim that *they* named the Oscar. But of course I did," claimed Bette Davis. "I named it after the rear end of my husband. Why? Because that's what it looked like." The first of her three husbands was bandleader Harmon Oscar Nelson, Jr.

What did the real Oscar think? He may have been flattered by the motive behind it, but not everyone who lends his or her name to a famous enterprise is pleased. "I know there are many times she wishes her name wasn't Wendy," said R. David Thomas, referring to his youngest daughter, who at age eight, redheaded, freckled, and buck-toothed, lent her name to his hamburger chain. "When you name something after someone, that's a lot of responsibility, good and bad. I remember she'd be very embarrassed sometimes. I'm not sure I'd do it again."

Charles Lubin likewise named his company after his daughter, Sara Lee. "I think that every dinner party we went to for the first five years I was married," she recalled, "the dessert made for me was cheesecake. . . . [O]nly I liked the Sara Lee cheesecake. I guess everybody felt that they could do it better."

Ian Fleming named his hero, James Bond, after a real-life leading American ornithologist. Fleming had spotted Bond's book *Birds of the West Indies* when he was in Jamaica writing a spy novel. As the author later wrote to Bond's wife, Mary Fanning Wickham Bond, "It struck me that this brief, unromantic, and yet very masculine Anglo-Saxon name was just what I needed, and so a second James Bond was born. . . . In return, I can only offer you or James Bond unlimited use of the name Ian Fleming for any purpose you may think fit. Perhaps one day your husband will discover a particularly horrible species of bird which he would like to christen in an insulting fashion by calling it Ian Fleming."

In the annals of naming, that's about as good a deal as you can get.

### NOTHING PERSONAL

1. "I personally did not shoot Dr. King, but I believe I may be partly responsible for his death."—James Earl Ray.

2. "I never had any feeling of hatred or dislike for Mr. Truman . . ." said Oscar Collazo, who tried to shoot the President to further the cause of Puerto Rican nationalism. After he was pardoned by President Carter at the age of sixty-four, he maintained, "I intend to continue where I left off, to keep on fighting for Puerto Rico's independence until I die."

3. "By the way I want to get one thing straight. I didn't know he had that many children. I didn't know he had so many children."—Sirhan Sirhan, RFK's assassin.

4. "I'm very sorry," John Hinckley wrote to President Reagan after trying to shoot him, ". . . I thank God no one died."

5. *"Do you know what you did? Do you?"* an arresting officer shouted at handcuffed Mark Chapman, John Lennon's assassin. From the backseat of the patrol car Chapman replied with heart-felt sincerity: "Listen, I'm sorry. I didn't know he was a friend of yours."

6. "Personally, I didn't kill any Vietnamese that day: I mean personally. I represented the United States of America. My country."—Lieutenant William Calley about My Lai, March 16, 1968.

7. "There is no borderline between one's personal world and the world in general."—Lee Harvey Oswald.

GREAT LINES FOR LOTS OF OCCASIONS

Worried about turning out clever phrases on cue? At a loss for witty things to say in meetings? Never fear. Here are some great lines to borrow for situations such as:

*DEALING WITH GOSSIPS.* "Once the toothpaste is out of the tube it's hard to get it back in."—H. R. Haldeman to White House counsel John Dean, who had just revealed he was talking to prosecutors in the Watergate investigation.

*GETTING THE SHOW ON THE ROAD.* "Tomorrow we shoot, whether it rains, whether it snows, whether it stinks."—movie mogul Samuel Goldwyn to director Leo McCarey.

*FIRING AN EMPLOYEE.* "Well, sometimes you just don't like somebody."—Henry Ford II to Lee Iacocca, who had just demanded to know why he had been fired.

*COUNTERACTING DOUBLE-TALK.* "What I want is an economist [substitute accountant, lawyer, doctor] with one arm—so he can't say on the one hand . . . but on the other."—Harry S. Truman.

*INSPIRING UNDERLINGS.* "Retreat, hell! We're just fighting in another direction."—General O. P. Smith in 1950 during the

Korean War when the Chinese unexpectedly poured across the border and drove his forces back.

*VENTING FRUSTRATION.* "Oh, sho-o-o-ot. Golly. Darn." —President Bush when he failed to sink a six-foot putt on the eighteenth hole in Kennebunkport, Maine.

*COMMENTING ON CURRENT EVENTS.* "People that are really very weird can get into sensitive positions and have a tremendous impact on history."—Dan Quayle.

*RECOVERING FROM A FAUX PAS.* "Man does not live by words alone, even though sometimes he has to eat them."—Adlai Stevenson.

### THE ART OF THE INSULT

It isn't hard to insult someone. All you have to do is throw a lot of bad language around. But delivering an insult without expletives that need deleting is an art. Among the remarks from the cutting edge of history:

1. "If you give me a week, I might think of one."—Eisenhower to reporters when asked an example of Nixon's major contributions to his administration.

2. "He squats when he pees."—LBJ on Adlai Stevenson.

3. Not "even dry behind the ears."—Harry Truman on JFK as a candidate.

4. "Just a twentieth-century Uncle Tom."—Malcolm X on Martin Luther King, Jr.

5. "More people died at Chappaquiddick than Three Mile Island."—former Texas Governor John Connally.

6. "You can't make a soufflé rise twice."—Alice Roosevelt Longworth on Thomas Dewey, when he was nominated by the Republicans for the second time in 1948.

7. "It was the goddamnedest thing, here was a young whippersnapper, malaria-ridden and yellah, sickly, sickly. He never said a word of importance in the Senate and he never did a thing. But somehow with his books and his Pulitzer Prizes he managed to create the image of himself as a shining intellectual, a youthful leader who would change the face of the country."—LBJ, then the Senate majority leader, on JFK.

8. "All his golfing pals are rich men he has met since 1945."—JFK on Ike.

9. "Can you imagine Jerry Ford sitting in this chair?" —Nixon on his Vice President.

10. On the second day of the Democratic National Convention in 1964, Hubert Humphrey was summoned to the White House. Lyndon Johnson kept him waiting in a limousine outside the south entrance. When Humphrey was finally let inside, LBJ told him, "If you didn't know that I had you picked a month ago, maybe you haven't got brains enough to be the Vice President."

11. "He went out the way he came in—no class."—JFK after Nixon finally conceded the very close 1960 election by sending out an aide, Herb Klein, to read a brief statement.

12. "Speak up, Bill," Lyndon Johnson commanded his press secretary, who was saying grace at the LBJ ranch. Moyers, who had been a Baptist minister, responded: "I wasn't talking to you, Mr. President."

# 24
# Film Versus Reality

*Whatever happened to real men in this world?*
*Men like Clark Gable? No one would have carried off my*
*daughter if there had been a* real *man there.*
—Catherine Hearst, Patty's mother, a former Atlanta belle who
had been up for the part of Scarlett O'Hara opposite Gable

Things do get a little confusing. In a world where JFK is both a movie and a man, a world where the star of *Bedtime for Bonzo* ends up sleeping at the White House, sometimes it's hard to tell where the movie stops and reality begins.

"Bonzo's death was a tough concept for me to get a grip on," Maureen Reagan once commented, and you can't help sympathizing. Her father walked through life as if it were a Hollywood set. After World War II ended, he said, "By the time I got out of the Army Air Corps, all I wanted to do—in common with several million other veterans—was to rest up awhile, make love to my wife, and come up refreshed to do a better job in an ideal world." Unlike millions of veterans, he had spent the war in the same city as his wife, Jane Wyman, making military promotional films.

On inauguration day 1981 Reagan stopped by House Speaker Tip O'Neill's office and admired his antique desk. O'Neill explained proudly that it had once belonged to President Grover Cleveland. "That's very interesting. You know I once played Grover Cleveland in the movies," said Reagan.

O'Neill corrected him. "No, Mr. President, you're thinking of Grover Cleveland *Alexander*, the ballplayer." O'Neill had recently seen the *The Winning Season* on TV starring Reagan as the famous pitcher.

With Reagan the line between film and reality was consistently thin. Asked if he'd been nervous debating President Carter in 1980, he replied, "Not at all. I've been on the same stage with John Wayne." When a TWA airline was hijacked by Shiite Muslims in 1985 and one American was killed and forty were held hostage, Reagan had it all figured out: "After seeing the

Diana Lynn looks on as Bonzo beds down with Ronald Reagan, a man who took a decidedly cinematic view of life even when his career took him away from Hollywood sets.

movie *Rambo*, I'll know what to do the next time something like this happens." He once interrupted a top-level White House briefing on MX missiles to recount the plot from the movie *War-Games*. It was his only contribution to the meeting. When he telephoned just-fired Oliver North, who stood at attention in his motel room to take the call, he said, "Ollie, you're a national hero. This is going to make a great movie someday."

Reagan knew implicitly that real life is the greatest movie ever made. Though he didn't get a chance to play a film version of his career, others did enact theirs. Audie Murphy, the most decorated American war hero in World War II, starred in a 1955 film of his autobiography, *To Hell and Back*. He guessed it was "the first time, I suppose, a man has fought an honest war, then come back and played himself doing it."

Jerry Ford lost an honest election and donned black tie to appear in an episode of *Dynasty* as himself. Dan Quayle acted vice presidential when he made a cameo appearance on *Major Dad*, a 1990 performance one reviewer dubbed "amazingly realistic."

Boxer Rocky Graziano left his life story to Paul Newman, who starred in the 1956 film *Somebody Up There Likes Me*, but he got his chance to play a version of himself. The producers of Martha Raye's 1950s TV show were brainstorming, looking for a loutish character like Rocky to be Martha's boyfriend. Finally one of them said, "Let's get Graziano," and they did.

Pete Rose, banned from baseball for gambling, wishes they'd make a film about him. "I hope I'll be around to see it," he said in 1991, "and . . . I think you'll agree, it will be a lot better movie if it ends up in Cooperstown. If I'm not mistaken, most of your good movies have good endings, happy endings." In his view, admittance to the Baseball Hall of Fame would be the perfect Hollywood ending to his life.

Rose may find out, however, that when you're up on the silver screen—whether you're playing yourself or someone like Jason Robards is doing the job for you—you look into an unexpected mirror. "There's nothing in my education that prepared me for seeing someone up there on the screen with the name of Bradlee using all those dirty words," said Ben Bradlee, the *Washington Post* editor with the notoriously tart tongue whose reporters, Bob Woodward and Carl Bernstein, broke the Watergate cover-up and inspired the movie *All the President's Men*.

Once immortalized on the screen, real people sometimes have trouble filling their own shoes. "Men go to bed with Rita Hayworth and wake up and find it's only me," lamented Rita Hayworth.

"A man can buy a poster, pin it on his locker, and imagine the most minute details about a slinky starlet. He'll know her through and through. He'll possess her external reality. So of course Hinckley 'knew' me," commented Jodie Foster in 1982.

"Here's the difference between being an actor and being a politician," said Kirk Douglas. "Gary Hart changed his name, lied about his age, and had a much publicized affair. And he was ruined. Well, I changed my name. I always lie about my age. And if I had a much publicized liaison, it would be the best thing that could happen to my career."

But sometimes film and reality are a perfect match. Just take Mary Martin and her son, Larry Hagman, who said, "She's very proud to have JR for a son and I'm very proud to have Peter Pan for a mother."

### HORSEMANSHIP AND THE HOLLYWOOD COWBOY

1. "The only time I get on a horse is when I make a movie. I hate the damn things."—John Wayne.

2. "Anytime I want to relax, I get on a horse."—James Drury, star of TV's *Virginian*.

3. "There's something about . . . having a horse between my knees that makes it easier to sort out a problem."—Ronald Reagan.

4. "I'm scared to death on a horse. You can't be sure that it isn't going to step into a gopher hole or something and throw you on your ass and break your neck."—Henry Fonda.

5. "The whole romance of being a cowboy is absurd because basically what you do is block cows," said actor Daniel Stern after playing an urban cowboy in *City Slickers*. "I mean, a cow wants to go this way, and you put your horse in front of him, and the cow is afraid of the horse, so it runs back the other way. And that's what you do for five hundred miles across Colorado is block cows because they're too stupid to go around you."

### LIFE IMITATES ART: ASSORTED CASE STUDIES

1. In the early seventies "nuclear energy became an issue, and when I'm preoccupied by an issue, I try to find a way to make a film about it," explained Jane Fonda of the impetus for *The China Syndrome*. A week after the film opened, an accident very like the one in the movie transpired at the Three Mile Island nuclear reactor in Pennsylvania.

2. Roman Polanski's pregnant wife, Sharon Tate, and four guests at his house were bizarrely murdered in 1969 and the crime remained unsolved for months. "It was shortly after *Rosemary's Baby* and *Rosemary's Baby* dealt with witchcraft in today's New

York," recalled the film's director. As a result, the press was rife with "stories of black magic and ritual orgies. Can you imagine an eight-and-a-half-month pregnant woman indulging in orgies and sex . . . ?" The stories persisted until Charles Manson was linked to the murder.

3. "Americans like to think that war is John Wayne. To get a grenade and a VC's throat, to shove the grenade right down it. Americans sit at television sets and say, 'One hundred bodies. Boy!' And they think, *Great,* and they think that I'm the ugly one."—Lieutenant William Calley of My Lai massacre fame.

4. "It was like going to a movie: we paid our money, we went to the theater, we laughed, we cried, the movie ended and an hour later we had forgotten about it."—Saudi financier Adnan Khashoggi after the Gulf War.

### TV: THE ULTIMATE TWILIGHT ZONE

*Before I was shot I always suspected I was watching TV instead of living life. Right when I was being shot, I knew I was watching television.*
—Andy Warhol, who was shot in 1968 by Valerie Solanis, a radical feminist/frustrated glory seeker

As generations of Americans have been reared in front of the TV, the boundaries between what's happening in the little box and what's happening in the living room tend to blur. Here are real-life episodes that seem to be borrowed from *The Twilight Zone.*

1. "I've seen Europe on television . . . so really it was nothing new to me."—George Wallace, who first visited there in the mid-seventies.

2. "The show was so real. A woman who follows her man anywhere is a real woman."—Eva Gabor about the TV show *Green Acres.*

3. "I must admit I'm glad to be out of the hospital. It's a little unsettling to turn on the news and see Peter Jennings pointing to a diagram of a heart with your name on it."—George Bush after he was hospitalized for heart fibrillations in May 1991.

4. "Back in that first year when I was so excited about the quality of the show [*Star Trek*], I suddenly realized my part was being cut down and I decided to leave the show . . . It just so

happened that is when I met Dr. King . . . I told him my feelings. I wanted to get on with my career." Nichelle Nichols, alias Lieutenant Uhura, expected King to say "bravo," but instead he said, "You must stay. You don't understand the effect you are having not only on black people but on everybody. Everybody's mind and attitude is changed immeasurably because you are there." She stayed, and on November 22, 1968, she and William Shatner engaged in TV's first interracial romantic kiss.

5. "I'd seen so many people and their sadness on television. I didn't want to see myself that way."—Gwen Kopechne, whose daughter, Mary Jo, drowned at Chappaquiddick. Television crews showed up at the funeral because Teddy Kennedy attended.

6. "I've just been robbed by the girl who played Kimberly on *Diff'rent Strokes*," said Heather Dailey, a clerk at the Lake Video store in Las Vegas, dialing 911 at 10:25 A.M. She'd recognized the sunglasses-clad woman who pulled a pellet gun and said, "Give me your money," as Dana Plato, former child-TV-star turned down-on-her-luck, out-of-work actress.

7. "It was a little disturbing when we did the Klan scene and some of the extras asked if they could bring their own robes."—actress Jennifer Grey, who played Mickey Schwerner's wife in a TV movie based on the murder of three civil rights workers killed by the Ku Klux Klan in Mississippi in 1964.

8. "People say that racing is dangerous, but I'll take my chances on the track any day than on the highway." James Dean was filmed, slouched in a chair, toying with a small lariat on the set of *Giant*, for a commercial on safe driving. "Take it easy drivin', uh, the life you save might be mine, you know?" After *Giant* was completed, Dean was killed in a car crash.

9. "I'm never going to have memories of Christmas with my father or of sitting in his lap, but I still feel I know him," said singer Jett Williams, the illegitimate daughter of Hank Williams, who died of a drug and alcohol overdose five days after she was born in 1953. The family feeling struck her "like a bolt of lightning" when she happened to see rare 1952 footage of her father on *The Kate Smith Evening Hour*. "It was the first time I ever saw him move. He's singing 'Hey, Good Lookin',' and when he turns to look at the camera, it felt like he was looking straight at me. When my eyes met his, I thought I was looking at myself."

10. "I think the opulence, the consumerism, the food, the

cars—these things made [people] want more than their government provided them," explained Larry Hagman, who thinks *Dallas* influenced world politics and hastened the demise of the Eastern bloc dictatorships. "You take people who don't have any food to a goddamned supermarket, they're going to want to stay."

11. "People will say to twenty million people what they won't say in their dining rooms."—Oprah Winfrey, who is no exception to her rule. While interviewing an incest survivor on a 1985 show, she suddenly started talking about her own experience as if she were sitting at home with a cup of coffee. "I had no idea of the impact or the power of that statement. I had no idea that years later, everywhere I went, women would come up to me. I've been crossing the street in downtown Chicago and have had women come up to me and whisper, 'Can I talk to you about something?' I always know what it's about."

### A CHILD'S VIEW

*I grew up at the studio behind the camera, climbing up ladders and running around the soundstage. But I understood right away about the difference between real life and television. I wasn't the one who was confused—other people were. They thought I was Little Ricky. But I knew Fred and Ethel didn't live next door —Jack Benny did.*
—Desi Arnaz, Jr., son of Lucille Ball

Not every child has it figured out quite so neatly. "I remember riding in a chariot at the age of three or four during *Ben-Hur*, and my father coming home in his gladiator outfit with blood all over him. I just thought he was a chariot driver, I imagine," said Fraser Heston, Charlton's son, who at two months played the infant Moses in *The Ten Commandments*.

"Christ, I saw my father as a gladiator nailed to the cross," said Michael Douglas of his father, Kirk. "I'd think, 'How can I be the man this man was?' "

"For the longest time I didn't know he was Captain Kangaroo," Bob Keeshan's son, Michael, said. " . . . My sister Maeve, who was about three and a half at the time, went into the studio with my mother where the show was being taped. When my father finished taping, he went back to his dressing room and then came back as himself. He asked my sister how it was, and she said, 'Oh, Daddy, Daddy! You just missed Captain Kangaroo!' "

"I know who you are," Dinah Shore's young daughter, Melissa, accused her one evening.

"Then who am I?" Dinah responded playfully.

"You're Dinah Shore."

"Of course I'm Dinah Shore," she said, but that wasn't the right answer. Melissa pouted until Dinah realized that "Mrs. George Montgomery" was the correct response. Dinah Shore was someone on TV. Finally she offered, "But I'm your mother, too," which helped.

"As long as you're not Dinah Shore," her daughter concluded, and gave her a kiss.

When Barbara Walters's adopted daughter, Jackie, was five, she announced, "That's not you, Mommy," when she saw her mother on TV. "I like you better here at home." When she was older, her mother interviewed Menachem Begin and Anwar el Sadat, interrupting the scheduled programming. When Walters called home, she was told, "It's unfair, Mommy. I was watching my program about cats, and just before it ended, they took it off and put *you* on."

"When I was little, I always used to sit in front of the television and scream, 'Daddy, out of the box! Daddy, come home!' " recalls Walter Cronkite's daughter, Nancy. "Well, one time Dad explained to me all about how the airwaves go out. I was nodding and nodding and agreeing, and at the end of his explanation I asked him, 'But, Daddy, how do you get in the box?' "

# 25
# What They Were Doing When

*"The day that Desi died, [Lucille Ball] and I were doing* Password *together,"* recounted Betty White, Ball's longtime friend. It was 1986, and *"she was being real funny on the show, but during a break she said, 'You know it's the damndest thing. Goddamn it, I didn't think I'd get this upset. There he goes.' "*

With brows furrowed about everyday concerns, with hearts full of common joys, we go about our lives. Then suddenly something happens—a death, a stock market crash, an award—that throws everything into stark relief. We look up and take note of where we are in the scheme of things. Sometimes it's not where we thought we'd be.

1. *Watching TV.* On election night 1960, Judith Campbell Exner was glued to the set. The Nixon-Kennedy contest was one of the closest in history. "[T]he one thought that kept going through my mind was '[W]here do we go from here? How the devil do you carry on a love affair with the President of the United States,' " mused JFK's lover. It was one thing to date a glamorous politician. It was another to go "to the White House for a rendezvous. I couldn't even fathom it."

2. *Taking a bath.* Ingrid Bergman was awakened at 7:00 A.M. in Paris "by Twentieth Century-Fox publicity men shouting into the phone, "You've won! You've won!" She'd won the Academy Award for *Anastasia*. To celebrate, she took a glass of champagne to her bath and was still soaking when her young son, Robertino, called, " 'Mama, they're talking about you!' . . . It was a repeat over the French radio of the Oscar ceremony in Hollywood, and Robertino had heard the announcement of 'Ingrid Bergman,' and then the applause. I could still hear the applause as he put the radio on the bathroom floor and Cary [Grant] began his speech: 'Dear Ingrid, wherever you are . . .' And I was saying, 'I'm in the bathtub!' 'Wherever you are in the world, we your friends, want to congratulate you. . . .' "

3. *In the shower.* As the October 1991 vote neared on his

UPI/BETTMANN

When news breaks, who knows where we'll be?
Harlem's Adam Clayton Powell, Jr., was playing
dominoes in the Bahamas when he discovered that
Congress had refused to seat him for ethics violations.

controversial appointment to the Supreme Court, Clarence
Thomas headed for the shower. Neither he nor his wife, Virginia,
turned on the radio. Finally she called her office, "and they said,
'Why aren't you watching TV? He has fifty-two votes.' I ran
upstairs to tell Clarence. He'd just gotten out of the shower, and
I said, 'You got fifty-two votes!' He kind of shrugged. It was the
oddest thing. It was like, 'Okay, thanks.' It was as if it didn't
matter anymore."

4. *In prison.* When the stock market plummeted more than
five hundred points on October 19, 1987, inside trader Dennis

Levine was monitoring the debacle in the TV room at the Lewisburg Penitentiary. Then two guards appeared, bearing a message that "one of the high-ranking prison officials wanted to see me." What could a prison official want from the man who had brought down Ivan Boesky and assorted other Wall Street power brokers?

"Dennis, can you give me some advice on what to do with my portfolio? Should I sell out and take my losses, or should I hold on?"

Levine, always eager to cut a deal, responded, "If I give you advice, is there any way I can go home sooner?"

"Oh, no, I can't do anything like that."

"Then I can't help you," he replied. There were no deals in prison. Levine served seventeen months of his term and was released on September 8, 1988.

5. *Eating ice cream.* CBS correspondent Bob Simon was picked up by the Iraqis during the Gulf War and held captive for forty days, but at times he managed to escape his circumstances. "At one point I heard somebody being brought up onto the floor and I heard him being kicked. Oomph. Four times he was being kicked. But I was so deep at that moment—so deep. I was walking down Broadway with an ice-cream cone in one hand and some popcorn in the other—that I couldn't pay attention to the kicking. You develop defense mechanisms you don't know you're capable of."

6. *In the Ceylon jungle.* When his grandfather John D. Rockefeller, Jr., died in 1960, John D., IV (now a senator from West Virginia), "happened to be in the middle of the Ceylon jungle—quite literally in the middle—visiting an old friend. I still don't quite know how they located me, but some way or another this native came walking up in the middle of this God-forsaken place and asked me if I was Mr. Rockefeller. I said I was. He gave me a telegram from my father."

7. *Driving to Marlon Brando's house.* "I stopped the car. I couldn't believe it. I was in a state of shock, actually," recalled *Life* photographer Gordon Parks. "I went into Marlon's place and Marlon was stretched out on the couch. And he said 'Hello.' I said, 'Hello. You know Dr. King is dead.' So Marlon didn't get up. He just looked at me with a rather steely look." Brando then "called his assistant. 'Order me some guns from my gunsmith.' . . . He called the Panther Headquarters in California. I don't know

what he said to them but I waited and then he came back. . . . He said, 'I feel like shooting my way all the way to Washington, D.C.' I said, well look at all those people down below. You're not going to shoot indiscriminately. They may feel exactly the same way you do." Brando calmed down, and Parks went back to his hotel room, where he got a call from *Life* assigning him the coverage of King's funeral.

8. *Skipping through Yale.* When a student called out, "Hey. Did you hear? Reagan got shot," Jodie Foster, a freshman in the class of 1984 at Yale, "was skipping hand in hand across campus with [her] best friend." Since the real world seldom makes a dent in campus life, Jodie didn't think much about the news until she returned to her dorm at ten-thirty that night. Before she could get her key in the lock, her roommate opened the door and announced: "John Hinckley."

"What about him? Did he write me again?"

"He's the one, I think. It was on the radio."

9. *Recovering from surgery.* "I felt dead. I kept thinking, I'm really dead. This is what it's like to be dead—you think you're alive but you're dead. I just *think* I'm lying here in a hospital," recalled Andy Warhol as he was recovering from five hours of surgery after a disgruntled feminist fired two bullets into his stomach in 1968. The next day Robert Kennedy was killed. "I heard a television going somewhere and the words *Kennedy* and *assassin* and *shot* over and over again. Robert Kennedy had been shot, but what was so weird was that I had no understanding that this was a *second* Kennedy assassination—I just thought that maybe after you die, they rerun things for you, like President Kennedy's assassination."

WHO WAS DOING WHAT, NOVEMBER 22, 1963

*"It didn't surprise me that Americans who visited [Kennedy's] grave would invariably tell you in minute detail what they were doing when they first learned of his death," said Kerri Childress, of Arlington National Cemetery's office of the historian, in 1989. "But . . . five Soviet war generals recently told me how old they were when it happened and what they were doing. I have had South Americans cry. It wasn't just an American tragedy. It affected people from all walks of life, all over the world."*

Almost anyone who was around on November 22, 1963, can tell you what he or she was doing when the news broke that John F. Kennedy was shot. Herewith a sampling of the places they found themselves.

1. *Weighing a load of grain.* "I remember that I climbed down from a tractor, unhooked a farm trailer, and walked into my warehouse to weigh a load of grain," said Jimmy Carter. "I was told by a group of farmers that the President had been shot. I went outside, knelt on the steps and began to pray. In a few minutes I learned that he had not lived. It was a grievous personal loss—my President. I wept openly for the first time in more than ten years—for the first time since my father had died."

2. *Finishing lunch.* Senator J. William Fulbright threw down his napkin and leaped up when he heard the news. "God *damn* it! I *told* him not to go to Dallas!" he cried. Indeed, he had told the President that "Dallas is a very dangerous place. I wouldn't go there. Don't you go." Texas wasn't Kennedy country. It was right-wing, conservative. But it was Democratic, and the President needed to hold his party together for the 1964 election.

3. *Swooning at the House restaurant.* Initial reports indicated that LBJ had been shot along with Kennedy. Next in line for the presidency was the Speaker of the House, seventy-one-year-old John McCormack, who was dining at the House restaurant. He said the possibility that he was President hit him with "a terrific impact." He tried to stand up but was attacked by vertigo. The room spun, and he feared he would faint. He sat down and was still shaky when someone passed the word that LBJ was unharmed.

4. *At the movies.* "We have just learned that the President of the United States, the Vice President, the Governor of Texas, and a Secret Service man have been murdered," announced the manager of a Nevada movie house. "We now continue with our matinee feature." The lights, which had been raised, were lowered, and the film continued. In the first hours after the assassination news was wildly inaccurate.

5. *Manning the switchboard at CBS.* "When President Kennedy was assassinated, people were actually upset because the soaps weren't on," recalled Chris Santana, switchboard operator at CBS television in New York City. "If the soaps weren't on, that generates more traffic than anything. If they're used to watching the

soap opera, they don't care about the President or anything else until that's all over. Put it on the six o'clock news."

6. *At a table by the pool.* Robert F. Kennedy was home at Hickory Hill. A workman who was painting a wing of the family house heard the news over a transistor radio. He shouted to Kennedy, but RFK didn't understand. Then the phone rang. It was J. Edgar Hoover, calling on extension 163—the poolside phone. "I have news for you," he said matter-of-factly. "The President's been shot." A few minutes later he called back and said, "The President is dead," and hung up. RFK commented later that Hoover's voice was "not quite as excited as if he were reporting the fact that he has found a Communist on the faculty of Howard University." The FBI director expressed no sympathy.

7. *On the floor of a limousine.* When the shots were fired, Secret Service Agent Rufus Youngblood hurled LBJ to the floor and jumped on top of him. He didn't let on what happened, but the Vice President knew something was up because he could hear conversations on the hand-held radios like "Follow that car. Dagger to Daylight. I'm shifting to Charlie [the President's channel]. Do the same."

All Youngblood told LBJ was "An emergency exists. When we get to where we're going, you and me are going to move right off and not tie in with the other people."

"Okay, partner," Johnson replied softly.

8. *Sitting in Spanish class.* A friend at the National Cathedral School for Girls in Washington, D.C., told Luci Johnson what happened to President Kennedy. "I thought she was kidding," Luci recalled. "Then the class began buzzing. The bells started ringing continuously. My teacher never said a word. The class stood up and walked to the chapel . . . everyone was so thunderstruck. My principal, Katherine Lee . . . said the best thing was to pray. My first reaction was that I was the only one who knew President Kennedy. It never entered my mind that I was the President's daughter."

# 26
# The Hand of Fate

*If I was gonna have to wait more than five or ten minutes, I was going back to the hotel. I just wasn't that desperate about it. I just wasn't that desperate to act that afternoon. That plan wasn't my plan. It was raining, misting. I wasn't going to stand around in the rain.*
—John Hinckley on his attempt to kill Ronald Reagan

Most of us don't fret the little things. How long we linger in a meeting, whether it's raining, whose turn it is to drive, what we should wear—every day we negotiate a hundred questions of this nature without thinking twice. Then tragedy strikes. Someone has a brush with mortality. Suddenly the "what ifs" of life kick in. We look back over our shoulders, analyzing the smallest details. What if Reagan had been late? What if it had poured? What if . . . ?

When Ronald Reagan finished his speech at the Hilton Hotel on March 30, 1981, his fate was not sealed. Yes, a young man intent on killing him was waiting in the crowd outside. But as Hinckley himself admitted later, "I didn't know what I was going to do. I had my little gun. I thought I'd see how close I could get."

Hinckley had stalked Carter when he was still President and even had managed to get within spitting distance. But the would-be assassin's guns had been confiscated at the airport. Hinckley had been to Ted Kennedy's office twice and waited patiently for the senator but never caught a glimpse of him. He'd watched Reagan go into the hotel, but he wasn't able to get within firing range.

Hinckley was used to seeing targets come and go. He "wasn't that desperate about it."

Finally, as Reagan headed back to his limo, amid the confusion caused by the press, Hinckley managed to slip in at the front of the police line. "Boy, has security fouled up," he said to himself. He "didn't really think it would work out." But the Secret Service men weren't even looking in his direction. Within three seconds

About three weeks before he aimed his gun at Ronald Reagan, John Hinckley sent this note to Jodie Foster at Yale.

he'd fired six shots. Press secretary Jim Brady was lying on the sidewalk in a pool of blood. Reagan, who didn't think he was hit, was pushed into the black limousine. "Jerry, get off me. You're hurting my ribs," the President told Secret Service man Jerry Parr. Reagan was sandwiched on the transmission hump and thought that accounted for the pain in his chest. He took out a napkin he'd saved from the convention hall lectern and wiped his lips. "I think I've cut my mouth," he said. Parr realized something else was going on. The President was coughing up blood. The limo took off at high speed for George Washington Hospital.

What if Parr hadn't told the driver to hit the gas? What if there'd been more traffic? "If ten minutes had gone by," said Dr. Joseph Giordano afterward, "the President would not have survived. My feeling is that the secret hero was Jerry Parr, who recognized the origin of that bright-red blood and got the president to G.W. immediately."

Life often hangs in the balance of a myriad of small details: the vagaries of the weather, the caprice of mood, the quirks of timing.

Little things end up making a tremendous difference. Things like who drives. James Chaney took the wheel the night in 1964 when he and his fellow civil rights workers Andrew Goodman and Michael Schwerner were stopped by the Ku Klux Klan on the back roads of Philadelphia, Mississippi. Schwerner, a Jew, was the most familiar to the Klan; he was the one who really bothered them. Had he been driving, he could have been charged with speeding and taken away separately. But as it was, all three young men were arrested and then let out of jail in the middle of the night, sitting ducks for a Klan vendetta.

Little things cast the die. Things like where you get out of the car. "Some time shortly before eleven o'clock, John Lennon and his wife arrived back at the Dakota [apartment building] in a limousine. They parked the limousine outside the Dakota. There is a driveway into which they might have gone, but on this occasion did not," New York Chief of Detectives James T. Sullivan told reporters at 2:00 A.M. in October 1980. "They got out and walked into the archway area of the Dakota. . . . This individual, Mr. Chapman, came up behind them and called to him, 'Mr. Lennon!' Then, in a combat stance, he fired. He emptied the Charter Arms .38-caliber gun that he had with him and shot John Lennon."

Little things can kill you—or protect you. Things like coming out to kiss your husband good-bye as he's about to head off for church. In December 1960 John F. Kennedy, then President-elect, was all set to head off for Sunday services in Palm Beach, Florida. Waiting for him out at the street was seventy-six-year-old Richard P. Pavlick, whose car had seven sticks of dynamite that could be activated with a switch. Angry that Kennedy, in his opinion, had "bought" the election, Pavlick intended to drive his car into JFK's on a suicide/assassination mission. But by chance, Jackie, little Caroline, and a nurse with baby John, Jr., in her arms, came out, smiling and laughing, to bid JFK good-bye. Pavlick was so struck by the scene, he said, "I decided to get him at the church or some other place." Before he could, he was picked up by the police.

Destiny seems to shift with as much rhyme or reason as the wind. Even the decision to go to church or not can tip the balance. "I actually started to church with my wife. I got to church and I said, 'You get out, I am going down and see if I can do something for Captain [J. Will] Fritz,' " recalled [Harry D.] Holmes, Dallas postmaster. He'd helped trace the money order Oswald used to purchase the gun he used to kill Kennedy. Holmes had "been in and out of Captain Fritz's office on numerous occasions during this two-and-a-half day period." He went back to help the head of the Dallas Police's homicide section one more time that Sunday. ". . . Captain Fritz motioned to me and said, 'We're getting ready to have a last interrogation with Oswald before we transfer him to the county jail. Would you like to join us?' I said, 'I would.' "

Holmes added what proved to be a critical half hour to the interrogation. At its completion Oswald was brought downstairs, where he encountered Jack Ruby, who shot him at 11:21 A.M. Only minutes earlier Ruby was nowhere to be seen. In fact, at 11:17 he had been at the Western Union office wiring money to a nightclub employee. If Holmes had decided to go to church with his wife, Ruby would have missed his moment in history.

Sara Jane Moore probably would have preferred to miss hers. A divorced housewife with a checkered past—she'd joined a radical group and then ratted on them to the FBI—she was trying to redeem her left-wing standing by shooting Gerald Ford. But he was late, and she needed to pick up her son at school. "This has to be the most ridiculous thing I have done in my entire life," she said to herself as she stood outside the St. Francis Hotel in San Francisco in 1975. "What the hell am I doing here, getting ready to shoot the President?"

She said, "I turned around to leave. Couldn't get through the crowd." Penned in by indecision and circumstance, she stayed and tried to fire her shots. Had the crowd been more obliging, she might have been on time at school and never pulled the trigger.

Fate's forecast is always partly cloudy, partly sunny. No assassin is one until he pulls the trigger. For example, between Oswald's purchase of a $19.95 mail-order rifle and the moment Kennedy came within his viewfinder there were probably a dozen variables—including something as simple as a kiss—that could have recast the outcome. The night before the murder Oswald had tried to repair his rocky marriage, but his Russian-born wife, Marina, had turned a cold shoulder. He slept little and in the morning kissed his two children, left his wedding ring in a demitasse cup, wrapped his rifle in brown paper, and went to work at the Texas Book Depository. It was a drizzly day. A chance of this, a chance of that. Meanwhile, Jackie Kennedy was worried about her hair. "Oh, I want the bubbletop," she said. The rain stopped. The bubbletop came off. Oswald had his moment.

Arthur Bremer initially missed his for the simplest reason of all: He was worried about what to wear. Bremer, who made headlines when he shot George Wallace in 1972, had aimed for the limelight even earlier. On April 22 of the same year he tracked President Nixon to Canada, his weapon loaded and his goal within sight. "All along the fucking Ottawa visit I cursed the damn 'demonstrators.' Security was beefed up—overly beefed up—because of these stupid dirty runts," he wrote in his diary. As he was walking down the street, "A woman, middle-age gave me an anti-war/anti-Nixon leaflet. I glanced it over & handed it back to her, politely. What could I say? You stupid bitch stop this useless protest, let the security slacken & I'll show you something really effective?"

Then opportunity knocked. "Shock! Shock! I saw what I took to be the President's car parked directly in front of the embassy! . . . I went immediately home, ran part of the way. . . . I stupidly took time to, I'm ashamed & embarrassed [*sic*] to say, brush my teeth, take 2 asperin [*sic*] & I think change from a salt & pepper knit suit into my black business one. . . . Car gone. . . . I will give very little if ANY thought to these things on any future attempt.

"After all does the world remember if Sirhan's tie was straight?

"SHIT, I was stupid!"

But it's foolish to curse fate. If someone's number's not up, it's just not up. Mark David Chapman, a plump, bespectacled security guard at a vacation condo at Waikiki Beach, had thought about killing lots of people besides John Lennon. Ronald Reagan, Jackie O, Liz Taylor, and his own father were all on his list. On Sunday, May 7, 1972, Bremer wrote in his diary, "Yesterday I even considered McGovern as a target."

What possessed LBJ, on a stopover at Pearl Harbor during World War II, to decline a lift back to California on the plane of Admiral Chester Nimitz? Who can say? But the next day Johnson said he "picked up the paper and saw where Admiral Nimitz's plane had landed on a log in San Francisco Bay, and the plane had turned over and the lieutenant who had taken my seat had drowned." LBJ's time just hadn't come.

Neither had Larry Speakes's. On March 30, 1987, it was his turn to escort Ronald Reagan to the speech at the Hilton Hotel. The trip was routine. Speakes tried to fast-talk his boss, Jim Brady, into taking on the chore, but Brady was trying to delegate unimportant matters. He refused, then at the last moment had a change of heart. He stuck his head in Speakes's office and said, "Catfish," as he called his Mississippi employee, "I think I'll go on the traveling circus today after all." Brady was shot by one of Hinckley's bullets.

Should we or shouldn't we? Do we or don't we? Only the person who spins the wheel of fortune knows for sure. We can cross our fingers, knock on wood, walk around ladders, and still be done in by the fine print.

"I did some of the big things rather well," said Richard Nixon, looking back on his presidency. "I screwed up terribly on what was a little thing. . . ." He meant Watergate—a small-time, bungled break-in. But the analysis can be taken farther. What really did Nixon in was the proof of a cover-up provided by his own tapes. Nixon's taping system ran continuously. LBJ, who also taped conversations, relied on a manually operated recorder. One Nixon staffer summed it up: "For want of a toggle switch, the presidency was lost."

It was Mies Van der Rohe who said "God is in the details." He was referring to architecture, but it's something to think about.

CAUGHT IN THE CROSS FIRE

*If John Hinckley hadn't shot my Dad, he [Dad] would be able to take me to karate this morning when you can't take me.*
—Scott Brady to his mother, Sarah

When fate lands even a pebble in the placid pool of one man's life, the shock waves span out. John Hinckley aims a gun at Ronald Reagan, press secretary Jim Brady is left permanently handicapped, and his son, Scott, aged two at the time of the shooting, grows up complaining, "If John Hinckley hadn't shot my dad, then you wouldn't be so tired, Mom, and you wouldn't fuss at me so much." As his mother, Sarah, explains, "Very often if he gets mad at me or his father, the blame immediately goes back to Hinckley."

It's a ripple effect that also turned Mary Ann Vecchio's world upside down. Familiar to anyone who has seen pictures from Kent State, Mary Ann is the girl who strikes a pose of graphic anguish, her arms outstretched above the body of slain student Jeffrey Miller.

John Filo, the student photographer who snapped the picture on May 4, 1970, won a Pulitzer Prize. As for Mary Ann, "It really destroyed my life." A fourteen-year-old runaway from Opa-Locka, Florida, she was spotted by her father, Frank, tracked down, and brought home, where she spent time in a juvenile home and was later arrested for loitering and marijuana possession. "I've been miserable since Kent State," she said in 1975. "Not for any political reasons, but after all the publicity I've received, I feel the police have been unnecessarily harassing me."

Her mother, Claire, explained that Governor Claude Kirk of Florida said Mary Ann "was planted there by the Communists and people wrote letters that she was responsible for murdering all those children. Can you imagine a fourteen-year-old girl having to deal with that?"

We react in the anguish of the moment—simple acts of human decency that suddenly propel us into the glare of TV cameras. "All I knew was that I was shaking so much I couldn't light a cigarette," said Oliver Wellington Sipple after he was questioned and congratulated by the Secret Service for knocking aside Sara Jane Moore's gun and most likely saving President Ford's life. A former marine living on disability pay from his Vietnam days, he mused, "Hero—everyone is calling me a hero. But what's a hero? It's just a word. All I did was react. I'm glad I was there. If it's true I saved the President's life, then I'm damn happy about it. But I honestly feel that if I hadn't reached out for that arm, somebody else would have."

Afterward he dearly wished someone else had. His reward: Ford wrote him a letter of thanks. The price he paid: It became national news that he was part of San Francisco's gay community. Sipple filed a fifteen-million-dollar invasion of privacy suit, naming *San Francisco Chronicle* columnist Herb Caen, seven newspapers, and fifty "John Doe" publishers as defendants. His suit charged that his family "learned for the first time of his sexual orientation and. . . abandoned the plaintiff." At a news confer-

ence announcing the legal action, which he said caused him
"great mental anguish, embarrassment, and humiliation," Sipple
explained, "My sexuality is part of my private life and has no
bearing on my response to the act of a person seeking to take the
life of another." The suit was dismissed. Sipple died a broken
man—his problems ranged from schizophrenia to alcoholism—
at the age of forty-seven in 1989.

His plight was echoed by a male hairdresser filmed frolicking
in the buff with a nude female friend in the documentary *Woodstock*. He filed a million-dollar suit claiming that being exposed as
a heterosexual was damaging his beauty business.

But when someone's life intersects with history, there can be
unexpected bonuses. Abraham Zapruder, a Dallas dressmaker,
initially set out to watch President Kennedy's motorcade on November 22, 1963, without his movie camera. He was told by his
secretary to "march right back" home and get it. "How many
times will you have a crack at color movies of the President?" she
told him.

Zapruder grumbled, "I'm too short. Probably I wouldn't even
get close." He complained that he was "chased home by my own
girl. It looks bad." Nonetheless, he heeded her advice. He caught
the assassination on film, and the timing of his frames have provided the basis for doubt that Kennedy was shot by a single
assassin. Time Inc. bought his 486 frames of Kodachrome for
$150,000 two days after the shooting. In 1975, unwilling to moni-
tor requests for the film's use, Time sold it back to Zapruder's
heirs for a dollar. Though bootleg copies exist, anyone who wants
to use the actual film must pay a fee—sometimes tens of thousands of dollars. "We could have made copies and peddled it on
street corners," commented Zapruder's widow, Lillian. "Someone
else would have made millions on it."

But even with restrained use, it's a pretty nice piece of change
for having been caught in the crossfire of fate.

### SECOND-GUESSING FATE

*"I see you will be President—in the lucky cycle of thirteen you will
be President," said a fortune-teller to Dwight D. Eisenhower in
1939. Thirteen years later, in 1952, he was elected President.*

\* \* \*

When Lieutenant Colonel Eisenhower and his wife, Mamie, were stationed in the Philippines, Mrs. Maurice Kahn held a dinner party and as entertainment invited Madame Hebibi, Manila's noted Gypsy fortune-teller. It was the eve of World War II. From the vantage point of Mrs. Kahn's well-set table, the future held the unimaginable—especially as far as a genial young military man was concerned.

Mrs. Kahn noted Madame Hebibi's prediction in her diary, but Ike didn't give it a second thought. If he had given credence to everything everyone said, he might have been teaching history at Yale—the fate forecast in his 1909 high school yearbook—and visiting his brother at the White House. Yes, it was Edgar Eisenhower, the future lawyer and businessman, whom the high school students of Abilene, Kansas, picked for President of the United States.

It's hard to resist getting out the crystal ball, even if you run the risk of getting your Eisenhowers crossed. High schools do it. Farmer's almanacs do it. Even men of God dabble at divining the future. One evening at the White House Billy Graham was all set to give his blessing on LBJ's vice presidential candidate—in fact, Johnson was handing him the list of fourteen contenders—but Ruth Graham kicked her husband under the dinner table. "Now, why'd you kick him?" LBJ inquired.

"I think Billy ought to limit his advice to you to religious and spiritual matters," she said firmly.

Johnson conceded the point. "But," as Graham recalled, "when dinner was over and the ladies had gone out ahead of us, he quietly closed the door and turned and asked me, 'All right, what's your choice?' I said. 'Hubert Humphrey.' He just nodded. And you know, I've often wondered since then. . . ."

It never hurts to try to skew fate's odds in our favor. Even Eisenhower, as president of Columbia University in 1948, applied for a permit to carry a concealed weapon and strolled Central Park with a derringer in his pocket. New York City is something you just don't leave to chance. Neither, apparently, is life with Ronald Reagan. Nancy Reagan once confessed that she kept a little gun in her bedside table.

If we can find an insurance policy to guard against the

demons of the night—or the insecurities of the day—most of us take it. "I had that superstition of putting gum on the button of my cap and only taking it off when we lost the game," recalled Phil Rizzuto, who played for the Yankees in the 1950s. "Like if we'd win six or seven in a row, I'd leave it on there. One time we won—we had set the record—I think it was like nineteen straight or something. Gum was getting a little rancid. No one would sit too close to me on the bench."

"I wasn't terribly short of money. I just decided I didn't ever want to worry where my next dollar was coming from," said Army Warrant Officer James W. Hall, who decided to supplement his income by spying for the Soviet Union and East Germany. In 1989 Hall was sentenced to forty years in prison. He gambled—and lost.

So did the Kennedys. But they gambled that character and breeding were enough to enable them to beat the odds. During World War II Joe, Jr.—who died in combat some months later—volunteered for a dangerous mission. He was climbing into the cockpit when another pilot told him he hoped his insurance was paid up. Joe flashed that Kennedy grin. "Nobody in my family needs insurance," he said. He was talking about money, but the confidence, the arrogance if you will, was pure Kennedy.

"You know, if I'm ever elected President, I'm never going to ride in one of those goddamned cars," said Robert Kennedy of bulletproof bubbletop vehicles. "If there is somebody out there who wants to get me, well, doing anything in public life today is Russian roulette."

His brother John had the same feeling. He had been warned that Dallas was nut country. It was the kind of place where newspapers ran full-page ads maligning the President on the day of his arrival. But Kennedy ignored the naysayers. His feeling about the Dallas trip was "If they are going to get me, they will get me even in church."

Harry Truman gambled and won. After he was nearly assassinated—in 1950 two Puerto Rican nationalists tried to shoot their way into Blair House where he was napping—he told Admiral William Leahy, "The only thing you have to worry about is luck. I never had bad luck."

Nancy Reagan's husband was lucky, too. No President before him had been struck by an assassin's bullet and lived. But Nancy wasn't willing to leave well enough alone. She was painfully aware that, as she put it, there was a "so-called twenty-year death cycle for American presidents. For more than a century, every president elected, or re-elected, in a year ending in zero had died in office." Nancy was frantic. "When Ronnie was in the hospital, I would lie on his side of the bed at the White House as a way of feeling closer to him, but I barely slept. Now that he was home, I still kept waking up during the night." Little bedside guns and ordinary lucky charms weren't going to help now. She needed higher powers: She dialed astrologer Joan Quigley.

"My relationship with Joan Quigley began as a crutch, one of several ways I tried to alleviate my anxiety about Ronnie," Nancy Reagan wrote in her memoir. "Within a year or two, it had become a habit, something I relied on a little less but didn't see the need to change. Because while I was never certain that Joan's astrological advice was helping to protect Ronnie, the fact is that nothing like March 30 [the date of Reagan's shooting] ever happened again."

But other strange things did. Like the announcement of Anthony M. Kennedy's appointment for the Supreme Court. It was timed for 11:32:25 A.M.—on the *second*. Quigley wrote in her memoir, "I knew, of course, from his horoscope that Kennedy would be confirmed, but the mood on Capitol Hill was not favorable for any nominee to the Supreme Court proposed by Reagan. Nancy felt it was wise to have me pick the time of the announcement." Finessing the announcement down to the precise second took careful engineering. "Nancy arranged to start a little early and stall until the person chosen to man the stopwatch gave the signal for the President to make the announcement." Kennedy was confirmed by a vote of 97–0 on February 3, 1988. But if it was all that easy, one wonders where Joan was on a lot of other occasions. For instance, where was Joan when Robert Bork's and Douglas Ginsburg's names were proposed for the Supreme Court? (Quigley explains part of the mystery: "Nancy had not asked me to look at Bork's horoscope until after the fact. . . . When I did . . . I knew the situation was hopeless.")

But hey, if you thought making political announcements by the stopwatch would get them through Congress, or putting gum on your baseball cap would appease the gods overlooking the World's Series, would you do it? Would you run your vice presidential choices by Billy Graham? Would you listen to Madame Hebibi? If you moved into a house that was number 666 on St. Cloud Road, would you worry that it bore the sign of the devil or would you have the street number changed to 668?

The residents of the latter address: former President and former First Lady Ronald and Nancy Reagan. Their decision: They changed the number.

# Notes

CHAPTER 1

GROWING UP IN AMERICA

*Page*

15   "Aren't you Senator . . . up my pants!" Barry Goldwater, *Goldwater* (New York: Doubleday, 1988), p. 365.

15   "Mrs. Roosevelt straightened . . . over her shoulder." Shirley Temple Black, *Child Star: An Autobiography* (New York: McGraw-Hill, 1988), p. 237.

15   "Son, I want . . . an old man!" *New York*, September 30, 1991, p. 42.

15   "If Mrs. Gorbachev . . . than my brother." *The New York Times*, December 7, 1988, p. A19.

16   "Are they on . . . Three days." Neil Armstrong et al., *First on the Moon* (Boston: Little, Brown, 1970), p. 104.

16   "Daddy, *why* do . . . go to prison." Jeb Stuart Magruder, *From Power to Peace* (Waco, Texas: Word Books, 1978), p. 90.

16   "Mom, if you . . . to rescue you." *Newsweek*, September 10, 1990, p. 22.

16   "When we become . . . and blue eyes." James McKinley, *Assassination in America* (New York: Harper & Row, 1977), p. 207.

16   "My tongue twisted . . . to colored children." Stephen Oates, *Let the Trumpet Sound: The Life of Martin Luther King, Jr.* (New York: Mentor, 1982), pp. 176–177.

16   "A bad man . . . coming back." William Manchester, *The Death of a President November 20–November 25, 1963* (New York: Harper & Row, 1967), p. 464.

17   "And my son . . . his name is." *Real Life with Jane Pauley*, NBC, July 14, 1991.

17   "My grandfather . . . won the war." *New York*, August 8, 1988, p. 33.

17 "It's no fun . . . your father stinks." Lester David, *The Lonely Lady of San Clemente: The Story of Pat Nixon* (New York: Crowell, 1978), p. 81.

17 "Dad would say . . . the umbrella rack." *Newsweek*, June 18, 1990, p. 54.

18 "I can deal . . . a last name." *Mirabella*, July 1991, p. 22.

18 "When I was . . . it to her." Peter Collier and David Horowitz, *The Rockefellers: An American Dynasty* (New York: Holt, Rinehart & Winston, 1976), pp. 526–527.

18 "It's a preposterous . . . wasn't my name." Ibid., p. 509.

18 "How would you . . . the robber barons?" Joan Braden, *Just Enough Rope* (New York: Villard Books, 1989), p. 31.

18 "didn't take American . . . about the Rockefellers." Collier and Horowitz, *The Rockefellers*, p. 527.

18 "To be truthful . . . it around anymore." Ibid., p. 509.

18 "I wanted that . . . thing as leisure." *The New York Times Magazine*, July 21, 1991, p. 20.

18 "I'm not going . . . how burdensome." *M Inc.*, January 1991, p. 71.

19 "Oh, no, how . . . this to me?" Ronald Reagan, *An American Life* (New York: Simon & Schuster, 1990), p. 565.

19 "Some parts . . . as his child." *People*, January 8, 1989, p. 42.

19 "Every girl should . . . like Charlie [Manson]." James Clarke, *American Assassins: The Darker Side of History* (Princeton, N.J.: Princeton University Press, 1982), p. 146.

19 "Well, I've got . . . I love her." Manchester, *The Death of a President*, p. 92.

19 "Boys, I'll . . . story—for money." Ibid., p. 285.

19 "I wouldn't say . . . the other girls." Susan Dworkin, *Miss America, 1945: Bess Myerson's Own Story* (New York: Newmarket Press, 1987), p. 152.

20 "But what do . . . she doesn't dance." Debbie Reynolds, *Debbie: My Life* (New York: Morrow, 1988), pp. 44–45.

20 "You would make . . . made of lightning." *People*, October 29, 1989, p. 86.

20 "To my knowledge . . . the screen." Joan Fontaine, *No Bed of Roses* (New York: Morrow, 1978), p. 114.

20 "I can't believe . . . my old age." *Cosmopolitan*, April 1991, p. 214.

20 "I hope not." *The New York Times Book Review*, March 26, 1989, p. 8.

20 "I'm rather . . . running for governor." *M Inc.*, January 1991, p. 69.

20 "My mother's been . . . percent of it." Ibid.

20 "My father would . . . the Communist Party." Ralph Martin, *A Hero for Our Time* (New York: Fawcett Crest, 1983), p. 128.

21 "If I walked . . . than anyone else." Doris Kearns Goodwin, *The Fitzgeralds and the Kennedys* (New York: St. Martin's Press, 1987), p. 812.

21 "need a new . . . language like that." J. Ronald Oakley, *God's Country: America in the Fifties* (New York: Dembner Books, 1986), p. 31.

21 "When those headlines . . . could I do?" *The American Experience*, "Nixon: The Quest, the Triumph, the Fall," PBS, October 15, 1990.

21 "I think he . . . on his side." Fawn Brodie, *Richard Nixon* (New York: Norton, 1981), p. 416.

21 "No, I never . . . change so little." Ibid.

21 "Amy's been arrested . . . CIA in Nicaragua." *The New York Times*, April 16, 1987, p. A17.

21  "Great! What for? . . . agreed with me." *People,* May 1, 1989, pp. 108–109.

22  "Sometimes when I . . . stayed a virgin." Robert Byrne, *The 637 Best Things Anyone Ever Said* (New York: Fawcett Crest, 1982), p. 278.

22  "I taught Ralph . . . thought of himself." Robert Buckhorn, *Nader: The People's Lawyer* (Englewood Cliffs, N.J.: Prentice-Hall, 1972), p. 36.

22  "I can't understand . . . than he does." Albert Goodman, *Elvis* (New York: McGraw-Hill, 1981), p. 230.

22  "If he had . . . senator by now." Roger Morris, *Haig: The General's Progress* (N.P.: Playboy Press, 1982), pp. 11–12.

22  "I'll give him . . . Frankie Satin crap." Kitty Kelley, *His Way: The Unauthorized Biography of Frank Sinatra* (New York: Bantam, 1986), p. 48.

22  "If all parents . . . and little vandals." *Life,* Fall 1990, p. 84.

22  "I am not . . . cookie-baking mother." Elaine Partnow, ed., *The Quotable Woman* (Philadelphia: Running Press, 1991), p. 76.

22  "Why can't you . . . or Pat Nixon." C. David Heymann, *A Woman Named Jackie* (New York: Lyle Stuart, 1989) p. 223.

22  "His father and . . . become a Christian!" Charles Colson, *Born Again* (Old Tappan, N.J.: Chosen Books, 1976), p. 169.

22  "Dear Ted: Did . . . types of desserts." Diana McLellan, *Ear on Washington* (New York: Arbor House, 1982), p. 107.

23  "I know a . . . You're adopted." Michael Reagan, *On the Outside Looking In* (New York: Zebra Books, 1988), p. 22.

23  "Your father and . . . what we wanted." Ibid.

23  "And do you . . . that far yet." Maureen Reagan, *First Father, First Daughter* (Boston: Little, Brown, 1989), p. 97.

23  "I was playing . . . until much later." Barbara Reynolds, *Jessie Jackson: America's David* (Washington, D.C.: JFK Associates, 1985), p. 23.

24  "A tabloid called . . . put it together." *People,* October 2, 1989, p. 94.

25  "I always wondered . . . watched *Bonanza*." *People,* December 9, 1991, pp. 69–70.

25  "[S]he asked about . . . and through adoption." Jerry Oppenheimer, *Barbara Walters: An Unauthorized Biography* (New York: St. Martin's Press, 1990), p. 307.

25  "first major shock . . . down and cried." Gerald R. Ford, *A Time to Heal* (New York: Harper & Row, 1979), p. 46.

26  "Every birthday I . . . this is her.'" *Vanity Fair,* April 1990, p. 166.

26  "Suddenly, in a . . . of it gone." Oates, *Let the Trumpet Sound,* p. 475.

26  "I was just . . . there is trouble." Arthur Schlesinger, *Robert Kennedy and His Times* (Boston: Houghton Mifflin, 1978), Vol. 2, p. 684.

27  "A child's death . . . just don't know." *People,* April 30, 1990, pp. 119–121.

27  "It took me . . . Nothing's too monumental." *20/20,* ABC, May 11, 1990.

27  "I got a . . . in the family." McLellan, *Ear on Washington,* pp. 286–287.

27  "I'll make more . . . I work harder." *People,* March 6, 1989, p. 74.

28  "I might say . . . what he does." Barbara Ketterman, *All the President's Kin* (New York: Free Press, 1981), p. 224.

28  "Sam Houston is . . . come home drunk." Ibid., p. 216.

28  "my poor damn, dumb brother." Brodie, *Richard Nixon,* p. 442.

28    "proper for a . . . the United States." Ibid., p. 220.

28    "Look, I want . . . keep him covered." H. R. Haldeman and Joseph Di-
Mona, *The Ends of Power* (New York: Times Books, 1978), p. 36.

29    "I want to . . . there is." Peter Collier and David Horowitz, *The Kennedys:
An American Drama* (New York: Summit Books, 1984), p. 60.

29    "Bobby's never practiced . . . have his chance." *M Inc.*, March 1991,
p. 97.

CHAPTER 2

FINANCIAL TEA LEAVES: FINDING CHARACTER IN A WALLET

31    "If you know . . . sleeping with them." *People*, December 4, 1989, p. 126.

31    "it's always been . . . think about money." Robert Buckhorn, *Nader: The
People's Lawyer* (Englewood Cliffs, N.J.: Prentice-Hall, 1972), p. 143.

31    "a salary of . . . dresses she wants." *Time*, January 16, 1989, p. 52.

31    "Lookit, Elvis . . . That's all." Jerry Hopkins, *Elvis: The Final Years* (New
York: St. Martin's Press, 1980), p. 1.

31    "Department store—$40,000 . . . a hundred thousand as President?"
Ralph Martin, *A Hero for Our Time* (New York: Fawcett Crest, 1983),
p. 353.

32    "It is estimated . . . classified as poor." *Eyes on the Prize,* "The Promised
Land, 1967–1968," PBS.

32    "There he was . . . bunch of clerks." *The New York Times Book Review,*
February 3, 1990, p. 12.

32    "Take an average . . . hundred thousand dollars." Joseph Persico, *The
Imperial Rockefeller: A Biography of Nelson A. Rockefeller* (New York: Simon
& Schuster, 1982), p. 165.

33    "There were three . . . we were closest." Peter Collier and David Horowitz,
*The            Rockefellers:          An          American          Dynasty*
(New York: Holt, Rinehart & Winston, 1976), pp. 518–519.

33    "Mother thought this . . . right of course." *The New York Times*, July 13,
1990, p. A8.

33    "If that's the . . . a lousy father." Arthur Schlesinger, *Robert Kennedy and
His Times* (Boston: Houghton Mifflin, 1978), Vol. 2, pp. 20–21.

33    "You just remember . . . can destroy him." James Steele, *Empire: The
Life, Legend, and Madness of Howard Hughes* (New York: Norton, 1979),
p. 451.

33    "You can buy those monkeys anyway." Mike Wallace and Gary Paul
Gates, *Close Encounters: Mike Wallace's Own Story* (New York: Morrow,
1984), p. 130.

33    "I'm telling . . . I'll sell you." *The New York Times*, August 6, 1991, p. A15.

33    "The old George . . . got his money." *People*, April 22, 1991, pp. 107–121.

34    "God, was I . . . were money-grubbers." Peter Wyden, *The Unknown
Iacocca* (New York: Morrow, 1987), p. 361.

34    "I think greed . . . good about yourself." *People*, March 6, 1989, p. 55.

34    "I am not sending . . . the old applause." Ibid., p. 51.

34    "Somebody said to . . . a swimming pool." *Newsweek*, January 29, 1990,
p. 23.

34   "I went through ... get it back." *The New York Times,* April 13, 1989, p. B12.

34   "There was a ... I just wasted." *Newsweek,* February 13, 1989, p. 13.

34   "I'm so naïve ... Then I understood." *People,* March 6, 1989, p. 54.

35   "If we stop ... closing up shop." *The New York Times,* April 3, 1991, p. c7.

35   "Who's a hippie? I'm Jewish." Abbie Hoffman, *The Best of Abbie Hoffman,* ed. Daniel Simon (New York: Four Walls Eight Windows, 1989), p. 21.

35   "I'm from ... lot more fun." Ibid., p. 22.

35   "I've always thought ... the real test." *The New York Times Magazine,* July 23, 1989, p. 30.

35   "What does Jackie eat for breakfast?" *People,* March 11, 1991, p. 100.

35   "We were just ... me a break." *People,* April 23, 1990, p. 123.

36   "I took it ... shower a day." *People,* August 6, 1990, p. 102.

36   $1,046 a minute. *The New York Times,* April 3, 1989, pp. D1, D4.

36   $1.40 an hour. *Newsweek,* October 7, 1991, p. 45.

36   "I'll be the ... for my job." *Prime Time Live,* ABC, April 4, 1991.

36   "I never *used* ... he did anyway." *The New York Times,* December 14, 1989, p. C18.

36   "I can't type ... answer the phone." *Cosmopolitan,* March 1991, p. 230.

37   "I was making ... you pricks." John Barron, *Breaking the Ring* (Boston: Houghton Mifflin, 1987), p. 158.

37   $110,000 a year. *Newsweek,* January 15, 1990, p. 19.

37   "fucking believe it. I've made it." Bob Woodward, *Wired: The Short Life and Fast Times of John Belushi* (New York: Simon & Schuster, 1984), p. 150.

37   "Since the President ... of them complained." *The New York Times Book Review,* October 1, 1989, p. 32.

37   "Well, when the ... is not illegal." David Frost, *I Gave Them a Sword: Behind the Scenes of the Nixon Interviews* (New York: Morrow, 1978), p. 183.

37   "I would ... on the presidency." *20/20,* ABC, November 17, 1989.

38   "I can't really ... from New Jersey." C. David Heymann, *A Woman Named Jackie* (New York: Lyle Stuart, 1989), p. 486.

38   "Do you think ... whenever she called." Ibid., p. 492.

38   "That sounds like ... like Monopoly money." *Newsweek,* November 27, 1989, p. 27.

38   $112 million. *Newsweek,* May 20, 1991, p. 59.

38   "For older women ... the opposite sex." *Time,* May 15, 1989, p. 72.

38   "Well, you see ... dollars a week." Don Hewitt, *Minute by Minute* (New York: Random House, 1985), p. 30.

39   "The news about ... they would know." Robert Lenzer, *The Great Getty* (New York: Crown, 1985), p. 121.

CHAPTER 3

POWER AND POLITICS: THE RULES OF THE GAME

41   "There is a ... to the other." *American Masters,* "Edward R. Murrow: This Reporter," Part II, PBS, August 6, 1990.

41    "Politics is just . . . of a closing." Paul Boller, *Presidential Campaigns* (New York: Oxford University Press, 1984), p. viii.

41    "It's times like . . . It's Wilson." Larry Speakes, *Speaking Out: The Reagan Presidency from Inside the White House* (New York: Scribners, 1988), p. 116.

41    "Now some men . . . to use it." Richard Goodwin, *Remembering America: A Voice from the Sixties* (Boston: Little, Brown, 1988), p. 270.

42    "[Y]ou know why . . . have been delighted." Curt Smith, *Long Ago: The Years of Turmoil Remembered* (South Bend, Ind.: Icarus Press, 1982), p. 211.

42    "How many of . . . six years ago." Frances Leighton, *The Search for the Real Nancy Reagan* (New York: Macmillan, 1987), p. 193.

42    "The pomp . . . our own." *A Conversation with the President*, CBS Special Report, December 28, 1977.

42    "I was eleven . . . I read it." *The New York Times*, March 16, 1990, p. A10.

42    "My God! He's . . . with a leper!" William Manchester, *One Brief Shining Moment: Remembering Kennedy* (Boston: Little, Brown, 1983), p. 216.

42    "Being in politics . . . think it's important." Morris Udall, *Too Funny to Be President* (New York: Holt, 1988), p. 20.

42    "Now here's what . . . reacting to them." *The New York Times*, July 26, 1989, p. 23.

43    "greeted the crowds . . . arms any higher." James Reston, *Deadline: A Memoir* (New York: Random House, 1991), p. 275.

43    "If the cameras . . . Where's Hal?" *The New York Times*, June 16, 1991, p. 18.

43    "Mrs. O'Brien met . . . to be thanked." *Vogue*, September 1987, p. 823.

43    "One thing I . . . threw it out." Winzola McLendon and Scottie Smith, *Don't Quote Me* (New York: Dutton, 1970), p. 25.

44    "with both feet . . . into rejoining us." H. R. Haldeman and Joseph Di-Mona, *The Ends of Power* (New York: Times Books, 1978), pp. 784–785.

44    "Mr. President, I've . . . make my point?" George Bush, *Looking Forward* (New York: Doubleday, 1987), pp. 100–101.

44    "We're going to . . . their own game." *Vanity Fair*, December 1990, p. 219.

44    "Kennedy speaks over . . . I'll murder Kennedy." Goodwin, *Remembering America*, p. 112.

45    "I moved into . . . field of politics." Brian Lanker, *I Dream a World: Portraits of Black Women Who Changed America* (New York: Stewart, Tabori & Chang, 1989), p. 106.

45    "You know the . . . in the nose." Goodwin, *Remembering America*, p. 493.

45    "This country has . . . on and on." *20/20*, ABC, February 15, 1991.

45    "I used to . . . steal to survive." Thomas Landess and Richard Quinn, *Jesse Jackson and the Politics of Race* (Ottawa, Ill.: Jameson Books, 1985), p. 8.

45    "People want a . . . would have died." *The New York Times*, November 19, 1990, p. A14.

46    "If you couldn't . . . it wasn't aired." *The New York Times*, April 22, 1990, p. 23.

46    "Get those goddamned . . . out of here." *Wilson Quarterly*, Spring 1988, p. 70.

46    "You won't have . . . kick around anymore." James Witover, *The Resurrection of Richard Nixon* (New York: Putnam, 1970), p. 22.

46 "You fellows won't . . . flog and insult." Arthur Schlesinger, *Robert Kennedy and His Times* (Boston: Houghton Mifflin 1978), p. 907.

46 "I've read about . . . number of continents." Peter Collier, *Famous in America: The Passion to Succeed* (New York: Dutton, 1985), p. 113.

46 "If you've seen . . . seen them all." Mike Wallace and Gary Paul Gates, *Close Encounters: Mike Wallace's Own Story* (New York: Morrow, 1984), p. 127.

46 "Known all over . . . marriage, practiced celibacy." Ernest B. Fergurson, *Hard Right: The Rise of Jesse Helms* (New York: Norton, 1986), p. 50.

46 "No more bullshit." *Insight,* October 28, 1991, p. 30.

47 "back into the . . . a nuclear weapon." Thomas A. Bailey, *Voices of America* (New York: Free Press, 1976), p. 470.

47 "Do I have . . . for mayor? No." *Newsweek,* October 14, 1991, p. 21.

47 "There is no . . . in Eastern Europe." Richard Reeves, *I'm a Ford, Not a Lincoln* (New York: Harcourt Brace Jovanovich, 1975), p. 145.

47 "I came out . . . as a prophet." *Newsweek,* January 1, 1990, p. 44.

47 "For seven and . . . have been setbacks." *The New York Times,* January 17, 1992, p. A28.

47 "Our future lies before us." William Leuchtenburg, *The Great Age of Change: The Life History of the United States* (New York: Time-Life Books, 1964,) p. 4.

47 "The question is . . . to the back." *Prime Time Live,* ABC, May 21, 1992.

47 "Don't worry, Jim . . . just confuse them." J. Ronald Oakley, *God's Country: America in the Fifties* (New York: Dembner Books, 1986), p. 160.

47 "I am in . . . a national answer." *The New York Times,* February 24, 1989, p. A33.

48 "Oh, Hubert, you . . . to be immortal." Reston, *Deadline,* p. 263.

48 "I shall try . . . to be interesting." *Adam Clayton Powell,* PBS, December 3, 1989.

48 "If Lincoln were . . . in his grave." Reeves, *I'm a Ford,* p. 145.

48 "Well, what do . . . Harvard, after all." Peter Collier and David Horowitz, *The Kennedys: An American Drama* (New York: Summit Books, 1984), p. 435.

48 "My position on . . . what I said." Joseph Persico, *The Imperial Rockefeller: A Biography of Nelson A. Rockefeller* (New York: Simon & Schuster, 1982), p. 71.

48 "You can't campaign . . . what they're buying." Udall, *Too Funny to Be President,* p. 20.

48 "Well, that's over . . . farmers after November." Goodwin, *Remembering America,* pp. 119–120.

48 "What would you . . . Demand a recount." John B. Judis, *William F. Buckley, Jr.: Patron Saint of the Conservatives* (New York: Simon & Schuster, 1988), p. 24.

48 "Republicans understand the . . . parent and child." Editors of *The Quayle Quarterly, The Unauthorized Autobiography of Dan Quayle* (Bridgeport, Conn., 1992), p. 3.

48 "I don't want . . . governor of Texas." *The New York Times,* March 22, 1990, p. B24.

49 "Won't it be . . . you mean *we*?" Paul Boller, *Presidential Wives* (New York: Oxford University Press, 1988), p. 358.

49    "I'm really very . . . okay or crash." Diana McLellan, *Ear on Washington* (New York: Arbor House, 1982), p. 22.

49    "Thank God that's . . . to come along." Jeb Stuart Magruder, *An American Life: One Man's Road to Watergate* (New York: Atheneum, 1974,) p. 220.

49    "I mean, like . . . President for years?" *Spy*, August 1988, p. 98.

49    "Did you ever . . . be Harry Truman?" Robert Shelton, *No Direction Home: The Life and Music of Bob Dylan* (New York: Morrow, 1986), p. 287.

50    "I always took . . . of my mind." Persico, *The Imperial Rockefeller*, p. 294.

50    "I am just not . . . for standby equipment." Ibid., p. 245.

50    "I go to . . . go to earthquakes!" Ibid., p. 262.

50    "filled with trips . . . it is nothing." Doris Kearns, *Lyndon Johnson and the American Dream* (New York: Harper & Row, 1976), p. 164.

50    "every time I . . . over his shoulder." Schlesinger, *Robert Kennedy and His Times,*, Vol. II, p. 649.

50    "I happen to . . . the Vice President." *Newsweek*, April 9, 1990, p. 17.

50    "Clare, honey, no . . . chance I got." Ralph Martin, *A Hero for Our Time* (New York: Fawcett Crest, 1983), p. 169.

50    "I couldn't help . . . the high five sign." *The New York Times Magazine*, December 18, 1988, p. 18.

51    "as governor of . . . seem very smart." Lee Iacocca, *Iacocca: An Autobiography* (Toronto: Bantam, 1986), p. 289.

51    "I have a . . . will be chosen." James B. Simpson, *Contemporary Quotations* (New York: Crowell, 1964), p. 45.

51    "I am not . . . high political office." Herbert Eaton, *Presidential Timber* (London: Free Press of Glencoe, 1964), p. 412.

51    "I cannot conceive . . . of the Universe!" Peter Wyden, *The Unknown Iacocca* (New York: Morrow, 1987), p. 285.

51    "The thought of . . . want the job." Christopher Cerf and Victor Navasky, *The Experts Speak* (New York: Pantheon Books, 1984), p. 287.

51    "I have no . . . change my mind." James Osborne, *White House Watch: The Ford Years* (Washington, D.C.: New Republic Books, 1977), p. xvii.

51    "Right now I . . . ambition at all." *20/20*, ABC, March 15, 1991.

51    "Getting all caught . . . fit for it." *The New York Times*, June 28, 1991, p. 40.

51    "I'm not . . . I'd win." *Spy*, October 1988, p. 88.

51    "It won't be . . . any more worry." William Seale, *The President's House* (Washington, D.C.: White House Historical Association, 1986) Vol. 2, p. 1006.

52    "The pay is . . . walk to work." Helen Thomas, *Dateline: White House* (New York: Macmillan, 1975), p. 22.

52    "At last I've . . . to stay home." Amy Jensen, *The White House and Its 34 Families* (New York: McGraw-Hill, 1965), p. 92.

52    "Before you get . . . it was advertised." Bobby Baker, *Wheeling and Dealing* (New York: Norton, 1978), p. 265.

52    "I've been criticized . . . don't completely comprehend." *A Conversation with the President*, CBS Special Report, December 28, 1977.

52    "It's full-time work . . . all hard work." *The New York Times Magazine*, July 29, 1990, p. 32.

52    "You go to . . . not aware of." *Newsweek*, July 3, 1989, p. 15.

52    "I'm an old-fashioned . . . me to do." Martin, *A Hero for Our Time*, p. 86.

53   "I'll do anything . . . me to do." Ibid., p. 182.
53   "Whatever you want . . . being courted again." Ibid.
53   "Well, I try . . . me to do." Barbara Kellerman, *All the President's Kin* (New York: Free Press, 1981), p. 242.
53   "But very rarely . . . than I am." *Newsweek*, January 23, 1989, p. 25.
53   "I made all the decisions." *Time*, January 23, 1989, p. 27.

## CHAPTER 4
## MATTERS OF DRESS (AND UNDRESS)

55   "I wear a . . . of great respect." Benjamin Spock and Mary Morgan, *Spock on Spock* (New York: Pantheon Books, 1989), p. 194.
55   "He would hide . . . for his back." Ralph Martin, *A Hero for Our Time* (New York: Fawcett Crest, 1983), p. 370.
55   "were dressed like . . . were denied service." *Eyes on the Prize*, "Ain't Scared of Your Jails, 1960–1961," PBS, 1991.
56   "People expect to . . . to disappoint them." *The New York Times Magazine*, November 17, 1991, p. 43.
56   "I'm not exactly grace in motion." Frances Leighton, *Search for the Real Nancy Reagan* (New York: Macmillan, 1987), p. 185.
56   "both resplendent in . . . am not interested." William C. Westmoreland, *A Soldier Reports* (Garden City, N.Y.: Doubleday, 1976) p. 37.
56   "dazzled the Committee . . . 'Around-the-Capitalist-World.' " Abbie Hoffman, *The Best of Abbie Hoffman*, Daniel Simon, ed. (New York: Four Walls Eight Windows, 1989), p. 93.
57   "with his shirt . . . for twenty years." J. Ronald Oakley, *God's Country: America in the Fifties* (New York: Dembner Books, 1986), p. 82.
57   "I'm not going to wear my uniform." *The New York Times Book Review*, February 24, 1991, p. 7.
57   " 'No,' she said . . . what they've done." William Manchester, *The Death of a President November 20–November 25, 1963* (New York: Harper & Row, 1967), p. 348.
57   "woman in the . . . talking about me." *Newsweek*, January 16, 1989, p. 33.
58   "Maybe he thought . . . a waiter, Jack." Peter Collier and David Horowitz, *The Kennedys: An American Drama* (New York: Summit Books, 1984), p. 196.
58   "Buy yourself a . . . the goddamn case." Leonard Katz, *Uncle Frank: The Biography of Frank Costello* (New York: Drake, 1973), p. 198.
58   "I had just . . . supposed to be." Paul Boller, *Presidential Wives* (New York: Oxford University Press, 1988), p. 468.
58   "That was how . . . the Presidential Seal." Richard Nixon, *RN: The Memoirs of Richard Nixon* (New York: Grosset & Dunlap, 1988), p. 1053.
59   "Look, I was . . . walking around naked." *Vanity Fair*, July 1991, p. 130.
59   "I'm not comfortable . . . reveal my body." *Mirabella*, January 1991, pp. 42–43.
59   "I suppose it . . . launch a career." Andrew J. Edelstein and Kevin McDonough, *The Seventies: From Hot Pants to Hot Tubs* (New York: Dutton, 1990), p. 117.

60    "I was so . . . my GOD, *SIR!*" Ray Charles and David Ritz, *Brother Ray* (New York: Dial Press, 1978) pp. 202–203.

60    "I was staying . . . room seventeen twelve!" Donnie Radcliffe, *Simply Barbara Bush: A Portrait of America's Candid First Lady* (New York: Warner Books, 1989), p. 10.

60    "I'd like to . . . a road map." Richard Goodwin, *Remembering America: A Voice from the Sixties* (Boston: Little, Brown, 1988), pp. 128–129.

61    "You should have . . . me to leave." *Cosmopolitan*, March 1991, p. 230.

61    "pasties and a . . . the First Amendment." *The New York Times*, June 22, 1991, p. 8.

61    "skin and beads . . . around the flame." *Vanity Fair*, May 1991, pp. 188–189.

61    "I can't kiss . . . I wear it." Carol Felsenthar, *Alice Roosevelt Longworth* (New York: Putnam, 1988), p. 245.

61    "some of the . . . as a hat." Jodi Shields, *Hats* (New York: Potter, 1991), p. 12.

62    "I will . . . I'll wear hats." *Vanity Fair*, January 1989, p. 94.

62    "I've got to . . . the hat industry?" William Manchester, *One Brief Shining Moment: Remembering Kennedy* (Boston: Little, Brown, 1983), p. 135.

62    "a grey fedora . . . by Drew Pearson." Jack Anderson, *Confessions of a Muckraker* (New York: Random House, 1979), p. 217.

62    "That whole year . . . let it go." *Vanity Fair*, April 1990, p. 222.

62    "They've got some . . . were washed out." Gordon Liddy, *Will: The Autobiography of G. Gordon Liddy* (New York: St. Martin's Press, 1980), p. 94.

63    "I refuse to . . . over a hat." Oakley, *God's Country*, p. 141.

63    "If you and . . . are so close." *People*, March 19, 1990, p. 33.

63    "My white suits . . . form of aggression." *Time*, February 13, 1989, p. 92.

63    "It's ridiculous to . . . building in shirtsleeves." Arthur Schlesinger, *Robert Kennedy and His Times*, (Boston: Houghton Mifflin, 1978), Vol. I, p. 268.

63    "The American people . . . one will notice." Martin, *A Hero for Our Time*, p. 134.

63    "see beneath the . . . but I'm not." *Dolly: Here I Come Again*, Leonore Fleischer (Toronto: PaperJacks, 1987), introduction.

64    "*Laugh-In* came in . . . was *already liberated.*" *People*, June 11, 1990, p. 83.

64    "I may be . . . is all about." *The New York Times*, December 16, 1990, Arts and Leisure, p. 38.

64    "I figured since . . . were up there." Henry Hampton and Steve Fayer, *Voices of Freedom: An Oral History of the Civil Rights Movement from the 1950s Through the 1980s* (New York: Bantam, 1980), p. 239.

65    "I knew where . . . lie about everything." Robert Caro, *The Path to Power: The Years of Lyndon Johnson* (New York: Knopf, 1982), p. 156.

65    "My biggest irritation . . . when they shampoo." Michael Deaver, *Behind the Scenes* (New York: Morrow, 1987), p. 98.

65    "I think it's . . . I look fantastic." *Smithsonian*, October 1991, p. 125.

65    "I've come up . . . sets me straight." *20/20*, ABC, November 23, 1990.

66    "During the week . . . to sleep on." *People*, April 15, 1991, p. 44.

67    "That way it . . . across the street." *People*, May 1, 1989, p. 158.

67    "I don't wear . . . It's *au naturel.*" *Prime Time Live*, ABC, June 24, 1991.

67    "I have never . . . a dark-haired person." *People*, March 6, 1989, p. 55.

67    "When it's short . . . the brown hair." *20/20*, ABC, November 17, 1989.

67   "I mean shit . . . loud and clear." David Farber, *Chicago '68* (Chicago: University of Chicago Press, 1988), p. 122.

67   "The thing that . . . John Wilkes Booth's?" Craig McGregor, ed., *Bob Dylan: A Retrospective* (New York: Morrow, 1972), p. 135.

67   "If truth is . . . in a library?" Elaine Partnow, ed., *The Quotable Woman* (Philadelphia: Running Press, 1991), p. 144.


CHAPTER 5
WHY ME? DISCRIMINATING POINTS OF VIEW


69   "I don't even . . . me?' Why not?" William L. Calley and John Sack, *Lieutenant Calley: His Own Story* (New York: Viking, 1971), pp. 169–170.

69   "Why me? Why . . . like Brooke Shields?" *Esquire*, December 1982, p. 104.

69   "Why me? . . . or ten minutes." *The New York Times*, November 9, 1991, p. 33.

69   "I think it . . . could understand it." Ralph Martin, *A Hero for Our Time* (New York: Fawcett Crest, 1983), p. 202.

69   "They're not like . . . bitches are saying." Thomas P. O'Neill and William Novak, *Man of the House: The Life and Political Memoirs of Speaker Tip O'Neill* (New York: Random House, 1987), p. 256.

70   "We have a . . . for a gun." Bill Russell and Taylor Branch, *Second Wind: The Memoirs of an Opinionated Man* (New York: Random House, 1979), p. 194.

70   "I'm waiting for . . . in this town." *The New York Times*, July 1, 1991, p. A13.

70   "The white man . . . but a Cadillac." Time-Life Editors, *This Fabulous Century, Vol. 7: 1960–1970* (New York: Time-Life Books, 1970), p. 148.

70   "I've got black . . . yarmulkes every day." *The New York Times Book Review*, July 14, 1991, p. 24.

70   "What can you . . . gave anyone AIDS." *Newsweek*, May 28, 1990, p. 17.

71   "Until everyone knows . . . improve the situation." *Nightline*, ABC, April 11, 1990.

71   "I'm anti-bigotry, anti-racist and anti-Semitic." Helen Thomas, White House correspondent, in a speech, June 18, 1989.

71   "Daddy, I go . . . colored people do?" Jack Olsen, *Black Is Best: The Riddle of Cassius Clay* (New York: Putnam, 1987), p. 145.

71   "every joke . . . lead to trouble." *The New York Times Book Review*, October 29, 1989, p. 3.

71   "getting beaten up . . . gantlet every block." *The New York Times*, August 24, 1988, p. C15.

71   "You are an . . . was too complicated." Jacques Levy, *Cesar Chavez* (New York: Norton, 1975), p. 24.

72   "One of my . . . hated my guts." Jim Haskins, *Richard Pryor: A Man and His Madness* (New York: Beaufort, 1984), p. 12.

72   "I was shocked . . . had told me." Kareem Abdul-Jabbar, *Giant Steps* (Toronto: Bantam, 1983), pp. 14–15.

72    "Why is my . . . think I'm beautiful?" J. Randy Taraborrelli, *Call Her Miss Ross* (New York: Birch Lane Press, 1989), p. 327.

72    "Mother, we've got . . . than Adrienne did." Arnold Shaw, *Belafonte: An Unauthorized Biography* (Philadelphia: Chilton, 1960), pp. 127–128.

73    "I was eleven . . . Dago and Wop." Lee Iacocca, *Iacocca: An Autobiography* (Toronto: Bantam, 1986), p. 13.

73    "We were in . . . city of Cleveland." *Eyes on the Prize*, "Power," PBS, 1991.

73    "How many blacks . . . black from white." Mike Wallace and Gary Paul Gates, *Close Encounters: Mike Wallace's Own Story* (New York: Morrow, 1984), pp. 213–214.

73    "How are you . . . in your city." Ronnie Dugger, *On Reagan: The Man and His Presidency* (New York: McGraw-Hill, 1983), p. 30.

73    "in every stage . . . unbearably stinking niggers." Stephen Oates, *Let the Trumpet Sound: The Life of Martin Luther King, Jr.* (New York: Mentor, 1982), p. 88.

73    "Everybody knows that . . . than white people's." Lester David and Irene David, *Bobby Kennedy: The Making of a Folk Hero* (New York: Dodd, Mead, 1986), p. 188.

74    "I want to . . . to get him." David Garrow, *Bearing the Cross: Martin Luther King, Jr., and the Southern Christian Leadership Conference* (New York: Morrow, 1986), p. 322.

74    "I haven't had . . . about the Negro." Victor Lasky, *J.F.K.: The Man and the Myth* (New York: Macmillan, 1963), p. 256.

74    "Reverend, there are . . . fixed and rigid." Oates, *Let the Trumpet Sound*, p. 130.

74    "These are not . . . big overgrown Negroes!" J. Ronald Oakley, *God's Country: America in the Fifties* (New York: Dembner Books, 1986), p. 195.

74    "those goddamn coons . . . just aren't any." Iacocca, *An Autobiography*, p. 289.

74    "I favor the . . . gunpoint if necessary." Christopher Cerf & Victor Navasky, *The Experts Speak* (New York: Pantheon Books, 1974), p. 26.

74    "I would have . . . Act of 1964." Ibid.

74    "You're a what? . . . I can't fight." Sammy Davis, Jr., *Yes, I Can* (New York: Farrar, Straus & Giroux, 1965), pp. 462–463.

75    "I remember when . . . hurtful, so vicious." *People*, October 15, 1990, p. 116.

75    "the new captain's . . . cut Jap hair." Daniel K. Inouye and Lawrence Elliot, *Journey to Washington* (Englewood Cliffs, N.J.: Prentice-Hall, 1967), pp. 207–208.

75    "was having a ball . . . a black side." Ray Charles and David Ritz, *Brother Ray* (New York: Dial Press, 1978), p. 125.

77    "all the crew . . . can fly airplanes." John Neary, *Julian Bond: Black Rebel* (New York: Morrow, 1971), p. 228.

77    "to make a . . . a stone wall." Susan Dworkin, *Miss America 1945: Bess Myerson's Own Story* (New York: Newmarket Press, 1987), p. 179.

77    "I wanted to . . . come back here." Reggie Jackson, *Reggie* (New York: Villard Books, 1984), pp. 59–60.

78    "Before I was . . . for his services." *Rolling Stone*, September 19, 1991, p. 21.

78    "at the far . . . the oil embargo." Richard Valeriani, *Travels with Henry*
      (Boston: Houghton Mifflin, 1979), p. 311.
78    "I had expected . . . fathers, don't we?" Taylor Branch, *Parting the Waters:*
      *America in the King Years 1954–1963* (New York: Simon & Schuster, 1988),
      pp. 366, 370.

## CHAPTER 6
### THE ART OF COURTSHIP

79    "He spent half . . . very spasmodic courtship." William Manchester, *One*
      *Brief Shining Moment: Remembering Kennedy* (Boston: Little, Brown, 1983),
      p. 63.
79    "I was at . . . got it back." Elaine Partnow, ed., *The Quotable Woman*
      (Philadelphia: Running Press, 1991), p. 45.
79    "This is it . . . with me kid." *People*, March 6, 1989, p. 34.
79    "I hate to . . . over the world." *People*, November 18, 1991, p. 154.
80    "How do you . . . for my answer." Shirley MacLaine, *Don't Fall Off the*
      *Mountain* (New York: Norton, 1970), pp. 33–34.
80    "What's the matter? . . . Clark Gable." Joe Hyams, *Bogart and Bacall: A*
      *Love Story* (New York: McKay, 1975), p. 66.
80    "You're rather *short* . . . down to size." Muriel James, *Hearts on Fire* (Los
      Angeles: Tarcher, 1991), pp. 26–27.
81    "That's why I'm . . . side of me." *The New York Times*, October 27, 1988,
      p. B15.
81    "The German and . . . aware of it." *Time*, January 23, 1989, p. 25
81    "You know, in . . . hundred million dollars." Frank Brady, *Hefner* (New
      York: Macmillan, 1974), p. 228.
81    "One time in . . . think it's wonderful." *People*, July 17, 1989, p. 34.
81    "Now there's a . . . wasn't feeling peppy." *People*, June 11, 1990, p. 63.
81    "How would you . . . still be married." Sandra Sherey, *The Marilyn Scandal*
      (New York: Morrow, 1987), p. 11.
82    "When are you . . . to marry you." Stephen Ambrose, *Nixon: The Educa-*
      *tion of a Politician* (New York: Simon & Schuster, 1987), p. 93.
82    "nuts or something." Ibid.
82    "Hey, baby, I'm . . . bright and sensitive." Dorothy Chaplick, *Up with*
      *Hope: Jesse Jackson* (Minneapolis: Dillon Press, 1988), p. 29.
83    "just flagged me . . . that marriage lasts." Ronnie Dugger, *The Politician:*
      *The Life and Times of Lyndon Johnson* (New York: Norton, 1983), p. 177.
83    "framed in the . . . a long time." Norman Vincent Peale, *The True Joy of*
      *Positive Living: An Autobiography* (New York: Morrow, 1984), p. 110.
83    "I swear to . . . Just that quick." Muhammad Ali, *The Greatest: My Own*
      *Story* (New York: Random House, 1976), p. 184.
84    "Whoever that girl is, hire her." David Oshinsky, *A Conspiracy So Immense:*
      *The World of Joe McCarthy* (New York: Free Press, 1983), p. 302.
84    "I loved her . . . this little girl?" James Simon, *Independent Journey: The*
      *Life of William O. Douglas* (New York: Harper & Row, 1980), p. 381.
84    "The only reason . . . any other way." Marcia Chellis, *Living with the*
      *Kennedys: The Joan Kennedy Story* (New York: Simon & Schuster, 1985),
      p. 34.

84    "She's the girl I want to marry." Barbara Kellerman, *All the President's Kin* (New York: Free Press, 1981), p. 187.

84    "in the rumble . . . they were engaged." Rosalynn Carter, *First Lady from Plains* (Boston: Houghton Mifflin, 1984), pp. 23–24.

84    "I'm away from . . . of anxiety reduction." David Garrow, *Bearing the Cross: Martin Luther King, Jr., and the Southern Christian Leadership Conference* (New York: Morrow, 1986), p. 375.

85    "Do you know . . . in a wife." Stephen Oates, *Let the Trumpet Sound: The Life of Martin Luther King, Jr.* (New York: Mentor, 1982), p. 42.

85    "He had quite . . . call intellectual jive." Garrow, *Bearing the Cross*, pp. 45–46.

85    "The four things . . . see you again." Taylor Branch, *Parting the Waters: America in the King Years 1954–63* (New York: Simon & Schuster, 1985), pp. 95–96.

85    "How BIG of you." Ralph Martin, *A Hero for Our Time* (New York: Fawcett Crest, 1983), p. 316.

85    "When I learned . . . had it all." Gordon Liddy, *Will: The Autobiography of G. Gordon Liddy* (New York: St. Martin's Press, 1980), p. 94.

86    "a full-blown nut . . . to marry you." Debbie Reynolds, *Debbie: My Life* (New York: Dial Press, 1978), pp. 427–428.

86    "I'd seen Mike . . . from this man." Michael Todd, Jr., and Susan McCarthy Todd, *A Valuable Property: The Life Story of Michael Todd* (New York: Arbor House, 1983), p. 313.

86    "I'm going to marry that man." *Cosmopolitan*, August 1991, p. 186.

86    "When I first . . . The Sensuous Man." *Vanity Fair*, December 1990, p. 226.

86    "The night I . . . have his child." Hilary Mills, *Mailer: A Biography* (New York: Empire Books, 1982), p. 237.

86    "Ronnie and I . . . man for me." Laurence Leamer, *Make Believe: The Story of Nancy and Ronald Reagan* (New York: Harper & Row, 1983), p. 154.

86    "I found myself . . . do just that?" Gerold Frank and Zsa Zsa Gabor, *Zsa Zsa Gabor: My Story* (Cleveland: World Publishing, 1960), pp. 106–107.

87    "My huge, happy . . . the English language." David Harrell, *Oral Roberts: An American Life* (Bloomington: Indiana University Press, 1985), p. 46.

87    "It's your engagement . . . what's it for?" Joan Collins, *Past Imperfect: An Autobiography* (New York: Simon & Schuster, 1984), p. 181.

87    "Bill, what do . . . finish my hand?" John B. Judis, *William Buckley, Jr.: Patron Saint of the Conservatives* (New York: Simon & Schuster, 1988), p. 69.

88    "We were about . . . director said 'Cut!' " Joe Morella and Edward Epstein, *Jane Wyman* (New York: Delacorte Press, 1985), p. 29.

88    "I don't think . . . we get married." Peter Collier and David Horowitz, *The Kennedys: An American Drama* (New York: Summit Books, 1984), p. 39.

88    "I couldn't visualize . . . talk about it." Ibid., p. 194.

88    "The day I . . . and not overplayed." Donald Spoto, *The Dark Side of Genius: The Life of Alfred Hitchcock* (Boston: Little, Brown, 1983), p. 65.

CHAPTER 7

THE WHITE HOUSE: LIFE ABOVE THE STORE

89    "More than once . . . do it again?" Ronald Reagan, *An American Life* (New York: Simon & Schuster, 1990,) p. 395.

89    "Honey, I'm still living above the store." Frances Leighton, *The Search for the Real Nancy Reagan* (New York: Macmillan, 1987), p. 201.

89    "I felt like . . . an office building." Ralph Martin, *A Hero for Our Time* (New York: Fawcett Crest, 1983), p. 263.

89    "I hated the . . . and ears everywhere." *Vanity Fair*, July 1991, p. 132.

89    "It's not the . . . on Pennsylvania Avenue." Hugh Sidey, *A Very Personal Presidency: Lyndon Johnson in the White House* (New York: Atheneum, 1968), p. 47.

90    "It was the . . . sleep at night." Curt Smith, *Long Time Gone: The Years of Turmoil Remembered* (South Bend, Ind.: Icarus Press, 1982), p. 216.

90    "Nobody could sleep . . . it's impossible." Lester David, *The Lonely Lady of San Clemente: The Story of Pat Nixon* (New York: Crowell, 1978), p. 133.

90    "It was like . . . troops sitting there." *The American Experience*, "Nixon: The Quest, the Triumph, the Fall," PBS, October 15, 1990.

90    "Those damned drums . . . up all night." *The New York Times*, January 29, 1991, p. A13.

90    "the Great White Prison." J. Ronald Oakley, *God's Country: America in the Fifties* (New York: Dembner Books, 1986), p. 33.

90    "there they were . . . back to bed." Betty Ford, *The Times of My Life* (New York: Harper & Row, 1978), pp. 241–242.

91    "I thought about . . . so to bed." Lady Bird Johnson, *A White House Diary* (New York: Holt, Rinehart & Winston, 1970), pp. 161–162.

91    "It's an official . . . is a museum." *The New York Times*, December 10, 1987, p. A1.

91    "Imagine what it . . . as they look." *The New York Times*, January 25, 1988, p. A16.

91    "my own car . . . how to drive." J. B. West, *Upstairs at the White House* (New York: Coward, McCann & Geoghegan, 1974), p. 79.

92    "It caused such . . . a shopkeeper again." Reagan, *An American Life*, p. 395.

92    "We barely get . . . to do that." David Frost interview, PBS, January 3, 1992.

93    "It's so boring . . . home from school." Peter Hay, *All the Presidents' Ladies* (New York: Penguin, 1989), p. 135.

93    "I'm not going . . . a gilded cage." *Parade*, August 12, 1990, p. 5.

93    "The best way . . . the White House." Diana McLellan, *Ear on Washington* (New York: Arbor House, 1982), p. 162.

93    "Mr. West, we . . . during the night." West, *Upstairs at the White House*, p. 112.

93    "It surprised the . . . the White House." William Manchester, *One Brief Shining Moment: Remembering Kennedy* (Boston: Little, Brown, 1983), p. 160.

93    "I even had . . . to step into." West, *Upstairs at the White House*, p. 141.

93    "Many times while . . . in plastic ones." Traphes Bryant, *Dog Days at the White House* (New York: Macmillan, 1975), p. 33.

94    "Well, sir, you . . . another full-grown man." Frank Cormier, *LBJ: The Way He Was* (Garden City, N.Y.: Doubleday, 1977), p. 135.

94    "Mr. West, you're . . . to do it." C. David Heymann, *A Woman Named Jackie* (New York: Lyle Stuart, 1989), p. 382.

94    "It was kind . . . way, Mr. President." Martin, *A Hero for Our Time*, p. 377.

94    "a civil servant . . . Everything is fine." Dennis McCarthy, *Protecting the President* (New York: Morrow, 1985), pp. 40–41.

95    "For two weeks . . . night to boot?" Paul Boller, *Presidential Wives* (New York: Oxford University Press, 1988), p. 415.

95    "Oh, Mary, do . . . these marvelous gifts." Mary Gallagher, *My Life with Jacqueline Kennedy* (New York: McKay, 1969), p. 223.

96    "He told me . . . I believe him." Martin, *A Hero for Our Time*, p. 270.

96    "Chili con-crete . . . washer to do it." West, *Upstairs at the White House*, p. 326.

96    "You don't ask . . . all over them." Sidey, *A Very Personal Presidency*, p. 265.

96    "It looks like . . . seasick green." Martin, *A Hero for Our Time*, p. 234.

97    "you couldn't even . . . ever been used." Ibid., p. 263.

97    "Ken, look at . . . a good reproduction." Peter Collier and David Horowitz, *The Kennedys: An American Drama* (New York: Summit Books, 1984), p. 263.

97    "I had a . . . for three months." Martin, *A Hero for Our Time*, p. 263.

97    "The dining room . . . most fascinating wallpaper." Maude Shaw, *White House Nanny* (New York: New American Library, 1966), p. 81.

97    "I don't give . . . money for wallpaper." Kitty Kelley, *Jackie Oh!* (Secaucus, N.J.: Lyle Stuart, 1978), p. 137.

97    "It was a . . . eating my soup." Ford, *The Times of My Life*, p. 174.

98    "mumble." *The New York Times*, June 7, 1991, p. A22.

98    "Get those goddamn squirrels out of here." Traphes Bryant, *Dog Days at the White House* (New York: Macmillan, 1975), pp. 10–11.

98    "The next time . . . and shoot it!" West, *Upstairs at the White House*, p. 162.

98    "He used to . . . after the weekend." Maureen Reagan, *First Father, First Daughter* (Boston: Little, Brown, 1989), pp. 325–326.

98    "Oh, gosh, Millie kills squirrels." *Millie's Book: As Dictated to Barbara Bush* (New York: Morrow, 1990), p. 25.

99    "After a few . . . the little bag." Reagan, *An American Life*, p. 274.

99    "the worst-looking thing . . . creamed chip beef." *The New York Times*, March 23, 1990, p. A14.

99    "I guess you'd . . . the White House." Chester Bowles, *Promises to Keep: Carter's First Hundred Days* (New York: Crowell, 1977), p. 124.

99    "Bird, let's have Congress over tonight." Charles Whalen and Barbara Whalen, *The Longest Debate: A Legislative History of the 1964 Civil Rights Act* (New York: Mentor, 1985), p. 90.

100   "the most extraordinary . . . Jefferson dined alone." Helen Thomas, *Dateline: White House* (New York: Macmillan, 1975), p. 15.

100   "Nothing is the . . . I can stand." Liz Carpenter, *Ruffles and Flourishes* (Garden City, N.Y.: Doubleday, 1970), p. 209.

## CHAPTER 8
## THE MORAL AND THE IMMORAL

101 "I'm reliable . . . was also exemplary." *Frontline,* "The Spy Who Broke the Code," PBS, April 10, 1990.

101 "I ran the . . . it with integrity." *People Weekly Extra,* Fall 1989, p. 100.

101 "One question among . . . certainly hope so." *Nightline,* ABC, May 14, 1990.

101 "see me typing . . . in the store." *The New York Times,* April 14, 1989, p. A17.

102 "I need him." *The New York Times,* June 26, 1991, p. A20.

102 "The trouble with . . . don't recognize integrity." *The Great Age of Change: The Life History of the United States* (New York: Time-Life Books, 1964) p. 133.

102 "A gift is . . . expression of friendship." Shelley Ross, *Fall from Grace* (New York: Ballantine Books, 1988), p. 186.

102 "The conflict of . . . apply to me." Ibid.

102 "I certainly don't . . . It's dangerous." *60 Minutes,* CBS, March 25, 1990.

103 "No major publication . . . left at Yale." Mort Sahl, *Heartland* (New York: Harcourt Brace Jovanovich, 1976), p. 86.

103 "Everyone's entitled to . . . vengeance of God." *M Inc.,* November 1991, p. 126.

103 "The idea was . . . 'a good job.' " Victor Navasky, *Naming Names* (New York: Viking, 1980), p. 147.

104 "I became an . . . Understanding. Information." *Prime Time Live,* ABC, March 21, 1991.

104 "Wow! Would I? . . . judge and jury." *7 Days,* March 14, 1990, p. 14.

104 "Mister, it's my . . . him in trouble." *The New York Times,* April 13, 1989, p. B12.

104 "We're all given . . . up on people." *People,* March 6, 1989, p. 51.

104 "Lieutenant Calley started . . . gettin' to me." *Mike Wallace: Then and Now,* CBS, September 26, 1990.

104 "I sent them . . . him a murderer." Mike Wallace and Gary Paul Gates, *Close Encounters: Mike Wallace's Own Story* (New York: Morrow, 1984), p. 234.

105 "I cannot and . . . this year's fashions." Robert P. Newman, *The Cold War Romance of Lillian Hellman and John Melby* (Chapel Hill: University of North Carolina Press, 1989), p. 179.

105 "I don't give . . . guidance and understanding." David Frost, *I Gave Them a Sword: Behind the Scenes of the Nixon Interviews* (New York: Morrow, 1978), p. 302.

105 "President Ford was . . . to her students." *The Presidency, the Press, and the People,* PBS, April 2, 1990.

105 "If it's possible . . . in my life." Milton Meltzer, ed., *The American Promise* (New York: Bantam, 1990), p. 50.

105 "Now . . . you have . . . soul is rested." Howell Raines, *My Soul Is Rested* (New York: Putnam, 1977), p. 61.

106    "Here, find out . . . not my size." *The New York Times Book Review,* May 28, 1989, p. 10.

106    "it is through . . . the modern world." David Garrow, *Bearing the Cross: Martin Luther King, Jr., and the Southern Christian Leadership Conference* (New York: Morrow, 1986), p. 376.

106    " 'tom cat' with . . . degenerate sexual urges." Richard Powers, *Secrecy and Power: The Life of J. Edgar Hoover* (New York: Free Press, 1977), p. 373.

106    "Catch him in . . . of his babes." Fawn Brodie, *Richard Nixon* (New York: Norton, 1981), p. 464.

106    "Did you have . . . candidate that question." *The Best of Nightline,* ABC, April 24, 1990.

107    "So you say . . . It wasn't *reported." Vogue,* September 1987, p. 823.

107    "What's going to . . . write about it?" Curt Smith, *Long Time Gone: the Years of Turmoil Remembered* (South Bend, Ind.: Icarus Press, 1982, p. 148.

107    "I think we . . . They liked him." *Richard Nixon Reflects,* PBS, May 4, 1991.

107    "We were standing . . . monuments and parks." Judith Exner, *My Story* (New York: Grove Press, 1977), p. 221.

107    "When he used . . . Kennedy was furious." Heymann, *A Woman Named Jackie,* pp. 281–282.

107    "Do we want . . . the White House." Ralph Martin, *A Hero for Our Time* (New York: Fawcett Crest, 1983), p. 292.

108    "And this is . . . with my husband." Ibid., p. 295.

108    "I don't think . . . good and evil." Paul Boller, *Presidential Wives* (New York: Oxford University Press, 1988), p. 347.

108    "that from now . . . hire faster ambassadors." Arthur Schlesinger, *Robert Kennedy and His Times* (Boston: Houghton Mifflin, 1978), Vol. 1, p. 267.

108    "Joe got up . . . I'm his age." Joan Fontaine, *No Bed of Roses* (New York: Morrow, 1978), p. 267.

109    "They can't touch . . . dead, who cares?" Martin, *A Hero for Our Time,* p. 290.

108    "Anyone who knows . . . golf everytime." *People,* May 20, 1991, p. 34.

108    "There is great . . . to $5 million?" *Frontline,* "High Crimes and Misdemeanors," PBS, November 27, 1990.

109    "[White House chief of staff] . . . an impeachable offense, Ibid.

109    "How much money . . . get $1 million' " *American Experience,,* "Nixon: The Quest, the Triumph, the Fall," PBS, October 15, 1990.

109    "the first bad nigger in Congress." *Adam Clayton Powell,* PBS, December 3, 1989.

110    "Is going to . . . to do it." Ibid.

110    "common practice . . . dreamed of making." *American Heritage,* May/June 1989, pp. 76–88.

111    "a new kind . . . antidote to Presley." Ibid.

111    "It was this . . . wasn't that *hard." 60 Minutes,* CBS, September 22, 1991.

111    "You get bolder . . . I'd get caught." Ibid.

CHAPTER 9

FAMOUS LAST WORDS

113 "I've got Bush by the balls." *Newsweek,* January 15, 1990, p. 20.

113 "I want you . . . me to do." *American History Illustrated,* March & April 1991, p. 41.

113 "Fighter-bomber planes . . . missiles like sausages." J. Ronald Oakley, *God's Country: America in the Fifties* (New York: Dembner Books, 1986), p. 343.

113 "If anyone wants . . . be very bored." *American History Illustrated,* March/April 1991, p. 54.

113 "We are not . . . home to fight." Jules Abels, *The Degeneration of Our Presidential Election* (New York: Macmillan, 1968), p. 7.

114 "Don't worry, Bobby . . . happen to me." Richard Goodwin, *Remembering America: A Voice From the Sixties* (Boston: Little, Brown, 1988), p. 101.

114 "If anybody shoots . . . to shoot me." William Manchester, *The Death of a President: November 20–November 25, 1963* (New York: Harper & Row, 1967), p. 520.

114 "That guy's got . . . He'll see us." Malcolm Forbes and Jeff Bloch, *They Went That-a-way . . .* (New York: Ballantine Books, 1988), p. 74.

114 "I know the . . . piled six deep." Oakley, *God's Country,* p. 82.

114 "I was an utter flop." Garry Wills, *Nixon Agonistes: The Crisis of the Self-Made Man* (Boston: Houghton Mifflin, 1970), p. 110.

114 "And you know . . . gonna keep it." American Heritage editors, *The American Heritage Pictorial History of the Presidents of the United States* (New York: American Heritage, 1968), p. 900.

115 "Time had run . . . should be sent." Wills, *Nixon Agonistes,* p. 110.

115 "I'm going to . . . sugar-crazed taxi driver." Forbes and Bloch, *They Went That-a-way . . . ,* p. 266.

115 "I've never been . . . all my life." James R. Hoffa, *Hoffa: The Real Story* (New York: Stein & Day, 1975), p. 235.

115 "Tip, I'm getting . . . of a gentleman." Thomas P. O'Neill and William Novak, *Man of the House: The Life and Political Memoirs of Speaker Tip O'Neill* (New York: Random House, 1987), p. 262.

115 "The Vice Presidency is . . . who needs experience." Victor Lasky, *J.F.K.: The Man and the Myth* (New York: Macmillan, 1963), p. 379.

115 "I can't imagine . . . never require it." Juan Williams, *Eyes on the Prize: America's Civil Rights Years, 1954–1965* (New York: Viking, 1987), p. 103.

116 "I don't answer charges; I make them." David Oshinsky, *A Conspiracy So Immense: The World of Joe McCarthy* (New York: Free Press, 1983), p. 405.

116 "I believe all . . . man a chance." *People Weekly Extra,* Fall 1989, p. 152.

116 "political convulsion." *Wilson Quarterly,* Spring 1988, p. 79.

116 "Don't pay any . . . mean a thing." Peter Collier and David Horowitz, *The Kennedys: An American Drama* (New York: Summit Books, 1984), p. 193.

116 "I have no . . . or my children." Ibid., p. 79.

116 "only for idiots." *People,* February 18, 1991, p. 51.

116 "I . . . recognized that . . . at age thirty-five." Lewis J. Paper, *Empire: William S. Paley and the Making of CBS* (New York: St. Martin's Press, 1987), p. 15.

116   "CWO-2 Walker is . . . sense of humor." John Barron, *Breaking the Ring* (Boston: Houghton Mifflin, 1987) p. 61.

117   "K Mart security . . . their top secrets." *Frontline,* "The Spy Who Broke the Code," PBS, April 10, 1990.

117   "All in all . . . hit the jackpot." *Newsweek,* May 21, 1990, p. 27.

117   "From the cradle . . . tomorrow! Segregation forever!" Stephen Oates, *Let the Trumpet Sound: The Life of Martin Luther King, Jr.* (New York: Mentor, 1982), p. 206.

117   "I really see . . . a safe program." *People,* August 5, 1985, p. 29.

117   "Ah, c'mon . . . be covered, too." Kitty Kelley, *Elizabeth Taylor: The Last Star* (New York: Simon & Schuster, 1981), p. 141.

117   "You don't understand . . . they know it." *Newsweek,* February 11, 1991, p. 64.

118   "To hell with . . . of this country." Ronnie Dugger, *The Politician: The Life and Times of Lyndon Johnson* (New York: Norton, 1982), p. 124.

118   "that no-account Johnson . . . and grubby politicians." Ibid.

118   "Honey, be careful . . . like to sunbathe." Leo Damore, *Senatorial Privilege* (Washington, D.C.: Regnery Gateway, 1988), p. 59.

118   "I am going . . . certain of this." Forbes and Bloch, *They Went That-a-way* . . . , pp. 210–211.

118   "This is going . . . me to live." William R. Witherspoon, *Martin Luther King, Jr.: To the Mountaintop* (Garden City, N.Y.: Doubleday, 1985), p. 150.

118   "Of course, somebody's . . . about doing anyway." Marshall Frady, *Wallace* (New York: World Publishing, 1968), p. 63.

119   "I am pretty . . . nuttiness, that's all." Arthur Schlesinger, *Robert Kennedy and His Times* (Boston: Houghton Mifflin, 1978), Vol. 2, p. 941.

119   "the man he . . . much about Elijah." Mike Wallace and Gary Paul Gates, *Close Encounters: Mike Wallace's Own Story* (New York: Morrow, 1984), p. 139.

119   "I probably am a dead man already." *Mike Wallace: Then and Now,* CBS, September 26, 1990.

119   "Turn me loose." *Esquire,* July 1991, p. 61.

119   "Goddamn the whole . . . but you, Carlotta." Forbes and Bloch, *They Went That-a-way* . . . , p. 97.

119   "Paul said there . . . this goddamn world." James Reston, Jr., *Our Father Who Art in Hell* (New York: Times Books, 1981) pp. 324–325.

119   "Where the hell . . . waiting for him." Forbes and Bloch, *They Went That-a-way* . . . , pp. 154–155.

120   "Hey! We've got . . . We're burning up." Buzz Aldrin and Malcolm McConnell, *Men From Earth* (New York: Bantam, 1989), p. 164.

120   "Don't come back . . . over the valley." Forbes and Bloch, *They Went That-a-way* . . . , p. 277.

120   "reached over for . . . in the face." Henry Hampton and Steve Fayer, *Voices of Freedom: An Oral History of the Civil Rights Movement from the 1950s Through the 1980s* (New York: Bantam, 1982), p. 268.

CHAPTER 10

HOW TO SUCCEED, WITH OR WITHOUT TRYING

121 "We had no . . . WHAT'S GOING ON." *People*, September 10, 1990, p. 75.

121 "the two slowest . . . the seventh grade." Ibid., p. 73.

121 "The professor didn't . . . not work harder." *Esquire*, August 15, 1978, pp. 10–11.

122 "If we don't . . . risk of failure." Editors of *The Quayle Quarterly, The Unauthorized Autobiography of Dan Quayle* (Bridgeport, Conn., 1992), p. 74.

122 "This very thin . . . a great vocalist." Kitty Kelley, *His Way: The Unauthorized Biography of Frank Sinatra* (New York: Bantam, 1986), p. 48.

122 "I always knew . . . born for greatness." *The New York Times Magazine*, June 11, 1989, p. 28.

122 "I'm one of the world's great humans." *Barbara Walters Special*, ABC, May 14, 1989.

122 "I'm going to heaven." Ibid.

122 "Everyone wants to . . . be Cary Grant." *Newsweek*, March 12, 1990, p. 76.

122 "I want to . . . let you broadcast." Don Hewitt, *Minute by Minute* (New York: Random House, 1985), p. 35.

122 "If I ever . . . be irreparably ruined." *The New York Times*, July 7, 1991, p. 12.

122 "Paley and his . . . him the money." Lewis J. Paper, *Empire: William S. Paley and the Making of CBS* (New York: St. Martin's Press, 1987), p. 177.

123 "I was so . . . a second month." Francis Brady, *Hefner* (New York: Macmillan, 1974), p. 74.

123 "If you ever . . . good for you." *Newsweek*, July 3, 1989, p. 50.

123 "I made over . . . my studying music." Albert Goodman, *Elvis* (New York: McGraw-Hill, 1981), p. 267.

123 "I had about . . . be a copywriter." *Vanity Fair*, June 1990, pp. 153–154.

123 "the skinniest legs . . . at the Apollo." *The New York Times*, February 12, 1990, p. C13.

124 "The Pulitzer is . . . definition 'distinguished commentary.' " *Time*, July 3, 1989, p. 68.

124 "You may know . . . 'Yes, of course.' " Joan Peyser, *Bernstein: A Biography* (New York: Morrow, 1987), p. 102.

125 "a little girl . . . 15-mile-an-hour collision." Robert Buckhorn, *Nader: The People's Lawyer* (Englewood Cliffs, N.J.: Prentice-Hall, 1972), p. 35.

125 "in the shower . . . time to think." *Prime Time Live*, ABC, December 6, 1990.

125 "I recall a . . . clear to me." *The New York Times*, March 2, 1991, p. 29.

125 "Ted's notebooks were . . . hell with them." *The New York Times*, September 26, 1991, p. D23.

125 "He'll ask for . . . I'll read it." Richard Valeriani, *Travels with Henry* (Boston: Houghton Mifflin, 1979), p. 61.

126 "Of course, it's . . . He was fired." *The New York Times Book Review*, March 8, 1987, p. 36.

126 "Deviates do that." Ibid.

126    "Listen, I called . . . house up." *The New York Times Magazine*, April 2, 1989, p. 30

126    "You would be . . . lot to say." *Donahue*, NBC, February 7, 1990.

127    "What did you . . . that happen again." Roger Morris, *Haig: The General's Progress* (Playboy Press, 1982), p. 274.

127    "We were handed . . . to feel awful." *Newsweek*, January 1, 1990, p. 11.

127    "I'd make them . . . or the other." Roy Blount, Jr., *Not Exactly What I Had in Mind* (Boston: Atlantic Monthly Press, 1985), p. 165.

127    "the menu is . . . spoonful of it." *Vogue*, March 1989, p. 564.

127    "I'm a woman . . . match went instead." *20/20*, ABC, November 23, 1990.

127    "Big breasts, big . . . be anything else?" Gloria Steinem, *Marilyn* (New York: Holt, 1986), p. 71.

128    "Every woman will . . . right to that." *New York*, March 20, 1989, p. 44.

128    "It's not the . . . know the letters." *People*, March 6, 1989, p. 55.

128    "When I started . . . cancer from sex." Anthony Summers, *Goddess: The Secret Lives of Marilyn Monroe* (New York: Macmillan, 1985), p. 34.

128    "Hollywood's wonderful . . . for making love." Thomas Kiernan, *Jane: An Intimate Biography of Jane Fonda* (New York: Putnam, 1973), p. 133.

128    "No question . . . secretary to LBJ." *ERA: The War Between the Women*, ABC, January 22, 1977.

128    "dogs, daughters, and delphiniums." *Seattle Post-Intelligencer*, May 5, 1991, p. 32.

128    "It's a good . . . a drag queen." *People*, March 6, 1989, p. 54.

128    "The thing women . . . just take it." Elaine Partnow, ed., *The Quotable Woman* (Philadelphia: Running Press, 1991), p. 161.

129    "If you give . . . in high heels." *Cosmopolitan*, April 1991, p. 124.

129    "living in Los Angeles . . . what to do." *People*, April 24, 1989, pp. 40–45.

129    "The man came . . . the lucky ones." *The New York Times*, April 10, 1989, p. B6.

129    "wreck both our careers." *Parade*, September 1, 1991, p. 2.

129    "That's what he . . . what I did." *The New York Times*, October 8, 1989, p. 39.

129    "It is only . . . down the drain." Ibid.

130    "We have a . . . get that raise." ABC News, September 13, 1991.

130    "were as close . . . of the guilts." *The New York Times*, January 22, 1991, p. A12.

130    "This was my . . . than my kid." *Barbara Walters Special*, ABC, September 10, 1991.

130    "When we were . . . going to happen." *People*, October 2, 1989, p. 91.

130    "It's obvious that . . . want to do." Peter Carroll, *Famous in America: The Passion to Succeed* (New York: Dutton, 1985), p. 195.

130    "I never knew . . . be liberated from." Paul Boller, *Presidential Wives* (New York: Oxford University Press, 1988), p. 347.

130    "Women's natural role . . . lose their mystery." Sarah Bedford, *Princess Grace* (New York: Stein & Day, 1984), p. 193.

131    "As important as . . . wish him well." *The New York Times*, June 2, 1990, p. A1.

131    "If you hire . . . *That's* loyalty." Robert Caro, *Means of Ascent: The Years of Lyndon Johnson* (New York: Knopf, 1990), pp. 117–118.

131 "Boy, it'd be . . . carry it out." Jeb Stuart Magruder, *An American Life: One Man's Road to Watergate* (New York: Atheneum, 1974), p. 175.

132 "You just give . . . a parking lot." *Newsweek*, October 23, 1989, p. 59.

132 "Ronnie just didn't . . . Haig finally left." *Newsweek*, October 23, 1989, p. 59.

132 "I started pulling . . . boots and back." *The New York Times*, March 24, 1989, p. A12.

132 "Sometimes you have . . . a written law." Helen Thomas, UPI White House correspondent, in speech, June 18, 1989.

132 "full of political . . . keep their integrity." *The New York Times Book Review*, September 15, 1991, pp. 3, 19.

132 "want to . . . arms control," *The New York Times*, March 31, 1989, p. A11.

133 "home of watermelons . . . in my hometown." *The New York Times*, November 5, 1990, p. B11.

133 "Do you know . . . What's *Ebony* magazine." *Black Stars in Orbit*, PBS, February 12, 1990.

133 "Everything I have, I owe to spaghetti." *Vanity Fair*, January 1991, p. 122.

133 "I learned in . . . deodorant like success." Kitty Kelley, *Elizabeth Taylor: The Last Star* (New York: Simon & Schuster, 1981), p. 234.

133 "Success for me . . . of each one." Partnow, *The Quotable Woman*, p. 29.

133 "Show me success without ego." *Time*, January 16, 1989, p. 54.

133 "I believe strongly . . . a new dream." *M Inc.*, October 1991, p. 114.

133 "But for [affirmative . . . second seventeen years," *The New York Times*, July 14, 1991, pp. 1, 16.

134 "For the Kennedys . . . no in-between." Francis Russell, *The President Makers* (Boston: Little, Brown, 1976), p. 387.

134 "It's not a . . . for the thrill." Kitty Kelley, *Jackie Oh!* (Secaucus, N.J.: Lyle Stuart, 1978), p. 297.

134 "Well, I think . . . could be done." *20/20*, ABC, February 23, 1990.

134 "Most people in . . . be this way." *Time*, May 20, 1991, p. 58.

134 "Of course if . . . to grow up." *The New York Times*, August 4, 1988, p. C23.

134 "If it hadn't . . . life of crime." Summers, *Goddess*, p. 106.

134 "Whoever heard of . . . unknown Swedish broad." Sammy Davis, Jr., *Hollywood in a Suitcase* (New York: Morrow, 1980), p. 106.

134 "If I had . . . in Dixon, Illinois." *20/20*, ABC, November 2, 1990.

134 "My daddy had . . . worth a damn." Jerry Hopkins, *Elvis: The Final Years* (New York: St. Martin's Press, 1980), p. 61.

135 "Personally, if I . . . to announce Mozart." *M Inc.*, October 1991, p. 38.

135 "I would have made a good pope." Christopher Cerf and Victor Navasky, *The Experts Speak* (New York: Pantheon Books, 1984), p. 288.

135 "If I hadn't . . . in a whorehouse." J. Ronald Oakley, *God's Country: America in the Fifties* (New York: Dembner Books, 1986), p. 24.

## CHAPTER 11
### ONLY IN AMERICA

137 "So this is . . . of their minds." *The New York Times Book Review*, December 31, 1989, p. 12.

137  "pull out a . . . country has changed." *Smithsonian*, December 1989, p. 80.

137  "Why am I . . . can destroy me?" Kitty Kelley, *His Way: The Unauthorized Biography of Frank Sinatra* (New York: Bantam, 1986), p. 255.

138  "Tell the old . . . there this afternoon." *The New York Times*, May 17, 1990, p. A19.

138  "I don't *care* . . . *can* light it." William Manchester, *The Death of a President: November 20–November 25, 1963* (New York: Harper & Row, 1967) pp. 550–551.

139  "funded and supported . . . of 1960s." *Mission Mind Control*, ABC, July 10, 1979.

139  "I walked into . . . Boardwalk for five hundred dollars." *Manhattan, inc.*, May 1988, p. 106.

139  "We had a twelve-thousand-dollar . . . the police department." David E. Koskoff, *The Mellons* (New York: Crowell, 1978), p. 467.

139  "It cost me . . . being—well spent." J. Paul Getty, *As I See It: The Autobiography of J. Paul Getty* (Englewood Cliffs, N.J.: Prentice-Hall, 1976), p. 282.

140  "Tony, what is . . . wanted at all." Tom Valentine and Patrick Mahn, *Daddy's Duchess* (Secaucus, N.J.: Lyle Stuart, 1987), p. 148.

140  "You can make . . . the rubber gloves." James Phelan, *Howard Hughes: The Hidden Years* (New York: Random House, 1976), pp. 45–46.

141  "Where's your clicker?" *M Inc.*, October 1990, p. 120.

141  "Frank thinks you . . . all he needs." Spiro Agnew, *Go Quietly . . . or Else* (New York: Morrow, 1980), p. 204.

141  "Rich people don't . . . the bank offices." Andy Warhol, *The Philosophy of Andy Warhol* (New York: Harcourt Brace Jovanovich, 1975), p. 129.

141  "I want them . . . me a ten." William Manchester, *One Brief Shining Moment: Remembering Kennedy* (Boston: Little, Brown, 1983), p. 37.

141  "I remember another . . . nothing to him." Joan Blair and Clay Blair, Jr., *The Search for J.F.K.* (New York: Berkley Publishing, 1976), p. 161.

141  "We met at . . . think about money." Ibid., p. 352.

141  "Oh, Dad, I . . . be the day." Peter Collier and David Horowitz, *The Kennedys: An American Drama* (New York: Summit Books, 1984), pp. 275–276.

142  "People attending parties . . . there and everywhere." Robert Lenzer, *The Great Getty* (New York: Crown, 1985), p. 128.

142  "I love quality . . . I don't chisel." *Time*, January 16, 1989, p. 48.

142  "Only the little people pay taxes." *Newsweek*, July 24, 1989, p. 11.

142  "You've got to . . . pay income taxes." Victor Lasky, *Never Complain, Never Explain: The Story of Henry Ford II* (New York: Marek, 1981), p. 176.

143  "I don't pay . . . what I want." Shawn Considine, *Barbra Streisand: The Woman, the Myth, the Music* (New York: Delacorte Press, 1985), p. 197.

143  "Can you possibly . . . Go to work." Armand Hammer, *Hammer* (New York: Putnam, 1987), p. 487.

143  "Uncle Nelson offering me Bobby Kennedy's seat." *The New York Times Magazine*, July 21, 1991, p. 21.

143  "Don't buy a . . . for a landslide." Hedley Donovan, *Roosevelt to Reagan* (New York: Harper & Row, 1985), p. 66.

144  "Bill, I've thought . . . the ball rolling." Lewis J. Paper, *Empire: William S. Paley and the Making of CBS* (New York: St. Martin's Press, 1987), p. 261.

144   "Well, I think . . . for 30 days." Peter Collier and David Horowitz, *The Rockefellers: An American Dynasty* (New York: Holt, Rinehart & Winston, 1976), pp. 281–282.

144   "Of course, he . . . of their fate." *The New York Times Magazine*, June 24, 1990, p. 60.

144   "For too long . . . a noble cause." Ronnie Dugger, *On Reagan: The Man and His Presidency* (New York: McGraw-Hill, 1983), p. 349.

145   "It's a . . . and for all." ABC News, March 1, 1991.

145   "If we get . . . his ass kicked." *Newsweek*, January 21, 1991, p. 37.

145   "Everything I knew . . . reward to aggression." *The American Experience*, "LBJ," Part 3, PBS, October 1, 1991.

145   "You have a . . . over very quickly." J. Ronald Oakley, *God's Country: America in the Fifties* (New York: Dembner Books, 1986), p. 215.

145   "Whatever happens in . . . except military victory." Gore Vidal, *An Evening with Richard Nixon* (New York: Random House, 1972), p. 78.

145   "I think he . . . is the place." *American Heritage,* November 1989, p. 46.

145   "I call it . . . begging for peace!" H. R. Haldeman and Joseph DiMona, *The Ends of Power* (New York: Times Books, 1978), p. 83.

145   "We were not . . . continue the war." *The New York Times Magazine,* June 24, 1990, p. 36.

146   "Westmoreland was wrong . . . Human beings!" Ibid.

146   "Any American commander . . . been sacked overnight." Ibid., p. 36.

146   "I'm not going . . . lost a war." Hugh Sidey, *A Very Personal Presidency: Lyndon Johnson in the White House* (New York: Atheneum, 1978), p. 211.

146   "We cannot accept a visible humiliation." David Halberstam, *The Best and the Brightest* (New York: Random House, 1972), p. 92.

146   "First I'd drop . . . or three weeks." *People,* February 13, 1989, p. 68.

146   "We won the . . . one but itself." *The New York Times,* January 25, 1991, p. A14.

CHAPTER 12

LIFE-STYLES

147   "He had this . . . I'm the greatest." Henry Hampton and Steve Fayer, *Voices of Freedom: An Oral History of the Civil Rights Movement from the 1950s Through the 1980s* (New York: Bantam, 1990), p. 323.

147   "Brezhnev, a collector . . . road very well." Richard Nixon, *The Memoirs of Richard Nixon* (New York: Grosset & Dunlap, 1988), p. 880.

147   "He got into . . . shouted, 'Okay, Harry.' " Desi Arnaz, *A Book* (New York: Morrow, 1976), p. 158.

148   "That's the closest . . . White House yet." Alfred Steinberg, *Sam Johnson's Boy: A Close-Up of the President from Texas* (New York: Macmillan, 1968), p. 673.

149   "you're always somewhat . . . where things are." *The New York Times,* January 12, 1989, p. B8.

150   "Everybody had been . . . know how many." Hampton and Fayer, *Voices of Freedom,* pp. 30–31.

150   "My wife made . . . was flamingo pink." Sugar Ray Robinson, *Sugar Ray* (New York: Viking, 1969), pp. 59–60.

150 "Nothing stops him . . . scared of anything." *American Masters*, "Ray Charles: The Genius of Soul," PBS, January 3, 1992.

151 "When you go . . . am sitting down." Betty Ford, *The Times of My Life* (New York: Harper & Row, 1978), p. 177.

151 "He was in . . . talks to me." Marcia Chellis, *Living with the Kennedys: The Joan Kennedy Story* (New York: Simon & Schuster, 1985), p. 183.

151 "We'd better talk . . . doesn't mean anything." Peter Collier and David Horowitz, *The Kennedys: An American Drama* (New York: Summit Books, 1984), p. 243.

151 "Mr. Ghorbanifar took . . . a million dollars." Jane Mayer and Doyle McManus, *Landslide: The Unmaking of a President* (Boston: Houghton Mifflin, 1988), p. 189.

151 "one of the . . . in the world." Richard Goodwin, *Remembering America: A Voice from the Sixties* (Boston: Little, Brown, 1988), pp. 258–259.

152 "Do you think . . . a hearing aid?" David Halberstam, *The Best and the Brightest* (New York: Random House, 1972), p. 74.

152 "(Arafat leaned over . . . floor with laughter." *Newsweek*, February 11, 1991, p. 66.

152 "Would you like . . . all right." Michael Deaver, *Behind the Scenes* (New York: Morrow, 1987), p. 115.

152 "Chuck, c'mere a . . . place has *everything*!" Marshall Frady, *Billy Graham: A Parable of American Righteousness* (Boston: Little, Brown, 1979), pp. 166–167.

153 "I went to . . . nothing had happened." Rosalynn Carter, *First Lady from Plains* (Boston: Houghton Mifflin, 1984), p. 106.

153 "I looked from . . . inside your house." Eartha Kitt, *Alone with Me* (Chicago: Regnery, 1976), p. 47.

153 "each Friday a . . . lords and earls." *Child Star: An Autobiography of Shirley Temple Black* (New York: McGraw-Hill, 1988), pp. 88–89.

154 "dashed into what . . . and dashed out." Shelley Winters, *Shelley II: The Middle of My Century* (New York: Simon & Schuster, 1989), p. 87.

154 "Do you want . . . door number three?" *Newsweek*, July 23, 1990, p. 13.

154 "I was at . . . hand, and left." Pearl Bailey, *Talking to Myself* (New York: Harcourt Brace Jovanovich, 1971), p. 109.

154 "Being a hero . . . convenience,' she suggested." Sugar Ray Robinson, *Sugar Ray* (New York: Viking, 1969) pp. 188–189.

154 "had a bladder . . . of a football." *The New York Times Book Review*, November 17, 1991, p. 24.

155 "Mr. President, he . . . That's my prerogative." George V. Higgins, *The Friends of Richard Nixon* (Boston: Little, Brown, 1975), p. 177.

155 "Are you ready? . . . in the can." Lauren Bacall, *Lauren Bacall by Myself* (New York: Knopf, 1978), pp. 155–156.

155 "I don't know . . . a professional southerner." Peter Carroll, *Famous in America: The Passion to Succeed* (New York: Dutton, 1985), p. 43.

155 "A woman who . . . be an inquest." Malcom Forbes and Jeff Bloch, *They Went That-a-way . . .* (New York: Ballantine Books, 1988), p. 72.

155 "I eat cottage . . . disguises almost anything." Gore Vidal, *An Evening with Richard Nixon* (New York: Random House, 1972), p. 82.

156 "They had incredibly . . . a good life." *M Inc.*, May 1991, p. 65.

156 "What kind of . . . over America today." Lee Iacocca, *Iacocca: An Autobiography* (New York: Bantam, 1984), pp. 13–14.

156 "a white lady . . . cook with, lady." Dick Gregory with Robert Lipsyte, *nigger!* (New York: Dutton, 1964), p. 48.

156 "They sounded like . . . an outdoor pit." *People*, May 6, 1991, p. 54.

156 "Jack's secretary called . . . cook's night out." Ralph Martin, *A Hero for Our Time* (New York: Fawcett Crest, 1983), p. 85.

157 "I wonder if . . . wonder and beauty." *Vogue*, September 1989, p. 798.

157 "I used alcohol . . . of the imagination." *Vanity Fair*, December 1989, p. 215.

157 "Well, with one . . . no holding me." Bacall, *By Myself*, p. 238.

157 "For me marijuana . . . conceptual boundaries." *Spy*, October 1988, p. 11.

157 "It was astounding . . . a trip abroad." Barry Miles, *Ginsberg: A Biography* (New York: Simon & Schuster, 1989), pp. 260, 262.

158 "An insulator against the pain of racism." *American Masters: "Satchmo— Louis Armstrong"*, PBS, October 22, 1990.

158 "Drugs have been . . . us a lot." *60 Minutes*, CBS, November 25, 1990.

158 "Marijuana is like . . . get a headache." Willie Nelson and Bud Shrake, *Willie: An Autobiography* (New York: Simon & Schuster, 1988), p. 197.

158 "I don't care . . . It works." C. David Heymann, *A Woman Named Jackie* (New York: Lyle Stuart, 1989), p. 296.

158 "invaluable senior partner . . . of my spirit." *Vanity Fair*, December 1989, p. 215.

158 "I probably encouraged . . . to relax him." Betty Ford, *Betty: A Glad Awakening* (New York: Doubleday, 1987), p. 33.

158 "The combination of . . . Senate in California." The *Presidency, the Press and the People*, PBS, April 2, 1990.

158 "I used to . . . my fucking mind." Jose Torres, *Fire and Fear: The Inside Story of Mike Tyson* (New York: Warner Books, 1989), p. 21.

159 "I drank nail . . . empty difficult day." *20/20*, ABC, September 7, 1990.

159 "I felt hypocritical . . . with this picture?" *Vanity Fair*, July 1991, p. 132.

159 "Only thing wrong . . . love with it." *Vanity Fair*, August 1989, p. 160.

159 "See that? It's . . . deaden the pain." *People*, September 3, 1990, pp. 57–58.

159 "Never once, until . . . from my stash." *Spy*, August 1989, p. 73.

159 "When I was . . . like vitamins." Gerold Frank, *Judy* (New York: Harper & Row, 1975), p. 460.

160 "Yeah, life's groovy . . . ain't groovy enough." Forbes and Bloch, *They Went That-a-way . . .* , p. 173.

160 "Can you imagine . . . live with it." Larry Geller, *If I Can Dream: Elvis's Own Story* (New York: Simon & Schuster, 1989), p. 80.

160 "I was walking . . . an AA meeting." *People*, August 14, 1989, p. 40.

160 "The hardest thing . . . feel all day." *The New York Times*, May 17, 1990, p. D28.

160 "the reason 90 percent . . . person in Harlem." *Vogue*, July 1988, p. 239.

160 "Some drug guy . . . like I'm President." *Newsweek*, April 3, 1989, p. 17.

161 "You know, a . . . the right time." Arthur Schlesinger, *Robert Kennedy and His Times* (Boston: Houghton Mifflin, 1978), p. 220.

161   "Sometimes I feel . . . I could cry." Robert Donovan, *Confidential Secretary: Ann Whitman's Twenty Years with Eisenhower and Rockefeller* (New York: Dutton, 1988), p. 43.

161   "You cry too . . . in a dictionary." Gloria Steinem, *Marilyn* (New York: Henry Holt, 1986), p. 106.

161   "Don't tell me . . . I'm Roe." Marian Faux, *Roe v. Wade* (New York: Macmillan, 1988), p. 304.

161   "another woman . . . lose my lunch." *The New York Times*, May 9, 1989, p. A18.

161   "One night they . . . started to cry." *Time*, December 16, 1991, p. 20.

161   "Grant after Shiloh . . . a little bit." *20/20*, ABC, March 15, 1991.

162   "walked only a . . . felt completely helpless." Dennis V. N. McCarthy, *Protecting the President* (New York: Morrow, 1985), pp. 19–20.

162   "I never cry except in public." Fawn Brodie, *Richard Nixon* (New York: Norton, 1981), p. 63.

162   "I do that . . . Here we go." *The New York Times*, June 7, 1991, p. A14.

162   "What does cry . . . the crying type." *The New York Times*, June 12, 1990, p. B4.

## CHAPTER 13

### LIFE IN THE PUBLIC EYE

165   "Now I have . . . to walk faster." *The Presidency, the Press and the People*, PBS, April 22, 1990.

165   "compact body . . . virile masculinity." *The New York Times Book Review*, September 15, 1991, pp. 3, 19.

165   "We'd always be . . . It was exciting." *The New York Times*, June 10, 1989, p. 11.

166   "I remember one . . . dog King Timahoe." *The Presidency, the Press and the People*, PBS, April 2, 1990.

166   "Good Christ," said . . . wearing *shoes*." Dan Rather and Gary Paul Gates, *The Palace Guard* (New York: Harper & Row, 1974), p. 244.

166   "That was our . . . with that situation." *The Presidency, the Press and the People*, PBS, April 2, 1990.

166   "the courage of . . . not coming through." *The New York Times Book Review*, November 24, 1991, p. 3.

166   "One effective . . . years from now." James Reston, *Deadline* (New York: Random House, 1991), p. 410.

166   "Something's going . . . to the question." *The New York Times*, November 28, 1991, p. A16.

167   "You smile discreetly . . . what you say." Editors of *The Quayle Quarterly*, *The Unauthorized Autobiography of Dan Quayle* (Bridgeport, Conn., 1992), p. 61.

167   "Sincerity is the . . . through on television." Time-Life editors, *This Fabulous Century* (New York: Time-Life Books, 1970), p. 96.

167   "That's my boy! That's my actor!" Fawn Brodie, *Richard Nixon* (New York: Norton, 1981), pp. 115–116.

167   "That bite of . . . of my mouth." Lester David, *The Lonely Lady of San Clemente: The Story of Pat Nixon* (New York: Crowell, 1978), p. 83.

168    "No, I didn't . . . it over television." *Mike Wallace: Then and Now*, CBS, September 26, 1990.

168    "He came back . . . tell you where." *People*, September 3, 1990, p. 69.

168    "I just saw . . . a Jesus freak." Charles Colson, *Born Again* (Old Tappan, N.J.: Chosen Books, 1976), p. 169.

168    "With my mind . . . not heard correctly." Laura Walker, *Daughter of Deceit* (Dallas: Word Publishing, 1988), pp. 180–181.

168    "Walter Cronkite came . . . calls back home." Henry Hampton and Steve Fayer, *Voices of Freedom: An Oral History of the Civil Rights Movement from the 1950s through the 1980s* (New York: Bantam, 1990), pp. 39–40.

169    "As I got . . . he'd believe me." Lynn Bloom, *Dr. Spock: Biography of a Conservative Radical* (Indianapolis: Bobbs-Merrill, 1972), p. 283.

169    "A headline caught . . . going to *do*?" Joan Collins, *Past Imperfect* (New York: Simon & Schuster, 1984), pp. 85–86.

169    "of the action . . . home at last." Douglas MacArthur, *Reminiscences* (New York: McGraw-Hill, 1964), p. 395.

169    "Hey, I didn't . . . telling the truth." Thomas Kiernan, *Jane: An Intimate Biography of Jane Fonda* (New York: Putnam, 1973), p. 50.

169    "I arrived home . . . I was leaving." Ronnie Dugger, *On Reagan: The Man and His Presidency* (New York: McGraw-Hill, 1983), p. 9.

170    "What's all this . . . and reasoned together." Helen Thomas, *Dateline: White House* (New York: Macmillan, 1975), pp. 100–101.

170    "When he got . . . as your President." *The American Experience*, "LBJ," Part 4, PBS, October 1, 1991.

170    "I—I couldn't . . . I was stunned." Ibid.

170    "In America, heroes . . . to the NRA." Lincoln Caplan, *The Insanity Defense and the Trial of John W. Hinckley, Jr.* (Boston: Godine, 1984), p. 45.

171    "Now, everyone will know me." James McKinley, *Assassination in America* (New York: Harper & Row, 1977), p. 122.

171    "From everything I . . . known in history." Leon Jaworski, *Confession and Avoidance* (Garden City, N.Y.: Doubleday, 1979), p. 191.

171    "But, hell, I . . . life to do." Robert Kaiser, *R.F.K. Must Die* (New York: Dutton, 1970). p. 540.

171    "I've decided Wallace . . . heard of Wallace." Arthur H. Bremer, *An Assassin's Diary* (New York: Harper's Magazine Press, 1973), p. 104.

171    "Just stay with . . . like I am." McKinley, *Assassination in America*, p. 122.

171    "I did not . . . up a gun." James W. Clarke, *American Assassins* (Princeton, N.J.: Princeton University Press, 1982), p. 143.

171    "I know every . . . in a rathole." *The New York Times*, November 3, 1988, pp. C30–C31.

171    "I would get . . . you than me." J. Ronald Oakley, *God's Country: America in the Fifties* (New York: Dembner Books, 1986), p. 164.

171    "You know, when . . . out of there." David Oshinsky, *A Conspiracy So Immense: The World of Joe McCarthy* (New York: Free Press, 1983), p. 490.

173    "If you'll cover . . . on a hydrant." Booth Moody, *LBJ: An Irreverent Chronicle* (New York: Crowell, 1976), p. 167.

173    "regarded the press . . . dump on it." James Reston, *Deadline: A Memoir* (New York: Random House, 1991), p. 302.

173    "I trust the . . . trust my wife." Hugh Sidey, *A Very Personal Presidency: Lyndon Johnson in the White House* (New York: Atheneum, 1968), p. 163.

173 "Rather, are you trying to fuck me?" Dan Rather, *The Camera Never Blinks* (New York: Morrow, 1977), p. 158.

173 "The press aren't . . . were really shootouts." *Richard Nixon Reflects*, PBS, May 4, 1990.

173 "The story had . . . to have worked." *The Presidency, the Press and the People*, PBS, April 2, 1990.

173 "There is in . . . because we're human." Reston, *Deadline*, pp. 426–427.

173 "There's some good in everyone." Helen Thomas, UPI White House correspondent, in a speech, June 18, 1989.

173 "You may have . . . to prevent leaks." *The New York Times*, May 15, 1989, p. B7.

CHAPTER 14

WHAT'S IT ALL ABOUT?: LIFE AND DEATH, ETC.

175 "I like thinking . . . well think big." *Time*, January 16, 1989, p. 48.

175 "I believe that . . . bed until noon." J. B. West, *Upstairs at the White House* (New York: Coward, McCann and Geoghegan, 1973), p. 178.

175 "Christ says, 'Don't . . . to his wife." *Newsweek*, October 4, 1976, pp. 70–71.

175 "Never doubt that . . . that ever has." *Utne Reader*, March/April 1991, p. 77.

175 "Service is the . . . on this earth." Brian Lanker, *I Dream a World: Portraits of Black Women Who Changed America* (New York: Stewart, Tabori & Chang, 1989), p. 106.

175 "If there is . . . you have one." *The New York Times Book Review*, June 23, 1991, p. 18.

176 "Retire? No one . . . Why should I?" *M*, December 1991, p. 119.

176 "The meek shall . . . the mineral rights." Robert Lenzer, *The Great Getty* (New York: Crown, 1985), p. 93.

176 "You gotta take . . . with the bitter." *Vogue*, March 1989, p. 318.

176 "You can never . . . who is he." ABC News, February 10, 1992.

176 "I enjoy shopping . . . than a psychiatrist." *The Best of Nightline*, ABC, April 24, 1990.

176 "If you can . . . a capitalist country." *Donahue*, NBC, February 7, 1990.

176 "If they said . . . back to Terry." ABC News, March 16, 1990.

176 "the day before . . . have a Daddy." Dick Gregory and Robert Lipsyte, *nigger!* (New York: Dutton, 1964), pp. 45–47.

177 "The United States . . . a little boy?" *People*, August 6, 1990, p. 38.

177 "Chairman, Chairman, wake . . . pigs are vamping." *Eyes on the Prize*, PBS, 1991.

178 "There is another . . . their fathers were." William Manchester, *Death of a President: November 20–November 25, 1963* (New York: Harper & Row, 1967), p. 635.

178 "Moneywise I got took." Ibid., p. 636.

178 "Our parents gave . . . were for *me*." Peter Collier and David Horowitz, *The Rockefellers: An American Dynasty* (New York: Holt, Rinehart & Winston, 1976), p. 520.

178   "We didn't see . . . and more parents." Peter Collier and David Horowitz, *The Fords: An American Epic* (New York: Summit Books, 1987), p. 283.

178   "Lou, you poured . . . million dollar judgment." *The Man Who Beat the Blacklist: John Henry Faulk*, PBS, August 1, 1990.

179   "I'm investing this in America, not you." Ibid.

179   "We shall pay . . . success of liberty." *The New York Times*, May 28, 1990, p. A21.

179   "save the taxpayers . . . for fourteen days." Stephen Oates, *Let the Trumpet Sound: The Life of Martin Luther King, Jr.* (New York: Mentor, 1982), p. 133.

179   "I am a . . . and human dignity." Arthur Schlesinger, *Robert Kennedy and His Times* (Boston: Houghton Mifflin, 1978), Vol. 1, p. 338.

180   "I have been . . . word I say." Richard Valeriani, *Travels with Henry* (Boston: Houghton Mifflin, 1975), p. 25.

180   "Deep down, I'm pretty superficial." Kitty Kelley, *His Way: The Unauthorized Biography of Frank Sinatra* (New York: Bantam, 1986), p. 139.

180   "I've never had . . . in my life." Ralph Martin, *A Hero for Our Time* (New York: Fawcett Crest, 1983), p. 499.

180   "You know, nobody . . . really an egghead." Gore Vidal, *An Evening with Richard Nixon* (New York: Random House, 1972), p. 52.

180   "My mouth was overshadowed by my ability." *The New York Times*, November 23, 1990, p. C8.

180   "What will be . . . lot by watching." Phil Pepe, *The Wit and Wisdom of Yogi Berra* (New York: Hawthorne Books, 1965), p. 76.

180   "There are two sorts . . . I'm a broad." *People*, March 6, 1989, p. 55.

180   "Being the author . . . a full-time job." Malcom Forbes and Jeff Bloch, *They Went That-a-way . . .* (New York: Ballantine Books, 1988), pp. 210–211.

180   "What's wrong with . . . kind of fellow." *Spy*, August 1988, p. 98.

180   "I'm a classic . . . in that category." *The New York Times Magazine*, June 25, 1989, p. 18.

180   "Caroline is very . . . for a father." Martin, *A Hero for Our Time*, p. 254.

181   "I was under oath, wasn't I?" *Life*, Fall 1990, p. 105.

181   "Looking back on . . . me from myself." Arthur H. Bremer, *An Assassin's Diary* (New York: Harper's Magazine Press, 1973), p. 142.

181   "Just destroy the tapes." *Esquire*, January 1992, p. 117.

181   "The great tragedy . . . the last battle." Ladislas Farago, *The Last Days of Patton* (New York: McGraw-Hill, 1981), cover.

181   "If I could . . . scheduled it differently." *People*, May 20, 1991, p. 3.

181   "I took my . . . part left out." *The New York Times Magazine*, June 9, 1991, p. 56.

181   "I didn't belong . . . been much easier." Elaine Partnow, ed., *The Quotable Woman* (Philadelphia: Running Press, 1991), p. 39.

181   "If I'd known . . . see your show." *People*, December 16, 1991, p. 97.

181   "Fuck the law! . . . would have happened." Robert Kaiser, *R.F.K. Must Die!* (New York: Dutton, 1970), p. 513.

181   "I worry sometimes . . . us killing then." William L. Calley, Jr., and John Sack, *Lieutenant Calley: His Own Story* (New York: Viking, 1971), p. 94.

182   "I was just . . . anything about anything." *New York*, August 8, 1988, p. 36.

182   "It was inconceivable . . . had come true." James W. Clarke, *On Being Mad or Merely Angry: John W. Hinckley, Jr., and Other Dangerous People* (Princeton, N.J.: Princeton University Press, 1990), p. 23.

182   "made me realize . . . thought I was." *Esquire*, January 1992, p. 116.

182   "There's no doubt . . . I were neck-and-neck." *The Village Voice*, May 21, 1991, p. 35.

182   "I didn't have . . . was going on." *Vanity Fair*, July 1991, p. 91.

182   "Was there anything . . . to my grave." *Mike Wallace: Then and Now*, CBS, September 26, 1990.

183   "Like anybody, I . . . of the Lord." William R. Witherspoon, *Martin Luther King, Jr.: To the Mountaintop* (Garden City, N.Y.: Doubleday, 1985), p. 221.

183   "A long life . . . and illusions shattered." Forbes and Bloch, *They Went That-a-way . . .* , p. 150.

183   "He drank himself . . . emptiness, after all." Barry Miles, *Ginsberg: A Biography* (New York: Simon & Schuster, 1989), p. 427.

184   "It wasn't suicide . . . then wilts away." Forbes and Bloch, *They Went That-a-way . . .* , p. 117.

184   "Before takeoff they . . . I've ever heard." Lynda Obst, ed., *The Sixties: The Decade Remembered Now, by People Who Lived It Then* (New York: Random House, 1977), p. 32.

184   "I wouldn't mind . . . to miss it." Forbes and Bloch, *They Went That-a-way . . .* , pp. 215–216.

184   "It's not that . . . when it happens." *The New York Times*, June 2, 1991, p. 19.

184   "I think about . . . just a waste." *Time*, May 20, 1991, p. 58.

184   "But, a friend . . . after you die.' " *People*, November 11, 1991, p. 56.

184   "I had a . . . religion at all." *20/20*, February 22, 1991, ABC.

184   "You know, when . . . what they mean." Joan Baez, *A Voice to Sing With* (New York: Summit Books, 1987), p. 87.

185   "Hey, life is . . . happy about it." *Time*, January 16, 1989, p. 54.

## CHAPTER 15
### WHO'S NOT WHO: MIXUPS, IDENTITY CRISES, AND BLOOPERS

187   "Yes, things went . . . the other fellow." *The Best of Nightline*, ABC, April 24, 1990.

187   "I talked to . . . had talked to." *Newsweek*, September 2, 1991, p. 17.

187   "Prime Minister Lee . . . an *opera* star!" Beverly Sills and Lawrence Linderman, *Beverly: An Autobiography* (Toronto: Bantam, 1987), pp. 229–230.

187   "Health, Welfare, and Whatnot." Piers Brandon, *Ike: His Life and Times* (New York: Harper & Row, 1984), p. 232.

187   "Could you explain . . . my military aide." *The New York Times*, February 23, 1990, p. A19.

188   "Mr. President . . . was Donald Duck." William Manchester, *The Death of a President: November 20–November 25, 1963* (New York: Harper & Row, 1967), p. 219.

188   "Jimmy who?" Lonnelle Aikman, *The Living White House* (Washington, D.C.: White House Historical Association, 1982), p. 18.

188  "Where do I . . . I'm a congressman." Victor Lasky, *J.F.K.: The Man and the Myth* (New York: Macmillan, 1963), p. 101.

188  "Sorry, son. These are reserved for Senators." William Manchester, *One Brief Shining Moment: Remembering Kennedy* (Boston: Little, Brown, 1973), p. 59.

188  "Get that car . . . I didn't recognize you." Thomas P. O'Neill and William Novak, *Man of the House: The Life and Political Memoirs of Speaker Tip O'Neill* (New York: Random House, 1987), p. 13.

189  "To . . . the great . . . Egypt, excuse me." Christopher Cerf and Victor Navasky, *The Experts Speak* (New York: Pantheon Books, 1984), p. 146.

189  "The senator has . . . you're in trouble." Mollie Dickenson, *Thumbs Up* (New York: Morrow, 1987), p. 155.

189  "You, I've been . . . I'm talking to?" David Halberstam, *The Best and the Brightest* (New York: Random House, 1972), p. 133.

189  "the governor of . . . was President Eisenhower." *People,* December 18, 1989, p. 160.

190  "Do you mind . . . Who is this?" Gerald Clarke, *Capote: A Biography* (New York: Simon & Schuster, 1988), p. 281.

190  "telling me she . . . I'm Judy Garland." Ray Charles and David Ritz, *Brother Ray* (New York: Dial Press, 1978), p. 247.

190  "Isn't this a . . . Robert Redford." O'Neill and Novak, *Man of the House,* p. 291.

191  "Don't you remember . . . you're George!" A. E. Hotchner, *Doris Day: Her Own Story* (New York: Morrow, 1976), p. 286.

191  "a tall, sort . . . a little confused." Shelley Winters, *Shelley II: The Middle of My Century* (New York: Simon & Schuster, 1989), pp. 310–311.

191  "Later in the . . . remorse and embarrassment." Everett Morrow, *Black Man in the White House* (New York: Coward, McCann & Geoghegan, 1963), p. 40.

191  "Lieutenant, let me . . . to a nigger?" Jackie Robinson and Alfred Duckett, *I Never Had It Made* (New York: Putnam, 1972), p. 26.

192  "Everyone sitting at . . . who he is." *7 Days,* February 14, 1990, p. 22.

192  "Obediently, I borrowed . . . Oh, her." Shirley Temple Black, *Child Star: An Autobiography* (New York: McGraw-Hill, 1988), pp. 499–500.

192  "You know, Mr. Bogart . . . you a newspaperman?" Joe Hyams, *Bogie: The Biography of Humphrey Bogart* (New York: New American Library, 1966), p. 190.

193  "I am looking . . . balls to balls." *The New York Times Book Review,* July 1, 1990, p. 3.

193  "We're supposed to . . . on her gown." Ronald Reagan, *An American Life* (New York: Simon & Schuster, 1990), pp. 390–391.

193  "The Next President . . . Crowded." *Wilson Quarterly,* Spring 1988, p. 48.

193  "The funnyest [sic] . . . Irony abounds." Arthur H. Bremer, *An Assassin's Diary* (New York: Harper's Magazine Press, 1973), p. 45.

193  "I had a . . . the grand scale." *The New York Times,* July 17, 1989, p. A17.

195  "You see, my . . . cure my cold." J. B. West, *Upstairs at the White House* (New York: Coward, McCann & Geoghegan, 1973), p. 142.

## CHAPTER 16

### LIVING THE LONELY LIFE

197    "How is school . . . a long time." *Eyes on the Prize,* PBS, 1991.

197    "When I traveled . . . and played cards." Jackie Robinson and Alfred Duckett, *I Never Had It Made* (New York: Putnam, 1972), p. 78.

197    "I was completely . . . most every day." Brian Lanker, *I Dream a World: Portraits of Black Women Who Changed America* (New York: Stewart, Tabori & Chang, 1989), p. 77.

197    "What to do about the nigger." ABC News, February 8, 1991.

197    "The only effect . . . into the army." *The New York Times,* February 20, 1991, p. C15.

198    "It was almost like . . . were they now?" *Eyes on the Prize II,* "Keys to the Kingdom," PBS, 1990.

199    "It's a very . . . I'd sit down." *The Man Who Beat the Blacklist: John Henry Faulk,* PBS, August 1, 1990.

199    "I can't characterize . . . go forward anyway." *The Public Mind,* "The Truth About Lies," PBS, November 28, 1989.

199    "A major public . . . your personal feelings." Tom Wicker, *One of Us: Richard Nixon and the American Dream* (New York: Random House, 1991), p. 651.

200    "Her strength? Jane . . . we say *solide.*" Thomas Kiernan, *Jane: An Intimate Biography of Jane Fonda* (New York: Putnam, 1973), p. 169.

200    "You know, I . . . to be loved." Barbara Leaming, *If This Was Happiness: A Biography of Rita Hayworth* (New York: Viking, 1989), p. 145.

200    "I am lonely . . . bed with you." James Spada, *The Divine Bette Midler* (New York: Collier Books, 1984), p. 58.

200    "I think he . . . Johnson to stop." *The New York Times,* January 26, 1989, p. B6.

200    "I was always very lonely." Doris Kearns, *Lyndon Johnson and the American Dream* (New York: Harper & Row, 1976) p. 79.

200    "The decision that . . . be made alone." Curt Smith, *Long Time Gone: The Years of Turmoil Remembered* (South Bend, Ind.: Icarus Press, 1982), p. 210.

200    "to that big . . . am I missing?" Ralph Martin, *A Hero for Our Time* (New York: Fawcett Crest, 1983), p. 314.

201    "Carl, if you . . . your friends are." Joseph Persico, *The Imperial Rockefeller* (New York: Simon & Schuster, 1982), p. 54.

201    "Colleen, I'm so scared . . . me to death." Paul Boller, *Presidential Wives* (New York: Oxford University Press, 1988), p. 449.

201    "Jackie, you're going . . . than freezing there." Martin, *A Hero for Our Time,* p. 533.

201    "I never said . . . be left alone." *Vogue,* February 1990, p. 354.

201    "You know, sometimes . . . to chicken dinners." Richard Goodwin, *Remembering America: A Voice from the Sixties* (Boston: Little, Brown, 1988), p. 530.

201    "Oh, boy! Listen . . . even beats screwing." Booth Moody, *LBJ: An Irreverent Chronicle* (New York: Crowell, 1976), p. 10.

202    "I miss what . . . find anymore." Lanker, *I Dream a World,* p. 94.

202   "You know, Bob . . . face going on." H. R. Haldeman and Joseph DiMona, *The Ends of Power* (New York: Times Books, 1978), p. 293.

202   "Be kind . . . their own disguise." Barry Miles, *Ginsberg: A Biography* (New York: Simon & Schuster, 1989), p. 331.

202   "the most downtrodden . . . minority in America." David Farber, *Chicago '68* (Chicago: University of Chicago Press, 1988), p. 128.

202   "The better we . . . of society's failures." Ibid., p. 29.

203   "Arresting them doesn't . . . usually stay there." Ibid., pp. 141–142.

203   "What would you . . . supposed to do?" Ibid., p. 254.

203   "The police are . . . been hit with." Ibid.

203   "He was never . . . achieve without him." Lanker, *I Dream a World,* p. 94.

203   "Where will we . . . all the country." William Manchester, *The Death of a President: November 20–November 25, 1963* (New York: Harper & Row, 1967), p. 350.

203   "George was off . . . week of interest." *Time,* January 23, 1989, p. 125.

204   "I spent my time . . . I was." *People,* May 1, 1989, p. 108.

204   "It was not . . . was all wrong." Martin, *A Hero for Our Time,* p. 86.

204   "I hardly ever . . . took up sex." *Life,* Fall 1990, p. 102.

204   "I saw him . . . tapes back and forth." *People Weekly Extra,* Spring/Summer 1991, pp. 6–8.

204   "The loneliness the . . . couple of years." Betty Ford, *The Times of My Life* (New York: Harper & Row, 1978), p. 122.

204   "I remember the . . . to the world." *Cosmopolitan,* August 1991, p. 193.

205   "How does it . . . a retired farmer." Margaret Truman, *Bess W. Truman* (New York: Macmillan, 1986) pp. 50–51.

205   "Knowing her, being . . . in the cold." *USA Today,* November 30, 1987, p. 4A.

205   "Some people think . . . so he is." *Newsweek,* October 23, 1989, p. 55.

## CHAPTER 17
### LIES AND OTHERS MISTRUTHS

207   "Now you here . . . we've ever known." *The New York Times Book Review,* February 24, 1991, p. 7.

207   "Taxes will go . . . I just did." *The New York Times,* July 2, 1990, p. A12.

207   "I told the . . . paid the price." *Newsweek,* July 9, 1990, p. 19.

207   "Sacrifice, patience, understanding . . . gains without pains." James Reston, *Deadline: A Memoir* (New York: Random House, 1991), p. 273.

207   "I'll never lie to you." *The New York Times,* July 2, 1990, p. A12.

208   "Today much of . . . science-fiction novel." Ibid.

208   "Miss Lillian, is . . . to see you?" *The Presidency, the Press and the People,* PBS, April 2, 1990.

208   "did something very . . . forget about it." Margaret Truman, *Bess W. Truman* (New York: Macmillan, 1986), p. 283.

208   "I see this . . . full and more." *The New York Times Magazine,* July 29, 1990, p. 48.

209   "The world rests . . . meeting here today." *The Presidency, the Press and the People,* PBS, April 2, 1990.

209    "out of the ballpark at 450 feet." Ibid.

209    "one time, President . . . to play golf." Ibid.

209    "My childhood was one of complete poverty." Joan Peyser, *Bernstein: A Biography* (New York: Morrow, 1987), p. 12.

209    "The idea that . . . were considered rich." Roger Morris, *Richard Milhous Nixon* (New York: Holt, 1990), p. 138.

209    "Now, Lyndon, you . . . of the farm." Booth Moody, *LBJ: An Irreverent Chronicle* (New York: Crowell, 1976), p. 166.

209    "My great-great . . . than the Alamo." Ronnie Dugger, *The Politician: The Life and Times of Lyndon Johnson* (New York: Norton, 1982), p. 33.

210    "All right now . . . then I'm dead." Victor Navasky, *Naming Names* (New York: Viking, 1980), p. 130.

210    "I was out." *The Wall Street Journal,* October 5, 1990, p. A16.

210    "I don't recall." *The New York Times,* March 23, 1990, p. A12.

210    "May I simply . . . been a diversion." ABC News, March 20, 1990.

211    "When you come . . . road, take it." Reston, *Deadline,* p. 349.

211    "Preposterous. I related . . . about tomorrow morning." *The Presidency, the Press and the People,* PBS, April 2, 1990.

211    "I had made up . . . Yes, there was." *Prime Time Live,* ABC, June 6, 1991.

212    "I want you . . . lives and lies." *The Public Mind,* "The Truth About Lies," PBS, November 28, 1989.

212    "I knew . . . was unlawful." *The New York Times,* April 8, 1989, p. 9.

212    "I lied, And . . . to their undertaking." *The Presidency, the Press and the People,* PBS, April 2, 1990.

212    "But what will . . . me was, 'Lie!' " Joan Quigley, *"What Does Joan Say?"* (New York: Birch Lane Press, 1990), p. 22.

213    "A couple of . . . had Addison's disease." Joan Blair and Clay Blair, Jr., *The Search for JFK* (New York: Berkley Publishing, 1976), p. 561.

213    "No one who . . . not have it." Ibid., p. 575.

213    "The Senator does . . . as Addison's disease." Victor Lasky, *JFK: The Man and the Myth* (New York: Macmillan, 1963), p. 376.

213    "Your friends on . . . take this job." Ralph Martin, *A Hero for Our Time* (New York: Fawcett Crest, 1983), p. 196.

213    "I have never had Addison's disease." J. Blair and C. Blair, *The Search for JFK,* p. 576.

213    "The clinical diagnosis . . . to be concealed." Ibid., p. 577.

213    "What happened was . . . a diabetic is." Ibid., p. 578.

214    "The gentleman informed . . . never has been." Michael Beschloss, *May Day: Eisenhower, Khrushchev, and the U-2 Affair* (New York: Harper & Row, 1986), p. 58.

214    "I was awakened . . . in your pocket." Armand Hammer, *Hammer* (New York: Putnam, 1987), p. 322.

215    "Yes, he did . . . a gorgeous bird." Allen Weinstein, *Perjury: The Hiss-Chambers Case* (New York: Knopf, 1978), pp. 20, 32.

215    "Tell the truth . . . don't ever lie." M. Hirsch Goldberg, *The Book of Lies* (New York: Quill, 1990), p. 90.

216    "I believe the . . . all the way." *The Public Mind,* "The Truth About Lies," PBS, November 28, 1990.

216    "Lyndon Johnson really . . . the pessimistic assumptions." *The Presidency, the Press and the People,* PBS, April 2, 1990.

216    "This is Jane . . . targets really are." *Vanity Fair*, December 1990, p. 216.

216    "Isn't it a possibility . . . right, all right." Mike Wallace and Gary Paul Gates, *Close Encounters: Mike Wallace's Own Story* (New York: Morrow, 1984), p. 436.

217    "We have been . . . force has increased." Ibid.

217    "You can fool . . . is big enough." *The New York Times*, October 11, 1990, p. A25.

217    "While I cannot . . . the State Department." Thomas A. Bailey, *Voices of America* (New York: Free Press, 1976), p. 440.

218    "authorize homosexual marriages . . . won't cause that." *ERA: The War Between the Women* ABC, January 22, 1977.

218    "People react to . . . but it's true." *The American Experience*, "Nixon: The Quest, the Triumph, the Fall," PBS, October 15, 1990.

218    "Just before the . . . of that fact." Ibid.

218    "Of course I . . . the important thing." Ibid.

218    "Pink right down to her underwear." Ibid.

218    "The essence of . . . simple as that." Ibid.

CHAPTER 18

THE HECK WITH IT: OATHS OF OFFICE AND OTHER LOCATIONS

219    "Goddamnit! I don't . . . words as adjectives." Lester David and Irene David, *Ike and Mamie* (New York: Putnam, 1981), p. 110.

219    "By darn we're going to win it." *The New York Times*, November 8, 1988, p. A18.

219    "We've got to . . . no matter what." Ronnie Dugger, *The Politician: The Life and Times of Lyndon Johnson* (New York: Norton, 1982), p. 364.

219    "Hey, by the . . . settle this thing." Diana McLellan, *Ear on Washington* (New York: Arbor House, 1982), p. 118.

219    "You know, George . . . for civil rights." Peter Carroll, *Famous in America: The Passion to Succeed* (New York: Dutton, 1985), p. 107.

220    "singing, laughing, printing . . . our own time." David Farber, *Chicago '68* (Chicago: University of Chicago Press, 1988), p. 17.

221    "I never gave . . . think it's hell." Richard Kenin and Justin Wintle, eds., *The Dictionary of American Biographical Quotation* (New York: Knopf, 1978), p. 743.

221    "I see mothers . . . the United States." Stanley Kutler, *The Wars of Watergate: The Last Crisis of Richard Nixon* (New York: Knopf, 1990), p. 52.

221    "What did that . . . her mouth again." Kitty Kelley, *Jackie Oh!* (Secaucus, N.J.: Lyle Stuart, 1978), p. 97.

221    "Now isn't that . . . only three letters." Bella Abzug, *Bella!: Ms. Abzug Goes to Washington* (New York: Saturday Review Press, 1972), pp. 11–12.

221    "You dirty bastard . . . country ever had." Lester David, *The Lonely Lady of San Clemente: The Story of Pat Nixon* (New York: Crowell, 1978), p. 162.

222    "get down or . . . motherfucking heads off." Andrew J. Edelstein and Kevin McDonough, *The Seventies: From Hot Pants to Hot Tubs* (New York: Dutton, 1990), p. 79.

222    "Who does that dame think she is?" *The New York Times*, May 31, 1990, p. A10.

222  "a four-million-dollar—I . . . rhymes with rich." *Time,* January 23, 1989, p. 24.
222  "the poet laureate has retired." Ibid.
222  "My whole life . . . by that bitch." Stephen Birmingham, *Jacqueline Bouvier Kennedy Onassis* (New York: Grosset & Dunlap, 1969), p. 48.
222  "I'm tough, ambitious . . . a bitch, okay." *People,* March 6, 1989, p. 25.
222  "I'm a woman . . . me a bitch." NBC News, February 7, 1990.
222  "I'll show that . . . he is—God?" J. Ronald Oakley, *God's Country: America in the Fifties* (New York: Dembner Books, 1986), p. 87.
222  "because he wouldn't . . . be in jail." Kenin and Wintle, eds., *The Dictionary of American Biographical Quotation,* p. 506.
223  "The son of . . . should be impeached." David Oshinsky, *A Conspiracy So Immense: The World of Joe McCarthy* (New York: Free Press, 1983), p. 194.
223  "a real son . . . the dirty work." Roberta Feurlicht, *Joe McCarthy and McCarthyism: The Hate That Haunts America* (New York: McGraw-Hill, 1972), p. 78.
223  "I guess he . . . for being one." Victor Lasky, *J.F.K.: The Man and the Myth* (New York: Macmillan, 1963), p. 416.
223  "I understand that . . . of a bitch." Arthur Schlesinger, *Robert Kennedy and His Times* (Boston: Houghton Mifflin, 1978), Vol. 1, p. 223.
223  "My private opinion . . . of-a-bitch." Ladislas Farago, *The Last Days of Patton* (New York: McGraw-Hill, 1981), p. 225.
223  "would never call . . . a self-made man." Traphes Bryant, *Dog Days at the White House* (New York: Macmillan, 1975), p. 65.
223  "President Johnson and I . . . uses the initials." Arthur Schlesinger, *Robert Kennedy and His Times* (Boston: Houghton Mifflin, 1978), Vol. 2, p. 773.
223  "How do you . . . in *public* yet." Ralph Martin, *A Hero for Our Time* (New York: Fawcett Crest, 1983), p. 284.
224  "Jackie's going to . . . "Oh, shit!" Peter Evans, *Ari: The Life and Times of Aristotle Socrates Onassis* (New York: Summit Books, 1986), p. 225.
224  "Sir, I think . . . Holy shit!" John Baron, *Breaking the Ring* (Boston: Houghton Mifflin, 1987), pp. 136–137.
225  "There's flashlights on . . . Shit!" Gordon Liddy, *Will: The Autobiography of G. Gordon Liddy* (New York: St. Martin's Press, 1980), p. 289.
225  "I was rather . . . Oh, shit." Jane Meyer and Doyle McManus, *Landslide: The Unmaking of the President* (Boston: Houghton Mifflin, 1988), p. 333.
226  "Good evening, the . . . Oh, shit." Debbie Reynolds, *Debbie: My Life* (New York: Morrow, 1988), p. 187.

CHAPTER 19
YOUR TAX DOLLARS AT WORK

227  "It was not . . . director, an actor." *People,* October 16, 1989, p. 38.
227  "I have enough . . . lasts a year." Ibid.
227  "Russia can't be worse than this." *Newsweek,* October 9, 1989.
227  "I wanted to . . . makeup won't hurt." *Prime Time Live,* ABC, August 9, 1990.
227  "told 'em it . . . Feature that." Ray Charles and David Ritz, *Brother Ray* (New York: Dial Press, 1978), p. 249.

228 "This does not . . . the Thirteenth Amendment." Ralph Abernathy, *And the Walls Came Tumbling Down* (New York: Harper & Row, 1989), pp. 306–307.

230 "Whatcha name? . . . 'You Watergate?' " Gordon Liddy, *Will: The Autobiography of G. Gordon Liddy* (New York: St. Martin's Press, 1980), p. 289.

231 "Occupation? . . . Urban guerilla." Patricia Hearst, *Every Secret Thing* (Garden City, N.Y.: Doubleday, 1982), p. 365.

231 "You know what . . . me back inside?" Nuel Emmons, *Manson in His Own Words* (New York: Grove Press, 1986), pp. 77–78.

231 "So they put . . . *would* be crazy." Donald Goddard, *Joey* (New York: Harper & Row, 1974), p. 30.

231 "It seems we . . . would be possible." Timothy Leary, *Flashbacks: An Autobiography* (Los Angeles: Tarcher, 1983), pp. 288–289.

232 "That's fine, Don." James Reston, *Deadline: A Memoir* (New York: Random House, 1991), p. 436.

232 "Throw a spitball . . . wake him up." *The New York Times,* November 10, 1989, p. A22.

232 "To be very . . . cold or diarrhea." *The New York Times,* February 20, 1989, p. A13.

232 "Constitutionally, gentlemen, you . . . Al, it isn't." Lawrence Barrett, *Gambling with History* (Garden City, N.Y.: Doubleday, 1983), p. 119.

233 "Have a brew . . . a station break?" *Spy,* December 1991, p. 63.

233 "Attention, please! All . . . for a quorum." Charles Whalen and Barbara Whalen, *The Longest Debate: A Legislative History of the 1964 Civil Rights Act* (New York: Mentor, 1985), pp. 164–165.

233 "I would get . . . in the process." Ibid., p. 196.

234 "I courted Dirksen . . . I did Muriel." Ibid., p. 204.

234 "Has Anybody Seen . . . and get dressed." *Cosmopolitan,* March 1991, p. 231.

234 "a locker-room male . . . black and blue." Ibid., p. 230.

234 "No politician feels . . . virtually no passing." *Newsweek,* July 8, 1991, p. 15.

234 "If there was . . . get one vote." Ibid.

235 "Whenever a person . . . served a purpose." *Adam Clayton Powell,* PBS, December 3, 1989.

235 "The telephone was . . . support the President." *The American Experience,* "LBJ," Part 3, PBS, October 1, 1991.

235 "rise in the . . . few other commissions." Ibid.

236 "When we got . . . saying they were." M. Hirsh Goldberg, *The Book of Lies* (New York: Quill, 1990), p. 151.

CHAPTER 20

SCHOOL DAYS: LEARNING THE ABCs OF LIFE

237 "Filming *The Conspirator* . . . Talk about humiliating." Elizabeth Taylor, *Elizabeth Takes Off* (New York: Putnam, 1987), p. 59.

237 "I'm not going . . . to Columbia Records." *20/20,* ABC, August 3, 1990.

237 "I was never . . . I got there." J. Randy Taraborrelli, *Cher: A Biography* (New York: St. Martin's Press, 1986), pp. 26–27.

237   "Lemme tell ya . . . wasted, totally wasted." Kitty Kelley, *Elizabeth Taylor: The Last Star* (New York: Simon & Schuster, 1981), p. 126.
238   "She sat behind . . . person on earth." Margaret Truman, *Bess W. Truman* (New York: Macmillan, 1987), p. 10.
238   "Mrs. Livingston thought . . . until she died." Kirk Douglas, *The Ragman's Son* (New York: Simon & Schuster, 1988), pp. 41–44.
239   "changed my life . . . tell anyone else." Ibid.
239   "She taught me . . . are my masterpiece." Joseph Persico, *Edward R. Murrow: The American Original* (New York: McGraw-Hill, 1988), p. 60.
239   "would let her . . . how could it?" *The New York Times Book Review*, June 9, 1991, p. 51.
239   "I just couldn't . . . couldn't believe it." Marshall Frady, *Billy Graham: A Parable of American Righteousness* (Boston: Little, Brown, 1979), p. 51.
240   "I could see . . . the school board." Ibid., p. 61.
240   "Yes, ladies and . . . that word right." Ibid., p. 218.
240   "absolutely no encouragement . . . my first job." *Prime Time Live*, ABC, September 13, 1990.
240   "was incapable of . . . be taught anything." *Life*, Fall 1990, p. 49.
240   "You *know* I'm . . . never make it." J. Randy Taraborrelli, *Call Her Miss Ross* (New York: Birch Lane Press, 1989), p. 55.
241   "You've got to . . . being a nigger." Henry Hampton and Steve Fayer, *Voices of Freedom: An Oral History of the Civil Rights Movement from the 1950s Through the 1980s* (New York: Bantam, 1990), pp. 242–243.
241   "showed no imagination or originality." *Time*, August 22, 1988, p. 24.
241   "knew very little . . . on his memory." Roberta Feuerlicht, *Joe McCarthy and McCarthyism: The Hate That Haunts America* (New York: McGraw-Hill, 1972), p. 12.
241   "Son, I watched . . . And you're *yellow!*" *The New York Times Book Review*, September 22, 1991, p. 21.
241   "I had been . . . total heart failure." George McGovern, *Grassroots: An Autobiography of George McGovern* (New York: Random House, 1977), p. 12.
242   "neatly dressed in . . . from the room." Eve Arden, *Three Phases of Eve: An Autobiography* (New York: St. Martin's Press, 1985), p. 314.
242   "This was just . . . cried each day." Lynn Bloom, *Dr. Spock: Biography of a Conservative Radical* (Indianapolis: Bobbs-Merrill, 1972), p. 17.
242   "In the third . . . where I belonged." Dave Marsh, *Born to Run: The Bruce Springsteen Story* (Garden City, N.Y.: Doubleday, 1979), p. 13.
242   "You'd leave your . . . boredom amd intimidation." *The New York Times Book Review*, June 9, 1991, p. 50.
242   "The closer we . . . on foot, anonymously." Peter Collier and David Horowitz, *The Rockefellers: An American Dynasty* (New York: Holt, Rinehart & Winston, 1976), p. 527.
242   "All the other . . . spoke Sicilian-Italian." Martin Gosch and Richard Hammer, *The Last Testament of Lucky Luciano* (Boston: Little, Brown, 1975), pp. 5–6.
243   "who had a . . . psychosis about it." Lawrence Grobel, *Conversations with Capote* (New York: New American Library, 1985), p. 51.
243   "We've got a . . . remotely resembling facility." Craig Claiborne, *Craig*

*Claiborne, A Feast Made For Laughter* (Garden City, N.Y.: Doubleday, 1982), p. 37.

243    "Well, we reduced . . . grateful to him." Joan Blair and Clay Blair, Jr., *The Search for J.F.K.* (New York: Berkley Publishing, 1976), p. 36.

243    "My God, my . . . with an M." Doris Kearns Goodwin, *The Fitzgeralds and the Kennedys* (New York: St. Martin's Press, 1987), p. 564.

244    "When I was . . . I couldn't do." *Time,* May 20, 1991, p. 57.

244    "Even in elementary . . . almost got expelled." Donald Trump and Tony Schwartz, *Trump: The Art of the Deal* (New York: Random House, 1987), p. 49.

244    "As he looks . . . the campus every day." Robert A. Caro, *The Path to Power: The Years of Lyndon Johnson* (New York: Knopf, 1982), p. 169.

244    "the very worst . . . I don't listen." C. David Heymann, *A Woman Named Jackie* (New York: Lyle Stuart, 1989), p. 26.

246    "I went to . . . was the truth." Taraborrelli, *Cher,* pp. 26–27.

246    "I quit school . . . nailed down." *The New York Times,* May 23, 1990, p. B7.

246    "firing off one . . . a doctor's appointment." *People,* December 2, 1991, p. 165.

246    "Most of my . . . to remain eligible." Ronnie Dugger, *On Reagan: The Man and His Presidency* (New York: McGraw-Hill, 1983), p. 3.

246    "I am so . . . down the answers." Mark Bego, *Linda Ronstadt: It's So Easy* (Austin, Tex.: Eakin Press, 1990), pp. 15–16.

247    "I got straight As . . . lynched in America." Abbie Hoffman, *Soon to Be a Major Motion Picture* (New York: Putnam, 1980), p. 18.

247    "There was a . . . were very normal." *20/20,* ABC, November 21, 1991.

## CHAPTER 21
### BELIEVE IT OR NOT AT THE WHITE HOUSE

249    "I do not . . . any more broccoli." *The New York Times,* March 23, 1990, p. A14.

249    "that my father . . . in her face!" Margaret Truman, *Bess W. Truman* (New York: Macmillan, 1986), pp. 284–285.

249    "as if it . . . down his vest." H. R. Haldeman and Joseph DiMona, *The Ends of Power* (New York: Times Books, 1978), p. 73.

250    "some far out . . . can dance to." Betty Ford, *The Times of My Life* (New York: Harper & Row, 1978), pp. 229–230.

250    "I danced with the President." Helen Thomas, *Dateline: White House* (New York: Macmillan, 1975), p. 83.

251    "Pierre, I have . . . down on Paris." Pierre Salinger, *With Kennedy* (Garden City, N.Y.: Doubleday, 1966), p. 165.

251    "to come up . . . an unlisted number." Benjamin Bradlee, *Conversations with Kennedy* (New York: Norton, 1975), pp. 106–107.

251    "Your fellows have . . . a tin can." Ronald Reagan, *An American Life* (New York: Simon & Schuster, 1990), pp. 277–278.

252    "Come show me . . . you do it!" Stephen Ambrose, *Eisenhower, Volume Two: The President* (New York: Simon & Schuster, 1984), pp. 616–617.

252   "Why did you . . . A big house?" J. B. West, *Upstairs at the White House* (New York: Coward, McCann & Geoghegan, 1973), p. 163.

252   "I will return." Stephen Ambrose, *Nixon: The Triumph of a Politician, 1962–1972* (New York: Simon & Schuster, 1989), p. 245.

252   "rounded up as . . . put any out." Maureen Reagan, *First Father, First Daughter* (Boston: Little, Brown, 1989), p. 323.

253   "a tremendous rat . . . cut that down." *Millie's Book: As Dictated to Barbara Bush* (New York: Morrow, 1990), p. 18.

253   "late at night . . . to smoke dope." Willie Nelson and Bud Shrake, *Willie: An Autobiography* (New York: Simon & Schuster, 1988), pp. 195–196.

254   "a small box . . . drop a bomb." C. David Heymann, *A Woman Named Jackie* (New York: Lyle Stuart, 1989), p. 375.

254   "The SOB, will . . . believe him!" Tom Wicker, *One of Us: Richard Nixon and the American Dream* (New York: Random House, 1991), pp. 634–635.

## CHAPTER 22

## THE AMERICAN LOVE STORY: THEMES AND VARIATIONS

255   "I married the . . . about throw up." *Time*, January 23, 1989, p. 25.

255   "He stopped dead . . . stop me now." Charles Shepard, *Forgiven: The Rise and Fall of Jim Bakker and the PTL Ministry* (New York: Atlantic Monthly Press, 1989), p. 31.

255   "I leaned over . . . was no asparagus." Ralph Martin, *A Hero for Our Time* (New York: Fawcett Crest, 1983), p. 72.

255   "We got to . . . in our hair." Abbie Hoffman, *The Best of Abbie Hoffman* (New York: Four Walls Eight Windows, 1989), p. 85.

257   "An eight-pound preemie . . . kind of cool." *Vanity Fair*, July 1991, p. 131.

257   "I have committed . . . heart many times." *Newsweek*, October 4, 1976, pp. 70–71.

257   "The big trouble . . . She was furious." Kay Summersby Morgan, *Past Forgetting: My Love Affair with Dwight D. Eisenhower* (New York: Simon & Schuster, 1976), p. 176.

257   "out of the Army . . . a peaceful breath." *The New York Times*, June 6, 1991, p. B4.

257   "I wanted to . . . *normal* to me." *Vanity Fair*, April 1990, p. 164.

258   "Hi. This note . . . Most sincerely." Rock Hudson and Sara Davidson, *Rock Hudson: His Story* (New York: Morrow, 1986), p. 252.

258   "Jodie, I would . . . the Hilton Hotel." Jack Hinckley and JoAnn Hinckley, *Breaking Points* (Grand Rapids, Mich.: Chosen Books, 1985), p. 169.

258   "Don't they make . . . virgin, aren't you?" Lincoln Caplan, *The Insanity Defense of John W. Hinckley, Jr.* (Boston: Godine, 1984), p. 42.

258   "If there were . . . a better place." *Time*, May 20, 1990, p. 58.

258   "Remember—never give . . . my head constantly." Lauren Bacall, *Lauren Bacall by Myself* (New York: Knopf, 1978), p. 59.

258   "I was fourteen . . . with great fondness." Sylvia Renick, *Burt Reynolds* (New York: St. Martin's Press, 1983), p. 8.

258   "This guy in . . . poised and smile." *People*, October 2, 1989, p. 69.

259   "naturally, I lost . . . into my pants." Tina Turner and Kurt Loder, *I, Tina* (New York: Morrow, 1986), p. 42.

259   "I said, 'When . . . was *hell* waiting." Bette Davis, *This 'n That* (New York: Putnam, 1987), p. 73.

259   "It is very . . . I was booked." *Film on Film,* "Roman Polanski," PBS, June 16, 1990.

259   "The good news . . . he isn't gay." *Newsweek,* April 15, 1991, p. 37.

259   "In today's society . . . my age anyway." *People,* August 12, 1991, p. 39.

260   "I love him better every day." Ibid.

260   "I just want . . . be his wife." Ibid., p. 39.

260   "Thirty or forty years." Ibid.

260   "This marriage will last forever." Ibid.

260   "We are stuck . . . feathers to tar." Ibid.

260   "I have never been so happy." Ibid.

260   "With God's blessings, this is it, forever." Ibid.

260   "I certainly told . . . to get involved." Sarah Bradford, *Princess Grace* (New York: Stein & Day, 1984), p. 124.

260   "The Prince comes . . . to Grace's titties." *Cosmopolitan,* April 1991, p. 213.

261   "Eddie was white . . . how fathers are." Helen Thomas, *Dateline: White House* (New York: Macmillan, 1975), p. 179.

261   "I think I've . . . wouldn't be overjoyed." Beverly Sills and Lawrence Linderman, *Beverly: An Autobiography* (Toronto: Bantam, 1987), p. 86.

261   "My family warned . . . word about women." Lee Israel, *Miss Tallulah Bankhead* (New York: Putnam, 1972), p. 72.

261   "I think you . . . with a woman." Martina Navratilova and George Vecsey, *Martina* (New York: Knopf, 1985), pp. 181–182.

261   "What's with this . . . a *Jewish* one?" Jane Kramer, *Allen Ginsberg in America* (New York: Random House, 1969), pp. 150–151.

262   "Marrying a man . . . with everything else." Elaine Partnow, ed., *The Quotable Woman* (Philadelphia: Running Press, 1991), p. 64.

262   "The problems were . . . to the bidet." Kitty Kelley, *His Way: The Unauthorized Biography of Frank Sinatra* (New York: Bantam, 1986), p. 175.

262   "My wives married . . . didn't marry them." Robert Lenzer, *The Great Getty* (New York: Crown, 1985), p. 40.

262   "I think . . . to men." *Spy,* August 1989, p. 73.

262   "The person you . . . in Intensive Care." *The New York Times,* August 4, 1988, p. C23.

262   "After all, I . . . pretty good wife." Lester David, *The Lonely Lady of San Clemente: The Story of Pat Nixon* (New York: Crowell, 1978), p. 190.

262   "Living with Marlon . . . anticipation." *People,* June 4, 1990, pp. 90–91.

262   "I went . . . difficult." *Vanity Fair,* April 1990, p. 208.

263   "I was telling . . . kind of stuff." *Elle,* August 1989, p. 46.

263   "The love of . . . age and experience." *The New York Times,* July 26, 1991, p. B5.

263   "Love does not . . . never forgive him." *Esquire,* December 1982, p. 108.

263   "Love is the . . . people can't reach." Muriel James, *Hearts on Fire* (Los Angeles: Tarcher, 1991), pp. 33–34.

263   "Few people know . . . to them." *20/20,* ABC, September 6, 1991.

264   "When a woman . . . answer is no." Peter Carroll, *Famous in America: The Passion to Succeed* (New York: Dutton, 1985), p. 251.

264    "I thought of . . . teachers, no classes." *People,* March 6, 1989, p. 34.

264    "These are sexy . . . at the world." *The New York Times Magazine,* June 9, 1991, p. 59.

264    "Porn killed stripping . . . I did it." *The New York Times,* December 14, 1989, p. C15.

264    "A lot of . . . to do that." *Donahue,* NBC, February 7, 1990.

264    "I wasn't blown . . . just kinda strange." *Insight,* September 18, 1989, p. 18.

264    "I visited him . . . best we've got." C. David Heymann, *A Woman Named Jackie* (New York: Lyle Stuart, 1989), pp. 284–285.

265    "If someone is . . . people abuse you." *The New York Times Magazine,* June 11, 1989, p. 48.

265    "I view it . . . anything but 'gay.' " *Time,* May 30, 1988, p. 50.

265    "picked me up . . . experiences, immensely varied." *American Heritage,* February 1989, p. 52.

265    "I think I am . . . their own sexuality." *Vanity Fair,* April 1990, p. 149.

265    "I never particularly . . . in a cage." Andy Warhol, *The Philosophy of Andy Warhol* (New York: Harcourt Brace Jovanovich, 1975), p. 48.

CHAPTER 23

MATTERS OF SEMANTICS

267    "Nobody goes there anymore, it's too crowded." Phil Pepe, *The Wit and Wisdom of Yogi Berra* (New York: Hawthorne Books, 1965), p. 64.

267    "We had to . . . to save it." *M Inc.,* May 1991, p. 65.

267    "We're going to . . . in the world." Editors of *The Quayle Quarterly, The Unauthorized Autobiography of Dan Quayle* (Bridgeport, Conn., 1992), p. 69.

267    "I knew that . . . was doing spying." Michael Beschloss, *May Day: Eisenhower, Khrushchev and the U-2 Affair* (New York: Harper & Row, 1986), p. 17.

267    "I am very . . . in my life." John Barron, *Breaking the Ring* (Boston: Houghton Mifflin, 1987), p. 159.

267    "If we didn't . . . working for us." *Newsweek,* March 5, 1990, p. 15.

267    "Mayor Daley, do . . . all our lives." Mike Royko, *Boss: Richard J. Daley of Chicago* (New York: Dutton, 1971), p. 24.

268    "I didn't have . . . it was removed." *The New York Times,* January 20, 1989, p. A30.

267    "We are dealing in facts, not realities!" *Vogue,* March 1989, p. 318.

267    "Ah, here is . . . you may not." Howard Teichman, *Alice: The Life and Times of Alice Roosevelt Longworth* (Englewood Cliffs, N.J.: Prentice-Hall, 1979), p. 197.

267    "I wish she . . . can't stand it." Lester David, *The Lonely Lady of San Clemente: The Story of Pat Nixon* (New York: Crowell, 1978), p. 81.

267    "Sweetheart, listen, Lady . . . think he is?" C. David Heymann, *A Woman Named Jackie* (New York: Lyle Stuart, 1989), p. 424.

268    "What's shakin', Chiefie baby?" *The New York Times,* June 28, 1991, p. A13.

268  "Boy, show me . . . I'm a man." Coretta Scott King, *My Life with Martin Luther King, Jr.* (New York: Holt, Rinehart & Winston, 1969), p. 83.

268  "We're not royal . . . me Lyndon sometimes." Hugh Sidey, *A Very Personal Presidency: Lyndon Johnson in the White House* (New York: Atheneum, 1968), p. 262.

269  "I am King . . . do no wrong!" *People*, March 6, 1989, p. 27.

269  "Would you like . . . remind you gentlemen." *Newsweek*, November 25, 1991, p. 17.

269  "Now we're all . . . so-and-so." *The New York Times*, November 19, 1990, p. B6.

269  "The one thing . . . as First Lady?" Peter Collier and David Horowitz, *The Kennedys: An American Drama* (New York: Summit Books, 1984), p. 281.

269  "You can't imagine . . . what to say." *Time*, December 16, 1991, p. 16.

269  "What can you . . . four beautiful sunsets?" Taylor Branch, *Parting the Waters: America in the King Years* (New York: Simon & Schuster, 1988), p. 562.

269  "He was too . . . much to laugh." James Reston, *Deadline: A Memoir* (New York: Random House, 1991), p. 275.

269  "saw people were . . . I was before." Isaac Bashevis Singer, PBS, 1990.

270  "Well, now what am I going to say?" *The Unauthorized Autobiography of Dan Quayle*, p. 53.

270  "Let's go get . . . You got it." Ibid.

270  "have a great day." *People*, May 20, 1991, p. 34.

270  "You all look . . . will always be." *Newsweek*, January 1, 1990, p. 47.

270  "nattering nabobs of negativism," Theo Lippman, Jr., *Spiro Agnew's America* (New York: Norton, 1972), p. 213.

270  "pusillanimous pussyfooting." Ibid.

270  "Verbosity leads to unclear, inarticulate things." *Mirabella*, May 1991, p. 12.

270  "Why don't you . . . finish the dinner?" *The New York Times*, January 9, 1992, pp. A1, A8.

270  "Honey, I forgot to duck." *Newsweek*, October 23, 1989, p. 53.

270  "I am leaving the . . . living than this." *The New York Times*, December 19, 1991, pp. C11, C24.

271  "As I was . . . I was interrupted." Ibid.

271  "You killed the President, you rat!" William Manchester, *The Death of a President: November 20–November 25, 1963* (New York: Harper & Row, 1967), p. 524.

271  "Here I am . . . me, Magic Johnson." *Newsweek*, November 18, 1991, p. 58.

271  "I feel like . . . played by giants." *Time*, April 17, 1989, p. 22.

271  "We would call . . . by the enemy." *The Public Mind*, "The Truth About Lies," PBS, Nov 28, 1989.

271  "It occurs to . . . personal in nature." *People*, May 1, 1989, p. 36.

271  "Today in the . . . how it worked!" Ralph Martin, *A Hero for Our Time* (New York: Fawcett Crest, 1983), p. 455.

272  "Don't shoot. We are your children." *Education Life*, The New York Times, January 7, 1990, pp. 62–63.

272  "I have a . . . before the speech." David Garrow, *Bearing the Cross: Martin*

*Luther King, Jr., and the Southern Christian Leadership Conference* (New York: Morrow, 1986), p. 283.

272   "The world has . . . that duty. Goodbye." William Manchester, *American Caesar* (Boston: Little, Brown, 1978), pp. 661–662.

272   "One hundred percent bullshit." Ibid.

273   "Now I find . . . behavior was inexplicable." Marcia Chellis, *Living with the Kennedys: The Joan Kennedy Story* (New York: Simon & Schuster, 1985), p. 86.

273   "I'm not . . . messed it up." David Frost, *I Gave Them a Sword: Behind the Scenes of the Nixon Interviews* (New York: Morrow, 1978), p. 251.

273   "I sorrowfully acknowledge . . . a female confederate." Charles Shepard, *Forgiven: The Rise and Fall of Jim Bakker and the PTL Ministry* (New York: Atlantic Monthly Press, 1989), p. 510.

273   "It was suggested . . . very serious mistake." *The Best of Nightline*, ABC, April 24, 1990.

273   "acknowledged wrongdoing. I . . . vote for him." *The New York Times*, January 28, 1992, p. A20.

273   "Poor George is . . . in a verb." *Spy*, August 1988, p. 100.

274   "New Hampshire values," *The New York Times*, January 17, 1992, p. A14.

274   "Remember Lincoln, going . . . all that stuff." Ibid.

274   "Grandkids. All of that. Very important." *The New York Times*, March 9, 1990, p. A14.

274   "We're ready to roll, yeah." *The New York Times*, February 24, 1989, p. A33.

274   "So, I'm glad . . . a spleen here." *The New York Times Magazine*, July 29, 1990, p. 48.

274   "But let me . . . about serious issues." *Spy*, August 1988, p. 102.

274   "Dear Ollie . . . thanks, George Bush." *Frontline*, "High Crimes and Misdemeanors," PBS, November 27, 1990.

274   "Did you come . . . a withdrawal thing?" *Spy*, October 1988, p. 88.

274   "How was the actual deployment thing?" *The New York Times Magazine*, July 29, 1990, p. 48.

274   "Cancel the word . . . Covenant House thing." *The New York Times*, June 27, 1989, p. A21.

275   "If they want . . . They got Jack." Collier and Horowitz, *The Kennedys*, p. 348.

275   "Boy, they were . . . weren't they?" *Time*, August 22, 1988, p. 27.

275   "I shall stop . . . invent something better." Diana McLellan, *Ear on Washington* (New York: Arbor House, 1982), p. 21.

275   "I hate it . . . on my *heart*." James Spada, *The Divine Bette Midler* (New York: Collier Books, 1984), p. 369.

275   "They fill your . . . for an exam." *Newsweek*, November 12, 1990, p. 36.

275   "They even told . . . the family clothes." *The New York Times*, December 14, 1989, p. B14.

275   "We went swimming . . . any of this." *The American Experience*, Radio Bikini, NJN, August 1, 1990.

275   "They seem to . . . answered a call." *Eyes on the Prize, 1967–1968:* "The Promised Land," PBS, 1990.

275   "A good man never has enough enemies." Carl Rowan, *Breaking Barriers* (Boston: Little, Brown, 1991), p. 286.

276    "I gave them . . . the same thing." Frost, *I Gave Them a Sword,* p. 72.

276    "I feel like . . . it to you." Gore Vidal, *An Evening with Richard Nixon* (New York: Random House, 1972), p. 81.

276    "They are drugging . . . the black community." *People,* September 17, 1990, p. 116.

276    "They're going to . . . they shot Bobby." Collier and Horowitz, *The Kennedys,* p. 369.

276    "He's dead, they've . . . I love you." James McKinley, *Assassination in America* (New York: Harper & Row, 1977), p. 117.

276    "What if when . . . no one went?" Abbie Hoffman, *The Best of Abbie Hoffman,* ed. Daniel Simon (New York: Four Walls Eight Windows, 1989), p. 95.

276    "How could anyone . . . name like Adlai?" Reston, *Deadline,* p. 276.

276    "I think Egbert . . . didn't look pretty." Alexander Kendrick, *Prime Time: The Life of Edward R. Murrow* (Boston: Little, Brown, 1969), p. 105.

276    "On November 12, 1934 . . . outlaw from birth." Nuel Emmons, *Manson in His Own Words* (New York: Grove Press, 1986), p. 28.

277    "I couldn't name . . . have been fair." *People,* April 22, 1991, p. 112.

277    "like a Tupperware . . . is a persona." *Barbara Walters Special,* ABC, September 10, 1991.

277    "That's a sweet . . . sweet as sugar." *People,* May 1, 1989, p. 155.

277    "Charles' will is man's son." *Esquire,* February 1992, p. 124.

277    "I got a . . . a new name." *People,* April 23, 1990, p. 101.

277    "The academy has . . . it looked like." *The New York Times,* October 8, 1989, p. 39.

278    "I know there . . . do it again." *People,* January 15, 1990, p. 51.

278    "I think that . . . do it better." *People,* September 25, 1989, p. 118.

278    "It struck me . . . it Ian Fleming." *The New York Times,* February 17, 1989, p. D19.

278    "I personally did . . . for his death." McKinley, *Assassination in America,* p. 175.

278    "I never had . . . for Mr. Truman." James Clarke, *American Assassins: The Darker Side of Politics* (Princeton, N.J.: Princeton University Press, 1982), p. 71.

278    "I intend to . . . until I die." Ibid., p. 75.

279    "By the way . . . so many children." Robert Kaiser, *R.F.K. Must Die* (New York: Dutton, 1970), p. 220.

279    "I'm very sorry . . . no one died." George Rush, *Confessions of an Ex-Secret Service Agent: The Marty Venker Story* (New York: Fine, 1988), p. 280.

279    "Do you know . . . friend of yours." Albert Goldman, *The Lives of John Lennon* (New York: Morrow, 1988), p. 687.

279    "Personally, I didn't . . . My country." William L. Calley, Jr., and John Sack, *Lieutenant Calley: His Own Story* (New York: Viking, 1970), p. 106.

279    "There is no . . . world in general." Clarke, *American Assassins,* p. 105.

279    "Once the toothpaste . . . it back in." *The American Experience,* "Nixon: the Quest, the Triumph, the Fall," PBS, October 15, 1990.

279    "Tomorrow we shoot . . . whether it stinks." *Vogue,* March 1989, p. 318.

279    "Well, sometimes you just don't like somebody." Peter Collier and David Horowitz, *The Fords: An American Epic* (New York: Summit Books, 1987), p. 411.

279 "What I want . . . on the other." *Esquire,* February 1992, p. 57.

279 "Retreat, hell!" . . . in another direction." Thomas A. Bailey, *Voices of America* (New York: Free Press, 1976), p. 442.

280 "Oh, sho-o-o-ot. Golly. Darn." *People,* September 2, 1991, p. 88.

280 "People that are . . . impact on history." *The Unauthorized Autobiography of Dan Quayle,* p. v.

280 "Man does not . . . has to eat them." *Esquire,* February 1992, p. 57.

280 "If you give . . . think of one." Paul F. Boller, *Presidential Campaigns* (New York: Oxford University Press, 1984), p. 297.

280 "He squats when he pees." Richard Goodwin, *Remembering America: A Voice from the Sixties* (Boston: Little, Brown, 1988), p. 294.

280 "even dry behind the ears." Evelyn Lincoln, *My Twelve Years with John F. Kennedy* (New York: McKay, 1965), p. 141.

280 "Just a twentieth-century Uncle Tom." Andrew J. Edelstein and Kevin McDonough, *The Seventies: From Hot Pants to Hot Tubs* (New York: Dutton, 1990), p. 81.

280 "More people died . . . Three Mile Island." *Prime Time Live,* December 6, 1990, ABC.

280 "You can't make a soufflé rise twice." Bailey, *Voices of America,* p. 435.

280 "It was the . . . of the country." Doris Kearns Goodwin, *The Fitzgeralds and the Kennedys* (New York: St. Martin's Press, 1987), p. 901.

281 "All his golfing . . . met since 1945." Time-Life editors, *This Fabulous Century 1950–1960,* Vol. 6 (New York: Time-Life Books, 1970), p. 34.

281 "Can you imagine . . . in this chair?" Richard Reeves, *I'm a Ford, Not a Lincoln* (New York: Harcourt Brace Jovanovich, 1975), p. 42.

281 "If you don't . . . the Vice President." Arthur Schlesinger, *Robert Kennedy and His Times* (Boston: Houghton Mifflin, 1978), Vol. 2, p. 692.

281 "He went out . . . no class." Ibid., p. 231.

281 "Speak up, Bill . . . you, Mr. President." Helen Thomas, White House correspondent, in a speech.

CHAPTER 24

FILM VERSUS REALITY

283 "Whatever happened to . . . *real* man there." Shana Alexander, *Anyone's Daughter* (New York: Viking, 1979), p. 94.

283 "By the time . . . an ideal world." Gary Wills, *Reagan's America: Innocents at Home* (Garden City, N.Y.: Doubleday, 1987), p. 168.

283 "That's very interesting . . . the ballplayer." Bob Schieffer and Gary Paul Gates, *The Acting President* (New York: Dutton, 1989), pp. 167–168.

283 "Not at all . . . with John Wayne." *American Heritage,* November 1989, p. 46.

283 "After seeing the . . . like this happens." *American History Illustrated,* March/April 1991, p. 52.

284 "Ollie, your're a . . . movie someday." Jane Meyer and Doyle McManus, *Landslide: The Unmaking of the President* (Boston: Houghton Mifflin, 1988), p. 351.

285 "the first time . . . himself doing it." Malcolm Forbes and Jeff Bloch, *They Went That-a-away . . .* (New York: Ballantine Books, 1988), pp. 218–219.

285    "Let's get Graziano." *The New York Times*, May 23, 1990, p. B7.

285    "I hope I'll . . . happy endings." *Real Life with Jane Pauley*, July 14, 1991.

285    "There's nothing in . . . those dirty words." *Prime Time Live*, ABC, August 29, 1991.

285    "Men go to . . . it's only me." *The New York Times*, March 24, 1991, p. 1.

285    "A man can . . . Hinckley 'knew' me." *Esquire*, December 1982, p. 108.

285    "Here's the difference . . . to my career." *M Inc.*, October 1991, p. 115.

286    "She's very proud . . . for a mother." *World News Tonight*, ABC, November 9, 1990.

286    "The only time . . . the damn things." G. Barry Golson, ed., *The Playboy Interview II* (New York: Putnam, 1983), p. 101.

286    "Anytime I want . . . on a horse." *People*, December 2, 1991, p. 179.

286    "There's something about . . . out a problem." *The New York Times Book Review*, November 18, 1990, p. 43.

286    "I'm scared to . . . break your neck." Golson, ed., *The Playboy Interview II*, p. 463.

286    "The whole romance . . . go around you." *People*, June 17, 1991, p. 96.

286    "nuclear energy became . . . film about it." *People*, April 19, 1990, p. 38.

286    "It was shortly . . . orgies and sex?" *Film on Film*, "Roman Polanski," PBS, June 16, 1990.

287    "Americans like to . . . the ugly one." William L. Calley, Jr., and John Sack, *Lieutenant Calley: His Own Story* (New York: Viking, 1971), p. 176.

287    "It was like . . . forgotten about it." *Newsweek*, May 20, 1991, p. 19.

287    "Before I was . . . was watching television." *The New York Times*, February 22, 1991, pp. C1, C8.

287    "The show was . . . a real woman." *New Woman*, June 1991, p. 118.

287    "I must admit . . . name on it." *The New York Times*, May 8, 1991, p. A21.

287    "Back in that . . . you are there." *Black Stars in Orbit*, PBS, February 12, 1990.

288    "I'd seen so . . . myself that way." Leo Damore, *Senatorial Privilege* (Washington, D.C.: Regnery Gateway, 1988), p. 140.

288    "I've just been . . . me your money." *People*, March 25, 1991, p. 34.

288    "It was a . . . their own robes." *People*, February 5, 1990, p. 52.

288    "People say that . . . mine, you know?" Malcolm Forbes and Jeff Bloch, *They Went That-a-way . . .* (New York: Ballantine Books, 1988), p. 74.

288    "I'm never going . . . looking at myself." *People*, September 17, 1990, p. 102.

288    "I think the . . . want to stay." *People*, May 6, 1991, p. 48.

289    "People will say . . . their dining rooms." *The New York Times Magazine*, June 11, 1989, p. 130.

289    "I had no . . . what it's about." *Newsweek*, October 7, 1991, p. 72.

289    "I grew up . . . Jack Benny did." *People*, August 14, 1989, p. 66.

289    "I remember riding . . . driver, I imagine." *People*, July 31, 1989, p. 74.

289    "Christ, I saw . . . this man was?" *The New York Times Magazine*, December 3, 1989, p. 107.

289    "For the longest . . . missed Captain Kangaroo!" Kathy Cronkite, *On the Edge of the Spotlight* (New York: Morrow, 1981), p. 46.

290    "I know who . . . not Dinah Shore." Bruce Cassidy, *Dinah!: A Biography* (New York: Franklin Watts, 1979), p. 125.

290    "That's not you . . . put *you* on." Jerry Oppenheimer, *Barbara Walters: An*

*Unauthorized Biography* (New York: St. Martin's Press, 1990), pp. 306–307.

290    "When I was . . . in the box?" Cronkite, *On the Edge of the Spotlight*, p. 58.

## CHAPTER 25
### WHAT THEY WERE DOING WHEN

291    "The day that . . . There he goes." *People*, August 14, 1989, p. 69.

291    "The one thought . . . even fathom it." Judith Exner and Ovid Demaris, *My Story* (New York: Grove Press, 1977), pp. 196–197.

291    "by Twentieth Century-Fox . . . to congratulate you." Ingrid Bergman and Allan Burgess, *Ingrid Bergman: My Story* (New York: Delacorte Press, 1980) pp. 350–351.

292    "Why aren't you . . . matter any more." *People*, November 11, 1991, pp. 112–114.

293    "one of the . . . can't help you." *New York*, September 16, 1991, p. 49.

293    "At one point . . . you're capable of." *60 Minutes*, CBS, March 31, 1991.

293    "happened to be . . . from my father." Peter Collier and David Horowitz, *The Rockefellers: An American Dynasty* (New York: Holt, Rinehart & Winston, 1976), p. 550.

293    "I stopped the . . . way you do." Interview with Gordon Parks, PBS, January 15, 1990.

294    "Hey. Did you . . . on the radio." *Esquire*, December 1982, p. 102.

294    "I felt dead . . . President Kennedy's assassination." *Manhattan, inc.*, May 1988, p. 102.

295    "I remember that . . . father had died." Harrison Rainie and John Quinn, *Growing Up Kennedy: The Third Wave Comes of Age* (New York: Putnam, 1983), p. 21.

295    "God*damn* it! . . . Don't you go." William Manchester, *The Death of a President: November 20–November 25, 1963* (New York: Harper & Row, 1967), p. 209.

295    "a terrific impact." Ibid., p. 247.

295    "We have just . . . our matinee feature." Ibid., p. 169.

295    "When President Kennedy . . . six o'clock news." *50 Years Together: Channel 2 and You*, CBS, July 9, 1991.

296    "I have news . . . of Howard University." Manchester, *The Death of a President*, pp. 195–196, 257.

296    "Follow that car . . . Okay, partner." Ibid., p. 166.

296    "I thought she . . . the President's daughter." Helen Thomas, *Dateline: White House* (New York: Macmillan, 1975), p. 97.

## CHAPTER 26
### THE HAND OF FATE

297    "If I was . . . in the rain." Mollie Dickenson, *Thumbs Up* (New York: Morrow, 1987), pp. 60–61.

297    "I didn't know . . . I could get." Ibid., p. 59.

297 "wasn't that desperate about . . . would work out." Ibid., pp. 60–61.

298 "Jerry, get off . . . hurting my ribs." Lou Cannon, *Reagan* (New York: Putnam, 1982), pp. 402–405.

298 "I think I've cut my mouth." Dickenson, *Thumbs Up*, p. 72.

298 "If ten minutes had . . . to G.W. immediately." Dickenson, *Thumbs Up*, p. 76.

299 "Some time shortly . . . shot John Lennon." Editors of *Rolling Stone, The Ballad of John and Yoko*, (Garden City, N.Y.: Rolling Stone Press, 1982), pp. 202–203.

299 "I decided to . . . some other place." C. David Heymann, *A Woman Named Jackie* (New York: Lyle Stuart, 1989), pp. 251–252.

299 "I actually started . . . 'I would.' " *The New York Times Magazine*, November 26, 1988, p. 76.

300 "This has to . . . through the crowd." James Clarke, *American Assassins: The Darker Side of History* (Princeton, N.J.: Princeton University Press, 1982), p. 164.

301 "Oh, I want the bubbletop." William Manchester, *The Death of a President November 20–November 25, 1963* (New York: Harper & Row, 1967), p. 122.

301 "All along the . . . something really effective?" Arthur H. Bremer, *An Assassin's Diary* (New York: Harper's Magazine Press, 1973), p. 74.

301 "Shock! Shock! I . . . I was stupid." Ibid., p. 76.

301 "Yesterday I even . . . as a target." Ibid., p. 119.

301 "picked up the . . . seat had drowned." Ronnie Dugger, *The Politician: The Life and Times of Lyndon Johnson* (New York: Norton, 1982), p. 250.

302 "Catfish, I think . . . today after all." Dickenson, *Thumbs Up*, p. 58.

302 "I did some . . . a little thing." Fawn Brodie, *Richard Nixon* (New York: Norton, 1981), p. 36.

302 "For want of . . . Presidency was lost." H. R. Haldeman and Joseph Di-Mona, *The Ends of Power* (New York: Times Books, 1978), p. 81.

302 "God is in the details." *New York Herald Tribune*, June 28, 1959.

302 "If John Hinckley . . . can't take me." *60 Minutes*, CBS, May 25, 1991.

302 "If John Hinckley . . . back to Hinckley." Ibid.

303 "It really destroyed . . . deal with that." *The New York Times*, May 6, 1990, p. 32.

303 "All I knew . . . else would have." *Time*, October 6, 1973, p. 20.

303 "learned for the . . . life of another." *Newsweek*, October 20, 1975, p. 20.

304 "How many times . . . It looks bad." Manchester, *The Death of a President*, p. 116.

304 "We could have . . . millions on it." *The New York Times*, November 26, 1988, p. B20.

304 "I see you . . . will be President." Dorothy Brandon, *Mamie Doud Eisenhower* (New York: Scribners, 1954), p. 199.

305 "Now, why'd you . . . wondered since then." Marshall Frady, *Billy Graham: A Parable of American Righteousness* (Boston: Little, Brown, 1979), p. 264.

306 "I had that . . . on the bench." *Phil Rizzuto: Holy Cow! Fifty Years*, WLN, July 3, 1990.

306 "I wasn't terribly . . . was coming from." *The New York Times*, July 19, 1989, p. A10.

306 "Nobody in my family needs insurance." Peter Collier and David Horo-

witz, *The Kennedys: An American Drama* (New York: Summit Books, 1984), p. 137.

306   "You know, if . . . is Russian roulette." Arthur Schlesinger, *Robert Kennedy and His Times* (Boston: Houghton Mifflin, 1978), Vol. 2, p. 493.

306   "If they are . . . even in church." Evelyn Lincoln, *My Twelve Years With John F. Kennedy* (New York: McKay, 1965), p. 365.

306   "The only thing . . . had bad luck." Margaret Truman, *Harry S. Truman* (New York: Morrow, 1973), pp. 487–488.

307   "so-called twenty-year . . . during the night." *Newsweek,* October 23, 1989, pp. 56, 59.

307   "My relationship with . . . ever happened again." Ibid.

307   "I knew of . . . make the announcement." Joan Quigley, *''What Does Joan Say?''* (New York: Birch Lane Press, 1990), pp. 170–171.

307   "Nancy had not . . . situation was hopeless." Ibid., p. 169.

# Index